Transactions of the Royal Historical Society

FIFTH SERIES

35

LONDON 1985

British Library Cataloguing in Publication Data

Transactions of the Royal Historical Society.
—5th series, vol. 35 (1985)
1. History—Periodicals
I. Royal Historical Society
905   D1

ISBN 0-86193-107-6

Made and printed in Great Britain by Butler & Tanner Ltd, Frome and London

CONTENTS

TRANSACTIONS OF THE
ROYAL HISTORICAL SOCIETY

PRESIDENTIAL ADDRESS

By Professor J. C. Holt, M. A., D.Phil., F.B.A., F.S.A.

FEUDAL SOCIETY AND THE FAMILY IN EARLY MEDIEVAL ENGLAND:
IV. THE HEIRESS AND THE ALIEN

READ 23 NOVEMBER 1984

THE topic is doubly important. First, the heiress was one of the fluid elements in the social structure. By marriage, families forged links with each other, landless knights and ambitious officials made their way into the noble hierarchy, and established lineages renewed their military reputation or improved their access to government circles.[1] If the bride was an heiress all this was underwritten by a territorial endowment far larger than the usual marriage-portion. She also brought to her husband title to office, all the legal and quasi-legal claims which came to be concentrated in her from her lineage, and sometimes even the family name of her forbears to be assumed, if not by him, then by the offspring of their marriage. So the heiress was special; she magnifies for us all the problems and consequences of marriage.

The problems were obvious. In what way was such a system to be controlled and by whom? What say in the matter was to be enjoyed by the parties to a marriage, by their families, by their lords? Who might be regarded as an heir? Which among a man's

[1] For recent studies see Georges Duby, *Medieval Marriage* (Baltimore, 1978); M. Sheehan, 'Choice of marriage partners in the Middle Ages: development and mode of application of a theory of marriage', *Studies in Medieval and Renaissance History*, n.s.i (1978), 3-33; Eleanor Searle, 'Women and the legitimisation of succession at the Norman Conquest', California Institute of Technology, Social Science Working Paper, 328 (1980), also in *Proceedings of the Battle Conference on Anglo-Norman Studies*, iii (1980), 159-70; C. N. L. Brooke, 'Marriage and Society in the Central Middle Ages', *Marriage and Society*, ed. R. B. Outhwaite (1981), 17-34; Georges Duby, *Le Chevalier, la Femme et le Prêtre* (Paris, 1981; Eng. trans. 1983); Ragena C. DeAragon, 'In pursuit of Aristocratic Women: A Key to Success in Norman England', *Albion*, 14 (1982), 258-66; Jack Goody, *The development of the family and marriage in Europe* (1983).

daughters might be regarded as an heiress? Some of the answers to these questions were reinforced by stern doctrine, others were slowly pieced together from practical experience and immediate convenience. But the answer to the last question—who might be regarded as an heiress?—was different from all the rest: it was altered. Up to the second quarter of the twelfth century the inheritance descended through one daughter or sister, usually the eldest: after that point it was divided among them all. This change was the result of a specific ruling, as near an act of legislation as could be achieved in England at that time. It is the one point where anything approaching a revision of substantive law can be investigated, the one point where motives and attitudes of all concerned can be probed both in general and in depth. This is the second good reason for studying the topic. There was a sudden, deliberate change of policy.

Women were subordinate. They were placed under the dominion of husband, head of family or lord. But the lawfully wedded wife played a crucial role: she was the sole source of legitimate heirs. In a society which, within a few generations at most, had been restructured around lineal descent, the bride was soon hedged about by a protective law which excluded illegitimate children from the succession, defined the acceptable degrees of affinity, and protected her in marriage against desertion and divorce.[2] All these rules were brought into play by the twelfth century. The woman's role might be thrown in doubt by the higher flights of the more insulated theologians who presented her as an unfortunate necessity, the originator of sin, who approached nearer to the ideal if in her later years she turned from her earthly husband to the heavenly embrace of Christ, repenting her days away that she had ever born men's children. But not all contemporary stereotypes were like that. Marriage was seen as a security for peace and legitimate succession: hence Rollo, first duke of Normandy, was made to marry Gisèle, daughter of Charles the Simple; Queen Emma was said to have brought half the realm to Cnut; and Duke William was made to convey his daughter, Adeliza, to Harold with the promise of half the kingdom of England.[3] Marriage and the continuation of the lineage

[2] Brooke, 23-7. See also the cases of Agnes of Ponthieu, who fled from the cruelty of her husband, Robert of Bellême (Orderic Vitalis, ed. Chibnall, iv. 300); Hildegarde, countess of Poitou, who appealed at the Council Rheims, 1119, against desertion by her husband (Orderic Vitalis, ed. Chibnall, vi. 258-60; F. Villard, 'Guillaume IX d'Aquitaine et le concile de Reims de 1119', *Cahiers de Civilisation Médévale*, xvi (1973) 295-302); and Agnes, countess of Oxford, who fought long and ultimately successfully against repudiation by her husband, Aubrey de Vere (*Complete Peerage*, x. 206-7; App. J. 116-17; Brooke, 31-2).

[3] For the fictitious marriage of Rollo see Dudo of St Quentin, *De moribus et actis primorum Normanniae ducum*, ed. J. Lair (Caen, 1865), 169, repeated in Orderic Vitalis,

were one and the same. A barren marriage was a tragedy, a motive though not a ground for divorce, to be explained away as the consequence of accident or more usually of sin.[4] Hence the Emperor Henry V died childless *peccatis exigentibus*, and women who abandoned the veil remained childless all their lives and in the words of Ordericus, 'for a short period of wordly happiness incurred the wrath of the heavenly bridegroom'.[5] Such fictions and exaggerations heightened the status and reinforced the role of the lawfully wedded wife.

Inheritance in the female line was determined by these circumstances. A woman inherited not because of any title, not because of the survival of more ancient legal arrangements which might allow her a determinate share of her father's lands, but because, in the absence of male heirs in the same generation, she was the only means of continuing the lineage, the only legitimate route whereby her father's blood could be transmitted. Her children were his grandchildren just as her brother's might have been. This determined the woman's position as heir. If there were legitimate male heirs to her father then she could not expect to succeed. If there were no male heirs then the inheritance was 'hers' in the sense that it was no one else's, that the claim which she embodied was stronger than anyone else's. But it was not hers in the sense that she could succeed as a spinster. She brought her lands to her husband and ultimately to her children. Her husband had charge of them and he might be followed by her son even in her lifetime.[6] It was only as a widow

---

ed. Chibnall, iii. 78; for Emma see Orderic Vitalis, ed. Chibnall, i. 157; for Adeliza see William of Jumièges, interp. Orderic Vitalis, *Gesta Normannorum Ducum*, ed. J. Marx (Paris, 1914), 191, but cf. Orderic Vitalis, ed. Chibnall, ii. 136.

[4] See for example the sixteenth-century register of Tewkesbury Abbey which explains the descent of Robert fitz Hamo as follows: Robert, at the summit of power, enjoying great riches and the friendship of King Henry I, had everything a man could desire but issue of his marriage, a lack which would sadden the heart of any man. So he and his wife sought a remedy through alms, pilgrimage and prayer until at last they came to pray to St Benignus at Glastonbury. They promised a 100/- of land if the Saint interceded to give them an heir and in a few days Robert's wife was heavy with child. However they cheated the Saint and as a result as long as Robert lived his wife bore female children only. Once he was dead she married at a lower status and had children of both sexes. (British Library, Add. MS 36985, f. 3v). For another example of analogous genealogical fiction see the case of Walter Espec, discussed below pp. 15-16.

[5] Orderic Vitalis, ed. Chibnall, v. 200; ii.102-4. Orderic's comment concerned Judith and Emma, sisters of Robert of Grandmesnil, abbot of St Évroult. Judith married Roger Guiscard and had at least two daughters. See Chibnall, ii 103-4n.

[6] S. F. C. Milsom, 'Inheritance by Women in the twelfth and early thirteenth centuries' in *On the Laws and Customs of England: Essays in Honor of Samuel E. Thorne*, eds.

that she might hope to gain sole control. That was a possibility which led the cautious beneficiary to associate her with her husband in acts affecting her lands, just as her title brought her into the courts alongside her husband if her rights were subject to litigation. But settled widowhood was a status only achieved with difficulty, usually after several marriages, and it was likely to be maintained only at considerable cost.

Norman and Anglo-Norman society in the eleventh and early twelfth centuries reveals these rules in operation. No spinster can be found in enjoyment of her inheritance. It was only very occasionally, after some disgrace of the male line, that a female was given precedence over a male heir.[7] Widows in possession of their inherited lands were rare birds. The social cross-cut provided by the Domesday Survey is revealing. The tenants-in-chief of 1086 included one great widow, the Countess Judith.[8] Queen Matilda, and less than ten wives of the leading tenants of the day, held land which had presumably been given to them in dower.[9] The daughters of two tenants-in-chief appear, each with a single estate which was probably her marriage-portion.[10] There was a scattering of English ladies still with possessions of their own, the residue of an older society in which women had held property in their own right. This last group was minute compared with what it has been in 1066. These women saw their time out enjoying a right which the Conquest had destroyed.

Morris S. Arnold, Thomas A. Green, Sally A. Scully and Stephen D. White (Chapel Hill, 1981), 60–89; cf. J. C. Holt (1983), 218.

[7] No statement about rules of inheritance in this period can be hard and fast. One obvious possible exception in this case is the descent of Bellême, where Mabel and her husband Roger of Montgomery succeeded to the family lands after much confusion over the rights of her father, William Talvas, and to the exclusion of his brother, Oliver, a monk of Bec, who may have been illegitimate. See Marjorie Chibnall's discussion in Orderic Vitalis, ii. 362–5 and ibid, i. 213 for a genealogical table, also G. H. White, 'The first house of Bellême.' *TRHS*, 4th ser., xxii (1940), 67–99. There are many examples of a female effectively legitimising the succession of her husband after some break in the descent through her male relations. See the case of Mowbray (*Charters of the Honour of Mowbray 1107–1191*, ed. D. E. Greenway, British Academy Records of Social and Economic History, n.s.i, 1972, xviii), and other examples noted in J. C. Holt, 'Politics and Property in early medieval England,' *Past & Present*, 57 (1972), 31n; cf. ibid., 22n.

[8] For Judith see Henry Ellis, *A General Introduction to Domesday Book* (1833), i. 440–1; *Complete Peerage*, vi. 639–40. Countess Godeva, widow of Earl Leofric, was dead by 1086 (Ellis, i. 370, 426).

[9] Ellis, i. 501–2.

[10] The daughter of Ralph Taillebois (D.B., i. 142b) and Roger de Rames (D.B., ii. 422b).

None of this means that women were unimportant. On the contrary, descent in the female line was common; indeed, it was the obvious course whenever the male line failed. The extent and importance of the inheritance did not affect the issue. The counties of Anjou, Maine and Évreux and the lordship of Breteuil all descended through the female line in various ways between 1060 and 1110.[11] Even an unconsummated betrothal could count. Giroie, the founder of the fortunes of the patrons of St Evroult, agreed to marry the only daughter of the knight, Heugon, and received Montreuil and Échauffour as the marriage portion. Then his betrothed died. Giroie had to seek the confirmation of Duke Richard, but he was given the land as a hereditary tenure. That story comes from the years before 1027.[12] Many descents were much less direct than this. The descent of Maine involved four arrangements or claims, all in the female line, spread over a period of twenty-seven years, from 1063 to 1090. It began with an agreement concluded by Herbert II, Count of Maine, with Duke William of Normandy whereby Herbert's sister Margaret was promised to William's son Robert, with the proviso that she would inherit Maine if Herbert had no children. It ended in 1090 with the succession of first one then another of Herbert's cousins, each of them the son of his aunts, sisters of his predecessor, Count Hugh IV. The first of these cousins was brought back from Italy where his father was Marquis of Liguria with the argument that 'no man was closer heir than he'. The second pressed his claim on the ground that 'I no less than you am sprung from the stock of Count Herbert' (*recte* Count Hugh). So at least Orderic Vitalis tells us.[13] His genealogy was not quite right, but it is none the less significant that he presented the succession in these terms.

Such was the system which the Norman brought to England. It was transplanted unchanged and undisturbed. By 1130 more than twenty baronies had descended in the female line.[14] By 1150 the number had risen to thirty.[15] Some underwent more than one such succession.[16]

[11] For Anjou see L. Halphen. *Le Comté d'Anjou au xie siècle* (Paris, 1906), 133 ff. For Maine see Orderic Vitalis, ed. Chibnall, ii. 116–18. For Évreux see *Complete Peerage*, vii. 709, 711. For Breteuil see ibid, vii. 529–30; ix. 574 and n.

[12] Orderic Vitalis, ed. Chibnall, ii. 22.

[13] Orderic Vitalis, ed. Chibnall, ii. 116–18; iv. 192–8. For corrections to Orderic's genealogy see R. Latouche, *Histoire du comté du Maine pendant le xe et le xie siècles* (Paris, 1910), 113–15.

[14] Aveley, Belvoir, Blagdon, Bourne, Brattelby, Castle Combe, Chester, Folkestone, Gloucester, Hockering, Hooton Paynel, Keevil, Malton, Much Marcle, Nether Stowey, Papcastle, Salwarpe, Stogursey, Tamworth, Wallingford and Witham.

[15] Bolinbroke, Bourn, Burgh by Sands, Dudley, Hanslope, Kempsford, Meschin, Okehampton, Stainton le Vale.

[16] Belvoir, Folkestone and Wallingford.

On both sides of the Channel and both before and after 1066 female succession was a source of much dispute. Some of the conflicts arose from the competing claims of sisters. Some were parentelic, between the husbands or descendants of niece and aunt. Some were quarrels in the half-blood, between the descendants of an heiress's successive marriages. The more distant successions were always more intricate and more difficult to regulate precisely.[17] But all were subject to the primacy of the male line. Few maidens at their betrothal were heirs apparent. Some were heirs presumptive. All were heirs potential. In any marriage, therefore, quite apart from the marriage-portion, there were chances to be weighed. In any family a maiden unbetrothed, unless devoted to the service of Christ, was a wasted resource. Worse still she was vulnerable. So she was betrothed at any early age. In 1103 Robert, Count of Meulan, pledged his daughter to Amaury, nephew of William, Count of Évreux, when she was aged one.[18] The same circumstances determined the position of the widow. She came complete with dowry. She might already be an heiress who had brought her inheritance to her previous husband. If not, like the maid, she was an heir potential to a succession more or less likely. The system was one which made it very difficult for a woman to enjoy estate in her own right, but used her to the full as a means of perpetuating the bond between tenure and lineage.

Such arrangements were controlled in two distinct ways. First there were conventions about who might betroth or give a bride in marriage. The coronation charter of Henry I presents a strictly defined system: barons arranged the marriage of their daughters and other women folk, but had to consult the king, who would neither

---

[17] For disputes involving distant relationships in the female line see the quarrel between Ascelin Goel and William of Breteuil for the castle of Ivry, the one possibly the great great grandson and the other certainly the great grandson of Aubrée wife of Ralph, county of Ivry. Aubrée reputedly built the castle. If the genealogy is correct, each party claimed through a female ancestor, granddaughter and daughter of Aubrée, i.e. a niece and aunt. The argument therefore seems to have involved seniority of line versus seniority of generation, i.e. parentelic precedence. (Orderic Vitalis, ed. Chibnall, iv. 199 n.4). For a similar though milder dispute, cut short by the death of both niece in the senior and aunt in the junior line, see the case of Maine (Orderic Vitalis, ed. Chibnall, ii. 116–18, 304). For the quarrel between Robert of Ballême and Rotrou, count of Perche, depending in part on claims from the cousins, Mabel and Adeline of Bellême see G. H. White (1940), 79; *Complete Peerage*, xi, appendix D, 122n; Orderic Vitalis, ed. Chibnall, i. 213; ii. 362–5; iv. 397. For examples drawn from England see Holt, *Past & Present* (1972), 22, n. 99. For descent in the female line where the division of estates was ultimately resolved see the honour of Bolingbroke (*Complete Peerage*, vii. 667–75; 743–6) and the lands of William of Arques, tenant of the archbishop of Canterbury (*Domesday Monachorum of Christ Church, Canterbury*, ed. D. C. Douglas (1944), 42–3; J. H. Round, *Geoffrey de Mandeville* (1892), 180, 397–8).

[18] Orderic Vitalis, ed. Chibnall, vi. 47.

take payment for his permission nor prohibit the match unless to one of his enemies; if a baron died leaving a daughter as heir the king gave her in marriage by the advice of his barons; the king also promised not to give widows in marriage against their wish; similar arrangements were to pertain between the barons and their men.[19] It is easy enough to illustrate all this in practice. Barons gave away daughters, sisters and nieces:[20] how far they consulted the duke in the years before the Conquest is uncertain; that they did so under Henry I is occasionally made clear.[21] The ruling house disposed of heiresses and widows; it also played a patronal role in other marriages.[22] Real life was not as neatly arranged as Henry I's charter suggests. The ducal or royal right was not always maintained; Adeliza, daughter of the Countess Judith, niece of the Conqueror, was given in marriage to Ralph de Tosny, not by the king but by her elder sister's husband, Simon de St Liz.[23] Conversely the king's influence could extend far beyond the limits indicated in 1100; in 1121 Henry I gave Sibilla, daughter of Bernard de Neufmarché, to Miles of Gloucester during her father's lifetime, under terms which provided for the transfer to Miles of a considerable portion of Bernard's lands as a marriage-portion.

This transaction was justified by the fiction that Bernard had surrendered all his acquisitions into the hands of the king, who was now granting them to Miles.[24] Such a special provision may point to a breach of current conventions, but it would be wrong to conclude that practice was intended to be hard and fast. Some of the evidence is contradictory. Sometime after 1107 Hawise, daughter of Richard de Reviers, was married to William de Roumare. Orderic states that she was given in marriage by Henry I, which would be

---

[19] Caps. 3,4. It should be noted that the charter distinguishes childless widows from those with children, leaving the latter or other relatives with the custody of land and children. It also implies that the widowed mother was less liable to remarriage.

[20] For daughters see the arrangements made by Heugon, Geoffrey of Mortagne and Hugh of Crépy (Orderic Vitalis, ed. Chibnall, ii. 22; iv. 160; v. 30). For a sister see Baudri of Bocquencé (ibid., ii. 84). For a niece see Gilbert of Brionne (ibid., ii. 82).

[21] See the case of Hugh de Gournay who discussed the future of his sister, Gundreda, with Henry I and, on the King's recommendation, gave her to Nigel d'Aubigny (ibid., vi. 192). This replicates the procedure envisaged in Henry's coronation charter.

[22] For an heiress see Aubrée, daughter of Guitmund of Moulins-la-Marche, given in marriage by Duke William (ibid., iii. 132). For a widow see Ada, widow of Herluin the elder of Heugleville, given in marriage by Duke Robert the Magnificent (ibid., iii. 252). For more general intervention by William I and Henry I see ibid., ii. 262; iv. 158; iii. 258-60.

[23] *Complete Peerage*, xii, pt. 1. 762; *Vita et Passio Waldevi Comitis*, ed. F. Michel, *Chroniques Anglo-Normandes*, 3 vols. (Paris, 1836-40), ii. 126.

[24] *Ancient Charters*, ed. J. H. Round, Pipe Roll Soc. 10 (1888), 8-10.

consistent with the rules of his charter.[25] The lady herself, however, subsequently in her widowhood, gave part of her marriage-portion to the monks of Twineham for the souls of several, including her dear brother Earl Baldwin, 'who gave me those lands in frank marriage when he gave me in marriage to my noble husband, William de Roumare'.[26] It is tempting to say that Orderic was wrong and that Hawise was right; she after all should have known; Orderic, in contrast, got her name wrong;[27] but both may reflect different aspects or stages of the same transaction. There is no need to assume that there was some kind of constitutional battle over who had the right to bestow a bride. It is more likely that there was reasonable give and take between king and baron, lord and man, so long as the result did not undermine due loyalty.

A second control was stricter. Apparently, descent in the female line was always to a single heiress. In all the instances of Norman and Anglo-Norman descent mentioned by Orderic Vitalis, none involves parceny among heiresses. In England, where baronies descended in the female line, as had occurred in twenty cases by 1130, they descended to a single heiress. The coronation charter of Henry I runs: 'and if a daughter remains an heir';[28] partition among several daughters was not considered. The Pipe roll of 1130 records twenty-seven fines for wardship and/or marriage. There is no hint in any of them that the inheritance was divided in the female line. The significance of this overwhelming accumulation of evidence depends, of course, on the assumption that in all these instances the heiresses were not single daughters. That can be settled beyond reasonable doubt by a few particular instances. The Countess Judith, niece of the Conqueror, widow of Earl Waltheof, left two daughters, Maud and Adeliza. Maud, the senior, married Simon de St Liz *c.* 1190. Adeliza seems to have remained in the custody of her elder sister and brother-in-law until her marriage to Ralph de Tosny in 1103. It is said on the strong authority of the *Complete Peerage* that the two were co-heiresses, but the sole evidence is that the manor of Walthamstow, which had passed from Waltheof to the Countess Judith, ultimately came to the younger sister, Adeliza.[29] That is inconclusive. The subsequent history of Judith's lands, which became the honour of Huntingdon, gives no hint of a division between the two sisters. Fees were lost from the honour but not on

[25] *Complete Peerage*, iv. 309–11; Appendix I, 771; Orderic Vitalis, ed. Chibnall, vi. 380.

[26] *Complete Peerage*, iv. 311, n.b.

[27] He misnamed her Matilda.

[28] Cap. 3.

[29] *Complete Peerage*, xii, pt. 1. 761–2.

this account. The inheritance descended through Maud. Walthamstow was probably Adeliza's marriage-portion.[30] The descent of the
lands of Robert fitz Hamo provide another example. These were
brought by his daughter Mabel to her husband Robert, illegitimate
son of Henry I; they came to constitute the honour of the earls of
Gloucester.[31] The marriage took place between 1107 and 1114. At
the time Mabel had at least two sisters; one became abbess of Shaf-
tesbury and the other probably abbess of Wilton.[32] Whether they
had already taken the veil at the time of their sister's marriage is
uncertain. Yet another example is provided by Rotrou, count of
Perche, who married Maud, illegitimate daughter of Henry I. Maud
died in the White Ship in 1120, leaving two daughters, Philippa and
Felicia. There is no indication of when Felicia died, but there is no
doubt that between 1120 and his second marriage, sometime before
1127, Rotrou treated Philippa and her husband as his sole heirs.[33]
Finally, there is the example of the extraordinarily complex descent
of the lands of Robert de Tosny, who died in 1088, and of his son,
Berenger, who died before 1116. These came, some directly, some
by circuitous routes, to Alice, daughter of Robert and sister of
Berengar, widow of Roger Bigod, who died in 1107. None passed
by inheritance to Alice's younger sister, Agnes and her husband
Hubert de Rye.[34] The import of each of these instances might be challenged; it is far from easy to determine when older sisters married
and when younger sisters took the veil or died. But they all point in
the same direction: only one female heiress succeeded at a time.

This was the rule which was altered. The change is mentioned in
a charter of Roger de Valognes in favour of the priory of Binham.
It refers to a *statutum decretum*, an established ruling,[35] that 'where
there is no son, the daughters divide their father's land by spindles,
and the elder cannot take from the younger her half of the land

[30] William Farrer. *Honors and Knights' Fees*, 3 vols. (Manchester, 1923–5), ii. 296–
301. Cf. J. H. Round, *Geoffrey de Mandeville*, 191–3, 264–5. See also the *Vita et Passio
Waldevi* which clearly refers to a marriage-portion (above, n.23).

[31] *Earldom of Gloucester Charters*, ed. R. B. Patterson (Oxford, 1973), 3.

[32] *The Heads of Religious Houses England and Wales 940–1216*, eds D. Knowles, C. N. L.
Brooke and Vera London (Cambridge, 1972), 219, 222. There is insufficient evidence
of a third younger sister said to have married the count of Brittany.

[33] *Complete Peerage*, xi, Appendix D, 112–13 and nn. See especially Rotrou's grant
to the abbey of Tiron made 'assensu generis mei Helie filieque mee Philippe ... Hoc
concessit gener meus Helias et filia mea Philippa'.

[34] *Early Yorkshire Charters*, i. 460–1, 466; HMC, *Rutland*, iv. 107, 144. 161; *The Leicestershire Survey*, ed. C. F. Slade (Leicester. 1956), 90.

[35] After much consultation I have settled on this as the best translation, inadequate
though it is. Stenton chose 'appointed law,' which seems altogether too biblical in
flavour (*The First Century of English Feudalism* (Oxford, 2nd edn, 1961), 39). 'Enactment' is perhaps too legislative in tone.

without violence and injury'. Stenton dated the charter *c.* 1145.[36] No date is given for the enactment to which it refers. The indications of the Pipe roll of 1130 are that it was not yet in force. It seems unlikely that it was the work of King Stephen. A tentative date of 1130–35 would seem the best, but for the present purposes the precise dating does not matter very much. It is sufficient to say that there was a change of policy at about this time and that it was formal and deliberate. Up to this point there was no sign of parceny; after this point it became the common practice. From the 1140s onwards there is no difficulty at all in finding examples.

Why was this done? We can only guess or reconstruct an answer; no contemporary provides an explanation. An essential preliminary is to understand how it was intended to take effect, and here there are too many answers. Glanville, writing some fifty years after the *statutum decretum*, was in no doubt. Where there were no sons the inheritance was divided among daughters, with the proviso that the eldest daughter was to retain the chief messuage. The husband of the eldest daughter performed homage for the whole fee. Husbands and descendants of the younger daughters need not perform homage until the third generation, when at last they where bound to do so. But they then performed homage and paid a reasonable relief not to the lord but to the heirs of the senior daughter. In like manner, though junior daughters and their husbands were bound to perform the due services to the lord they did it by hand of the eldest daughter.[37]

What Glanville prescribed was derived from Norman *parage* as legal historians have long recognised.[38] He has been taken seriously. In fact he leads us up the garden path. Putting it at its lowest, his scheme is a method of tax avoidance, for it deprives the lord of wardships and reliefs. Putting it at its highest, what Glanville described certainly occurred; it engendered much litigation; but it is likely that it was still a novel procedure when Glanville described it as part of the law of the realm;[39] and it certainly was not the only way of arranging a partition. In 1236 King Henry III answered an enquiry from Ireland on these matters as follows:

> In our realm of England ... it was always the law and custom in such cases that if there was any holding of us in chief, having

[36] F. M. Stenton (1961), 261.
[37] Glanville, ed. G. D. G. Hall (1965), 76.
[38] F. Pollock and F. W. Maitland, *History of English Law* (Cambridge, 1898), ii. 276.
[39] Milsom (1981), especially 69–78. The earliest surviving record of such *parage* is in final concords concluded in the King's court. One of these is dateable to 1174–9, before Glanville became Chief Justiciar (*Curia Regis Rolls*, xi. no. 869); another of less certain date also belongs to Henry II (ibid., viii. 387).

daughters as his heirs, our ancestors and we, after the death of the
father, have always had and received homage of all the daughters,
and every one of them in such a case holds of us in chief; and if
they happen to be under age we have always had the wardship
and marriage of every one of them.

So much for tenants-in-chief. For tenants of others it was a different
matter. The ruling in their case was infected to some degree by
Glanville's doctrine; the younger sisters performed service by the
hand of the elder and the elder alone did homage; but the elder
sister was not allowed to take homage from the younger, as Glanville
required.[40] So there is a plain difference between Glanville and the
statement of 1236, in the case of tenants-in-chief a striking one. It is
possible that Glanville was right for 1189 and Henry III's advisers
were right for 1236. But it is also possible that Glanville is and was
misleading.

For his own generation and for the period stretching back to the
statutum decretum, Glanville's doctrine leads to obvious factual questions. Were the service and the performance of the service attached
to eldest co-heiress or were they divided, like the land? Was relief
paid to the senior line or to the lord? Was homage paid to the senior
line or to the lord? In sum was there *parage* or complete partition?
It is only in the case of homage that the answers are at all difficult
and even there there they can be implied.

The *statutum decretum* is a good starting point, for the charter which
Stenton discussed is not the only evidence. The cartulary of Binham
Priory, daughter house of St Albans, from which it was taken, includes some twenty documents relevant to the transaction.[41] The
first of these is a straightforward notification by Walter de Valognes
that he and his daughter Agnes, with the consent of this wife Roesia,
had granted Barney and Thursford in perpetuity to the monks of
Binham.[42] It is obvious that Agnes had an interest in the grant and
the lack of any reference to a husband indicates that she was as yet
unmarried. The second document is Stenton's charter. It is in the
name of the chief lord of the fee, Roger de Valognes, probably
Walter's first cousin. It makes plain that the land was granted with
all solemnity, in the presence of the abbot of St Albans and of clerks
and knights; Agnes and her father Walter gave seisin by placing a
knife on the altar before the assembled company. Both charters, it
should be noted, bear the marks of ecclesiastical draughtsmanship

[40] *Statutes of the Realm*, i. 5. The 1236 statement also excluded the elder from the
wardship of the younger, a matter not specifically discussed by Glanville.

[41] B. L., Cotton Claudius D. xiii, ff. 49–59v. These are not included in *Monasticon*,
iii. 345–53, where the Valognes charters are confined to those of the senior line.

[42] Binham Cartulary, f. 53.

and were most probably the work of the beneficiaries; this accounts for the peculiar term *statutum decretum*.[43] In this second charter Agnes remains unmarried, for there is still no reference to a husband, and she is now stated to be heir to her father in Barney according to the terms of the *statutum decretum*. The obvious implication is that she was the younger of two daughters who were dividing the inheritance. But the existence of an older daughter is no more than implied and the charter leaves it far from clear whether the whole, or merely half of Barney and Thursford was being conveyed; it also fails to explain why. At this point there had been some reference to Theobald, Archbishop of Canterbury, by whose admonition and laudation the gift was made. That the Archbishop's interest went beyond personal advice is made clear by the third document. This is a mandate of 1152-61 in which he informed Richard Bishop of London and William Bishop of Norwich that Richard of Colne and Geoffrey Tresgoz had contemned their agreement concluded before him concerning Barney and had withdrawn the gift of Walter de Valognes; the Bishops were instructed to pronounce anathema and impose an interdict if the matter was not amended within eight days.[44] So there were indeed two daughters and they were now married. The elder remains anonymous throughout; her husband, Richard of Colne, was a leading tenant of the Valognes barony.[45] The younger, Agnes, who benefited from the *statutum decretum*, married Geoffrey Tresgoz.[46] The Archbishop's intervention was effective. Agnes's grant was confirmed by her husband[47] and subsequently by her successor, her daughter Petronilla, both with her husband and in her widowhood.[48] The charter of Geoffrey Tresgoz records that an agreement had been concluded before the Archbishop after which the land was divided and partitioned by measurement. The exact bounds were given both in his charter and in a subsequent confirmation of his daughter and son-in-law. The division was car-

[43] Ibid., f. 49-49v; F. M. Stenton (1961), pp. 38-40; 260-1. The first charter (f. 53) includes—'Concedimus igitur et statuendo sanctimus ut monarchi ...' and 'Quicunque ergo hanc donacionem enervare presumpserit deleatur de libro vivencium et descendet ad inferni novissima; amen.' Compare the more elaborate anathema in the second (Stenton, 261).

[44] Binham Cartulary, ff. 51v-52, printed Avrom Saltman, *Theobald Archbishop of Canterbury* (1956), 247-8.

[45] He was the Richard de Calum or Calne who held $7\frac{1}{2}$ fees of Robert de Valognes in 1166 (*Red Books of the Exchequer*, i. 360).

[46] Binham Cartulary, f. 50v. The archbishop's letter, coupled with the clear implication of Roger de Valognes' charter, surely places Agnes as the younger sister. Milsom, (1981), 78, takes the other view to the point of doubting the existence of a younger sister.

[47] Ibid., f. 51.

[48] Ibid, ff. 50v, 51-51v.

ried out in the presence of both Geoffrey and his wife, Agnes; his confirmation of the grant was executed in the monks' chapter at Binham, in which he was admitted to the spiritual benefits of the house.[49] The grant was of half Binham, to be held by the service of a third of a knight; this service was subsequently conceded to the monks by the chief lord, Peter de Valognes.[50]

What interest did this leave to the older sister and her descendants? Certainly not the other part of Barney; that was a tenement which Geoffrey Tresgoz held of a different barony and conceded to the monks in his own right.[51] The senior sister retained some interest in the advowson, which her daughter, Sibilla of Colne, and Sibilla's husband conceded to the monks after final concord concluded before Peter des Roches and other justices in 1214;[52] but the advowson was not part of the original grant.[53] Sibilla of Colne was also vouched to warranty in a grand assize between Richard prior of Binham and Robert of Horkesley, concerning a carucate in Barney and Thursford, which was concluded by concord in 1235.[54] But that this was not part of the junior daughter's portion is demonstrated by a charter of Sibilla's grandson, which distinguished the gift of Walter de Valognes from that of Walter and Robert of Horkesley.[55] This charter, whereby Walter, son of Walter, son of John Bernard, great grandson of Walter de Valognes's elder daughter, abandoned all claim in Barney and Thursford wherein the monks of Binham held by gift of Walter de Valognes, Walter of Horkesley, Robert his son, or any other, is the first indication that the senior sister or her heirs had any interest whatsoever in the lands which the younger sister, Agnes, conceded to Binham c. 1145. It dates from the late thirteenth century. Prior to that the senior sister and her heirs never intruded into the acts of the junior; the junior line confirmed Walter de Valognes's grant repeatedly without any reference to the senior; their acts were attested by different witnesses. It is difficult to avoid the conclusion

[49] 'Notifico vobis per presentia scripta in capitula fratrum ecclesie [sancte] Marie de Binham, accepta societate eorundem et beneficio loci me confirmasse predicte ecclesie de Binham dimidium partem ville que Berneya vocatur in terris, pratis, silvis, pascuis et hominibus et insuper advocacionem et dominium ecclesie ipsius ville sicut coram Theobaldo archiepiscopo inde fuit facta composicio deinde divisa et in fundo (*recte* funiculo) distributionis partita' (Ibid., f. 51).

[50] Ibid, f. 55.

[51] Ibid., f. 50.

[52] Ibid., ff. 52v, 56; *Curia Regis Rolls*, vii. 286.

[53] See n. 49 above where the grant of the advowson was made *insuper*. There is no specific mention of the advowson in the charters of either Walter or Roger de Valognes.

[54] Binham Cartulary, f. 56–56v; *Curia Regis Rolls*, xv. no. 521.

[55] Binham Cartulary, f. 59v.

that originally there had been no *parage*, that the division of *c.* 1145 had been absolute.[56]

The documents concerning Barney reveal nothing about the division and performance of feudal service. This is best examined at baronial level where division among heiresses began to take effect in the very same period. The Domesday holdings of Arnulf de Hesdin descended to his second son who was probably hanged at Shrewsbury in 1138. Thereafter part descended through the marriage of one of Arnulf's daughters to the Fitzalans of Oswestry and part through the marriage of another to the Chaworths and the earls of Salisbury.[57] The two parts constituted distinct baronies each accounting separately for feudal service.[58] The same happened to the lands of William le Meschin when his son died without issue in 1135-40: one part of his lands descended through one daughter to the counts of Aumale, to become the honour of Skipton; another descended through a second daughter to the Courcys; yet another smaller portion went through a third daughter to the Mortimers.[59] Once again the service was divided.[60] The pattern was repeated in 1147-8 in the case of the lands of William Peverel of Dover and Bourn (Cambridgeshire) which were divided first among four and then among three sisters,[61] and yet again in the division which followed the death of Robert Trussebut in 1193.[62] In both these instances the feudal service was divided and accounted separately to the Exchequer by each of the parceners, her husband and her heirs.[63] When portions were subsequently divided further among a later generation of heiresses the service was further fragmented.[64]

---

[56] This argument has to assume that Walter Bernard's charter was occasioned by circumstances not revealed in the cartulary. Another interpretation might be that the partition had reached the third generation, that the junior line performed homage to the senior and that the senior line's confirmation was now sought. Unfortunately, although it is clear that the senior line was now in the third generation, I have not been able to establish that this was true of the junior line. Moreover, the charter is a quitclaim not a confirmation and embraces other grants besides that of Walter de Valognes. In any case such an interpretation would not necessarily mean that *parage* had been intended *ab initio*. Notions derived from *parage* may have crept in as Glanville's doctrine took hold.

[57] J. H. Round. *Studies in peerage and family history* (1907), 115-129; I. J. Sanders, *English Baronies* (Oxford, 1961), 124-5.

[58] *Red Book of the Exchequer*, i. 274; 297-8.

[59] *Early Yorkshire Charters*, vii. 7-9.

[60] *Red Book of the Exchequer*, i. 225; 430-2; *Books of Fees*, 97, 425.

[61] W. Farrer, *Feudal Cambridgeshire* (Cambridge, 1920), 159-166, R. W. Eyton, *Antiquities of Shropshire*, 12 vols. (1853-60), ix. 64-77.

[62] *Early Yorkshire Charters*, x. 13-19.

[63] For Peverel see *Red Book of the Exchequer*, i. 366-9, 372. For Trussebut see *Pipe Roll 6 Richard*, 154; *Pipe Roll 13 John*, 31, *Book of Fees*, 157, 191.

[64] For Peverel see Eyton, *Shropshire*, ix, 72-7; I. J. Sanders, *Baronies*, 19.

And just as the service was partitioned so also were the incidents. Where the payment of relief can be traced and isolated from the husband's it was paid separately by each parcener and her heirs.[65]

In view of this it is easy enough to say that, in the case of tenancies-in-chief, Glanville was simply wrong, or was at least guilty of an error of omission. But it is not quite so simple. First, divisions and expectancies were biased by political interests. In 1176 for example, the earldom of Gloucester and the lion's share of the Gloucester lands were diverted to Earl William's youngest daughter, Isabella, who was to marry Henry II's youngest son John, the future king. The arrangement was concluded by King Henry and William earl of Gloucester, whose son had died ten years earlier. Isabella's two elder sisters and their husbands simply received £100 per annum from the estates.[66] An even less equitable distribution was made between the co-heiresses and husbands of William de Say in 1185. In this case the younger daughter, Matilda, and her husband William of Buckland received the manor of Brunnington, the service of two tenants and the promise of land worth £10 from future acquisitions in return for abandoning any claim to such further acquisitions to the elder sister, Beatrice, and her husband, Geoffrey Fitz Peter. Those further acquisitions would include the honour of Mandeville and the earldom of Essex. The division was confirmed before Henry II at Melksham and attested by Ranulf Glanville.[67]

Secondly, it is extremely difficult to penetrate behind the formal results of a partition to the decisions which led to it. The one early case where this is possible provides some basis for understanding the line which Glanville took. This concerns Walter Espec, one of the chief agents of Henry I in northern England, a leader of the baronial army which defeated the Scots near Northallerton in 1138, who lived on to retire to the cloister in 1153 before his death two years later. Walter must in all probability have been a party to the *statutum decretum*; it would be astonishing if a man of his weight had not been consulted. He may have had a particular concern; a later tradition at Rievaulx provided him with a fictitious son who died in a riding accident, as a result of which he founded three monasteries and divided his lands among his three sisters.[68] But what in fact hap-

---

[65] See in particular the relief of Gilbert Pecche of 200m. in 1241, which included 50m. for a third of Bourn (*Excerpta e Rotulis Finium*, ii. 17). Gilbert represented the senior coparcener. Compare the direct statement concerning Agatha, youngest of the Trussebut sisters that she held Kirk Deighton, part of the Trussebut inheritance, in chief of the Crown (*Cal. Inq. p.m.*, i. no. 97; *Yorkshire Inquisitions*; no. 11).

[66] *Earldom of Gloucester Charters*, 5.

[67] Public Record Office, D L, 10/29, *Pipe Roll 10 Richard*, 139.

[68] *Cartularium Abbathiae de Rievalle*, ed. J. C. Atkinson (Surtees Society, 1889), 263-4.

pened was different, for sometime between Walter's death in 1155 and the completion of the Pipe roll of 1158 Robert de Ros, son of one of the sisters, fined in 1000m. for the inheritance of Walter Espec, and the sons of the other two sisters each fined in 100m. for the division of the land against Robert de Ros.[69] A confused entry on the Charter roll of 1200 which largely repeats a charter of Henry II spells out the resulting terms.[70] Robert received the whole honour of Walter Espec on the understanding that he gave £30 of land to each of his cousins, William de Bussy and Geoffrey de Trailly, and a life-interest in £50 of land to Jordan, William de Bussy's brother. The corroboration clause of this charter is a model of muddled or ambivalent thinking. Robert de Ros and his heirs were to have the whole of the honour which had belonged to Walter Espec in Northumberland and elsewhere 'except for those £30 of land which William de Bussy has thence with five enfeoffed knights and except for the other £30 of land which Geoffrey de Trailly has thence with five enfeoffed knights.' It would take a Glanville perhaps to comment on the precise meaning of the exception and the sense of 'has thence' and that of course, more generally, is what Glanville did. But the record of feudal service presents less ambivalence. Robert de Ros retained Wark, Helmsley and one fee in Walter Espec's patrimony of Old Wardon; Bussy and Trailly divided the rest of Old Wardon, with the service of five knights each.[71] In 1161 the sheriff accounted for the scutage of the knights of the whole of Old Wardon, but William de Bussy accounted for his own portion alone in 1162 and this was also presented separately in the cartae of 1166.[72] By 1185 the Bussy portion had been further divided between coheiresses; so also was the service.[73]

Within the arrangements which confronted Glanville there were embedded several general problems: the distinction between inheritance and acquisition, which may sometimes have influenced a partition;[74] the possible confusion of inheritance in the female line with

[69] *Pipe Roll 2-3-4 Henry II*, 140, 146.

[70] *Rot. Chartarum*, 32b.

[71] For Helmsley see *Early Yorkshire Charters*, x. 15. For the division of Old Wardon see William Farrer, 'The Honour of Old Wardon', *Publications of the Bedfordshire Historical Record Society*, xi (1927), 6ff; Sanders (1960), 133.

[72] *Pipe Roll 7 Henry II*, 12; *Pipe Roll 8 Henry II*, 42; *Red Book of the Exchequer*, i. 335-6.

[73] *Rotuli de Dominabus*, 11, 45; Sanders (1960), 133.

[74] This could well help to explain the division of Walter Espec's estates. The descendants of his two elder daughters shared his inheritance of Old Wardon. Robert de Ros, descendant of the youngest, received merely one fee of Old Wardon, but took all Walter's acquisitions. Robert probably got the lion's share on other grounds, but the distinction between inheritance and acquisition explains how the shares were defined. That Robert was descended from the youngest daughter is generally accepted. See *Beds. Historical Record Soc.*, xi. 4; *Early Yorkshire Charters*, x. 144.

marriage-portions,[75] and above all the need to determine *aesnecia*, *aînesse* or seniority. Now priority did not always go to the eldest heiress as the word *aînesse* implied and Glanville assumed.[76] It might be argued that it should go to the youngest if she was still resident and unmarried in her father's household at his death;[77] sometimes it went to the husband or descendant, who like Robert de Ros, had the greatest pull.[78] It might even be divided, as it was when Richard I split the Giffard inheritance between Richard de Clare and William Marshal with the proviso that Richard should have the *aînesse* and the *caput* in England and William the same in Normandy.[79] But it always had to be settled in order to allocate the chief messuage, *caput* or castle. That was easy. It was much more difficult to determine what to do about jurisdiction. Glanville's scheme provided one solution; first *parage*, then tenancy of the senior line. In these circumstances the original jurisdictional structure would be preserved; the acts of the junior lines would be confirmed and warranted by the senior; and this indeed is how Glanville's system came to be reflected in the records of the King's court.[80] But in these circumstances the junior heirs would be less free agents, with regard both to themselves and their beneficiaries. How could they dispose of land in perpetuity until they had performed homage for it? The alternative was to allow the partition to break the pattern of jurisdiction or at least to supplement it as more and more enactments and litigation sprang from the new tenurial conditions. If this happened it was reflected not so much in actions in the King's court, since there was far less need to argue about warranty, as in attestation of the charters of the parceners and their descendants. Sisters and their husbands may sometimes confirm each other's acts, cousins less frequently, their descendants rarely. By the same token witness lists may overlap at first; then they too move apart. The process was determined by no rule, merely by the convenience of benefactors and beneficiaries. It signalled the reordering of jurisdiction, in all that stemmed from the granting and confirmation of charters, around lines of tenure changed by the consequences of partition.

[75] For the relationship between partition and previous marriage-portions and actions arising therefrom see Milsom (1981), 81 ff.

[76] Glanville, ed. Hall. 75-6. For a straightforward example see the arrangements envisaged for the earldom Devon, 1200 (*Rot. Chartarum*, 52b).

[77] See the case of the succession to William of Buckland, 1218 (*Bracton's Note Book*, ed. F. W. Maitland, 3 vols. London 1887, i. no. 12), discussed with other possible cases by Milsom (1981), 66.

[78] See above, 15-16.

[79] *Cartae Antiquae Rolls 11-20* (Pipe Roll Society, N. S. xxxiii, 1957) no. 564.

[80] Milsom (1981), 71-2.

The process is admirably illustrated in the descent of the lands of
Hamo Peverel, which passed with those of his brothers Pain and
Robert, to three co-heiresses.[81] None seem to have had seniority;
Henry II addressed all three of their husbands jointly in a mandate
ordering them to restore to the monks of Shrewsbury the land in
Crudgington which has been given by Hamo Peverel whose heirs
they were.[82] The charters in which they restored the land were
identical in form and shared some of the witnesses.[83] It was a con-
vincing example of the solidarity of heirs, the occasion no doubt
engineered by the monks of Shrewsbury. But it soon weakened.
There is no evidence of such co-operation in the next generation.[84]
The same is broadly true of the descendants of Walter Espec and
Robert Trussebut: occasional and apparently haphazard confirmation of each other's acts or shared action in the courts, usually in
the first generation; thereafter separation.[85] At Barney, where the
consequences of partition were accentuated by the immediate alienation of the portion of Agnes de Valognes to the monks of Binham,
the division seems almost tangible. There was a market place and
courthouse with a garden to its south and a cross to the east before
its door. These were the landmarks from which the demarcation
of Agnes's lands began.[86] Her portion was transferred to the monks
with sake and soke and all free customs; the monks were to deal
with men, lands and goods *per sectam ecclesie* as seemed best to them
with prohibition from no-one.[87] In this case the linked effect of

[81] Farrer, *Feudal Cambridgeshire*, 160.

[82] Henry II to Hamo Pecche, Geoffrey of Waterville and Hugh of Dover—'Precipio
quod juste et sine dilatione reddatis Abbatie Salop ... terram suam de Crugeltona
quam Hamo Peverellus cujus hèredes vos estis eis dedit' (Eyton, *Shropshire*, ix. 67).

[83] *The Cartulary of Shrewsbury Abbey*, ed. Una Rees (2 vols., Aberystwyth, 1975), i.
nos. 29-31.

[84] Compare the charters of Hugh of Dover, Gilbert Pecche and Geoffrey and Asceline de Waterville (Eyton, *Shropshire*, ix. 67, 72, 76). For analogous action in a yet
further generation, between co-heiresses of Asceline de Waterville, see ibid. ix. 77, 79.

[85] In the case of Espec the descendents of one of the families, Bussy, now represented
by heir's general in the next generation, viz. Builly and Wake, were parties to an
action in 1198-1200 concerning the church of Old Wardon against the abbot of Old
Wardon. One of the other original participating families, Trailly, figured in this but
not as a party and the action was resolved against the heir's general of Bussy (*Beds.
Historical Record Soc.*, xi. 9-11). In the case of Trussebut, Cecily and Agatha made
fine for land in Newsome in 1197 (*Early Yorkshire Charters*, x. 48-9); all three co-heirs
combined in litigation against Henry du Puiset concerning Market Weighton in 1204
(*Curia Regis Rolls*, x. 42); and sometime after 1227 Hilary, who was not the senior,
confirmed a gift to the Temple by her dear nephew, Robert de Ros, who died in
retirement as a Templar (*Early Yorkshire Charters*, x. 42).

[86] The bounds appear in their earliest form in the charter of Agnes de Valognes'
husband Geoffrey Tresgoz and in greater detail in the confirmations of her daughter
and son-in-law (Binham Cartulary, ff. 51, 50v, 51v).

[87] Ibid., ff. 50v, 51v.

partition and alienation in alms was the fragmentation of jurisdiction. The relevance of this to the expansion of royal jurisdiction
will not be lost. One effect of the *statutum decretum* was to aid the
work of Henry II.

The reasons for Glanville's choice will now be obvious. The lands
which he left to his children were largely accumulated during his
own lifetime as an administrator; it is reasonable to imagine that he
would seek to give them some unity.[88] He knew as he wrote that
they would descend to his three daughters. After his death the eldest
of the daughters enjoyed seniority; she and her husband were primarily accountable for her father's debts. Occasionally the Exchequer wavered and took an interest in the other heirs, but the main
weight of the evidence suggests that *parage* was in operation among
Glanville's descendants.[89] Glanville had described as the custom of
England what he wanted to see as the custom of England. He must
have been a powerful influence in implanting such a custom. This
assumes, of course, that the law book we know as Glanville was
written by Glanville. If we transfer the authorship to the next likely
candidate, Geoffrey fitz Peter, the same point arises in a different
but perhaps even weightier form, for on the seniority of his wife
depended the honour of Mandeville and the earldom of Essex.[90]

This long *excursus* on how the *statum decretum* took effect helps to
explain why it was enacted. There was a much wider choice of
action than that indicated by Glanville. Baronies were divided into
distinct entities. Feudal incidents were thereby preserved and multiplied. Lords and individual heirs might conclude arrangements
which gave one of the heirs a lion's share. But heirs could go their
own separate ways, thereby fragmenting the old pattern of justice
of a single united fief. These effects may not all have been foreseen
with equal clarity. But they provide the grounds for understanding
motive.

It is best to begin with the lord of a fief, who was not only a lord
but also a father of sons and daughters, and one conscious that there
were other lords, also fathers. So the question which he faced was
not just one of whether to divide his own lands among co-heiresses,
were he to be placed in that predicament. He would also be con-

---

[88] R. Mortimer, 'The family of Ranulf Glanville', *Bull. Inst. Hist. Research*, liv
(1981), 1-16, especially 14-15.

[89] S. J. Bailey, 'Ranulf de Glanville and his children', *The Cambridge Law Journal*
(1957), 163-181, especially 173-6. See also J. N. L. Myres, 'Notes on the History of
Butley priory, Suffolk' *Oxford Essays in medieval history presented to H. E. Salter* (Oxford,
1934), 190-206, especially 190-3, which traces the descent of the patronage of Butley
in the senior line.

[90] *Complete Peerage*, v. 120-22.

scious of the greatly increased opportunities which the division of other baronies would create for his younger sons, for the market of actual or likely heiresses would be greatly expanded, and that at a time when his capacity to provide for younger sons was reduced as the flow of acquisitions, from which he and others had benefited, dwindled.[91] And partition could do no harm so long as seniority was applied to castles, office and title. Indeed, it might well multiply the incidents of marriage, wardship and relief if each parcener and her heirs were made directly dependent on the lord. It diversified the exercise of patronage and probably added to the profits. Looked at from the point of view of the lord, especially if the lord were king, parceny was a bargain. He could scarcely lose.

The same was true for potential husbands. To be sure, the lucky one who might have married an heiress sole would lose something. But all the others would gain part of an inheritance or a chance thereof, and usually this would be far more extensive than a bride's marriage-portion. And there may have been consequent advantages for others. There was less need for families to provide for younger sons if heiresses could be found to sustain them.

Finally there were advantages for the potential heiresses. They were now heiresses in parallel rather than in series. Younger sisters stood a better chance of better marriages, with more hope of inheriting and less dependence on the paternal or fraternal charity of the marriage portion. Since we have suffered so long with the Oedipus complex we might dub this the Cinderella syndrome. Who knows what ranged through the imagination of young girls and women, some of whom must have been raised on the varied sexuality of the *Lais* of Marie de France, a woman poet composing for an audience of women?[92]

However, if the change might be expected to bring benefits for all, those who disposed of marriages and controlled succession benefited more, for it multiplied their resources; and the king benefited most of all. For him the change was one of degree; an enactment which could transform the life of the younger womenfolk was for him little more than fine tuning which improved the performance of his incidents. Kings and their officials soon took note. In 1176 an enquiry into women in the king's gift was included in the articles of the eyre.[93] From 1185 the record of a similar enquiry survives as the

[91] In the event the conflicts of Stephen's reign increased the flow of acquisitions but this could not have been foreseen when the *statutum decretum* was agreed, as I suggest, 1130–35.

[92] So Elizabeth Williams in Christine Fell, *Women in Anglo-Saxon England* (1984), 175–9, to whom I should not attribute my assessment of the audience. The *Lais* are ed. A. Ewert (Oxford, 1947).

[93] Assize of Northampton, cap. 9.

Rotuli de Dominabus et Pueris et Puellis.[94] From 1130 onwards the Pipe
rolls provide systematic information on the Crown's exploitation of
rights of wardship and marriage. From 1199 the Fine rolls illustrate
the system in even greater detail. The abundance of this evidence
creates the impression that the system not merely yielded profit but
was designed for financial exploitation, and that the king's right of
marriage was used not simply to ensure loyal vassals but to provide
parvenus of unknown, low or alien extraction with the permanent
status which marriage to an heiress could provide.[95] Such is the
standard picture. It still leaves room for some discussion.

It is common ground that the king's control of wardship and
marriage established a kind of market with some very grubby characteristics. The coronation charter of Henry I implies that Rufus
had charged for his approval of marriages.[96] Henry's promise to
abandon the practice was vain. The Pipe roll of 1130 reveals a brisk
trade. The Exchequer already distinguished between widows who
brought their husbands dower and marriage portions and heiresses
who brought 'land'.[97] Through one large proffer of 1000m. William
Pont de l'Arche obtained the daughter and office of Robert
Mauduit, who had been one of the chamberlains.[98] Another proffer
was plainly speculative: William Maltravers offered 1000m. and
£100 for the widow of Hugh de Laval, to hold the whole of Hugh's
lands (the honour of Pontefract) for fifteen years and her dower and
marriage-portion thereafter.[99] These were not small transactions;
how the offers were assessed the roll does not reveal. The *Rotuli de
Dominabus* of 1185, however, illustrates the system of assessment in
detail. The justices now took evidence of the value and annual yield
of a woman's lands and the number and sex of her children. They
received estimates of her age and her childrens' ages. Some of the
returns assess her social standing and the potential of the incidents
to be derived from her by indicating that she was of baronial or

[94] Ed. J. H. Round, Pipe Roll Society, 35 (1913). The *Rotuli* are the returns made
by the justices of the evidence presented in court. See Round ibid, pp. xvii–xix. They
are not, as they are sometimes presented, a record of Exchequer administration,
although they were used by the Exchequer for the subsequent management of the
estates of some heiresses.

[95] A. L. Poole. *Obligations of Society in the XII and XIII centuries* (Oxford, 1946), 97–
100; Sidney Painter, *Studies in the history of the English feudal barony* (Baltimore, 1943)
66–72.

[96] Cap. 3.

[97] The terminology of the Pipe roll and the coronation charter is identical. Only
one entry on the roll, a proffer of Williams Maltravers, associates a woman with
hereditas (*Pipe Roll 31 Henry I*, 87). She was his wife.

[98] Ibid., 37.

[99] Ibid., 34.

knightly stock.[100] That was not the end of the story. By the reigns of Richard and John it is not unusual to find instances of competitive bidding or of charges placed so high that they can only be regarded as financial and political extortion.[101]

The seamier side of the system is even better revealed in a tale told by Adam of Eynsham.[102] It starts with Agnes, wife of the Lincolnshire knight, Thomas of Saleby. She was young, he was old, and their marriage was barren. She was determined that, if he were to die, she should not come into the custody of his brother, William of Hartshill. So she pretended pregnancy, padded herself well out, took to her bed in pretended labour and, with the connivance of a woman of the neighbourhood, produced a supposititious daughter whom she had christened, with appalling candour, Grace. All details were attended to; her aged husband was well briefed and the real mother was brought into the household as nurse and foster-mother. However, her brother-in-law was not to be put off and he carried the case to the royal court whence it was claimed by Bishop Hugh of Lincoln as a matter for ecclesiastical jurisdiction; Hugh investigated the matter, pronounced on it sternly from the pulpit and threatened excommunication against the offenders, but the aged husband died before he could confess his complicity. Grace was now an heiress and she was transferred with her lands to Adam de Neville, brother of Hugh, the chief forester. Adam of Eynsham tells us that he married her though she was less than four years old. Meanwhile the Bishop, reinforced by a confession of complicity from the real mother, ordered that sentence of excommunication should be pronounced every Sunday from all the neighbouring churches. In 1199 William of Hartshill launched an action in the *curia regis* against Adam de Neville; Adam was able by trickery to bring the case to the favourable judgment of the royal court but was snatched away by death before he could hear of his triumph. He was immediately followed by others, apparently undeterred by the accumulation of fatalities which were coming to be associated with the wretched Grace. Before the year was out she was given in marriage to a second husband, one of the king's chamberlains. He too died, and at the time at which Adam of Eynsham wrote she had been passed to a third who was worse than all the rest. Now the main points in Adam's story are undoubtedly correct.[103] The only serious

[100] A. L. Poole (1946), 100–103; D. M. Stenton, *The English Woman in History* (1957), 38–40.

[101] A. L. Poole (1946) 99–100; J. C. Holt, *Magna Carta* (Cambridge, 1965), 107–8.

[102] *Magna Vita Sancti Hugonis*, ed. Decima L. Douie and Hugh Farmer, 2 vols. (1961), ii. 20–27.

[103] It is succinctly stated in the first record of the action in 1194 (*Rot. Curiae Regis*, i. 78).

criticism is that Adam de Neville was Grace's guardian, not her husband.[104] However, she had certainly been married to the second intruder in the story, Norman de Camera, at the point at which she passed to the third, Brian de Lisle, in 1205.[105] So she was certainly a widow at the age of ten. The action concerning the supposititious child and the inheritance came before the royal court between 1194 and 1199.[106] William of Hartshill backed his claim with an offer of 500m.[107] Norman de Camera acquired his young wife at the cost of 200m. and she was passed on to Brian de Lisle for 300m.[108] Brian reinforced his proffer with some potent guarantors, including the bishops of Salisbury and London, Hugh, archdeacon of Wells, William, earl of Salisbury, William Marshal, earl of Pembroke and Saer de Quency; a wise precaution given the history of the case.[109] But nothing availed against the damnation threatened by Bishop Hugh. All the marriages were barren and the lands ultimately reverted to the line of the rightful heir.[110]

It was not all like that. First, a fair proportion of proffers came from relatives of the heir or heiress, or from widows seeking to continue control of their children.[111] Secondly, the evidence of resistance to the system requires careful handling. The murder in 1135 of William Maltravers, the royal official who intruded by the purchase of a marriage into the honour of Pontefract, was an expression of acute hostility among the tenants of the honour, but it was an isolated incident.[112] The more frequent and obvious objections came not from tenants, but from widows seeking to maintain their widowhood. Sometimes these sprang from real conflict. In 1194 the stock of the widowed Countess of Aumale was sold because she had refused to marry William de Forz: she married him.[113] In 1205 King John seized the dower lands of Alice, widow of John Belet, because she refused to marry according to his will; a proffer for her had been made by Ralph Ridel. Ultimately her father stepped in and paid

---

[104] Ibid., i. 452.
[105] *Rot. de Oblatis et Finibus*, 240.
[106] *Rot. Curiae Regis*, i. 78, 452.
[107] *Rot. de Oblatis et Finibus*, 20.
[108] Ibid, 40, 240.
[109] Ibid., 240–1.
[110] *Rotuli Hundredorum*, i. 294; *Magna Vita Sancti Hugonis*, ii. 27n. I am indebted to the careful annotation of the editors for much of the detailed record of the case.
[111] The exact proportion would be difficult to calculate because family relationships are not always stated in the record of the proffers on the Pipe or Fine roll. My impression of the Fine rolls of the early years of John's reign is that roughly 50% of the proffers involved some family relationship. This is likely to be an underestimate.
[112] W. E. Wightman, *The Lacy Family in England and Normandy 1066–1194* (Oxford, 1966), 68–73.
[113] *Pipe Roll 6 Richard*, 163; Doris M. Stenton (1957), 36.

to preserve her widowhood and recover her dower.[114] But these issues seem more contentious than they were in general because of the official jargon of the Exchequer; widows made fined 'that they should not be compelled', or 'that they should not be distrained to marry', and it is chiefly from this common form of words that the general impression of compulsion arises. In reality these daunting phrases must often have meant no more than that a widow had decided to buy exemption from the royal right of marriage. When she did so she was bidding not just for freedom but also for power, power over her inheritance, her dower and her marriage-portion. One of the first great ladies to do so was the Countess Lucy, thrice widowed after the death of Ranulf le Meschin, earl of Chester, before 1130.[115] She offered 500m. that she should not take a husband for five years. She also offered an additional 100m. that she might do justice in her court amongst her men; already by 1130 there was an appeal to the king from her jurisdiction. Finally she offered a further large sum for the recovery of her patrimony which had been dispersed when her last husband became earl of Chester.[116] In this too she was successful. There is a strong suspicion that the Countess Lucy fined for widowhood in order to put her house in order.

So the widow's fine is ambiguous evidence. Contemporary comment is equally unhelpful. We know from the letters of Archbishop Lanfranc that some English ladies fled to monasteries after 1066 'for fear of the French'.[117] Orderic commented that:

> Noble maidens were exposed to the insults of low-born soldiers and lamented their dishonouring by the scum of the earth. Matrons, highly born and handsome, mourned the loss of their loving husbands and almost all their friends, and preferred death to life.[118]

But he was not particularly concerned that a woman might be demeaned by marriage to one of lower status. He was surprised when Matilda de Grandmesnil widow of Hugh de Mt. Pincon abandoned friends and kindred in Normandy to accompany her new love, a young knight called Matthew, on the journey to Jerusalem, but he made no comment to suggest that the association was socially

---

[114] *Rot de Oblatis et Finibus*, 226, 287; *Curia Regis Rolls*, iii. 257; A. L. Poole (1946), 98.

[115] *Complete Peerage*, vii, Appendix J, 743-6.

[116] *Pipe Roll 31 Henry I*, 110, 114.

[117] *The Letters of Lanfranc Archbishop of Canterbury*, ed. H. Clover and M. Gibson (Oxford, 1979), no. 53 (1077-89).

[118] Orderic Vitalis, ed. Chibnall, ii. 268; cf. William of Poitiers, ed. Raymonde Forville, 232.

demeaning.[119] The same is true of his famous description of the men whom King Henry I raised from the dust. They were 'of base stock' or 'low birth'; they were ennobled, 'set on the summit of power,' rendered formidable to the chief men of the land; but Orderic, so conscious of their social and political promotion, did not allude to their marriages.[120] Yet one of those he named, Richard Basset, and many whom he did not name, who enjoyed rapid promotion under Henry I, William and Nigel d'Aubigny, William d'Aubigny of Belvoir, Miles of Gloucester, Pain fitz John, Eustace fitz John, William Maltravers, William Pont de l'Arche, owed much of their new found fortune to the marriage of a well endowed lady, usually an heiress.[121] Orderic's silence in the matter was not unusual. The vernacular literature which entertained the twelfth-century noble household contains only one clear example of an heiress demeaned in marriage. That was Gaimar's heroine Argentille, heiress to the kingdom of Lindsey, forced by her wicked uncle to marry a cook, so that the uncle could usurp the realm. The cook turned out to be Havelock prince of Denmark, so all ended well. Gaimar wrote about 1140; the tale was repeated in the *Lai d'Haveloc* of c. 1200.[122] That apart, one or two tales turn on forced marriages in which the woman feels disgraced, but without any element of social disparity between husband and wife.[123] The possibility of disparity was recognised. In the case of the supposititious heiress, Grace, Bishop Hugh of Lincoln pointed out to one of the intending husbands that the girl was a serf and that he would not enjoy her for very long,[124] but no-one apart from Gaimar made much of the theme.

[119] Orderic Vitalis, ed. Chibnall, iii. 166.
[120] Ibid., vi. 16.
[121] For Nigel d'Aubigny, William d'Aubigny of Belvoir, Miles of Gloucester, William Maltravers and William Pont de L'Arche see above pp. 7 n., 9, 21, 23. William d'Aubigny married Maud, daughter of Roger Bigod (*Complete Peerage*, i. 233); Pain FitzJohn married Sybil, daughter of Hugh de Lacy (Wightman, 175-83); Eustace fitz John married first Beatrice, daughter and heiress of Ivo de Vescy and, secondly Agnes, sister and co-heiress of William FitzNigel, constable of Chester (*Complete Peerage*, xii. pt. ii. 273-4). For general comment see R. W. Southern *Medieval Humanism and other Studies* (Oxford, 1970), 214-20.
[122] Geffrei Gaimar, *L'Estoire des Engleis*, ed. A. Bell, Anglo-Norman Text Society, 14-16 (1960), especially lines 96-167. For the *Lai d'Haveloc*, *Havelok the Dane* and other derivations see L. H. Loomis, *Medieval Romance in England* (New York, 1963), 103-114.
[123] Enforced marriage and misalliance are themse in the *Roman d'Eneas*, *Orsan de Beauvais*, *Raoul de Cambrai* and *Daurel and Beton* but without any emphasis on disparagement. In Chretien of Troyes' *Yvain* Laudine de Landuc is eager to secure the hand of Yvain because such a marriage will be no disgrace for the daughter of a duke (ed. T. Reid, lines 1815-18), but that scarcely present disparagement as a burning issue. I am indebted to Dr Peter Noble for bringing these sources to my attention.
[124] *Magna Vita S. Hugonis*, ii. 26.

All this has skirted round the term disparagement, and for good reason. For the word has come to play a quite inappropriate role. To put it in rough and ready terms: in 1215 King John promised in Magna Carta, following a demand in the Articles of the Barons, that heirs would be married without disparagement and after consultation with the nearest relative; this must therefore have been a ground for complaint; King John and perhaps others must therefore have disparaged heiresses; the cry of 'no disparagement' is therefore yet one more example of baronial protest. Such is the usual interpretation.[125] It is quite wrong. First the derivatives of the word *disparagare* seem not to have been used in England before 1194. In that year two proffers were entered on the Pipe roll, each concerning the marriage of a male heir on the understanding that he was not to be disparaged.[126] The same word was applied to both heirs and heiresses on the roll of 1195 and the following years;[127] it occurs more frequently, but still sporadically, on the Fine rolls of John's reign. The evidence leaves no room for doubt: 'no disparagement' was a condition imposed by the crown; there is no evidence at all that it was a requirement of the suppliant. The first evidence comes from 1194; it provides yet one more example of a possible initiative by the new justiciar, Hubert Walter. The words seem to occur at random, a few instances each year. There is no obvious reason why they should have been attached to one proffer and not another. But coming as they do from the Exchequer there can be little doubt about the purpose: they were intended not so much to protect the heir or heiress but to state the conditions on which the proffer had been agreed and to exclude the *parvenu* not because he was a social threat (although he might well be that) but because his intrusion would alter the terms of the negotiation. 'No disparagement' was a financial constraint, not a social complaint. It was invented by the Crown. King John lost little when it was included in Magna Carta.[128]

What then was disparagement? It is easier to say what it was not. Through his wife Isabel de Clare, the 'bachelor' William Marshal, fourth son of a knight, became Earl of Pembroke.[129] No-one objected. Through marriage Geoffrey fitz Peter, knight, justice of the

---

[125] A. L. Poole (1948), 97-8; S. Painter, *The reign of King John* (Baltimore, 1949), 217-19.

[126] *Pipe Roll 6 Richard*, 238.

[127] *Pipe Roll 7 Richard*, 177, 222, 246.

[128] I by-pass here the letter of 1212 of William the Lion of Scotland conceding the marriage of his son Alexander to King John 'ita quod non disparagetur' since it is of doubtful authenticity. See E. L. G. Stones, *Anglo-Scottish Relations 1174-1328* (1965), 12-13; *Regesta Regum Scottorum*, ii. ed. G. W. S. Barrow (Edinburgh, 1971), no. 505.

[129] *Complete Peerage*, x. 358.

forest and sheriff, acquired the honour of Mandeville and the earldom of Essex. No-one objected except the Walden chronicler and
that not on the grounds of disparagement.[130] In the next generation
Geoffrey's sons married the daughters of Robert fitz Walter, after
Richard of Clare the greatest of the barons of East Anglia.[131] No-
one forced Robert fitz Walter into these alliances. Sometime before
1210 Gilbert de Gant, one of the leaders of the Lincolnshire rebellion
in 1215 who laid claim to the earldom of Lincoln, married off his
daughter Juliana to a tenant, Geoffrey de Armenteres, whose father
held ten fees of the Gant honour. The agreement was attested by a
choice selection of tenants of the Gant honour.[132] They can scarcely
have found the alliance unacceptable. Plainly all these marriages
came within the social pale. But there was one which did not. On
1 September 1216 Baldwin de Redvers, son and heir to the Earl of
Devon, died aged sixteen. Within a month his widow, Margaret, who
was a double heiress, both to Warin fitz Gerold and William de
Courcy, was given in marriage to Fawkes de Bréauté, the Norman
knight who was one of King John's most vigorous commanders in
the civil war.[133] The reaction to this marriage determined much that
followed. The scandal was threefold. First, there was a wide social
gap between the status of husband and wife; the instances I have
mentioned suggest that this might have been bridged. Secondly,
there may have been an element of violence in the arrangement.
When Margaret sought dissolution of the match in 1224 she
apparently claimed that she had been seized in time of war and
married against her will, or so at least we are told by Roger Wendover.[134] If so, it was a matter not of disparagement but of enforced remarriage. Third, Fawkes, though of respectable Norman
extraction, called down on his own head all that hostility which
was directed against the officials and soldiers whom King John
brought to England from the Touraine and Poitou. All those influences and instincts, political and administrative, legal, artistic, literary and linguistic which were steadily distinguishing England from
France and giving definition to a sense of Englishness, came to be
concentrated against him. He was seen not simply as a *parvenu*, an
intruder, but as an alien, a foreigner. He was the first layman of
Norman extraction to be damned as such. This was entirely the
work of Roger Wendover and Matthew Paris. During the civil war

---

[130] Ibid., v. 122–3, 124 n.b.
[131] Ibid., v. 127, 132.
[132] *Sir Christopher Hatton's Book of Seals*, ed. L. C. Lloyd and D. M. Stenton (Oxford, 1950), no. 298.
[133] *Complete Peerage*, iv. 316.
[134] *Chronica Majora*, iii. 87–8.

of 1215–17 Fawkes offended St Alban by levying 'tenseries' on the Abbey; in return St Alban's two historians pilloried him. At Margaret's death in 1252 Matthew could still recall—'Noble though she was, she was married to this ignoble creature, the pious to the impious, beauty to the foul, unwilling and coerced, she was handed over by the tyrant John to whom no evil was abhorrent'.[135] That was disparagement fiercely denounced. It was largely generated after the event. It stands in sharp contrast to a strictly contemporary document. Sometime, and probably quite soon after the marriage Warin FitzGerold mortgaged the manor of Wootton Courtenay to his new son-in-law in return for 200m. 'pro necessitate sua'. The deed acknowledges Fawkes and Margaret as man and wife and makes prospective arrangements for their heirs. It is attested by Peter des Roches, bishop of Winchester, William Marshal, earl of Pembroke, William Longsword, earl of Salisbury and others.[136] For the moment, at any rate, Fawkes enjoyed the blessing of the establishment.

Fawkes' case never had an end. He was driven out of England in 1224. Pope Honorius intervened on his behalf to sustain the matrimonial bond, but Archbishop Stephen Langton, who was well aware that the political situation in England made Fawkes's restoration impossible, dragged his feet. The case was resolved by Fawkes' death in 1226.[137] It never had an end in yet another sense. It has cast a lurid retrospective light on the provisions of Magna Carta ever since, so that it is sometimes used to help explain the provision against disparagement of 1215 even though it occurred a year later.[138] At the time it may have given the terms of Magna Carta a posthumous importance. The defeat of Fawkes may have made it easier for Ella, Countess of Salisbury, to reject the importunities of the young knight Raymond, nephew of Hubert de Burgh, when it was thought that her husband had died on the Crusade in 1226. But this too is a tale told by Wendover and repeated by Matthew Paris, and one which smacks too much of romance to ring true.[139]

These stories were symptoms. King John may easily have allowed the provision on disparagement in 1215 with the thought that it referred to little ill. He was probably right at the time. But within a few years those ills were being revealed as a disease.

[135] *Chronica Majora*, v. 323.

[136] H. M. C., *Rutland*, iv. 55–6.

[137] F. M. Powicke, *King Henry III and the Lord Edward*, 2 vols. (Oxford, 1947), i. 61–6.

[138] S. Painter, *The Reign of King John* (Baltimore, 1949), 218.

[139] *Chronica Majora*, iii. 101–2.

THE IDEA OF 'CHARACTER' IN VICTORIAN POLITICAL THOUGHT

By Stefan Collini, M.A., Ph.D., F.R.Hist.S.

READ 3 FEBRUARY 1984

I

WHEN in the summer of 1902 Helen Bosanquet published a book called *The Strength of the People* she sent a copy to Alfred Marshall. On the face of it, this might seem a rather unpromising thing to have done. Mrs Bosanquet, an active exponent of the Charity Organisation Society's 'casework' approach to social problems, had frequently expressed her dissatisfaction with what she regarded as the misleading abstractions of orthodox economics, and in her book she had even ventured a direct criticism of a point in Marshall's *Principles*. Marshall, then Professor of Political Economy at Cambridge and at the peak of his reputation as the most authoritative exponent of neo-classical economics in Britain, was, to say the least, sensitive to criticism, and he had, moreover, publicly taken issue with the C.O.S. on several previous occasions. But perhaps Mrs Bosanquet knew what she was about after all. In her book she had taken her text from the early nineteenth-century Evangelical Thomas Chalmers on the way in which character determines circumstances rather than vice versa, and, as the historian of the C.O.S. justly remarks, her book 'is a long sermon on the importance of character in making one family rich and another poor'.[1] Although Marshall can hardly have welcomed the general strictures on economics, he was able to reassure Mrs Bosanquet that 'in the main' he agreed with her: 'I have always held', he wrote to her, 'that poverty and pain, disease and death are evils of greatly less importance than they appear, except in so far as they lead to weakness of life and character'.[2] It may now seem hard not to detect a tone of wilful moralism here: one would scarcely have to be an abandoned materialist to feel that the evil of death, in particular, was

---

[1] Helen Bosanquet, *The Strength of the People: A Study in Social Economics* (1902), iv, 120, 129. C. L. Mowat, *The Charity Organisation Society: 1869–1913: Its Ideas and Work* (1961), 125.

[2] The correspondence is reprinted in the Preface to the 2nd edition of *Strength of the People* (1903), quotation at p. viii.

being somewhat underrated by this remark. But we can confidently exonerate Marshall from any charge of having disingenuously adopted the language of his correspondent just for the occasion, for both his theoretical writings and his more direct contributions to the economic and political debates of the previous twenty-five years had displayed a pervasive concern with the shaping and the efficacy of character under modern industrial conditions, and he had always insisted that it was a central part of the economist's professional task to identify those forces which 'will help to build up a strong and righteous character'.[3]

In seeking to understand this exchange, we shall not, I think, get very far if we explain away our two correspondents' affirmation of the crucial importance of character simply as the coincidence of peculiarly personal preoccupations, and yet it is hard to know quite where to turn for further enlightenment. Such limited notice as historians have taken of the role of character in Victorian political argument has tended to suggest that it should be understood as an ideological device for imposing middle-class values upon a potentially disruptive working-class.[4] Whatever truth this description may contain, it surely cannot be very near to the whole truth. Socialists, too, justified their preferred economic arrangements on the grounds that they would produce 'a higher type of character', and argued that 'the end of the State ... is, in fact, the development of character'.[5] As one Socialist commentator put it in the 1890s: 'Today the key word ... in economics is "character". ... [The reason] why individualist economists fear socialism is that they believe it will deteriorate character, and the reason why socialist economists seek socialism is their belief that under individualism character is deteriorating'.[6] Moreover, although invocations of the ideal of character

---

[3] Alfred Marshall, *The Principles of Economics*, Ninth (Variorum) Edition, with annotations by C. W. Guillebaud, 2 vols. (1961) (1st ed, 1890), I. 1; **II.** 17; **I.** 723-5, 740-4. For fuller discussion of Marshall's views on this topic, see Stefan Collini, Donald Winch, John Burrow, *That Noble Science of Politics: A Study in Nineteenth-Century Intellectual History* (Cambridge, 1983), 309-337.

[4] For the most sophisticated discussion along these lines, see Gareth Stedman Jones, *Outcast London: A Study in the Relationship between Classes in Victorian Society* (Oxford, 1971), part III.

[5] W. P. D. Bliss (ed.), *The Encyclopaedia of Social Reform* (1898), 1271; Sidney Ball, 'The Socialist Ideal', *Economic Review* IX (1899), 437. Ball's testimony is particularly relevant here because he had taken issue with the Bosanquets' 1895 volume: see esp. his 'The moral aspects of Socialism', *International Journal of Ethics* VI (1896), 291-322. Although Ball, founder of the Oxford Branch of the Fabian Society, was not by this date a typical Fabian, it is worth recalling that the stated 'Object' of The Fellowship of the New Life, out of which the Fabian Society had grown in 1883, had been 'The cultivation of a perfect character in each and all'; see Edward R. Pease, *The History of the Fabian Society* (1916), 32.

[6] *Encyclopaedia of Social Reform*, 895.

undeniably possessed a special polemical force in the arguments about the role of the state which dominated political debate in the late nineteenth century, it would be a mistake not to recognise the privileged place occupied by that ideal in the political thought of the previous half-century. Even if we confine ourselves to the established canon of Victorian Liberal political theorists, we find Spencer urging that 'the end which the statesman should keep in view as higher than all other ends is the formation of character', or Mill that 'the problem of character is the determining issue in the question of government', or Green, in typically more tortured prose, that the state must secure those 'powers ... necessary to the fulfilment of man's vocation as a moral being, to an effectual self-devotion to the work of developing the perfect character in himself and others'.[7]

Now, needless to say, each of these authors, as well as the many others one could cite to the same purpose, was deploying the term to suit his own requirements, but *that* only raises the larger question. The very fact that these politically and theoretically diverse declarations should take this common form points to the extraordinary status and centrality of the cluster of assumptions and values which the term denoted. It would, of course, be naive to assume that it always involved an appeal to exactly the same values or to an identical ideal of human life: on this subject, John Stuart Mill's writings are most vulnerable to having representative status thrust upon them, so we would do well to remember that his famous plea for individuality was couched as a *protest* against what he called 'the pinched and hidebound type of character' which he took to be enjoying an insidious popularity in the moral reflection of the time.[8] But such differences may be taken as providing further testimony to the standing of the category itself: it represented a prize worth fighting for. In other words, I am suggesting that the ideal of character, in a sense of the term that I shall analyse in a moment, enjoyed a prominence in the political thought of the Victorian period that it had certainly not known before and that it has, arguably, not experienced since. In this paper I want briefly to explore the ramifications of that centrality and to enquire into the psychological and cultural assumptions which conferred such authority on the moral ambitions it represented. I hope my title has not raised expectations of a rigorous conceptual analysis of the role of the term in the abstract political theory of the period, for that is not what I am

[7] Herbert Spencer, *The Principles of Ethics*, 2 vols (1893), II, 251; Mill as paraphrased in L. T. Hobhouse, *Liberalism* (1911) (reprinted N.Y., 1964), 61; T. H. Green, *Lectures on the Principles of Political Obligation*, ed. by Bernard Bosanquet (1895), para 21.

[8] John Stuart Mill, *On Liberty* (1859), repr in *Collected Works* vol XVIII (Toronto, 1977), quotation at p. 265.

proposing. It is a question, rather, of attending to some of the ways in which this concentration on the political importance of forming character accorded with various non-political aspects of Victorian sensibility and belief, and of considering how these correspondences affected some of the more general political preoccupations of the period. What I have to say is unashamedly impressionistic and unsystematic, not, I like to think, simply as a result of my own failings of character, but also because this is an extensive, rambling sort of subject whose larger dimensions and even significance may elude a more tightly-focused and fine-grained approach.

II

As a prelude to attempting to isolate the distinctiveness of this subject, we should acknowledge that there is presumably some, albeit often implicit, conception of human nature in any body of professedly systematic political thinking, and in several cases we can find an explicit concern with the ways in which the moral formation of citizens may be effected by the political arrangements and practices of their communities. The example of ancient Sparta provided an unfailing source of reflection for those who entertained the most ambitious aspirations of this kind, while a more restrained and less specific commitment to fostering the moral qualities appropriate to a citizen in a free state was a constitutive element in the long tradition of civic republicanism which derived from Aristotle, was renewed by Machiavelli, and which featured significantly in European, and particularly Anglo-American, political thinking down to at least the end of the eighteenth century.[9] It is not so much that, by contrast to such traditions, the Victorian concentration on character introduced a radically new conceptual element, as that it gave a new form to an old concern, and did so in a way that traded upon certain distinctive nineteenth-century cultural resonances. Tom Brown, though he had to learn to defend himself, was not trained to be a member of a landholding militia, and Samuel Smiles, though Shaw called him 'that modern Plutarch', portrayed other qualities than those needed to keep a republic from succumbing to the temptations of luxury.

Part of the elusiveness of this subject arises from the fact that the dominant Victorian sense of the term 'character' embraced what we may for expository purposes distinguish as a descriptive and an evaluative element. The nineteenth-century compilers of the *OED*

---

[9] E. D. Rawson, *The Spartan Tradition in European Thought* (Oxford, 1969); J. G. A. Pocock, *The Machiavellian Moment: Florentine Political Thought and the Atlantic Republican Tradition* (Princeton, N.J., 1975).

attempted to capture this complexity by discriminating two senses of the term. In the first, it was said to mean 'the sum of the mental and moral qualities which distinguish an individual or race viewed as a homogeneous whole; the individuality impressed by nature and habit on man or nation; mental or moral constitution'. This definition refers us to an individual's settled dispositions (and suggests something about their formation to which I shall return) but does not in itself involve a judgement on the goodness or otherwise of these dispositions. The definition of the second sense, however, suggests just this evaluative use of the term when it refers to 'moral qualities strongly developed or strikingly displayed'. There is, of course, a potential ambiguity here, in that the term 'moral' itself can be used in two different senses: in the more inclusive, neutral sense the vices as well as the virtues are classified as moral qualities, while in the narrower affirmative sense 'moral' qualities are confined to those which meet with ethical approval, and there can be no doubt that 'character' was used to refer to the possession of certain highly-valued moral qualities in just this way. Those familiar secular homilies calling for 'the development of character' were, after all, doing more than recommending merely that a man get on with the business of establishing his identity whatever it was.[10]

At the same time, the cogency of these recommendations depended upon the very large causal role the Victorians assigned to character in the purely descriptive sense. For it was, notoriously, the favoured explanatory element in the analysis of different human fates, just as, the OED definition reminds us, national character enjoyed a special status in accounting for the variety of historical outcomes on a larger scale. In the classic late-nineteenth-century discussion of the most celebrated literary representation of human fate, it is taken for granted that tragedy follows from the deeds of men 'and that the main source of these deeds is character'. Indeed, A. C. Bradley, whom I am quoting here, praised Shakespeare for not allowing extraneous or accidental elements to weaken 'the sense of the causal connection of character, deed, and catastrophe', and he clearly found a congenial moral vision at work in the way that 'the concentration of interest, in the greater plays, on the inward struggle emphasizes that [the action] is essentially the expression of character'.[11]

[10] Cf. Anthony Quinton's reference, in making a similar point about the twentieth-century use of 'personality', to 'the alleged usage of Hollywood press agents ...: "this girl has a terrific personality" being a euphemistic formula for conveying the fact that she had large and well-shaped breasts'. *Thoughts and Thinkers* (1982), 21–2.

[11] A. C. Bradley, *Shakespearean Tragedy* (1904) (repr. 1965), 7, 9, 13. The book was based on lectures Bradley had been giving for some years previously.

The transition from this descriptive or explanatory sense to the evaluative sense—or, better, the blurring of the distinction between them—was facilitated by the assumption that the possession of settled dispositions indicated a certain habit of restraining one's impulses. The contrast was with behaviour which was random, impulsive, feckless; and where the impulses were identified, as they so often were, with the 'lower self' (conceived as purely appetitive and hence selfish), then a positive connotation was conferred on the habit of restraint itself.[12] Where cultural attitudes accord a higher standing, or even priority, to the gratification of impulse, this passage between the two senses is bound to appear more strained or contrived. One may be in danger of labouring the obvious here, but it would certainly be a more serious failing to neglect the particularly strong hold exercised over the moral and political thought of the period by the Manichean view of the self.

The relations between habit and the will premised by the local version of this view are particularly crucial for my theme. A long tradition of political theorists had pondered the paradoxes of trying to contrive that citizens should pursue aims which were only of value if pursued voluntarily. Speaking very generally, we may say that the nineteenth century's distinctive preoccupation with the shaping power of time, with the slow, sedimentary processes of development, be it of geological layers or legal customs or whatever, produced an intensified awareness of the role of habit. This could, of course, be taken in a determinist direction, as several notable nineteenth-century social theorists took it. But when married to the unreflective Kantianism of Victorian moral commonplaces, it issued in a concern with the long-term determinants of the will which particularly took the form of anxiety about the insidiously corrosive power of habit. The note of anxiety is well caught in this passage from William James cited by Mrs Bosanquet:

> The hell to be endured hereafter, of which theology tells, is no worse than the hell we make for ourselves in this world by habitually fashioning our characters in the wrong way. Could the young but realise how soon they will become mere walking bundles of habits, they would give more heed to their conduct

[12] A residue of this is very evident in the definition of 'character' given in the self-consciously 'value-free' language of the *Encyclopaedia of the Social Sciences* (N.Y., 1930), 335: 'An enduring psychophysical disposition to inhibit instinctive tendencies in accordance with regulative principles. ... Some other phrase, such as "prepotent impulses" or "firmly ingrained habits" may be substituted for "instinctive tendencies", but the implication remains that the more resistance there is to overcome in order to achieve a desirable end, the more character is to be ascribed to the successfully inhibiting individual'.

while in the plastic state. We are spinning our own fates, good or
evil, and never to be undone. Every smallest stroke of virtue or of
vice leaves its never-so-little scar.[13]

If occasionally Victorian political commentators seem to be concerned with what look like the implausibly distant consequences of
proposed measures, we must remember the prevalence of a psychological model that predisposed discussion towards indirect effects
and long-term results. What gave added force to this sort of anxiety
about cumulative damage to an individual's moral psychology was
the suggestion that it might have a physiological basis. Those mid-
Victorian psychologists and physiologists who obtained a wide
non-professional readership, such as Bain, Spencer, Carpenter and
Maudsley, all toyed with the notion that habit could modify or leave
a deposit in the nervous system itself. This needs to be seen in the
context of that more general appeal of a diluted Lamarckianism to
a scientifically semi-educated audience, which nurtured a fascination
with the idea that in properly exercising the muscles of the will the
individual might be acquiring a new capacity that could operate
instinctively on future occasions and, through the related Lamarck-
ian belief in the inheritance of acquired characteristics, could determine the behaviour of future generations. And even where no
physiological basis for this was fully elaborated, as for the most part
it was not, this concern still shifted the analytical focus away from—
perhaps 'behind' is the appropriate preposition—the situation in
which the individual found himself in the present. As Maudsley put
it in 1867, with the air of one summarising the current state of
scientific knowledge on the subject: 'The strong or well-formed
character which a well-fashioned will implies is the result of good
training applied to a well-constituted original nature; and the
character is not directly determined by the will, but in any particular act determines the will.'[14]

There was clearly an unresolved tension between voluntarism
and determinism in all this. It was an unclarity which surfaced most
famously in John Stuart Mill's repudiation of the Owenite doctrine
that 'our characters are made *for* us, not *by* us'. Mill, anxious to
be free of what he saw as the fatalistic implications of this, argued
that man's character is not simply formed by *external* circumstances
(including therein the influence of other people), for 'his own desire

---

[13] William James, *The Principles of Psychology*, 2 vols (1890), I. 127; cited in Bosanquet, *Strength of the People*, 32-3.
[14] Quoted in Bruce Haley, *The Healthy Body and Victorian Culture* (Cambridge, Mass.,
1978), 44. Cf. Alexander Bain, *The Study of Character* (1861), esp. Chap. 7.

to mould it in a particular way is one of those circumstances'. Subsequent critics have always seen a vicious regress here, in that the very desire to mould our own character may itself be regarded as a product of circumstances beyond our control, and so on. I do not wish to suggest that Mill makes a satisfactory escape from this regress; but it is revealing that he accepts, and indeed insists upon, the premise that 'our actions follow from our characters', and that he perpetuates the basic ambiguity. For he proceeds by denying that other people have been directly able to mould our character: 'They made us what they did make us, by willing not the end but the requisite means; and we, when our habits are not too inveterate, can, by similarly willing the requisite means, make ourselves different'.[15] Mill is not, therefore, challenging determinism by asserting our freedom at any given moment to act differently from the way we in fact choose to act; he accepts, in other words, that character determines the will. He also accepts that character can only be shaped indirectly. His sticking-point is that the individual's own desire to be different is an effective force in this shaping process. But it is so, note, only when (in a phrase which Mill did not subject to further analysis) his 'habits are not too inveterate'. The spectre of habit as a prison from which there is no escape still haunts the discussion. And this basic unclarity constantly cropped up in the political uses of the language of character. On the one hand, each individual is regarded as the ultimate author of his own fate: overwhelmingly unfavourable social circumstances are an inadmissible plea. On the other hand, political proposals are constantly challenged on the grounds that they will weaken character, by presenting temptations which the individuals in question will be *unable* to resist, and thereby warping the habits that will ineluctably govern their actions in the future.

There is no great obscurity about the basic core of qualities invoked by the evaluative sense of character: self-restraint, perseverance, strenuous effort, courage in the face of adversity. What is perhaps less obvious is the intimate dependence on a prior notion of duty. Samuel Smiles is a witness whom it would be unthinkable not to call at this point, if only because he published one book called *Duty* and another called *Character* and it is more or less impossible to tell without looking at the title-page which is which. Both books tirelessly urge that 'the abiding sense of duty is the very crown of character', and whereas Smiles' earlier work had come in for some criticism on the grounds that it might seem to have been encouraging the pursuit of merely material gain, these later books were praised for inculcating 'that honest and upright performance of in-

[15] John Stuart Mill, *A System of Logic* (1843), *CW*, VIII. 840-1.

dividual duty which is the glory of character'.[16] What all this indicated, I would suggest, was that the constant invocations of the
virtues of character in fact presupposed an agreed moral code.[17] The
fear was not moral relativism but weakness of will. For the most
part it was not even suggested that the dictates of conscience were
obscure or internally inconsistent, but rather that the required moral
effort might not be forthcoming were the will once allowed to fall
into disrepair. Smiles' favourite hortatory device was the exemplary
life, and his books celebrate a succession of worthies with the manners of an iron-master and the morals of the *corps*. A particularly
monotonous feature of his stylised portraits was the emphasis upon
his subjects' unselfishness and even altruism, a reminder that the
accepted understanding of character was far removed from the
stereotype of the resolutely self-interested or callously indifferent
figure of subsequent criticism. Here we have that moral tissue that
was assumed to provide the flesh on the otherwise abrasively bare
skeleton of the Individualist idea of the state.

Of course, the somewhat narrow vision of human potential displayed in such literature was not without its critics. I have already
remarked how Mill's famous essay *On Liberty* was a protest against
that 'pinched and hidebound type of human character' which he
saw being promoted in the chapels and meeting-houses of provincial
England, and this in turn reminds us of Arnold's no less celebrated
denunciation of a narrow Hebraism in the name of a Goethean ideal
of classical harmony and roundedness. It is worth pausing to point
out that Mill's ideal here was subtly different from Arnold's, though
both looked to aspects of German Romanticism for their inspiration,

---

[16] Samuel Smiles, *Character* (1871), 189; Kenneth Fielden, 'Samuel Smiles and
self-help'. *Victorian Studies*, XII (1968), 165. *Duty* was published in 1880. Even in
Self-Help, published in 1859, Smiles had insisted that 'elevation of character' was
more important than mere 'getting-on'; cf. the judgement that 'it is character, not
wealth, that the book glorifies as the end of human existence', in George Watson,
The English Ideology: Studies in the Language of Victorian Politics (1973), 51-2.

[17] Cf. the remark of an historian of nineteenth-century America, which he describes
as 'a culture of character':

'It is significant in this context to call attention to the other key words most often
associated with the concept of character. A review of over two hundred such items
reveals the words most frequently related to the notion of character: citizenship,
duty, democracy, work, building, golden deeds, outdoor life, conquest, honor,
reputation, morals, manners, integrity, and above all manhood. The stress was
clearly moral and the interest was almost always in some sort of higher moral law.
The most popular quotation—it appeared in dozens of works—was Emerson's
definition of character: "Moral order through the medium of individual nature".'
Warren I. Susman, '"Personality" and the making of twentieth-century culture', in
New Directions in American Intellectual History, eds. John Higham and Paul K. Conkin,
(Baltimore, 1979), 214.

in that Mill was urging the more Humboldtian ideal of self-culti-
vation and the expansion of experience; an ideal, in short, of *Bildung*.[18] For my purposes, it is particularly revealing that the feature
of *On Liberty* to which contemporary critics took strongest exception
was its perceived glorification of individual caprice and selfish indulgence at the expense of the stern demands of duty which were,
it was indignantly affirmed, the true school of character.[19] This
underlines the very considerable distance between the dominant
Victorian ideal of character and any ideal of *Bildung* which it may
at first sight seem to resemble. *Bildung*, at least in its purest Romantic
form, suggests an openness to experience, a cultivation of the sub-
jective response, an elevation of the aesthetic, and an exploratory
attitude towards one's own individuality and potential, all of which
carry a different, perhaps more self-indulgent, certainly more private, message and political bearing. Dilettantism may, it has been
suggested, be 'a possible parody of *Bildung*',[20] but it is clearly the
very antithesis of character.

III

Tracing the aetiology of this idea of character and the cluster of
values it embraced, and, what might be of greater interest, charting
the ways in which concepts long available came to acquire a new
prominence and resonance, partly in response to the rise of new
political preoccupations, would require a major effort of intellectual
history which will be a constitutive part of the task facing any future
historian of the Making of the English Respectable Class. But even
the much more limited enterprise of identifying the place of this idea
in Victorian political language demands that we have an eye to the
more general intellectual currents of which it was a part, to moral
and social developments which may be regarded as pre-conditions
rather than sources. One could not, for example, go very far into
this subject without mentioning the wider cultural impact of Evangelical Christianity, though it must be said that the most directly
relevant feature of that legacy—the vision of life as a perpetual
struggle in which one's ability to resist temptation and overcome
obstacles needed to be subject to constant scrutiny—was, with only
minor changes of emphasis, a feature shared by otherwise theologi-

---

[18] The best account of Arnold's view is still Lionel Trilling, *Matthew Arnold* (N.Y.,
1939); there is a helpful comparison with Mill in Edward Alexander, *Matthew Arnold
and John Stuart Mill* (1965).
[19] See J. C. Rees, *Mill and His Early Critics* (Leicester, 1956).
[20] See 'Editor's Introduction' to Wilhelm von Humboldt, *The Limits of State Action*,
ed. J.W. Burrow (Cambridge, 1969), xxii.

cally diverse groups who also left their mark on the early-Victorian educated classes, such as the Tractarians and the Arnoldians.[21] Of particular consequence for our theme was the way in which an essentially Evangelical moral psychology penetrated the discussion of economic life early in the century. As Boyd Hilton's analysis of the economic policy debates of the 1820s makes clear, economic activity was widely portrayed as a proving-ground of moral discipline where the existence of the possibility of debt and bankruptcy, or, lower down the social scale, of unemployment and destitution, operated as a check on that financial imprudence which was only the outward sign of moral failure.[22] Mrs Bosanquet was acknowledging a genuine affinity in taking her text on the economic power of character from Thomas Chalmers, however far apart they would have been on other matters.

In exploring this issue, we also need to note a significant shift away from eighteenth-century ideas of the moral and cultural primacy of leisure. For the Georgian gentleman, and thus for all those who aspired to that status, the most prized human qualities could only be developed in the enjoyment of 'society' in the older meaning of the term; mechanics were rude and scholars monkish precisely because, whether from necessity or choice, they spent so little time cultivating the virtues of sociability.[23] By contrast, for the respectable Victorian—who might, of course, belong to a much larger and less leisured class—work was the chief sphere in which moral worth was developed and displayed. It is not hard to see, for example, how the virtues of character spoke to the economic experience of those groups who made up the urban middling rank. That experience was above all of individual ventures under conditions of uncertainty with no financial safety-net. Stories of businesses which had 'gone down' and of modest fortunes lost in speculations which were imprudent or worse, furnished the moralist with particularly telling illustrations. It was, at all levels, an economic world in which reputation played a powerful part: to be known as a man of character was to possess the moral collateral which would reassure potential business associates or employers. Victorian lexicographers assigned a' correspond-

[21] See Walter E. Houghton, *The Victorian Frame of Mind 1830-1870* (New Haven, Conn., 1957), 233-4.

[22] Boyd Hilton, *Corn, Cash, Commerce: The Economic Policies of the Tory Governments 1815-1830* (Oxford, 1977), esp. 'Conclusion'.

[23] For some perceptive remarks on this ideal, see Sheldon Rothblatt, *Tradition and Change in English Liberal Education: An Essay in History and Culture* (1976), and Nicholas Phillipson, 'Culture and society in the eighteenth-century province: the case of Edinburgh and the Scottish Enlightenment', in *The University in Society*, ed. L. Stone, 2 vols. (Princeton, N.J., 1974), II. 407-48.

ingly prominent place to reputation in their definitions of character: 'good qualities or the reputation of possessing them' was how one laconically and revealingly put it.[24] Although the classic scenes of character-testing are essentially private—facing the discouragement of an empty order-book, coping with the failure of one's inventions and projects, studying deep into the night to acquire by hard labour what seemed to come so easily to the expensively-educated—it was also true that character was an ascribed quality, possessed and enjoyed in public view.

The increased circulation of the language of character also represented part of a wider reaction against the alleged vices and indulgences of the territorial aristocracy, especially in their metropolitan form. At its most general this involved a revolt against convention, artificiality, and mere outward polish, a post-Romantic assertion of authenticity as well as a puritan taste for austerity. More specifically, this repudiation of the ethics of the *salon* fed into a protest against the politics of patronage, in which the long-celebrated value of 'independence' acquired a new force. It is noticeable how often— Smiles could again be called to the witness-stand, but so could many others—the early- and mid-Victorian panegyrics on character occur in the context of homilies on how true worth is unrelated to social position, or, conversely, how the justifiable pride of the man of noble character is contrasted with, even provides the criterion for criticism of, the tawdriness of wealth and station and the snobbery of that sham gentility which pretended to them. Here we are beginning to back into the larger question of the sources of Victorian Liberalism, for accompanying the self-assertion of new groups in the political nation there developed something of a vogue for candour and manliness, a revulsion from the degrading nature of dependence and the social pretences which dependence demanded.

I shall return in a moment to the political form taken by these emotions, but first I want to draw attention to a very different strand in the fabric, to a tradition of political reflection in which the relevant contrast to talk of 'character' was not a moral posture of dependence or inauthenticity, or even just a state of chronic weakness of will, but such terms as 'political machinery' and 'paper constitutions'. It was, that is to say, part of a vocabulary of political analysis, with a very wide currency among the educated classes in post-Napoleonic Britain, which insisted on the inadequacy of merely

---

[24] *Century Dictionary* (1889); cf. the *OED*: 'the estimate formed of a person's qualities; reputation; when used without qualifying epithet, implying "favourable estimate, good repute"'. See also R. G. White, *Words and their Uses* (1870), 99: 'Character is like an inward spiritual grace of which reputation is, or should be, the outward and visible sign'.

constitutional or legal changes when unaccompanied by the necessary qualities and habits in the people. In practice, this usually slid
into a celebration of England's good fortune by contrast to the
unhappy experiences of politically less gifted nations (the French
provided the main source of cautionary tales), and there was certainly a congratulatory element in the way 'national character'
acted as the chief explanatory concept in these meditations on comparative political fortunes.[25] Mill, in self-consciously scientific vein,
maintained that 'the laws of national character are by far the most
important class of sociological laws', even insisting that national
character was 'the power by which all those of the circumstances of
society which are artificial, laws and customs for instance, are altogether moulded'.[26] (It is worth noting that character is being regarded as the very bedrock of explanation when even 'customs' are
classed as 'artificial'.) But Mill, too, raised his glass to that 'point of
character which beyond any other, fits the people of *this* country for
representative government', and Alfred Marshall was simply one of
many who extended this analysis from political stability to economic
prosperity: 'The same qualities which gave political freedom gave
[the English] also free enterprise in industry and commerce'.[27]

We have here again that blending of descriptive and evaluative
elements: progress is analysed in terms of the causal power of national character, and at the same time the development of a certain
type of character is itself an index of progress, a specification of
modernity where what Bagehot described as the 'cake of custom'
has been broken. Progress, after all, was still regarded as a rarity in
world history, a fragile achievement born of countless acts of initiative, acts which shape that character which in turn becomes the
chief, perhaps the only, guarantee of future progress. Here is the
anxiety about the long term once more. The fear of returning to a
'Chinese stationariness' was more than just a cultural cliché.

One way to bring out the distinctiveness and interdependence of
the elements in the Victorian language of character is to contrast
that language very briefly with comparable strands in the political
discourse of the preceding century. The two strands that could most
plausibly be seen as comparable are the language of virtue and the
language of sociability or politeness, for unlike, say, political thinking which remained in the austere language of natural law or pressed
one of the various radical or utopian cases in the language of rights,

---

[25] For examples, see Collini, Winch and Burrow, *That Noble Science of Politics*, 151–
9, 170-4, 185-205, 317-329.
[26] Mill, *System of Logic, CW*, VIII. 904-5.
[27] John Stuart Mill, *Considerations on Representative Government* (1861), *CW*, XIX. 421;
Marshall, *Principles*, I. 744.

these two dealt primarily with a comparable kind of concern and level of analysis—the moral qualities of the citizen and the habits and manners of a member of civil society. In making such a contrast, I do not mean to preclude the possibility of tracing survivals and mutations of these languages into the nineteenth century, but I take it that this is just what they would be—survivals and mutations rather than the chief structuring vocabularies of the political reflection of the age.

In both the language of virtue[28] and the language of character there is a similar emphasis on the moral vigour of the citizens as the prime requirement for the health of the body politic, though the civic humanist tradition tended to portray this as instrumental to the maintenance of political liberty whereas in the nineteenth century the cultivation of character could more readily be represented as an end in itself. But the simplest way to bring out the chief contrast between them is to look at their different visions of nemesis. Putting it in a single phrase, one might say that the politics of virtue was haunted by the fear of corruption, while it was stagnation that figured as the chief threat in the politics of character. As this suggests, the former was primarily concerned with maintaining an existing balance and was essentially backward-looking, in that it understood its political fate in terms of a well-established cycle, frequently enacted in the relevant ancient history, of liberty, opulence, corruption, loss of liberty; a cycle it was doomed to repeat if the valour and public spirit of its free-holding, militia-serving citizenry should once be sapped. By contrast, the striving, self-reliant, adaptable behaviour endorsed by the imperatives of character is inherently tied to movement and progress, to a future which must be regarded as to some extent open-ended (a point I shall return to in a moment). Both, of course, are strenuous ideals, containing a generous dash of asceticism, yet they stand in an interestingly different relation to the private pursuit of wealth. In the civic humanist tradition, it is a pre-condition of political liberty that those classed as citizens should be able to devote their energies to participation in public affairs free of the need to engage directly in productive activity; and luxury is an agent of decay precisely because it diverts men's concerns from the public to the private sphere. In character discourse, the individual is not primarily regarded as a member of a political community, but as an already private (though not there-

---

[28] For my understanding of 'the language of virtue' I am primarily indebted to Pocock, *Machiavellian Moment*: for its relation, particularly relevant to my theme, to political economy, see *Wealth and Virtue: The Shaping of Political Economy in the Scottish Enlightenment*, eds. Istvan Hont and Michael Ignatieff (Cambridge, 1983), esp. the essays by Robertson and Pocock himself.

by selfish) moral agent whose mastering of his circumstances is indirectly a contribution to the vitality and prosperity of his society.
Here, the getting of wealth, even in quite substantial quantities, is
a salutary moral experience, provided the emphasis is placed on the
getting; the civic humanist ideal of an *assured* independence would
figure rather as a temptation to indulgence than as a guarantee of
political commitment. Furthermore, for the civic humanist, uniform-
ity of material conditions is conducive to the practice of virtue,
whereas the growth of character is inherently tied to a situation of
diversity. In both traditions there is an abhorrence of apathy: it is
the obverse of their common strenuousness. But whereas in the civic
humanist eschatology apathy is what leads to a decline from public
to private, in Victorian individualism apathy, in the form of lack or
weakness of character, is more likely to figure as the force propelling
the otherwise self-maintaining individual into a state of dependence
and in *that* sense into the public sphere.

Somewhat similar contrasts can be made between the
eighteenth-century language of politeness and sociability[29] and the
nineteenth-century language of character. In this case we are dealing with a cultural or moral ideal which coloured political discussion
without issuing in a systematic programme in the way that civic
humanism did, but this arguably brings it nearer to the role of
character in Victorian political thought. In general terms, of course,
there is an obvious contrast between the emphasis they respectively
placed on the outer and the inner man (though as I have mentioned,
character was also bound up with reputation). This is evident even
where the same term is invoked, as in the praise for the way in
which the founding of the Poker Club of Edinburgh in 1762 not
only served 'national purposes' by bringing together representatives
of different social groups, but also had 'Happy Effects on Private
Character by Forming and polishing the Manners which are suitable
to Civilis'd Society'.[30] Here, 'private' means 'individual' as contrasted with 'national', but it clearly involves social qualities far
removed from character as the Victorians celebrated it. Where the
autodidact, for example, was the archetypal Smilesian hero, Geor-
gians deplored him as likely to be obtuse or crotchety, lacking the
urbanity and moderation imparted by extensive experience of sociability. Similarly, where 'getting on' suggested to the Victorian the
overcoming of adverse circumstances and engaging in wholesome
competition, for the Georgian 'getting along' required more attention to the arts of winning esteem and cultivating connections. The

[29] For 'the language of sociability' see the sources cited in fn. 23 above, and Nicholas
Phillipson, 'Adam Smith as civic moralist' in Hont and Ignatieff, *Wealth and Virtue.*
[30] Quoted in Rothblatt, *Liberal Education,* 73.

Georgian fear of isolation or eccentricity as a sign of a rude, un-
civilised way of life can be contrasted with the Victorian anxiety
about the way in which the pressures of opinion in a commercial
society made for conformity and lack of enterprise. 'Independence',
to be sure, was highly valued in both traditions, but even here its
ramifications differed somewhat. In eighteenth-century England, as
one historian has well put it, 'the sinecure was the favourite mode
of achieving independence in the heyday of the patronage system',[31]
whereas the holding of a 'place' came to be treated with opprobrium
by Victorian moralists, scenting in the lack of fair competition
damning evidence of both dependence and deceit.

These contrasts are clearly part of much larger developments: both
of my chosen eighteenth-century languages were, for example,
addressed to a smaller class that any nineteenth-century political
idiom could plausibly be. Although none of these languages was
exclusively the possession of a party, it is already evident that I am
trenching on the larger question of the development of Whiggism
into Liberalism, a story which, at the level of political argument,
remains largely untold. The language of character encapsulated a
substantial passage in this development. One of G. M. Young's remarks is, as so often, the starting-point of wisdom here: the Whigs,
he wrote, 'came from the eighteenth century where privilege was
taken for granted'.[32] Although in the history of political thought
Liberalism is mostly treated as a theory of the priority of liberty or
of the defence of the rights of the individual, its expression in the
political culture of mid-nineteenth-century England suggests its
fundamental emotional dynamic was something more like hostility
to unreflective and unjustified privilege and a related hatred of being
patronised. That somewhat prickly touchiness which characterised
several leading Liberals—Bright is a particularly conspicuous example—was an expression of this resentment of unmerited superiority and a fear of being slighted. It is now almost twenty years since
John Vincent taught us to see a vehicle for the expression of such
emotions in the electoral Liberalism of the bootmakers of Rochdale
and the shipwrights of Whitby,[33] but something similar remains to
be said, I think, due allowance being made for differences of register,
about the theories of the likes of Spencer and Green. From one point
of view, the lofty stoic ideal of self-command inculcated by the
language of character may seem very far removed from that spirit

[31] Rothblatt, *Liberal Education*, 28.

[32] G. M. Young, *Victorian England: Portrait of an Age* (1936), annotated edition by
George Kitson Clark (1977), 31.

[33] John Vincent, *The Formation of the British Liberal Party 1857-68* (1966); *idem. Poll-
books: How Victorians Voted* (Cambridge, 1967).

of self-righteous, mean-minded *ressentiment* which marked much of provincial dissenting Liberalism. But for many of those who read Smiles and admired Bright the language of character could produce a certain *frisson*; it allowed a vicarious form of self-assertion, a public affirmation of one's own worth in the face of a daily experience of the condescension of the well-born and well-connected.

As a body of political thought, Whiggism had been formatively and enduringly shaped by a view about the nature, and certainly by a conviction about the importance, of the constitution, and in the course of the nineteenth century many of these matters inevitably lost their political immediacy. An increasingly attenuated Whiggism still spoke to the one great recurrent constitutional issue, namely the extension of the franchise, yet even here it is interesting to see that the language of 'interests' and 'balance', which still occupied the centre of the stage in 1832, had ceded considerable ground to the language of character by 1867. Discussion of the Second Reform Bill, both in and out of Parliament, turned to a considerable extent on the question of whether the moral qualities of the respectable urban artisan were such that he should be entrusted with the vote. Proponents of reform argued that his exclusion could no longer be justified because he had revealed—whether in his regular contributions to Friendly Societies or in what Gladstone termed 'that magnificent moral spectacle', his supposed support against his own economic interest of the North in the American Civil War—that he had now developed that strength of character which would prevent him from misusing the vote in recklessly short-sighted or self-interested ways.[34] 'Self-command and the power of endurance' had been among the desirable qualities of a potential elector enumerated by Mr Gladstone in the debate on Baines' Bill, and it is an indication of the hold of the language of character that so much of the discussion in 1867 was not about the respectable workman's rights but about his habits.

At a different social level, there was a considerable vogue among the professional and preaching classes at this time for what was simply termed 'manliness'. That mingling of ethical and physiological properties which character-talk always involved was particularly pronounced here: bodily and moral vigour could be cultivated by the same means, expressed by the same actions. The quality most

[34] Ian Bradley, *The Optimists: Themes and Personalities in Victorian Liberalism* (1980), 154–5. There is much interesting material on the educated classes' views of reform in 1867 in Christopher Harvie, *The Lights of Liberalism: Academic Liberals and the Challenge of Democracy* 1860–1886 (1976), but for some reservations about Harvie's interpretation of it see Stefan Collini, 'Political theory and the "science of society" in Victorian Britain', *Historical Journal*, 23 (1980), esp. 212–18.

unsparingly denounced by the apostles of manliness was 'sentimentalism', and it is interesting to see that this, too, could issue in what might be called a political aesthetic. Theories and policies that were definite, sharp-edged, and did not shrink from acknowledging their painful consequences recommended themselves accordingly. Part of the appeal of classical political economy to the generation of intellectuals who were young in the 1850s and 1860s lay in its subliminal power to gratify these tastes, and both Tories and, later, Socialists could fall foul of this aversion to sentimentality. Leslie Stephen's *Life of Henry Fawcett* is an extended meditation on the political significance of manliness, in which the virtues of character that Fawcett displayed in overcoming the handicap of his blindness were displayed in more or less equal measure in his continuing love of exercise and in his refusal to indulge his working-class constituents by supporting any relaxation of the workhouse test.[35] Weakness of will, of which sentimentalism was a variety, could be walked or climbed out of the system, an attitude which in many cases found expression in what can only be called 'Muscular Liberalism'.

IV

By the late-nineteenth century the sectarian resonances of character were drowned out by the swelling chorus of politicians of all parties who professed to stand in the same relation to any scheme which might be said to weaken character as the preacher did to sin. One feature of the framework of assumptions which gave vitality and persuasiveness to these repeated invocations of character, a feature I have left implicit so far, was that it was an ideal peculiarly suited to a future of unknown circumstances. This applied with felt power to economic life as the individual member of the middle- and working-classes might experience it; it was part of the anxiety of those contemplating an extension of the franchise, as all the catchphrases about 'shooting Niagara' and 'a leap in the dark' remind us; and it seemed to be almost a defining characteristic of the many forms of colonial experience towards which so much of late-nineteenth-century character-training was directed. In travelling to these unknown futures, well-maintained habits and a breakdown-free will were essential. Victorian intellectuals were self-consciously members of a society in the van of progress: the first arrivals in the future cannot be sure what to expect, and no particular technical expertise can be guaranteed in advance to be relevant. Where cir-

[35] Leslie Stephen, *The Life of Henry Fawcett* (1885). Note the terms of Stephen's endorsement of Fawcett's views: 'Whoever professes to raise the position of a class without elevating its character is a charlatan'. (p. 152).

cumstances are known or can reliably be predicted (possibly a more common frame of mind before the nineteenth century's historicising of all experience, or in a society of more stable roles and statuses), then particular substantive virtues tend to figure more prominently among the moralist's desiderata. Seen thus, character may be said to represent a set of 'second-order' virtues, or even an acquired form of what a later age would call a 'personality-type', which would provide the best chance of first-order virtues being upheld in unknown circumstances.[36] It seems to me a little misleading to represent the Victorian emphasis on character-formation, as at least one distinguished cultural historian has done, as indicative of 'a society without a consensus of values'.[37] It is surely nearer the mark to speak of a society which paradigmatically envisaged the individual—often an isolated individual, whether literally so, in a remote hill station, or only subjectively so, surrounded by those who seemed to have succumbed to various forms of temptation—confronting the task of maintaining his will in the face of adversity. 'When England's far and honour a name', the temptation is to duck the obligation to 'play up and play the game'; but the obligation itself is not actually called into doubt.

In a fuller account, one would need to say much more here about those great *ateliers* for turning out well-made characters, the late-Victorian public schools. The potential anti-intellectualism and philistinism which Mill, Arnold and others had protested against in the ideal of character cherished among the dissenting provincial commercial classes was realised here in a new form, especially once the cult of organised games got under way from the 1870s onwards.[38] Adopting Arnold's terminology, this was very much a case of the Barbarians taking over an idol of the Philistines and re-making it in their own image.

[36] Cf. Alasdair Macintyre's remark about Adam Smith's moral philosophy: 'On Smith's view Knowledge of what the rules are, whether the rules of justice or of prudence or of benevolence, is not sufficient to enable us to follow them; to do so we need another virtue of a very different kind, the Stoic virtue of self-command which enables us to control our passions when they distract us from what virtue requires'. *After Virtue: A Study in Moral Theory* (1981), 218.

[37] Rothblatt, *Liberal Education*, 135.

[38] Cf. Haley's remarks on the 'Hebraic' ethic of the games-cult (*Healthy Body*, 260-1):

> The imposed moral imperatives of the game are few and simple: one does not cheat, take unfair advantage, shirk, or give up. Although this represents a type of seriousness, it is nothing like Arnold's "high seriousness". The player who lives by these lights on or off the field does not need the developing vision, the mental receptivity, or the imaginative or philosophic grasp—qualities most Victorian intellectuals considered necessary for a healthy mind. Those qualities he does need—tenacity, daring, and moral decisiveness—are not so much mental traits as traits of the mind-body, constitution, or "character".

Part of the function of organised games was, of course, the artificial provision of adversity. Edward Lyttleton (classified in the *DNB* as 'schoolmaster, divine, and cricketer') insisted on this point even in a game like cricket: the removal of the element of pain which came with the development of smooth pitches made the game, he announced, 'comparatively worthless'.[39] As one might expect, the specification of the moral contribution of sport could be adapted to fit various value-hierarchies. For example, the *Pall Mall Gazette* treated the Eton and Harrow match of 1866 as the occasion for reading a lesson on some quintessentially mid-Victorian values:

> Cricket is a game which reflects the character—a game of correct habits, of patient and well-considered practice—the very last game in the world in which any youth without the power of concentrativeness—nine-tenths of education but voted a bore at Eton—is ever likely to excel. To any lover of education the play of Harrow was a treat, and that of Eton a disappointment. In Harrow we saw care and discipline, and patient labour; in Eton a wild erratic performance, no sign of training or mental effort.

Over a quarter of a century later, Hely Hutchinson Almond, fresh-air fanatic and Headmaster of Loretto, eulogised rugby football in terms more expressive of *late*-Victorian preoccupations:

> Games in which success depends on the united efforts of many, and which also foster courage and endurance, are the very life-blood of the public school system. And all the more self-indulgent games or pursuits contain within themselves an element of danger to school patriotism and might, if they permanently injured the patriotic games, cause public schools to fail in their main object, which we take to be the production of a grand breed of men for the service of the British nation.[40]

Character was not, it perhaps needs to be said, merely a weapon fashioned to suit the purposes of middle-class moralists frightened by the possible consequences of the poor's apparent indifference to respectable values. It was an expression of a very deeply ingrained perception of the qualities needed to cope with life, an ethic with strong roots in areas of experience ostensibly remote from politics.

---

[39] Quoted in J. A. Mangan, *Athleticism in the Victorian and Edwardian Public School: The Emergence and Consolidation of an Educational Ideology* (Cambridge, 1981), 187. The cult of organised games is treated in very similar terms in Haley, *Healthy Body*, Chaps. 6–9.

[40] Both quoted in Mangan, *Athleticism*, 69–70, 56; see also Almond's article on 'Football as a Moral Agent', in *The Nineteenth Century* for 1893, cited in Haley, *Healthy Body*, Chap. 8.

Where cricket or rugby could be spoken of in these terms without the slightest hint of irony or defensiveness, it would be surprising if the implied reservoir of cultural values were not tapped by various forms of political argument as well.

By the end of the century, the imperial and military resonances of this ethic were widely recognised, as Almond's reference to 'the service of the British nation' suggests. It was the stuff of which many an Edwardian prize-day address was made, in which the values of teamwork and self-reliance, of concentration and courage, of obedience and initiative, were presented as unproblematically compatible. No doubt it contributed to the portrayal of 1914 as one big away match, where *homo Newboltiensis*, his character moulded by those early experiences of 'a bumping pitch and a blinding light', displayed the loyalty, bravery, narrowness, and unquestioning commitment which the situation demanded.[41] There would be a satisfying neatness in being able to say that the games-playing ethic of Harrow was lost on the battlefields of the Somme, but cultural change has happened more slowly than that even in twentieth-century Britain.

Quite how far such change *has* gone in this matter and what the main agents of it have been, are questions I shall not pursue. Clearly, deeper diggings by psychology into the ego's early career, and the diffusion of profoundly sociologised notions of 'society' and its powers, have both proved inhospitable to the explanatory power of character; the will has been effectively disenfranchised in political discussion, and habit dissolved into the less voluntarist language of complexes and conditioning. It is also true that the growth of security for all classes has given the qualities represented by character less purchase in everyday economic life. And as a political ideal it was naturally less congenial to a Labour Party committed to remedying structural defects in the distribution of wealth and power, and less central to a political debate dominated by concern about mass unemployment and the establishment of a welfare state. When the National Insurance Act was passed in 1911, C. S. Loch, the Secretary of the Charity Organisation Society and Mrs Bosanquet's closest political ally, remarked that it indicated a great change of

---

[41] For the term '*homo Newboltiensis*', see Patrick Howarth, *Play Up and Play the Game: The Heroes of Popular Fiction* (1973), 14. For the understanding of the First World war in sporting terms, see Paul Fussell, *The Great War and Modern Memory* (N.Y., 1975), Chap. 1, which also cites Lord Northcliffe's explanation of why the German soldier cannot be capable of acts of individual initiative like his British counterpart: 'He has not played individual games. Football, which develops individuality, has only been introduced into Germany in comparatively recent times.' (p. 26).

[42] Quoted in Mowat, *Charity Organisation Society*, 170.

social principles: 'The fear of moral injury which state dependence may cause is decreasing'.[42] Underlying this remark was the ideal of moral health and its priority which I have been exploring in this paper, an ideal which had itself to be in a pretty rude state of health if the language of character was to have a more than merely decorative role in political argument. And if that is true, it suggests the mischievous concluding thought that those who talk airily and ignorantly of reviving 'Victorian values' may be in line to get rather more than they bargain for.

LONDON AND THE NATION IN THE NINETEENTH CENTURY

The Prothero Lecture

By Francis Sheppard, M.A., Ph.D., F.R.Hist.S.

READ 16 MARCH 1984

THE relationship between London and the rest of the nation is an important but perhaps somewhat neglected aspect of English history. In recent years this theme has, it is true, directly or indirectly, engaged the attention of a number of distinguished scholars,[1] but it is still not generally recognised to be as vital an ingredient in the history of this country as is the rôle of Paris in the history of France. Henry James even went so far as to say that 'all England is in a suburban relation' to London,[2] and the standpoint of this paper is equally metropolitan. Its theme is that the loss of its normal pre-eminence which London seemed to sustain in the nineteenth century was in reality short-lived, and more apparent than real.

At the outset there are two general points which, however obvious and familiar they may be, nevertheless need to be made at the start of any discussion of London and the nation. Firstly, London's geographical position at the lowest crossing point of the largest river in the land, the estuary of which feeds one of the great commercial cross-roads of continental Europe, has always, from the days of the Romans onwards, been a major ingredient in the economic growth of London. This geographical advantage was, moreover, enhanced by the general accessibility of the country. In England there are virtually no important barriers to good communications. Distances

---

[1] T. C. Barker, 'London and the great leap forward', *The Listener*, lxxvii, 29 June 1967, 845-7; Asa Briggs, *Victorian Cities* (Penguin edn, 1968); H. J. Dyos, 'Greater and Greater London: Notes on Metropolis and Provinces in the Nineteenth and Twentieth Centuries', in *Britain and the Netherlands*, ed. J. S. Bromley and E. S. Kossmann (vol. iv of Papers delivered to the Anglo-Dutch Historical Conferences, London and The Hague, 1971), 89-112; F. J. Fisher, 'The Development of London as a Centre of Conspicuous Consumption in the Sixteenth and Seventeenth Centuries', *Transactions of the Royal Historical Society*, 4th ser., 30 (1948), 37-50; Donald Read, *The English Provinces c. 1760-1960, A Study in Influence* (1964); E. A. Wrigley, 'London and the great leap forward', *The Listener*, lxxvii, 6 July 1967, 7-8, and 'A Simple Model Of London's Importance in Changing English Society and Economy 1650-1750', *Past & Present*, 37 (1967), 44-70.

[2] Henry James, *English Hours* (1905), 34.

are small, and the sea provides an unchanging frontier. So geography has also had a powerful influence in the emergence at a very early date of a self-contained and stable political entity in England.

But if advantageous geographical position has since Roman times been a fundamental constituent in London's evolution, a second almost equally important component, with a history extending back over the last nine hundred years, has been the peculiar internal anatomy of London itself. Edward the Confessor's building of a royal palace beside the great Benedictine monastery at Westminster made a profound mark upon both the evolution of London itself and upon London's position within the realm. Westminster gradually became the main place of residence of successive sovereigns, and by the fourteenth century had become the political and administrative capital of the nation, as well as the seat of the royal courts of justice. The ancient city, already some three times as large as any other town in England, had meanwhile become the principal centre of manufacture, commerce and finance, and its port the main centre of foreign trade.

So throughout much of its history, and indeed until relatively recently, London has been two cities—the cities of London and Westminster, as the cartographers always entitled their maps until well into the nineteenth century—each immensely powerful in its own field, yet usually suspicious of and even hostile towards each other; and at least in Victorian times this internal dichotomy was to have important consequences both for London and indirectly for the nation. Viewed from outside, on the other hand, the cities of London and Westminster were only one great mass, London, embodying that dense concentration of all the basic functions of a nation which was first achieved so long ago and which has given London its never-threatened pre-eminence at home.

This pre-eminence of London has been clearly recognised by the French historian, François Bédarida.

> In spite of all the divergencies in the urban history of the two countries, it is worth pointing out that for six centuries [France and England] have had one fundamental trait in common—the unchallenged predominance of the capital city. In population, economic activity, in its monopoly of political and administrative function, in its dominating influence over the region or the country, this is the case with London—contrary to the belief of some— as it is with Paris.[3]

[3] François Bédarida, 'Towns in England and France', *Britain and France*, eds Douglas Johnson, François Crouzet and François Bédarida (1980), 228.

For the seventeenth and eighteenth centuries, this 'dominating influence over the region or the country' has been demonstrated (or at any rate, touched upon) by several eminent historians. Professor Fisher, writing on 'The Development of the London Food Market, 1540–1640', has shown 'that it is possible to watch the city's tentacles spreading over the provinces until by the middle of the seventeenth century they reached to Berwick, Cornwall, and Wales', and that this demand for food 'gave a definite stimulus to English agriculture.' He has also shown that in the early seventeenth century London handled some two-thirds or three-quarters of the nation's foreign trade, and has drawn attention to the importance of London's function as 'a centre of consumption where men expended the revenues which they had acquired elsewhere'.[4]

Towards the end of the seventeenth century London had become the largest city in Europe. In dealing with the century from 1650 to 1750 Professor Wrigley has suggested that one adult in every six in England had at some stage of their lives 'had direct experience of London life', and that 'this must have acted as a powerful solvent of the customs, prejudices and modes of traditional, rural England'. He too has pointed out the fundamental importance of the port in London's growth, and in addition to the ever-growing food market cites the enormous demand for coal from Tyneside as another example of London's influence upon some of the most distant extremities of the country.[5] Finally, Professor Barker has concluded that 'London almost certainly dominated the economic life of the country in this pre-industrial period far more than historians have so far brought out'. It is, however, what he calls the 'dramatic upsurge of activity outside London during the eighteenth century', mainly in the north of England, 'that has caught the imagination of historians'. But, he continues,

> Even during this upsurge, London continued to be of enormous importance, particularly in the financial field. We still need to keep our eyes on the place where there was the greatest concentration of economic wealth as well as on those other places where economic growth was fastest.[6]

The three historians quoted above were mainly concerned with the rôle of London in what is sometimes referred to as 'the Great

[4] Fisher, 'The Development of the London Food Market, 1540–1640', *Economic History Review*, v, (1934–5), 50–1; 'London's Export Trade in the Early Seventeenth Century', *Ec. Hist. Rev.*, 2nd ser., iii (1950), 152; 'The Development of London as a Centre of Conspicuous Consumption' etc., 38.
[5] Wrigley, 'A Simple Model', 50, 55–9.
[6] Barker, 845–7.

Leap Forward.' But by the beginning of the nineteenth century this famous leap had already taken place, or was at least in full flight. The pace of change, in the widest sense, had already begun to accelerate, and the theme of London and the nation therefore becomes more complex. The unprecedented size of London, changes in London's political influence, the problem of the government of London, the effect of the nineteenth-century revolution in communications, all provide new elements for examination in the ever-changing equation of London and the nation. Nevertheless, the problem which has preoccupied historians of the previous centuries—the dynamics of the economic relationship between metropolis and provinces—still presents itself for the nineteenth century; but the answer to the question posed by Professor Dyos in 1969, whether London's influence on the provinces in the nineteenth century 'amounted to a major stimulus to the economic growth of particular regions of the country, or whether it constituted some kind of drag on progress in the larger sense', will remain as obscure as ever until the full-scale economic history of Victorian London for which Professor Dyos called, has been written.[7]

If sheer size is any guide to the extent of the influence of the metropolis, the figures of population do not suggest that there was any relative decline in the nineteenth century. In 1801 London's population of a little under one million was more than eleven times as great as that of the second city, Liverpool, and on the night of the census more than one in ten of all the people of England and Wales were living in London. For several decades thereafter, however, the rate of increase of population in the principal towns (e.g. those numbering over 20,000) exceeded that for London, and whereas in 1801 London had been the only town with a population of over 100,000, by 1871 there were no fewer than sixteen such provincial towns, all but three in the midlands or the north.[8] But London's rate of increase was, nevertheless, hovering around the twenty per cent mark in every decade throughout the first half of the nineteenth century, and it has been calculated that in the three decades between 1841 and 1871 an average of about 300,000 immigrants came into the capital in each decade, balanced by an exodus of some 116,000 to 160,000.[9] London was, in fact, throughout the whole of the nineteenth century, the hub of enormous and con-

[7] Dyos, 103.

[8] R. Price Williams, 'On the Increase of Population in England and Wales', *Journal of the Statistical Society*, 43 (1880), 464–89, and 'The Population of London, 1801–81', ibid., 48 (1885), 349–440.

[9] H. A. Shannon, 'Migration and the Growth of London, 1841–91', *Economic History Review*, v (1934–5), 79–86.

tinuous movements of people, and by 1901 the population of Greater London (for the built-up area had long since expanded beyond the original confines of the Registrar General's metropolitan area) amounted to over 6,500,000. This figure was only barely exceeded by the total aggregate population of what later became known as the five provincial conurbations of South-East Lancashire, West Midlands, West Yorkshire, Merseyside and Tyneside. Expressed differently, these figures mean that whereas at the beginning of the nineteenth century one in every ten of the peoples of England and Wales lived in London, by the end of the century the proportion had doubled to one in every five.[10] In words written by Sidney Webb in 1891, London was, indeed,

> more than a city: it is a whole kingdom in itself, with revenues exceeding those of mighty principalities. With its suburbs it exceeds all Ireland in population: if it were emptied tomorrow the whole of the inhabitants of Scotland and Wales together could do no more than refill it: the three next largest cities in the world could almost be combined without out-numbering its millions.[11]

One certain fact embedded in all the endless ramifications of these figures is the colossal demographic influence exerted by London—so colossal, indeed, that it is very difficult to apprehend. In the mid nineteenth century nearly forty per cent of all Londoners had been born elsewhere—had their origins, in fact, somewhere else—and even at the end of the century this figure had only fallen to thirty-five per cent. At the time of their departure from their provincial town or village, many of these migrants were young, and in the words of H. Llewellyn Smith, written in the early 1890s, they were drawn up to London by the hope of work and economic advantage, and by

> the contagion of numbers, the sense of something going on, the theatres and the music halls, the brightly lighted streets and busy crowds—all, in short, that makes the difference between the Mile End fair on a Saturday night and a dark muddy lane, with no glimmer of gas and with nothing to do. Who could wonder that men are drawn into such a vortex, even were the penalty heavier than it is?

Such, or something like it, was the magnetic power of London, expressed in human terms. And the interviews conducted by Llew-

---

[10] Ken Young and Patricia L. Garside, *Metropolitan London. Politics and Urban Change 1837–1981* (1982), 342; Peter Hall, Harry Gracey etc., *The Containment of Urban England* (2 vols., 1973), I. 64.
[11] Sidney Webb, *The London Programme* (1891), 2.

ellyn Smith in the agricultural Eastern Counties with villagers who
had stayed at home there provide a vivid microcosm of the effect of
this metropolitan power upon the surrounding region. '"We shall
soon be all old men," says the village blacksmith mournfully,' all his
three sons having already settled in London, '"and yet what is the
use of the lads staying here? There is nothing to do; they had better
seek their luck elsewhere." '[12]

Yet despite this overwhelming metropolitan numerical prepon-
derance there were senses in which London's position suffered eclipse
throughout much of the nineteenth century. The centre of gravity
of the Industrial Revolution was not in London but in the north
and the midlands, the great new towns of which occupied much of
the limelight of the national stage until the 1880s. It was in Stockton
and Darlington and in Liverpool and Manchester, not in London,
that the earliest railways using steam locomotives were built; and
the middle years of the century saw the great age of provincial civic
pre-eminence, the age of the Manchester Free Trade School, of
Leeds Town Hall, and in the 1870s of Joseph Chamberlain's
Birmingham.

Politically, London was also in eclipse. It did not provide the
main driving force behind many of the most important agitations—
for the Reform Act of 1832, for factory legislation, for Chartism, for
national elementary education, or for the repeal of the corn laws;
nor was London's influence particularly effective in the early years
of the co-operative and trade union movements. If one ignores Sir
Francis Burdett, who was more a survivor from the days of Wilkes
than a portent of the future, London never had a great leader of its
own, like Thomas Attwood or Joseph Chamberlain or Richard Cobden or John Bright. Until 1885 London was, moreover, grossly
under-represented in the House of Commons, for even after the
Reform Act of 1832, when the number of Members of Parliament
representing the whole metropolitan area was increased from ten to
twenty-two, London's share was only about one-thirtieth of the
whole House—far below its 'true' share, whether calculated in terms
of wealth or population. As the capital city, too, London's rôle was
inevitably diminished in the heyday of *laissez-faire* economics, and
when the dangers of centralisation were a popular bogey. Lastly,
London's vast size, its rôle as capital, and the attitude of the City
Corporation—London's unique internal anatomy, in fact,—all made
the remodelling of London's own institutions peculiarly difficult.
The whole process of metropolitan municipal reform was, indeed,

[12] H. Llewellyn Smith, 'Influx of Population', in Charles Booth, *Life and Labour of the People in London*, 1st ser., *Poverty*, 3 (1902), 75, 130, 143.

greatly retarded in relation to the rest of the country, and London's political influence was much reduced thereby.

This relative recession in the extent of metropolitan political influence may in part be attributed to the small scale and infinite variety of London's industries. Despite the Industrial Revolution London was still, as it had been for centuries, the largest centre of manufacturing industry in the country, but with coal and iron deposits and water power all at a distance in the north, and without any staple industry suitable for adaptation to large-scale mechanical methods of production, the factory system did not establish itself widely in London until after the nineteenth century. In 1851, for instance, only twenty-one per cent of all industrial establishments in London employed over four workers.[13] London's typical industrial premises were often to be found in the back-street workshop, the back room, the sweat shop, the attic and even the cellar. Many of the principal trades were concerned in the manufacture or finishing of luxury goods or goods of very high quality, and because such demand was closely related to fashion or to the peregrinations of the royal court, it was often highly seasonal. So the peculiar structure of London's industries was, without doubt, in substantial measure due to the fact that London was the capital city, and had evolved to serve the peculiar demands of the capital. But in consequence of this diverse and fragmented structure London's work-force was peculiarly difficult to organise. Until the 1880s there was therefore no persistent, effective working-class movement in London, and metropolitan political influence suffered accordingly. The absence of a powerful organised working-class presence in London was, indeed, of profound importance in determining the course of national events in such critical times as 1832 and 1848.

But if the small scale and great variety of London's industries partly explains why metropolitan influence was in recession, another reason, perhaps even more important, was, paradoxically, the sheer prodigious size of the place, never previously known anywhere in the world. For Flora Tristan, a Frenchwoman recording her visits to London in the 1830s, it was 'the monster city', 'out of all proportion to the area and population of the British Isles'. For Henry James, recalling his first vivid impressions of the capital in the late 1860s, 'The immensity was the great fact'. London was 'above all overwhelming'; and comments of this kind could be multiplied indefinitely.

Both these perceptive Victorian foreign observers went on, however, to point out an important effect which this vast size had on

[13] Lynn Lees, 'Metropolitan Types. London and Paris compared', *The Victorian City*, eds H.J. Dyos and Michael Wolff (2 vols., 1973), I. 421.

the everyday life of London's inhabitants. For Flora Tristan the advantages which London offered to industry were

> offset by the inconvenience of the enormous distances one has to travel; the city is several cities in one and has become too large for people to meet or get to know one another. How is it possible to maintain close relations with father, daughter, sister or friends, when for a visit lasting an hour, one has to spend three hours on the journey and eight francs on a cab? The extreme fatigue of life in London can only be understood by those who have lived there for some time, whether in pursuit of business or diversion. Any journey is likely to be of five or six miles, so however trifling one's business, one is obliged to travel over fifteen miles a day. . . . When the Londoner returns home in the evening, weary and exhausted by the day's travel, he is incapable of wit or gaiety and disinclined for the pleasures of conversation, music or dancing.

And Henry James was making much the same point when he wrote of London that

> it is her incurable misfortune that there is really too much of her. . . . as the monster grows and grows for ever, she departs more and more . . . from the ideal of a convenient society, a society in which intimacy is possible, in which the associated meet often and sound and select and measure and inspire each other, and relations and combinations have time to form themselves. The substitute for this, in London, is the momentary concussion of a million of atoms.[14]

The suave and sophisticated 'relations and combinations' which Henry James had in mind when he wrote this passage in 1888 were certainly very different from the political connexions described by Francis Place nearly fifty years earlier, but the successful formation of all 'relations and combinations' was nevertheless in both cases impeded by the same cause—the sheer immensity of London. Writing in 1840 to Richard Cobden about the lack of metropolitan support for the Manchester-based Anti-Corn Law League, Place stated that

> London differs very widely from Manchester, and, indeed, from every other place on the face of the earth. It has no local or particular interest as a town, not even as to politics. Its several [parliamentary] boroughs in this respect are like so many very populous places at a distance from one another, and the inhabitants of any one of them know nothing, or next to nothing, of the proceedings in any other, and not much indeed of those of their own. London in my time, and that is half a century, has never

---

[14] *The London Journal of Flora Tristan 1842*, transl. Jean Hawkes (1982), 16, 18; Henry James, *English Hours* (1905), 3, 8, 42, 43.

moved [politically]. A few of the people in different parts have moved, and these, whenever they come together, make a considerable number—still, a very small number indeed when compared with the whole number—and when these are judiciously managed, i.e. when they are brought to act together, not only make a great noise, which is heard far and wide, but which has also considerable influence in many places. But, isolated as men are here, living as they do at considerable distances, many seven miles apart, and but seldom meeting together, except in small groups, to talk either absolute nonsense or miserable party politics, or to transact business exclusive of everything else, they will tell you they have no time to give to the Association to help repeal the Corn Laws, while the simple fact is that, with the exception of the men of business (and even they lose much time), four-fifths of the whole do nothing but lose their time.[15]

The effect which London's vastly increased size was having upon the social relationships and political influence of the capital's inhabitants was a matter of frequent comment in the middle years of the nineteenth century. It was a new phenomenon, still quite unknown in the later eighteenth century to (for instance) either James Boswell, who in his incessant comings and goings in London (many of them on foot) never complained of the capital's excessive size, or to John Wilkes, who had had no difficulty in arousing widespread political support there. London was in fact becoming the prototype of all those other cities, both at home and abroad, whose great size has reduced much of the social life of their inhabitants to Henry James's 'momentary concussion of a million of atoms'.

But in London this social disintegration was aggravated by the capital's peculiar internal anatomy, to which reference has already been made. In the seventeenth century the already long-standing mutual suspicion and hostility generally prevalent between the cities of London and Westminster had acquired a new dimension when in 1633 and again in 1634 the City Corporation had refused the Privy Council's request to 'accept part of the suburbs into their jurisdiction and liberty for better government'. This event, sometimes known as 'The Great Refusal', was to be of cardinal importance in the history of London, for it set back by some two hundred and fifty years the establishment of a rational system of local government throughout almost the whole of the metropolis.[16] In the long run it also deprived the people of London of the natural focal point for their civic loyalties. In 1891 'The greatest need of the metropolis' was, according

[15] Graham Wallas, *The Life of Francis Place 1771–1854* (1925 edn), 393–4.
[16] I. G. Doolittle, *The City of London and its Livery Companies* (Dorchester, 1982), 6–7.

to even such an unsentimental person as Sidney Webb, 'the growth among its citizens of a greater common life'.[17] And these two losses profoundly affected London's position in the nation throughout much of the nineteenth century.

In the eighteenth century the ever-growing chaos in the ever-growing suburbs had not yet had any great extra-metropolitan political significance because the predominantly Whig or Radical and anti-ministerial City could still provide a semblance of leadership for the whole of London. But in the mid 1780s the City began to support Pitt's administration, and although it resumed its old anti-government stance in 1807 it never regained its previous pre-eminent position in London's politics. In this interim period the parliamentary constituency of Westminster became and for many years remained the principal stronghold of London radicalism, and the City's subsequent petitions and addresses on such matters as parliamentary reform, the Corn Law Bill of 1815 or Queen Caroline's affairs no longer possessed the force which widespread popular support had conferred in the days of Wilkes. The sheer size and social complexity of London were beginning to prevent the re-emergence of any generally acknowledged metropolitan leadership. The days of the riotous Wilkite crowd were over, but (as previously mentioned) the days of a stable, organised working-class movement had not yet arrived; and it was in this confused period extending over some fifty years, from the early 1830s to the early 1880s, that London's political influence was in eclipse.

The situation was aggravated by successive governments' perplexity about how to deal with the administrative problems of London. Clearly, something had to be done, but what, and how? For mid-Victorian governments as well as for mid-Victorian Londoners, experience (in Donald Olsen's words) 'offered no guide, history no parallels. Victorian London was not only unique but unprecedented'.[18] The City Corporation, on the other hand, had one simple aim—the maintenance of the status quo—which, against all the odds, it achieved with a remarkable degree of success.

The Reform Bill crisis of 1830-2 proved to be the last occasion of national significance when the Corporation allied itself with the forces of popular radicalism. But with the establishment very shortly afterwards of the Royal Commission to 'inquire into the existing state of the Municipal Corporations in England and Wales' the great Corporation of London itself became a prime target for reform. When, however, the Commissioners at last presented their

---

[17] Webb, *London Programme*, v.

[18] Donald Olsen, 'Introduction: Victorian London', in David Owen, *The Government of Victorian London 1855–1889* (Harvard and London, 1982), 2.

report on London in 1837, two years after all the other larger municipal corporations throughout the country had been reformed, they
did little but point to the difficulties of the situation. There was no
reason, they said, to justify 'the present distinction of this particular
district [i.e. the City] from the rest, except that in *fact* it is, and has
long been, so distinguished'. Nor was there any reason why the
suburbs, now massive in their physical extent, should not be embodied within the original nucleus of London, as had already been done
in all the great provincial municipalities, unless the sheer magnitude
of the change would convert what elsewhere would 'be only a practical difficulty into an objection of principle.' Clearly the suburbs
should not be converted into a galaxy of new corporations in perpetual orbit around the City, but if on the other hand a single
municipality for the whole capital were to be set up, 'a new and
very important question' would arise, namely 'the proper division
of municipal authority between the Officers of Government and a
municipal body which might be established in the Metropolis' on
lines analogous to those of the provincial towns. The Commissioners
were, in fact, baffled, and in conclusion they could only point out
that the precedent of Peel's Police Act of 1829 had shown that there
was no middle course between 'placing the whole under a Metropolitan Municipality, and entrusting the whole to Commissioners
... under the immediate control of Your Majesty's Government'. So
Lord Melbourne's administration did nothing, and the City of London, alone among the great municipal corporations, survived unreformed.[19]

   This failure to deal with the metropolis was of crucial importance,
for it set a new scene in the perennial tragi-comedy of the history of
the government of London, which is still running today, as freshly
as ever. In the seminal ten or twelve years which began in 1842
with the publication of Edwin Chadwick's *Inquiry into the Sanitary
Condition of the Labouring Population of Great Britain*, the foundations of
national sanitary institutions were being laid. But in still unreformed
London the struggle for improved sanitation necessarily involved the
reform of the whole field of metropolitan administration as well; and
no government was willing either to take on the City Corporation,
which thanks to the ability of its first Medical Officer of Health,
Dr John Simon, had acquired a short-lived fame for civic virtue, or
to give whole-hearted support to Chadwick, who at least had definite ideas about the sanitary institutions needed for London. So by
1852, when another Royal Commission was appointed to inquire
into the state of the City Corporation, even such an ardent defender

[19] *P.P.* 1837, XXV (239), Second Report on the Municipal Corporations: London
and Southwark, 4.

of the established order as Joshua Toulmin Smith could declare without exaggeration that

> The present condition of this huge metropolis exhibits the most extraordinary anomaly in England. Abounding in wealth and intelligence, by far the greater part of it is yet absolutely without any municipal government whatever.[20]

This state of affairs was not satisfactorily corrected by the creation of the Metropolitan Board of Works in 1855. The Metropolis Management Act was, it is true, the first legislative attempt to tackle the problem of metropolitan local government as a whole—or at any rate, almost as a whole, for the City was still unreformed. It put an end to both select and open vestries, to innumerable paving and lighting trusts and commissions, it gave London a sanitary code roughly analogous to that of the rest of the country, and the Board did in due course provide London with a fine system of sewerage. But with thirty-eight district authorities still in existence, metropolitan administration was still absurdly fragmented; the Board's powers were extremely limited, particularly at first; and the system of indirect election to the Board, coupled with the continuing existence of the City Corporation, guaranteed ceaseless bickering between Board, vestries and Corporation, most of it conducted by the mainly very second-rate members who took charge of London during the sour and spleenful life-span of the Board.[21] Yet even such exiguous powers as the Board did possess were regarded as excessive by some Members of Parliament, one of whom, during the debates of 1855, denounced 'this system of centralization' as 'repugnant to our principles and our taste, which have hitherto always encouraged local self-government'.[22]

Attitudes of this kind were widely prevalent in the mid 1850s. The metropolis was regarded as an agglomeration of disparate new suburbs surrounding the ancient City, and having no overall coherence of their own. The Corporation could therefore turn its back upon ninety-five per cent of the people of London; and until the creation of the Metropolitan Boroughs in 1899 it systematically blocked either the creation of a ring of new municipalities around the ancient nucleus, or the expansion of its own jurisdiction over the whole built-up area. Inquiries by yet another Royal Commission and by half-a-dozen Select Committees, and Parliamentary Bills almost without number were all deftly circumvented or defeated by the Corporation. So not only was the City of London the sole great

[20] Joshua Toulmin Smith, *The Metropolis and Its Municipal Administration* (1852), 6.
[21] Owen, *Government of Victorian London, passim.*
[22] *Hansard*, 3rd ser., 138, 14 May 1855, col. 570.

corporation to survive unreformed, but it was also the only one to reject its own suburbs; and the consequence of the Lord Mayor, and the value of all the ancient traditions and trappings of the Corporation, which might have served as valuable adjuncts for metropolitan loyalties, and thereby in some measure counter-balanced the centrifugal forces prevalent within Victorian London, were thereby (and still are) largely squandered.

With London presenting such a spectacle of confusion it is indeed hardly surprising that in the middle years of the century the main focus of municipal attention shifted away from London to the north. But there were nevertheless two areas of public administration where London led the way. The first of these was the regulation of buildings, the history of which extended back within the City to medieval times and even in the suburbs back to the long series of Elizabethan and Jacobean proclamations against building. The great London Building Act of 1774, which codified standards of structure and safety and through the District Surveyors provided an efficient inspectorate, was still being used as a model in provincial towns in the early 1840s. The Metropolitan Building Act of 1844 attempted for the first time to regulate the relationship between the width of a street and the height of the buildings in it, and many of the provisions in the Towns Improvement Clauses Act of 1847, which was later adopted in large numbers of provincial towns, were based upon the example of the London Acts. In later years the two sets of model building bye-laws produced in 1858 by the Local Government Act Office and in 1877 by the Local Government Board both drew heavily upon the provisions of the London Building Acts.[23]

The other area of public administration where, despite the City, London was in advance of the rest of the nation, was in the matter of public order. The health, education, housing and general sanitary condition of the metropolitan labouring classes could all be, and indeed were to a large extent, neglected for many years, but public order could not be so treated, for, as Lord Liverpool had said, one 'serious insurrection in London, and all is lost'.[24] The Metropolitan Police Act of 1829 was a turning point in one of the great historic processes of the nineteenth century—the elimination of riot and disorder as an endemic feature of British life; but it had other significance as well. So far as London's internal anatomy was concerned, it has already been stated that in 1837 the Royal Commissioners inquiring into the City Corporation had the example of Peel's Act

---

[23] S. Martin Gaskell, *Building Control. National Legislation and the Introduction of Local Bye-Laws in Victorian England* (1983), 5, 14–15, 18–19, 44–6.

[24] *The Memoirs of François René Vicomte de Chateaubriand*, trans. Alexander Teixeira De Mattos (6 vols., 1902), IV. 92.

very much in mind in making their inconclusive report, and the omission of the City from the Act of 1829 had, indeed, established a precedent which proved all to easy to follow in later schemes of metropolitan reform. But more importantly it transferred one of the principal functions hitherto discharged by the London local authorities (i.e. the vestries) to the central government in the person of the Home Secretary. This too set an important precedent, which was followed in 1834 when the Poor Law Amendment Act removed another of the principal functions of the parish vestries to Chadwick's new centrally-controlled Poor Law Unions (though in some recalcitrant London parishes this central control was not fully established until the 1860s). In Peel's Act of 1829 may be seen the first significant example of the reassertion of those centripetal forces which exerted themselves with increasing power in the later nineteenth century, and to which attention must now be turned.

First of all, of course, there was the tremendous general extension of the operation of government in the nineteenth century. Even in the heyday of liberalism the English administrative system was in many ways becoming more centralised. Victorian legislation on prisons, factories, mines, railways, steamships, education and public health, to mention only a few of the most obvious examples, all conferred ever-increasing powers upon the state and its head-office staff and directors (so to speak) in London. Administrative contacts, either in writing or in person, between London and all parts of the country increased enormously, as thousands of departmental files now reposing in the Public Record Office can testify; and although by no means all public officers were based in the capital, the rise in their number from less than 17,000 in 1797 to over 107,000 in 1902 provides some indication of the scale of the growth of government action in the nineteenth century, all of it ultimately directed from London.[25]

This enlargement of the field of government action was in great measure a response to the rise of industrial and urban society, and was therefore a new factor in the relationship between the metropolis and the provinces. It was closely related to a second new factor which also exerted an increasingly powerful pull towards London— the nineteenth-century revolution in communications. Although most of the earliest railways were built in the north, London very soon—within some twenty years of the opening of the Stockton and Darlington line in 1825—became the hub of the new railway network, and through the greatly improved ease of movement of both goods and passengers even the largest provincial towns began to feel

[25] Emmeline W. Cohen, *The Growth of the British Civil Service 1780-1939* (1941), 23, 164.

the growing power of metropolitan influences (not to mention a similar process in even such remote places as the Scilly Isles, where spring flowers were being sent up to Covent Garden as early as the 1870s). In the south-eastern part of the country, where there were no such great regional centres as Birmingham or Leeds or Manchester, this metropolitan influence was, of course, particularly strong, the railways radiating out from London to a ring of towns along the south coast from Bournemouth to Margate and out into the wide open spaces of East Anglia, extending the ascendancy of the capital throughout the whole area. The mails, which greatly increased in quantity after the introduction of the penny post in 1840, were delivered more quickly, the London newspapers were nightly dispatched far afield to the provinces, and during the Chartist emergencies the speed with which troops and police could be sent from one part of the country to another greatly assisted in the preservation of order. So too, in the long run, the new precision of practice and behaviour required and provided by the railways increased centralisation, and hence the pre-eminence of London.

Comparable in importance to the building of the railways was the development of electricity. The commercial supply of electricity for lighting and power dates only from the 1880s, but the use of electricity in the field of communications dates back to the 1840s, when the first public electric telegraph line was laid from Paddington to Slough on the Great Western Railway in 1843. At first the use of the telegraph was almost entirely confined to the railways, but in 1850 telegraphic money orders were inaugurated, and after a cable had been laid between Dover and Calais the stock exchanges of London and Paris were able to compare prices during the business hours of the same day.

At home the electric telegraph transformed internal communications during the second half of the nineteenth century. By 1870–1 over nine million messages were being sent per annum, but thirty years later their number had increased nearly ten-fold to almost ninety million. Transatlantic cables were laid in the 1860s, and in the 1890s a world-wide network was being established. It was in the 1890s, too, that Marconi's experiments were leading to the successful transmission and reception of the first transatlantic message by wireless telegraphy in 1901, and to the inauguration of a public service in 1907. By that time the telephone had been ringing with mounting insistence for some thirty years, and in 1906 London, with a population of between six and seven millions, had nearly as many telephone subscribers as the whole of France, with a population of thirty-nine millions.[26]

[26] *Encyclopaedia Britannica*, 11th edn (1910–11), XXVI. 525, 554–6.

The centralising effects of all these new systems of electrical communication is particularly apparent in relation to the press, where the changes taking place towards the end of the nineteenth century provide a third London-oriented ingredient in the ever-shifting balance between metropolis and provinces. It is true that after the repeal of the newspaper stamp duty in 1855 and of the tax on paper in 1861 provincial journalism began to flourish; but so too did the London press, the *Daily Telegraph*, for instance, achieving in 1870 a circulation of 240,000—at that time the largest in the world for a daily paper. As the new electrical systems of communication took over all the transmission of news, a vast increase in the sheer quantity of information presented to the public was taking place, and between 1870 and 1900 the number of words handed in to the Post Office for transmission for press purposes rose from 22 million to 835 million.[27]

The purveying of information on this colossal new scale was made commercially possible by the cheapening of paper (through the introduction of wood pulp), the use of greatly improved printing machinery and the growth of newspaper advertising. But the success of the 'new Journalism' of the 1890s, epitomised in Alfred Harmsworth's *Daily Mail*, founded in 1896, was also the result of what was called in 1910 'the democratic movement produced by the Education Act of 1870 and the Reform Act of 1885'.[28] More information, collected by electrical or wireless telegraphy and by mass-production methods of printing regurgitated out to the nightly newspaper trains, and a public more literate and more concerned with politics, national and even international affairs than ever before—the one created a mass supply and the other a mass demand; and London was the natural place for the servicing of this great new market.

The daily newspaper industry is, after all, an essentially metropolitan business, best situated at the national centre of both events and of communications. Even in the 1870s, in their heyday, many of the provincial dailies had found it necessary to open offices in Fleet Street. Their employment of the London news agencies for much of their material was apt to produce 'sameness', and their habit of securing simultaneous publication of contributions specially prepared for the London papers was almost an acknowledgement of their secondary status. Even their admirable reporting of parliamentary debates, which (except in the case of *The Times*) was often fuller than that of the London papers, tended to divert their readers' attention away from local affairs towards the metropolitan scene.

[27] Ibid., XXIII. 108.
[28] Ibid., XIX. 547, 550.

When in 1902 the *Daily Mail*, already having a circulation of over one million copies, invaded the heartland of the provinces and started to print in Manchester as well as London, the whole contents of each issue being telegraphed nightly, the ultimate ascendancy of Fleet Street was not far away.[29]

In the intellectual and cultural fields London's long-standing pre-eminent position in the nation had traditionally been the preserve of a relatively small circle of people. But through the vast concentration of the well-to-do middle classes in the metropolis during the nineteenth century, far more people were able to enjoy this favoured situation than hitherto; and through the revolution in communications metropolitan standards and modes of thought and behaviour percolated outwards with greater ease and on a greater scale than previously. Before the days of fast easy travel by railway had even begun, Robert Southey had said in 1807 that 'London is now so often visited, that the manners of the metropolis are to be found in every country gentleman's house'.[30] The gentlemen's clubs of the West End, which proliferated throughout the nineteenth century and which drew their members from the country as well as from 'town', provided an important channel for the working of this process; and as the 'society' of the London Season became ever larger and less exclusive, so did its influence affect more and more people ever further down the social scale.

More specifically, London acquired its own university, which by 1914 had made outstanding contributions to industrial science, greater than those of any other British university, and which possessed in the London School of Economics (started in 1895) a pioneering institution of formidable influence.[31] London housed the headquarters of all the new more specialised professions, such as the surveyors, auctioneers, accountants, civil and mechanical engineers, as well, of course, as those of medicine and the law; and it was there that almost all of the learned or religious or philanthropic societies which proliferated in the nineteenth century had their origins and their places of meeting. In scientific research many of the pathfinders worked principally in London, notably Sir Humphry Davy and Michael Faraday. Rather unexpectedly, it was at his laboratory in St Pancras, not up in the north, that Henry Bessemer devised his revolutionary process for making steel; and it was in a little workshop in Clerkenwell, in London's ancient centre of clock, watch and precision instrument making, that Hiram Maxim constructed his first automatic gun. It fired six hundred rounds a minute, and within

[29] Ibid., XIX. 560, 564, and XXIII. 107; Read, 248.
[30] Robert Southey, *Letters from England* (3 vols., 1807), I. 291.
[31] Michael Sanderson, *The Universities and British Industry 1850-1970* (1972), 120, 190.

a short while Maxim had used over two hundred thousand cartridges at his premises in Hatton Garden in demonstrating the gun to such influential visitors as the Prince of Wales, the Duke of Cambridge (commander-in-chief of the British Army) and General Wolseley, all of whom were enchanted with it.[32] The advantages of being in London were, indeed, great, and very varied.

In the world of the theatre, opera and music, London's pre-eminence was absolute; while in the field of art it was not far short of absolute after the foundation of the National Gallery (1824), the National Portrait Gallery (1856) and the South Kensington Museum (1857), this last founded partly on the profits of the Great Exhibition, which had provided the occasion for millions of Englishmen and women to make their first visit to the capital. More important still, London was also the traditional centre of the fine art trade, nearly all the dealers having their galleries in the West End, mostly in or adjacent to St James's. It was because of this high degree of metropolitan concentration of artistic interests that most artists who exhibited at the Royal Academy had at least a pied-à-terre in London, and often a studio or a house as well. The Pre-Raphaelites all had their headquarters in London, and even Constable spent many years there. Blake and Turner were both Londoners by birth, and lived there throughout most of their lives.

In the literary world too the residence in London for substantial periods of many of the greatest writers, including Keats, Byron, Coleridge, Lamb, Carlyle, Thackeray, Browning, George Eliot, Macaulay and, of course, Dickens, demonstrates the capital's power of attraction; and many even of those writers who never lived there, such as Jane Austen or the Brontë sisters, nevertheless had business dealings with their publishers there, for only Edinburgh could rival London in the book trade. Whatever its limitations in other fields might be, London was throughout the nineteenth century indisputably the intellectual and cultural capital of the nation.

The ever-changing nature of London's economic position within the realm is rather less clear; and a full-scale economic history of Victorian London is still awaited. During the course of the nineteenth century the proportion of the peoples of England and Wales who lived in London doubled (as previously mentioned), from one in every ten to one in every five; and despite the collapse of such traditional industries as silk-weaving and ship-building, London's share of the national total of workers in either manufacturing or service industries was also rising, at any rate after 1861.[33] In that year no less than ten per cent of the male adult working population

---

[32] Sir Hiram Maxim, *My Life* (1915), 159–72.
[33] P. G. Hall, *The Industries of London since 1861* (1962), 21.

in London was employed on what the census called 'houses and buildings', and (although this figure must be regarded with caution) London had twenty-four per cent of all 'builders' in England and Wales, as well as thirty-eight per cent of the architects. Most building work in London was, of course, done speculatively by small firms, but by the middle of the century there were a few large-scale speculators as well. Large chunks of Victorian Kensington were built by such moguls as C. J. Freake, Charles Aldin or the Radfords; and in the erection of nearly a thousand houses in the Redcliffe Square area Corbett and McClymont used mechanical methods of mass-production, which had been pioneered by William Cubitt and Company.[34] Building speculators of this class may have had their counterparts in a few large provincial towns, but the great contracting builders like Alexander Copland or Samuel Peto and Thomas Grissell were certainly a breed of London origin; and even though the London men soon faced stiff provincial competition, it seems that they successfully maintained their leading position, for by the end of the century they were taking on work all over the country and overseas.[35]

But while London's share of industry was rising in the later nineteenth century, and metropolitan building capacity was certainly very great in relation to the rest of the country, the Port of London's share of Britain's foreign trade fell considerably, though its absolute value nevertheless increased over twelve-fold during the whole century. In 1909 twenty-nine per cent of all Britain's foreign trade still passed through London, and the total net tonnage of the vessels entering the port exceeded that of any other port in either Britain or continental Europe by some fifty per cent.[36]

In the City the physical landscape of the place was transformed from around 1860 onwards by the incursion (above and below ground) of the railways, the formation of new streets and the building of palatial new offices for the headquarters of banks, insurance companies and other commercial institutions; and this outward transformation reflected the rapidly changing functions of the City. The great growth in the scale and scope of business in such fields as insurance and the stock exchange, the development of joint-stock banks each with their own numerous branch offices, and changes in the short-term money market brought about after the appearance there of discount companies, all tended to strengthen the City's central position in the national economy; and City lawyers often

---

[34] John Summerson, *The London Building World of the Eighteen-Sixties* (1973), 9, 16–17; *Survey of London*, XLI (1983), 195.

[35] Marian Bowley, *The British Building Industry* (1966), 335–40.

[36] Douglas Owen, *Port of London Authority* (1914), 97–8.

provided the link for the investment of provincial capital in mort-
gages in metropolitan suburban bricks and mortar. But it was above
all in international trade and finance that the City's rôle was changing. It was through the City that much of the surplus wealth of
Britain was channelled into investment overseas, and it was in the
City that many of the nation's foreign trade partners held their large
sterling balances, much to Britain's advantage. By the end of the
nineteenth century, British banks had been established all over the
Empire, nearly thirty of them having branches in London.[37] The
provision of much of the cheap foreign food needed to feed Britain's
industrialised and urbanised population owed much to the financial
services provided by the City; and if by the end of the century
Britain had ceased to be able to claim to be 'the workshop of the
world', it was in large measure due to the men in the City, to such
people as H. L. Bischoffscheim, Sir Ernest Cassel, the Rothschilds,
and to numerous other less well known men, that Britain's claim to
be at any rate the world's banker and trader could still be convinc-
ingly sustained.

It was to the work of these City men that Dr W. D. Rubinstein
was pointing when he referred to the central importance of the City
in the occupational and geographical distribution of Britain's
wealth-holders. His researches have shown that a very substantial
proportion of the large fortunes made throughout the country in the
nineteenth century was made in finance and commerce rather than
in manufacturing industry, and that much of it was made in London, and in the City in particular, rather than in the provinces.
Furthermore, this concentration of wealth was not confined to a
small number of very rich people, but extended far down to quite
low levels of income. London's middle classes were, in fact, richer
per capita than their provincial counterparts; and due to their great
numbers, distributed in varying proportions throughout most of the
metropolitan area, London possessed by far the greatest single concentration of personal wealth in the nation.[38]

But London also possessed by far the greatest concentration of
poverty in Britain, and it was above all the revelation of this stark
fact, and of the deep-seated social problems attendant upon it, which
in the early 1880s firmly focused the national attention upon London
once more. It was in London that the widest extremities of wealth
and poverty were to be found, and there that the geographical
segregation of different social classes had reached its extreme limit.

[37] S. G. Checkland, *The Rise of Industrial Society in England 1815–1885* (1964), 203–10.
[38] W. D. Rubinstein, *Men of Property. The Very Wealthy in Britain since the Industrial Revolution* (1981), 61, 102–10.

The Bitter Cry of Outcast London, published in October 1883, the findings of the Royal Commission on the Housing of the Working Classes, published in 1884–5, and Charles Booth's *Life and Labour of the People in London*, the first volume of which was published in 1889, all exposed metropolitan social conditions hitherto either unknown or largely ignored. For a relatively short period in the mid 1880s, particularly at the time of the riots in the West End in February 1886 and of the demonstrations in Trafalgar Square in November 1887, there was even fear for the safety of the metropolis. This fear largely evaporated after the Dock Strike of 1889; but despite the relative outward calm which prevailed throughout the metropolis in the 1890s, the renewed ascendancy in the national regard which London had commanded during the traumas of the 1880s nevertheless continued; and when C. F. G. Masterman was considering the 'Problems of Modern City Life in England' in 1901, he felt able to discuss the whole subject of the 'Condition of the People' as it manifested itself in London alone, 'in the centre of culture and government, the home of literature, art, and religion, the spot whither all men pilgrimage to seek stimulus and pleasure, the capital of the greatest empire that the world has ever seen'.[39]

Politically, London was still weak and disorganised until the 1880s, and so too were the trade unions in relation to their strength in many of the great provincial cities; but in the 1880s there were numerous signs that the long period of metropolitan ineffectiveness would soon come to an end.[40] There seems to have been at this time a change in Parliament's attitude towards London. The metropolis was no longer the bogey which it had seemed to be in the 1850s, radical opinion had veered round to demanding a unified system of metropolitan government, and the Bill introduced in 1884 by Sir William Harcourt as Home Secretary would even, by extending the limits of a reformed City Corporation, have provided a single municipality for the whole of London. The withdrawal of this Bill—one of the great lost opportunities in London's history—was not, however, due to fear of centralisation but to the crisis provoked by the Lords' rejection of the Franchise Bill;[41] an odd irony, for it was from this measure as ultimately passed, and its companion, the Redistribution Act of 1885, that London was at last granted an adequate representation in Parliament.

On several occasions in the past, fear had provided an important

---

[39] C. F. G. Masterman, 'Realities at Home', in *The Heart of the Empire. Discussions of Problems of Modern City Life in England* . . . (1901), 48.

[40] See Paul Thompson, *Socialists, Liberals and Labour. The Struggle for London 1885–1914* (1967), chap. iii.

[41] Doolittle, 107.

stimulus to metropolitan reform—a fear of fire, leading to the London Building Acts; fear of disorder, leading to the Metropolitan
Police Act of 1829; and fear of disease, particularly of cholera,
leading to the establishment of the Metropolitan Board of Works in
1855. So far as London is concerned, the Reform Act of 1884 and
the Redistribution Act of 1885 may either be regarded as the last of
these fear-inspired reforms or the first of a new series, taken without
such a disagreeable stimulus. Either way, London's weight in the
nation was no longer ignored. It was no longer possible to say, as
Sir Edward Sugden, later Lord Chancellor, had said in the House
of Commons during the debates on the Reform Bill in 1832, 'One of
the principal things which they had to dread was the giving too
much power to the Metropolis ... let them take care how they made
the fate of the country depend on the will of the Metropolis';[42] nor
even to say, as Lord Halifax, a former Chancellor of the Exchequer,
had admitted in the Lords during the debates on the second Reform
Bill in 1867, 'I do not consider the representation of the metropolis
exactly on the same footing as that of the large constituencies in
different parts of the country'.[43] Instead the matter was at last to be
considered dispassionately. A vast new metropolitan working-class
electorate was created, and after metropolitan representation in the
Commons had been increased from twenty-nine to seventy-two
members—equivalent to about one tenth of the whole House—
London finally acquired a potential political significance in
rough measure commensurate with its size. And with the gradual
enlargement of metropolitan trade unions to include semi-skilled
and unskilled workers, the amalgamation of many London trade
organisations into national unions, and the foundation with trade
union support of the London Labour Party in 1914, London became
after the Great War a major centre of Labour power, and hence of
national political influence.

The three decades between the mid 1880s and the outbreak of
war in 1914 were, in fact, a period of rapid metropolitan political
re-awakening. It was in London that two of the most influential
socialist bodies in late Victorian and Edwardian times—the Socialist
Democratic Federation and the Fabian Society—had their origins
in the early 1880s.[44] Due to the greater personal mobility within
London made possible by the much enlarged and improved public
transport system,[45] sheer size was probably a less formidable obstacle

[42] *Hansard*, 3rd ser., X, 28 Feb. 1832, 923.
[43] Ibid., CLXXXIX, 29 July 1867, 268.
[44] Thompson, 93; Read, 194.
[45] T. C. Barker and Michael Robbins, *A History of London Transport* (2 vols., 1963–74), II. 208.

to metropolitan political activity than hitherto. Between 1885, when the metropolitan electorate numbered some 594,000 voters, and 1910, when it had risen to over one million, there were no less than eight general elections.[46] From 1889 onwards there were also triennial elections to the London County Council, besides numerous lesser elections for the vestries, Boards of Guardians and the London School Board, all these local contests being fought more and more on party lines. Between Sir William Harcourt's unsuccessful attempt in 1884 to set up a unified system of government for the whole of London, and the resolution of the matter (for some years, at any rate) in 1899 by the establishment of the twenty-eight metropolitan borough councils, the crisis of London's affairs was seldom far from the attention of either the Government or the general public. The findings in 1887 of the Select Committee on the 'improper use and Malversation of Public Funds of the Corporation of London', followed in 1888 by those of the Royal Commission on corruption within the Metropolitan Board of Works, titillated public interest;[47] and awareness of the importance of the creation of the County of London and the L.C.C. was stimulated by this timely contrast between the old and the new municipal dispensations. London's first directly elected municipal body was at once seen to be something entirely new in English politics. Lord Rosebery became its first chairman, and the Progressive party's 'London Programme' was able to claim that 'Metropolitan reform has become a national if not an international question'.[48] The days of provincial municipal pre-eminence, the pioneering days of Birmingham or Manchester, were over; and by the end of the Victorian era, after the celebration of the two royal jubilees and after what Masterman called 'a wave of "Imperialism"' had swept over the country, London had become the cynosure of both the nation and the Empire—the capital city of that Empire upon which the sun was said never to set.[49]

The raucous tone of later Victorian imperialism jars on some modern ears, and (to vary the metaphor) was anyway perhaps only the froth which overlay a more deep-seated and widely prevalent sense of foreboding for the future. But for anyone whose memory of London extends back to the 1930s, the London of around 1900 has in many respects a curiously familiar feel about it. The vast size, the anonymity, the lack of local community feeling, the social segregation of one district from another, the unsettling presence of a recently

[46] Thompson, 69; Henry Pelling, *Social Geography of British Elections 1885-1910* (1967), 4.

[47] David Owen, 181-92, 256.

[48] Webb, *London Programme*, 6.

[49] Masterman, 'Realities at Home', 3.

arrived immigrant community, the widespread practice of commuting daily between home and work, the growth of office employment and service industries and the relative lack of heavy industry—all these, as Dr Paul Thompson has pointed out, were already features of the metropolitan scene at the turn of the century.[50] London had, in fact, already become the first conurbation, and in all these ways was to be the precursor of similar developments in many of the great provincial cities of mid-twentieth-century Britain.

[50] Thompson, 2, 13, 294.

PLUNDER AND TRIBUTE IN THE CAROLINGIAN EMPIRE

By Timothy Reuter, M.A., D. Phil.

READ 13 APRIL 1984

IN 882 the Emperor Charles III was forced to break off his siege of the Norsemen's camp at Asselt and make peace with them.[1] One of their leaders, Gottfried, got a Carolingian wife and the benefices in Frisia formerly held by Rorich; the other, Siegfried, got a large sum in gold and silver. Commenting on these events, the Mainz cleric who composed this section of the Annals of Fulda wrote:[2]

> and what was still more of a crime, he did not blush to pay tribute, against the custom of his ancestors, the kings of the Franks, and following the advice of evil men, to a man from whom he ought to have exacted tribute and hostages.

This is undoubtedly polemic in intention, but the accusation is not, or not directly, that Charles III should have fought the Northmen, but that he should have taken tribute and hostages from them like a proper Frankish king. In saying this, the annalist was following a long tradition; earlier writers liked to demonstrate the power of the kings they wrote about by listing the tribute they took. For the Merovingian period we know of tribute-payments by the Lombards, the Bretons, the Thuringians, the Saxons, the Frisians and the Basques, as well as by other smaller German tribes. Such payments could be made in gold and silver, or in kind. The Lombards had to pay 12000 *solidi* annually; these *solidi* predate the Carolingian monetary reform, which makes the sum a very large one indeed. The pre-monetary Saxons and Thuringians paid tributes in cows (later horses) and pigs respectively.[3] For the Carolingian period we have

---

[1] I am grateful to Wilfried Hartmann, Janet Nelson, Ernst Tremp and Ian Wood for their comments and suggestions.

[2] '... et quod maioris est criminis, a quo obsides accipere et tributa exigere debuit, huic pravorum usus consilio contra consuetudinem parentum suorum, regum videlicet Francorum, tributa solvere non erubuit.', *Annales Fuldenses*, ed. F. Kurze (MGH, SRG, Hannover, 1895) *s.a.* 882, p. 99 (cf. also pp. 108–9). See E. Dümmler, *Geschichte des ostfränkischen Reiches* (2nd. edn., 3 vols., Leipzig, 1887–8), ii. 202ff.

[3] G. Waitz, *Deutsche Verfassungsgeschichte*, (8 vols. in 9, Berlin, 1880–1896) II.ii.250–254. On Merovingian tribute-taking see also I. Wood, *The Merovingian North Sea* (Occasional papers on medieval topics, 1, Alingsas, 1983), 11–12.

75

rather fewer reports of tribute-payments, largely because many of the regions from which the Merovingians had extracted tribute had been incorporated into the Carolingian empire. Nevertheless, we hear of the Beneventans paying 350 lbs of silver per year, and the Bretons paying 50 lbs;[4] what sums the tributary Slav tribes along the eastern frontier paid is not recorded, but the larger groups like the Abodrites, the Sorbs and the Bohemians were probably good for payments on the Breton scale, and the Great Moravian Empire will have paid—after 874[5]—rather more. Such payments were usually annual, but they could also be once-off affairs. In 756 the Lombard king Aistulf had to hand over a third of his treasure to the Franks, while in 787 and again in 844 the Beneventans bought off Frankish attacks with large payments—in 844 it was a *multa*, a fine, of 100,000 *aurei*.[6]

Tribute was, so to speak, the gilt-edged income of the Franks from warfare; plunder was less calculable, but in the heyday of the Carolingian empire no less important. The annalistic sources for the eighth century regularly mention *praeda* and *spolia* (normally without maintaining the classical distinction between the two). One can of course dismiss this as a topos, but one should not do so. The majority of these writers had probably never heard of a topos; what they used were clichés and formulae,[7] and these, unlike topoi, which have a literary function, are used to make the description of reality easier. Even if formulae like *cum praeda multa* are only intended to mean that the Franks won, it is still significant that victory and plunder were more or less coterminous. The sources are sparing with details; the more utilitarian the object of plunder, the less likely it is to be explicitly mentioned. The taking of victuals, for example, is hardly ever mentioned in Frankish accounts of Frankish raiding (though it is for the Norsemen)[8], but must be taken for granted, particularly in the fast punitive raids of destruction the Carolingians came to specialise in, which were generally carried out by a *scara*, a rapid

---

[4] *Annales regni Francorum*, ed. F. Kurze (MGH, SRG, Hannover, 1892), *s.a.* 814, p. 141 (cf. also the entry for 812, p. 137); *Annales Bertiniani*, eds F. Grat, J. Vielliard, S. Clémencet and L. Levillain (Société de l'histoire de France, 1964) *s.a.* 863, p. 96; 864, p. 113.

[5] For the treaty of Forchheim between Zwentibald of Moravia and Louis the German see *Annales Fuldenses*, *s.a.*, pp. 82-3.

[6] *The Fourth Book of the Chronicle of Fredegar with its Continuations*, ed. J. M. Wallace-Hadrill, (1960), c. 38, p. 108; *Annales regni Francorum*, *s.a.* 787, p. 74; *Annales Bertiniani*, *s.a.* 844, p. 46.

[7] On the formulaic nature of Carolingian annalistic writing cf. H. Hoffmann, *Untersuchungen zur karolingischen Annalistik*, (Bonner Historische Forschungen, 10, Bonn, 1958), 69-75.

[8] E.g. by *Annales Bertiniani*, *s.a.* 861, p. 86.

deployment force—fast-moving because without a baggage train, and living off the land.[9] How Frankish armies behaved in enemy territory is shown quite adequately by the frequent complaints about how they behaved before they got there.[10] A further important form of plunder was slaves. The enslaving of Saxons is mentioned in 748 and 796, for example.[11] It also recurs in the reports of the expeditions against the Slavs in the ninth century. Here we have enslaving of heathens (though Saxony in the 790s ought to have been stretching a point), but the enslaving of Christians did not call for particular restraint, if reports of the Breton campaigns of 818 and 824 are anything to go by; Christian slaves are an object of continuing concern in Carolingian church legislation.[12] Whether slaves were taken as *servi casati*, as appears to have been the case with many of the Saxons, or sold off to slave-traders, they represented a substantial part of the profits of warfare. Apart from these things, the hoard of the enemy ruler is often mentioned: so in Frisia in 735, in Lombardy in 755 and 774, in the Avar empire in 795 and 796 and in the Great Moravian empire in 870.[13] Temple treasures were also a preferred object of plunder: gold and silver were taken when the Irminsul was burnt in 772,[14] and temple-plundering probably took place in the early raids on Frisia[15] and in the raids on the

---

[9] F. L. Ganshof, *Frankish Institutions under Charlemagne* (Providence, Rhode Island, 1968), 64, 68; J. F. Niermeyer, *Mediae Latinitatis Lexicon Minus* (Leiden 1954-1976), 943-4, *s.v.* scara, scarire, scaritus. A study of the origin and use of this term would be worthwhile.

[10] In 860 the armed followings of the three Carolingian rulers who met at Koblenz laid the surrounding countryside waste, cf. *Annales Xantenses*, ed. B. von Simson (MGH, SRG, Hannover, 1909), s.a. 861, p. 19, and for the behaviour of Charles the Bald's army in 866, *Annales Bertiniani*, *s.a.*, pp. 132-3. For the Merovingian evidence, see J. P. Bodmer, *Der Krieger der Merowingerzeit und seine Welt*, (Geist und Werk der Zeiten, 2, Zürich, 1967), 94-7.

[11] Continuator of Fredegar (ed. Wallace-Hadrill), c. 31, p. 101 (748); *Annales Laureshamenses*, ed. E. Katz, (St. Paul, 1889), *s.a.* 796, p. 41 and *Chronicon Laurissense Breve*, ed. H. Schorr von Carolsfeld, *Neues Archiv der Gesellschaft für ältere deutsche Geschichtskunde*, 36 (1911), 15-39, here IV, 26, p. 34.

[12] Ermoldus Nigellus, *Carmen in honorem Hludovici*, ed. E. Faral (Classiques de l'histoire de France au moyen âge 14, 2nd. edn., Paris, 1964), ll. 1599-1600, 2020-1; for the legislation, Ch. Verlinden, *L'esclavage dans l'Europe médiévale, 1: péninsule Ibérique - France*, (Bruges, 1955), 706ff.

[13] Continuator of Fredegar (ed. Wallace-Hadrill), c. 17, p. 92 (Frisia); ibid. c. 39, p. 108 and *Annales regni Francorum*, *s.a.* 774 p. 38 (Lombardy); S. Abel and B. von Simson, *Jahrbücher des fränkischen Reiches unter Karl dem Großen*, (2 vols., Leipzig, 1883-8), ii. 98-104, 106-7, for references to the Avar treasure; *Annales Fuldenses*, *s.a.* 870 p. 71: (Carloman) 'ditatusque gaza regia revertitur'.

[14] *Annales regni Francorum*, s.a. 772, p. 34.

[15] The treasure collected by Liudger in Frisia and given by him to Charlemagne perhaps belongs in this category: *Vita Liudgeri* i.14, (MGH, SS, 2), 408, lines 49-52.

various Slav tribes in the ninth century; in view of the sacral nature of Avar kingship[16] we should perhaps see the treasures heaped up in the Avar *hring* as falling in this category. Here also belong the *thesauri* which Charles the Bald collected on his first Italian expedition in 875[17]: the Vikings were not the only church-robbers in Francia any more than they were in Ireland. Apart from treasure, the form of plunder most frequently mentioned explicitly is arms and horses. Horses are referred to particularly often: in Gascony in 763, in Moravia in 871, and after the battle of Andernach in 876.[18] With these last categories we reach the point where plunder and tribute show noticeable similarities: the sources are most generous with details and obviously most interested when the object of plunder was trophies and luxury goods: gold, silver, precious stones and cloths, horses, arms. These were 'noble' items, which were valued, as we shall see, not just for their utilitarian worth.

Who benefited from all this? Tribute came to the king; the question of what happened to the plunder is less easy to answer. It appears certain that the hoards were reserved to the king, even if he did not himself take part in the campaign. The Avar campaign shows this well: Charlemagne had led the first Avar expedition in 791 in person, but the expeditions of 795 and 796 which captured the *hring* and the accumulated Avar loot of over two centuries were commanded by his son Pippin and the margrave Eric of Friuli. Nevertheless, the treasure was shipped in cartloads to Aachen.[19] It seems likely that a lot of the more ordinary plunder also came to the king, even when he was not with the army. Spoils were sent to him as the trophies of victory—so after the Bretons were defeated in 799 for example, when their leaders' arms, inscribed with their names, were sent to Charlemagne, or in 865 when Robert the Strong presented trophies taken from the Norsemen to Charles the Bald.[20]

---

[16] J. Deer, 'Karl der Große und der Untergang des Awarenreiches', *Karl der Große. Persönlichkeit und Geschichte*, ed. H. Beumann (5 vols., Düsseldorf, 1965–7), i. 758–62, 777.

[17] *Annales Fuldenses*, s.a. 875, p. 84: 'omnes thesauros, quos invenire potuit, unca manu collegit.'; cf. also ibid., p. 75.

[18] Continuator of Fredegar (ed. Wallace-Hadrill), c. 44, p. 113; *Annales Fuldenses s.a.* 870, p. 75; 876, p. 89 (on this battle cf. also the comments by Hincmar, *Annales Bertiniani, s.a.*, p. 209).

[19] Abel-Simson, *Karl der Große, loc. cit.* It should be noted, however, that the king's control was not always complete: Louis II, according to Prudentius of Troyes, failed to press the siege of Bari in 852 because he had been told it contained a large treasure and he did not want his warriors to loot it (*Annales Bertiniani, s.a.*, p. 65).

[20] *Annales regni Francorum, s.a.* 799, p. 108 (the E-text, p. 109, here offers no significant alterations); *Annales Bertiniani, s.a.* 865, p. 122. Cf. also the Spaniard John, who offered a share of the spoils to Louis the Pious when he was subking of Aquitaine,

Possibly the loot sent by Louis the Pious to his father in Aachen after the sack of Barcelona in 801 should be interpreted as trophies, but it seems to have been on a rather larger scale than that: Ermold was able to use it for panegyric purposes to present Louis the Pious as a generous war-lord.[21] The only time when plunder definitely stayed with those who took it was, paradoxically, after home matches. Those who were lucky enough to catch Vikings loaded with plunder and defeat them seem to have kept it: the Frisians who fought a Viking band in 885 found 'such a mass of treasure in gold and silver and other movables that all from the greatest to the least were made wealthy'.[22] Of course, some of what was taken will have stuck to the fingers of those who took it at all times. But all the same it would seem that here the Carolingians had made some advances over their Merovingian predecessors. One would dismiss Gregory of Tours' well-known anecdote about the vase of Soissons, in which so powerful a ruler as Clovis appears unable to claim anything more than the share of the plunder which falls to him by lot, as mere saga, were it not for the fact that division of booty by casting lots is recorded elsewhere.[23] Moreover, both Gregory of Tours and Fredegar record a number of incidents which suggest that in Merovingian times the armies could plunder and hold on to what they had plundered. 'Follow me', says Theuderich to his warriors, 'and I will lead you into a country where you may find gold and silver as much as you may desire, whence you may take cattle, slaves and clothing in abundance.'[24] The Austrasians complain about a peace made by Sigebert with Guntramn: 'Do as you promised and give us a chance to fight and take plunder, otherwise we won't go back home'.[25] Such incidents imply kings as providers of opportunities for plundering, rather than as distributors of plunder. The Carolingians were more active: not only are they themselves recorded as taking plunder, which may simply be a convention among annalists, we have other

---

'equum obtimum et brunia obtima et spata India cum techa de argento parata', and received land in return: *Die Urkunden der Karolinger*, (MGH, Diplomata, Hannover, 1906), i. 242, no. 179 (795).

[21] *Carmen in honorem Hludovici*, ll. 678–9: 'Vidistis quae olim Maurorum funere misit:/ Regem, arma et vinctos, magna trophea simul' (spoken by Charlemagne to the Franks before Louis' coronation as emperor in 813).

[22] *Annales Fuldenses*, s.a. 885, p. 103; cf. also ibid., s.a. 876, p. 98: 'Frisiones ... cum Nordmannis dimicantes victores extiterunt omnesque thesauros ... abstulerunt atque inter se diviserunt.'

[23] Gregory of Tours, *Historiae*, 2.27, edd. B. Krusch and W. Levison, (MGH, SRM, 1.1, Berlin, 1937–51), 72; on division by lot cf. Bodmer, *Krieger*, 100–1.

[24] Gregory of Tours, *Historiae*, 3.11, pp. 107–8.

[25] Fredegar, *Chronicon*, 3.71, ed. B. Krusch, (MGH, SRM 2, Berlin, 1878), 112.

indications as well. In 847, for example, the three sons of Louis the Pious met at Meerssen and decided to send an embassy to the king of the Danes to persuade him to stop his subjects from raiding Frankish territory.[26] This certainly reflects a Frankish belief that a king should be capable of controlling his subjects, and indeed Louis the German had been able to negotiate successfully with Horic for the return of loot and captives after the sack of Hamburg,[27] but it also in my view says something about the Carolingians' view of plundering-expeditions—they were, or should be, under royal control and direction. Whoever drew up the *Ordinatio Imperii* thought so too.[28] A further indication that the Carolingians benefited more from warfare than their Merovingian predecessors is their attitude to their hoards. The Merovingians, at least until the end of the sixth century, had a regular if declining income from taxation and tribute, and their hoards were certainly there for distribution as well as for impressing people—Merovingians set up as subkings, like Sigebert III, got a hoard of their own to start them off.[29] But they do not seem to have been so lavish as the Carolingians were (though here as in so much else Dagobert I may have anticipated later developments): the hoards came intact to their heirs, whereas both Charlemagne and Louis the German are recorded as having distributed the bulk of their treasure in alms to the poor and the church.[30] Some of this sharing out was done by these kings during their own lifetime (without objection from their heirs, so far as we know), but in Charlemagne's case it was left to Louis the Pious to fulfil the terms of the will—which he largely did.[31] Evidently the expected inflow was so large and reliable that rulers could here afford to be lavish.

The pious and the poor and needy were not the only or even the primary recipients of the king's bounty. According to the *Chronicon Laurissense Breve* Charlemagne divided the Lombard treasure among his army after the capture of Pavia in 774. The Avar booty was also shared out. Some went to Rome, some to England and perhaps Ireland,[32] but the main beneficiaries recorded were the Franks, and

---

[26] *Annales Bertiniani*, s.a., pp. 54-5; MGH, Cap., ii. 70, no. 204, c. 3.

[27] *Annales Bertiniani*, s.a. 845, p. 51; Dümmler, *Ostfränkisches Reich*, i. 283-4.

[28] MGH, Cap., i. 271, no. 136, c. 6.

[29] Fredegar (ed. Wallace-Hadrill), iv. 75, p. 63; cf. Waitz, *Verfassungsgeschichte*, II. i. 182-3, and R. Doehaerd, 'La richesse des Merovingiens', *Studi in onore di Gino Luzzato* (Milan, 1949), i. 30-46, on Merovingian hoards.

[30] Einhard, *Vita Karoli*, c. 33, ed. O. Holder-Egger, (MGH, SRG, Hannover, 1911), 37-41; *Annales Fuldenses*, s.a. 869, p. 69.

[31] A. Schultze, 'Das Testament Karls des Großen', *Aus Sozial- und Wirtschaftsgeschichte. Gedächtnisschrift für Georg von Below* (Stuttgart, 1928), 46-81.

[32] Abel-Simson, *Karl der Große*, ii. 107; J. M. Wallace-Hadrill, 'Charlemagne and England', *Early Medieval History* (Oxford, 1975), 165-6.

in particular the Frankish nobility. The Royal Frankish Annals in the original version talk of sharing out among the *optimates, clericis sive laicis, ceterisque fidelibus*; in the revised version this has become, more precisely, 'he shared out the rest (i.e. apart from what went to Rome) among the *optimates* and *aulici ceterique in palatio suo militantes*'.[33] The Lorsch annals talk of division among 'churches, bishops, abbots and counts, as well as all his faithful men'.[34] The recipients, in other words, were Charles' own following and the magnates commended to him, his following in a wider sense—which corresponds roughly to the *leudes* and *antrustiones* of Merovingian times. These share-outs were once-off affairs, as were the gifts by rulers to their children and to ambassadors; but there was also regular gift-giving, as we learn from Notker the Stammerer, with gifts graded according to the recipients.[35] Hincmar goes so far as to describe the annual assembly as a place where gifts were 'generally' exchanged, and it is a very moot point whether the *dona militum* he mentions in another passage are the *annua dona*, to which we shall come shortly, or gifts made *to* the *vassi dominici*.[36] The context on the whole implies royal expenditure rather than income. Similar things occurred lower down the political ladder: annual gifts to vassals are described in an admittedly not quite kosher diploma of Charles the Bald's for Saint-Benoit-sur-Loire as an obligation incumbent on the abbot, along with royal service and the upkeep of buildings.[37] Here we can see magnates passing gifts on to their own followings, by which I mean those vassals of theirs of some independent standing plus their military households—bodyguards who accompanied their lords without being given grants of land in benefice or otherwise. The latter are

[33] *Annales regni Francorum, s.a.* 796, pp. 98, 99.

[34] *Annales Laureshamenses, s.a.* 795, pp. 40–1.

[35] Notker Balbulus, *Gesta Karoli Magni Imperatoris*, ii. 21, ed. H. Haefele, (MGH, SRG, nova series, Berlin, 1961), p. 92.

[36] *De ordine palatii*, edd. T. Gross and R. Schieffer, (MGH, Fontes Iuris Germanici Antiqui, 3, Hannover, 1980), ll. 478–9: 'propter dona generaliter danda'; ibid., l. 360: 'De honestate vero palatii seu specialiter ornamento regali nec non et de donis annuis militum, absque cibu et potu vel equis, ad reginam ... pertinebat ...' Schieffer and Gross argue in their edition (p. 72, n. 165) that these are the normal *dona annua*, against Waitz, *Verfassungsgeschichte*, iii. 549, who saw them as gifts *to* the *milites*. The sentence as a whole is undoubtedly talking about the queen's responsibility for outgoing expenses, and as there are Anglo-Saxon parallels Waitz' interpretation seems the more plausible. Cf. J. Nelson, 'The church's military service in the ninth century: a contemporary comparative view?', *Studies in Church History*, 20 (1983), 24 with n. 36, though I am not sure I agree with her that the gifts to the warriors must have been in cash; cf. the evidence for non-monetary gifts by the king to warriors assembled by Waitz, *Verfassungsgeschichte*, iv. 250.

[37] *Recueil des actes de Charles le Chauve*, ed. G. Tessier (3 vols., Paris, 1943–55) i. 468 no. 177.

known to us from the times of Tacitus and Gregory of Tours but their existence in the Carolingian period, though acknowledged, has been somewhat neglected in favour of the constitutionally more interesting development of beneficed vassals.[38] It is often assumed that the normal professional fighting-man in the Carolingian era was a vassal with a benefice, that is, the holder of a small fief (a 'knight's fee' or a 'Rittergut'). But most of the vassalitic[39] benefices whose size is mentioned in the Carolingian era are large: generally the benefice consists of one or more *villae*, that is, an estate of anything from twenty to two hundred *mansi*, generally several times the amount specified in capitularies as the minimum for military service.[40] Benefices smaller than this seem to have been the exception rather than the rule, and in any case one should not automatically assume that they represented the entire land-holding of their owner. Beneficed vassals, whether of the king or of magnates, were generally big men themselves, a minority compared with fighting-men who lived as a following at the expense of their lords, though such followings in the field will generally have included beneficed vassals as well. Hincmar, in *De ordine palatii*, talks of the fighting-men in the palace without fixed positions or incomes, who lived from gifts of food and clothing, 'gold and silver, horses and arms—'frequent' gifts, be it noted, which in Hincmar's view made them enthusiastically willing to serve the king.[41] The Carolingians were not the only people to maintain such warbands. True, they legislated against *trustis* and *collecta*,[42] but only against their misuse—and what that was, they decided. Certainly they must have been prepared to tolerate the

---

[38] For instance M. Bloch, *Feudal Society* (1961), 163ff., F. L. Ganshof, *Feudalism* (3rd. edn., 1964), 35, to cite only two classic discussions; both authors see the unbeneficed vassal as an increasingly marginal phenomenon. More recently B. S. Bachrach, 'Charles Martel, mounted shock combat, the stirrup, and feudalism', *Studies in Medieval and Renaissance History*, 7 (1970), 70-2 and Nelson, 'Military service', *passim*, have laid more stress on unbeneficed warrior followings.

[39] As opposed to the precarial benefices which were often granted in return for gifts of land to a church and were frequently recorded in the Bavarian *traditiones*, for example; here we find much smaller pieces of property and the use of the word *beneficiolum*, cf. *Mittellateinisches Wörterbuch*, *I. A-B*, (Munich, 1959-67), cols. 1432-3, *s.v.*

[40] MGH, Cap., i. 134-5, no. 48, c. 2 (807): all with three or more *mansi* are to serve; i. 137, no. 50, c. 1 (808): all with four or more *mansi*.

[41] *De ordine palatii*, 11. 439-446.

[42] O. G. Oexle, 'Gilden als soziale Gruppen in der Karolingerzeit', *Das Handwerk in vor- und frühgeschichtlicher Zeit*, eds H. Jankuhn and others, (Abhandlungen der Akademie der Wissenschaften zu Göttingen, phil.-hist. Klasse, dritte Folge, 122, Göttingen, 1981), i. 301-8, 339-41. The objection was to the use of armed bands in improper ways—e.g. attacks on *missi dominici* or intimidating county courts—and perhaps also to armed bands bound together by mutual oaths; on the Carolingians' fear of *coniuratio* see S. Epperlein, *Herrschaft und Volk im karolingischen Imperium* (Forschungen zur mittelalterlichen Geschichte, 14, Berlin(E.), 1969), 42-50.

thing itself, because there are numerous references to warbands led by ecclesiastics. In 830, for instance, during the first crisis of Louis the Pious' reign, Hilduin of Saint-Denis was accused of turning up to an assembly *hostiliter* when he had been asked to come *simpliciter*.[43] The *acta* of the council of Douzy record a similar charge against Hincmar of Laon, and Hincmar of Rheims in the course of his extensive writings frequently presupposes the existence of such followings.[44] Archbishop John of Ravenna, according to Nicholas I, went about with 'nearly five hundred men and as many horses'.[45] The charge in such cases was not that such things were per se illegal but merely that they were inappropriate or improper under the circumstances. One would naturally expect lay magnates to have had such followings as well, and indeed they did. Hincmar talks of the *pueri* (note the term 'the boys', familiar from Merovingian sources) *vel vassalli*; everyone sought to maintain as large a following of these as was possible without theft and robbery.[46] The author of the *Epitaphium Arsenii*, a generation earlier, thought that this was impossible: writing about Bernard of Septimania he commented that 'nowadays no-one leads fighting-men at his own expense, but instead maintains them through violence and theft'.[47] Note here incidentally that the author has non-beneficed followings in mind: expenses, *stipendia* are direct payments, not benefices. We can see such gangs of warriors in action frequently in the annals and hagiography of the Carolingian era, just as we can in the pages of Gregory of Tours. It was presumably such a band which *Bernardus filius Bernardi* had with him when he left a royal assembly *armata manu* in 864, and the *comites* of Count Gerald who joined him in an attack on the house of Egfrid in 868 were 'companions' rather than counts.[48] Similarly, it was because he had been rash enough to send all his warriors out to spy on the enemy that Count Robert was surprised by the Normans in 885 and killed.[49] It is true that we cannot always say with certainty that such followers were unbeneficed, but it is generally clear from the context that they were the constant companions of their lord, and the one presumably implies the other. The fate of Hugo's followers in 885 certainly does not suggest that they held land: they

[43] Astronomus, *Vita Hludovici*, c. 45, (MGH, SS, 2), 633.

[44] Nelson, 'Military service', 22-4.

[45] MGH, Epp., vi. 615, no. 105.

[46] *De ordine palatii*, ll. 455-458.

[47] Radbert, *Epitaphium Arsenii*, ed. E. Dümmler (Berlin, 1900), 83; for *stipendia* cf. also Hincmar, *Ad Carolum Calvum*, Migne, PL 125, col. 1050D.

[48] *Annales Bertiniani*, s.a. 864, pp. 113-4; 868, p. 141.

[49] Abbo, *Le siège de Paris par les Normands*, ed. H. Waquet (Les classiques de l'histoire de France au moyen âge 20, Paris, 1942) 1. 442-59 pp. 48, 50.

escaped with their lives, but lost their clothes, horses and weapons.[50] Nothing is said about their land being confiscated, and the inference is that they had none. Such bands, then, though they may have included some beneficed fighting-men, were essentially the *comitatus* of Tacitus' time, a warrior following. The references by Hincmar and the author of the *Epitaphium* to theft and robbery are thus not accidental or merely polemical. It is in the nature of a warrior following that its members need constant rewards. Germanic *Treue* may be enough for modern constitutional historians,[51] but was certainly not enough to enable a Carolingian ruler or magnate to keep a following together. This is forcefully demonstrated by the account in the Annals of Lorsch of Charlemagne's behaviour after the discovery of the conspiracy headed by his eldest son Pippin in 792:[52]

> King Charles held an assembly at Regensburg; and when he saw his faithful men, bishops, abbots and counts, who were with him there, and the rest of the faithful people, who had not joined with Pippin in that terrible conspiracy, he rewarded them many-fold with gold and silver and silks and other gifts.

The rewards expected were once again the same luxury goods I have already mentioned. The basic pay, so to speak—clothing, food, drink, accommodation—was expected, and by no means taken for granted, as is shown by the frequent occurrence in Carolingian sources of such words as *nutrire, nutritor, nutrimen* to describe all kinds of relationships between persons: lord and follower, teacher and pupil, abbot and monk.[53] But what really counted was the 'noble' gifts, though the distinction is not always easy to make: for the professional warrior, for instance, arms and horses were a necessity, and should perhaps be considered as basic pay.

---

[50] *Annales Fuldenses*, s.a. 885, p. 103. On Hugo's uprising see now G. Tellenbach, 'Die geistigen und politischen Grundlagen der karolingischen Thronfolge. Zugleich eine Studie über kollektive Willensbildung und kollektives Handeln im neunten Jahrhundert', *Frühmittelalterliche Studien*, 13 (1979), 286-8; for similar followings in Ottonian Saxony, K. J. Leyser, *Rule and conflict in Ottonian Saxony* (1979), 17-21.

[51] W. Kienast, 'Germanische Treue und "Königsheil"', *Historische Zeitschrift*, 227 (1978), 265-324, attempts a nuanced defence of the notion against the attacks by F. Graus, but it is so nuanced that I find it impossible to follow over large stretches.

[52] 'fecit rex Carlus conuentum apud Reganesburug; et cum cognovisset fideles suos, episcopos, abbates, et comites, qui cum ipso ibi aderant, et reliquum populum fidelem, qui cum Pippino in ipso consilio pessimo non erant, eos multipliciter honoravit in auro et argento et sirico et donis plurimis.', *Annales Laureshamenses*, s.a. 793, p. 38.

[53] In connection with education the usage is classical; but it appears to be in the Carolingian period that such words begin to be used of the relationship between lord and follower: cf. e.g. Einhard, *Vita Karoli*, preface, p. 1: 'nutritoris mei Karoli' and p. 2: 'nutrimentum in me inpensum'; Ermold, *Carmen in honorem Hludovici*, ll. 166, 658, 1144; MGH, Cap., ii. 283, no. 256, c. 4.

We must, then, think of a very large-scale circulation of goods on this level of gift-giving and tribute-payment, which ran largely parallel to and independently of the normal 'economic' circulation of goods (though there were naturally interfaces between the two).[54] It was motored by the inflow of tribute and plunder from beyond the borders, and it was largely, if not exclusively, controlled by the king. It provided a language in which to express power-relationships; like all good languages, it had the advantage of being ambiguous. In 798 Alfonso II of Asturias sent Charlemagne trophies following his capture of Lisbon: *loricae*, mules and captured Moors. The Royal Frankish Annals call these *insignia victoriae*; the revised version glosses this: *licet pro dono mitterentur, magis tamen insignia victoriae videbantur*.[55] The implication seems clear: one sends trophies to one's lord, and even if Alfonso thought he was just sending Charlemagne presents, that was not how the Franks viewed the matter. And yet the implication is not as clear as all that, for only a couple of years earlier Charlemagne himself had sent similar trophies to Offa and perhaps other rulers in the British Isles; no-one, least of all Offa, would have taken these gifts as signs of subjection. We should here note the similarities between such tribute and the internal tribute which seems to have begun and ended with the Carolingians, the *dona annua*,[56] which were paid in the same 'currency' of precious things as tribute and plunder. Like the income from tribute, they must have amounted altogether to very considerable sums. Louis the German says in a charter for St Gallen that the monastery should pay 'like the other monasteries' no more than two horses with shields and lances per year, and a diploma of Louis the Pious for Brioude specifies half this amount.[57] We know that there were exemptions and monasteries which never had such gifts required

[54] Among the numerous provisions in the capitularies regulating sales, there is one of particular interest in this context, MGH, Cap. i. 142, no. 55 c. 2: 'ut nullus audeat in nocte negotiare in vasa aurea et argentea, mancipia, gemmas, caballos, animalia . . .', an almost complete list of 'noble' items. It is significant that they could be sold at all, though by daylight only and before reliable witnesses; the prohibition of night (i.e. secret) sales was perhaps intended not only as a general measure against fencing stolen goods, but also to try to prevent feuds arising over the possession of such items.

[55] *Annales regni Francorum, s.a.* 798, pp. 104,105.

[56] Waitz, *Verfassungsgeschichte*, iii. 591, iv. 107–110; Ganshof, *Frankish Institutions*, 43 with n. 321. Although they are described in Carolingian sources as an ancient institution, the earliest datable reference is c. 6 of the council of Ver (755), MGH, Cap., i. 34. The reference in *Formulae Bituricenses*, ed. K. Zeumer (MGH, Formulae Merowingici et Karolini Aevi, Berlin 1882–6), 178 no. 18, is Carolingian. The last mention of them, so far as I can see, is at Quierzy in 877: MGH, Cap., ii. 363 no. 282.

[57] *Die Urkunden der deutschen Karolinger*, ed. P. Kehr (MGH, Diplomata, Berlin, 1934), i. 100, no. 70 (852); J. F. Böhmer, *Die Regesten des Kaiserreichs unter den Karolingern. 751–918*, 2nd. edn. by E. Mühlbacher (Innsbruck, 1908), no. 797 (825).

of them,[58] but nevertheless one can still extrapolate from this an annual 'income' of at least 200 horses and shields, possibly more. The bishoprics paid more substantial amounts—Zwentibold *reduced* Trier's obligation to six horses per year[59]—and recovered at least some of their costs by themselves requiring annual gifts from monasteries in their diocese.[60] Like tribute, such gifts could scarcely be described as voluntary—though in passing one may wonder whether in a society like that of Carolingian Francia the notion of a voluntary gift has much meaning. Hincmar referred to them as a tax for the upkeep of the army, and they are equated with taxation in an Italian capitulary of Louis II's.[61] But—like tribute—they were not an ordinary form of tax. They were called *dona* and treated as such: that is, they were 'noble' and handed over in public, as chroniclers noticed,[62] with ceremony—at the same time and in the same way as tribute (indeed, poets like Hibernicus Exul and Dungal as well as annalists often make no distinction between 'internal' and 'external' tribute).[63] In this way the Carolingians overcame, at least for a while, the hostility to public taxation which existed both before and after their time, in Austrasia at least. Just as the Franks salved their pride by making gifts rather than paying taxes, so the tribes around the Frankish empire probably preferred to see themselves as making gifts rather than paying tribute. Even in Frankish sources the distinction between tribute and gifts is not a fixed one: Aistulf's demands from the papacy in the 750s are described by the continuator of Fredegar as *tributa vel munera* for example, and there is a similar ambiguity in

---

[58] See the *Notitia de servitio monasteriorum*, ed. P. Becker, in *Initia Consuetudinis Benedictinae* (Corpus Consuetudinum Monasticarum, 1, Siegburg, 1963), 485-99; Böhmer-Mühlbacher, no. 929 (3 July 834) for Kempten is a diploma of exemption.

[59] *Die Urkunden der deutschen Karolinger*, ed. T. Schieffer, (MGH, Diplomata, Berlin, 1960) iv. 50-1 no. 18 (898).

[60] Cf. the charter of Archbishop Wenilo of Sens for Saint-Rémy, Sens, *Die Konzilien der karolingischen Teilreiche 843-859*, ed. W. Hartmann, (MGH, Concilia, Hannover, 1984), iii. 59, no. 10: 'Episcopus quoque in exigendis muneribus abbatem eiusdem loci non gravet, sed sufficiat ei ad annua dona equus unus et scutum cum lancea'; diploma of Charles the Bald for Saint-Pierre, Rouen (ed. Tessier, ii. 410, no. 407 (876)).

[61] MGH, Cap., ii. 93-4, no. 217, c. 4 (865); Hincmar, *Ad Carolum Calvum*, Migne, PL 125, cols. 1050D-1051A.

[62] Continuator of Fredegar (ed. Wallace-Hadrill), c. 48 p. 116; *Annales sancti Amandi*, s.a. 807 (MGH, SS, 1. 14); *Annales regni Francorum*, s.a. 827, p. 173, 829, p. 177; *Annales Bertiniani*, s.a. 832, p. 8, 833, p. 10, 835, p. 17, 836, p. 19, 837, p. 21, 864 p. 113, 868 p. 150, 874 p. 196; *Fragmentum Chronici Fontanellensis*, s.a. 851 (MGH, SS, 2. 303).

[63] Hibernicus Exul, *Ad Karolum Regem*, ed. E. Dümmler (MGH, Poetae Latini medii aevi, 1, Berlin, 1881), 396; cf. also Dicuil, *Versus*, ed. K. Strecker, (MGH, Poetae Latini medii aevi, 4, Berlin, 1923), 917. *Annales Fuldenses*, s.a. 870, p. 72: '... Francorum iudicio et Baioariorum necnon Sclavorum, qui de diversis provinciis regi munera deferentes aderant ...'. The Breton prince Salomon also handed his tribute over at the same time as the Franks presented the *dona* in 864: *Annales Bertiniani*, s.a., p. 113.

the various accounts of Charles III's payment of 882 with which I began.[64] On the other hand it was possible, for purposes of panegyric, to go further and see tribute as expressing not only submission but possession: Ermoldus Nigellus describes the Frankish demands for tribute-payment from the Breton ruler in terms appropriate for a peasant paying for his *mansus*: Murman is to pay a *census* for cultivating Frankish fields.[65] I do not want to suggest that consciousness determined being, however; tribute was not *just* a language for expressing or concealing political relationships. Payment was enforced: when a Slav tribe on the borders of the east Frankish kingdom refused its customary tribute, an army was instantly sent to collect it and to take reprisals.[66] Tribute was in practice institutionalized plunder, for the recipient particularly attractive because the victim plunders himself. The payments may have expressed or concealed subjection and dependence, but they were in the first instance *payments*. The precious things circulating as tribute, plunder and gifts had a vital political function not only at the level of *Selbstverständnis*: they served to create and reinforce political relationships, to determine military and hence political power.

All this has consequences for our understanding of the Carolingian era. In the first place, we may look again at the Carolingian army. The question of how the Carolingians recruited their fighting-men has generally been considered from the point of view of military *obligation*: the general duty of military service incumbent on all free men, or perhaps on all free land-holders, and the specific duty defined in terms of what would later be called feudal law, incumbent on all vassals. Attempts to deal with the inherently slightly improbable notion of a general obligation of military service by arguing that the 'free men' of the capitularies were a particular group, the *liberi regis*, who had special obligations, are looking increasingly unconvincing.[67] It seems worthwhile considering the question of *incentive*: what were the gains to be expected from warfare and who could profit from them? From this point of view it is immediately evident

---

[64] Continuator of Fredegar (ed. Wallace-Hadrill), c. 36 p. 104: *tributa vel munera quod ... requirabant*; for 882 see above, p. 75, n. 2.

[65] Ermoldus Nigellus, *Carmen in honorem Hludovici*, ll. 1328-30, p. 104: *En mea rura colit late .../...Nempe tributa vetat*; cf. also l. 1392, 1465-7.

[66] *Annales Fuldenses*, s.a., 874, p. 81; 877, p. 89.

[67] For objections to the theory see E. Müller-Mertens, *Karl der Große, Ludwig der Fromme und die Freien* (Forschungen zur mittelalterlichen Geschichte, 10, Berlin (E), 1963); H. K. Schulze, 'Rodungsfreiheit und Königsfreiheit. Zu Genese und Kritik neuerer verfassungsrechtlicher Theorien', *Historische Zeitschrift*, 219 (1974), 529-50; J. Schmitt, *Untersuchungen zu den Liberi Homines der Karolingerzeit* (Europäische Hochschulschriften, Reihe III, 85, Berne, 1977). I hope to deal more fully elsewhere with the problems discussed in the following section.

that the profits of Carolingian warfare were of a kind which could not easily benefit the small land-holder without a following of his own. Lacking such a following he could not turn the profits of warfare into political capital. Slaves were perhaps more worthwhile—Duby has shown how widespread was the possession of slaves in the Carolingian period[68]—but here also the advantage of slave-taking was definitely with the magnate with large estates to exploit. Unless the small man himself joined a following he had to fight at his own expense without much likelihood of getting something in return: we have already seen that the kings distributed the returns of warfare to the *optimates*. There are hints in the sources that people made such cost-benefit analyses: a fragmentary Italian capitulary of Charlemagne's complains that those who lived near the border were unenthusiastic or hostile when raids were being contemplated.[69] Evidently they did not expect the gains to outweigh the certain losses: the expenses of warfare and the danger of reprisals. For the leaders of warbands from further away the profit and loss calculation was a quite different one. Even where the results of warfare included territorial expansion, the Carolingians generally hung on to the gains themselves or distributed them in large parcels to members of the high aristocracy, as in Bavaria and Alemannia, where the gains were distributed among a small number of Austrasian magnate families,[70] or in Lombardy, where the 'Northerners' who came in after Hrodgaud's rising in 776 came in at a high level and the land-holders of intermediate rank were left largely undisturbed.[71] There was not much in the way of military colonisation by small land-holders, apart from the special case of the *aprisio*-regime on the Spanish border.[72] The expense of military service on the other hand

[68] G. Duby, *The growth of the early European economy*, (1974), 32, 86.

[69] MGH, Cap., i. 208, no. 101 c. 3: 'Quomodo causam confinales nostri odio semper habent contra illos qui parati sunt inimicis insidias facere et marcam nostram ampliare'; cf. also ibid., i. 206 no. 99 c. 3.

[70] Cf. I. Dienemann-Dietrich, 'Der fränkische Adel in Alemannien im 8. Jahrhundert', *Probleme der alemannischen Geschichte*, ed. T. Mayer (Vorträge und Forschungen ...,1, Lindau, n.d. [1955]), 149–92; M. Mitterauer, *Karolingische Markgrafen im Südosten* (Archiv für österreichische Geschichte, 123, Vienna, 1963), 78–84.

[71] D. Bullough, '*Europae pater:* Charlemagne and his achievement in the light of recent scholarship', *EHR*, lxxxv (1970), 82–3. For the 'Northerners' see the prosopography by E. Hlawitschka, *Franken, Alemannen, Bayern und Burgunder in Oberitalien (774–962)*, (Forschungen zur oberrheinischen Landesgeschichte, 8, Freiburg im Breisgau, 1960). On pp. 310ff. Hlawitschka gives a list of small men (*Staatssiedler*) found in Italian sources who came from north of the Alps, but there are surprisingly few of them before the end of the ninth century.

[72] There is a good discussion of the *aprisio* system in Müller-Mertens, *Karl der Große, Ludwig der Fromme und die Freien*, 61–6; for the evidence—very scanty apart from Italy—for military colonists elsewhere see *ibid.*, 74–8 and Schmitt, *Liberi Homines*, 110–35.

was considerable. This has little or nothing to do with the introduction of cavalry service and its supposed costliness[73]: warfare of the kind waged by the Franks in the eighth century—which was on a scale and intensity different from anything previously attempted, in spite of the parallels with the formation of the first Frankish empire in the late fifth and sixth centuries—was extremely expensive for the participants, however they fought. If we accept then that the small freeman would have lost rather than gained from Carolingian warfare it seems improbable that he can at any time have formed the backbone of the Carolingian army. This conclusion appears at first sight to contradict the evidence from the capitularies. From 800 onwards a series of provisions regulate the military service due from *liberi homines*; only those with more than a certain amount of property had to serve, while those with less had to club together to support one of their number. These provisions have generally been interpreted as a reduction in obligations which shows that towards the end of Charlemagne's reign the burden of military service had become unsupportable for the *pauper liber homo*;[74] before that, all free men had been obliged to perform military service. It is difficult to see, however, why such service should have become problematic only after nearly a hundred years of almost continuous wars of aggression; and in fact the evidence is misleading. Almost all the passages refer to specific situations in which *defensio patriae* is envisaged: the provisions in Charlemagne's capitularies, for example, fall within the period between 802 and 811, when Danish invasions were expected.[75] Most of the other provisions come from times of crisis as

[73] The importance of 'heavy cavalry' in Carolingian warfare continues to be overestimated; for a useful corrective see Bullough, '*Europae pater*', 84-89, who rightly points to the Carolingians' ability to move armies and mount effective sieges.

[74] This is common ground: cf. Schmitt, *Liberi Homines*, 211-24; Müller-Mertens, *Karl der Große, Ludwig der Fromme und die Freien*, 120-133; J. Fleckenstein, 'Adel und Kriegertum und ihre Wandlung im Karolingerreich', *Settimane di studi sull'alto medio evo*, 27(1981), 82. There is disagreement only about whether Charles' measures were primarily intended to maintain Frankish military power (so Müller-Mertens and Fleckenstein) or were rather an expression of a new *Herrscherethos* (so Schmitt).

[75] For *defensio patriae* cf. H. Dannenbauer, 'Die Freien im karolingischen Heer', *Grundlagen der mittelalterlichen Welt* (Stuttgart, 1958), 242-3. The earliest specific reference I have found is the Olonna capitulary of 822 (MGH, Cap., i. 319, no. 125, c. 18), but the context of Charlemagne's military preparations in the last decade of his reign is quite clearly a defensive one; cf. H. Sproemberg, 'Die Seepolitik Karls des Großen', *Beiträge zur Belgisch-Niederländischen Geschichte* (Forschungen zur mittelalterlichen Geschichte, 3, Berlin(E), 1959), 1-30. The one apparent exception is a capitulary which deals with the possibility that the Saxons might be sent into Aquitaine or against the Bohemians (MGH, Cap., i. 136, no. 49, c. 2), but what could be demanded of a recently-conquered tribe is not necessarily a guide to what could be done elsewhere.

well: the expedition against Corsica in 825 and Benevento in 866, or the general alarm of 828-9 after the failures on the Danish and Spanish borders.[76] Not all of these campaigns could be classified as *defensio patriae* in the strictest sense—then as now the word defence had ambiguities—but they were not normal plundering-expeditions. It is likely that the resources of military manpower provided by the warbands were not adequate for such defensive warfare, and hence recourse was had to other means of raising troops. This seems all the more likely as such warfare—coast watch and boatbuilding[77]—would have brought little gain for warbands and their leaders, and at the same time considerable risk if it should actually come to any fighting. Similarly, it was in 832, at a moment of crisis when his ordinary resources failed him, that Louis the Pious attempted a mass mobilisation.[78] The evidence for a general obligation to serve in the army—apart from *defensio patriae*—is much thinner and more ambiguous for the period before 800 than is often supposed, and it may well be that the demands made in the capitularies represented an increase on previous practice, not a reduction. It should also be noted that at such moments of crisis there was not just a general duty incumbent on all free men to fight; slaves and the unfree could also be mobilised or subjected to penalties for failing to fight, which should make us rethink the idea that the 'freedom' of the ordinary Frank depended on his right and duty to bear arms.[79] I do not want to exaggerate, and we are still some way away from the total specialisation between those who fight and those who plough which we find in the eleventh and twelfth centuries; this can be seen not only in the evidence of the capitularies, which because of its normative character is hard to interpret, but also in the occasional references to spontaneous resistance to the Vikings by the rural population,

[76] Corsica: MGH, Cap., i. 325, no. 162, c. 3; Benevento: ibid., ii. 94-5, no. 218, c. 1; 828/9: ibid., ii. 5, no. 185, 7, no. 186, c. 7. On these years see F. L. Ganshof, 'Am Vorabend der ersten Krise der Regierung Ludwigs des Frommen. Die Jahre 828 und 829', *Frühmittelalterliche Studien*, 6 (1972), 40-5.

[77] Sproemberg, 'Seepolitik', 20-24

[78] *Annales Bertiniani, s.a.* 832, pp. 7-8: 'denuo annuntiatum est placitum generale kalendas septembris Aurelianis habendum, ibique unumquemque liberum hostiliter aduenire'. So far as I can see, this is the only occasion in the whole of the Carolingian period when such a mass mobilisation is unambiguously and explicitly referred to in a narrative source.

[79] In 832 Louis the German was thought to be raising an army of all the Bavarians, free and unfree (*Annales Bertiniani, s.a.*, p. 5); in 802 Charlemagne laid down penalties for the unfree as well as for freemen, should they fail to give help when required in the event of a coastal attack: W. A. Eckhardt, 'Die Capitularia missorum specialia von 802', *Deutsches Archiv für Erforschung des Mittelalters*, 12 (1956), 502, c. 13b.

even if here also it is not always easy to say what strata of society the annalists have in mind.[80]

A further point concerns the nature of Carolingian society, or perhaps better the flavour. In spite of the pessimistic (or realistic) view taken by such scholars as Fichtenau and Duby, the Carolingian period still seems to us as somehow more advanced, more civilised, less archaic than the Merovingian era: after the heroic age, to borrow a phrase used by Mr Grierson in a similar context.[81] But this is probably an optical illusion; what we lack is the anecdotalised savagery provided by Gregory of Tours, Fredegar and the other authors of the *Scriptores rerum Merovingicarum*. Much is concealed by the classicising renewal of Carolingian intellectual and spiritual life, which is nevertheless apparent at a second glance: the nomadic or semi-nomadic existence of the Carolingian élite, involving much travelling and fighting punctuated by large-scale feasts with conspicuous consumption of meat and alcohol. The Lives of Louis the Pious by Thegan and the Astronomer are here a better guide than Einhard's stately tableaux. Such things would be more apparent if we had more in the way of Beowulf or Icelandic saga: but the *Hildebrandslied* and (perhaps) *Waltharius* point the way; such things may well have been found in the *antiquissima et barbarissima carmina* which Charlemagne tried to collect and Louis the Pious tried to forget.[82] We have heard much about the destructive effects of the Vikings on Frankish society in the ninth century: we forget that for most of Europe in the eighth and ninth century it was the Franks who were the Vikings,[83] and that the existence of a Frankish empire presupposes Frankish imperialism. It was not, however, a Byzantine imperialism. The Franks too could harbour pretenders and make 'chequerboard' alliances with the tribes beyond their immediate enemies. But they did not distance themselves from their neighbours as the Byzantines did. The clashes were not clashes between radically different worlds: the two sides understood each other very well. Bretons, Danes, Moravians and Franks shared to a surprising extent a common political culture. Disaffected Frankish princes may not normally have fled

[80] *Annales Bertiniani*, s.a. 859, p. 80 (where, incidentally, the discussion in note 1 is superfluous: the text means what it says, namely that the *coniuratio* was suppressed by powerful Franks); Regino of Prüm, *Chronicon*, ed. F. Kurze, (MGH, SRG, Hannover, 1890), s.a. 882, p. 118.

[81] P. H. Grierson, 'Commerce in the Dark Ages: a critique of the evidence', *Transactions of the Royal Historical Society*, 5th ser., 9 (1959), 139.

[82] This is a minefield, however: see the cautions issued by D. Geuenich, 'Die volkssprachige Überlieferung der Karolingerzeit aus der Sicht des Historikers', *Deutsches Archiv für Erforschung des Mittelalter* 39 (1983), 113-16.

[83] Note the Byzantine proverb quoted by Einhard, *Vita Karoli*, c. 16, p. 20: 'If a Frank is your friend, then he is not your neighbour'.

across the frontier—though Louis the German did just that in 840[84]—but that was only because they generally had uncles to turn to who had a more direct interest in offering help and more to offer. When this was not the case, they were quite prepared to take help from Viking bands or from their neighbours if it was forthcoming—look at Pippin of Aquitaine or Hugo of Lotharingia, both of whom allied themselves with Vikings, or at Louis the German's sons, who when it suited them allied themselves with the Moravian ruler Rastiz.[85] These relationships across the border can be found among the high nobility as well. The rulers of Brittany and Moravia could, at least under favourable circumstances, hope to maintain a clientele among their immediate Frankish neighbours;[86] and for disaffected aristocrats or estranged spouses, going into exile across the border was a real possibility.[87] The alliance between Nominöe and the Widonid margraves of Brittany is paralleled in the other direction by the 'Frankicization' of the Moravian prince Pribina.[88] Such things would not have been possible, or at least would have had to have taken different forms, if both sides had not been playing essentially the same game.

One should also look to the nature of Carolingian warfare for an explanation of the differences in the development of east and west Francia. There can be no question that west Francia even after two generations of raiding by Norsemen and Saracens still had a more advanced economy at the end of the ninth century than did east Francia; but this was not reflected in political power. The east Frankish kings were able to impose their will in the settlement of the Lotharingian succession, and to intervene three times in west Francia (if without any very notable success). It was certainly coincidence that the Carolingian kingdoms were reunited under an east Frankish ruler, Charles III; but it is significant that he spent comparatively little time in the west—two or three months at the begin-

[84] *Annales Fuldenses*, s.a. 840, pp. 30–1.

[85] On Pippin see *Annales Bertiniani*, s.a. 859, p. 81 and 864, p. 105; on Hugo see above, pp. 83–4 n. 50 and Regino, *Chronicon*, s.a. 885, p. 123; on Carloman and Louis the Younger see *Annales Bertiniani*, s.a. 861, p. 85, and *Annales Fuldenses*, s.a. 866, p. 65.

[86] L. Levillain, 'La marche de Bretagne, ses marquis et ses comtes', *Annales de Bretagne*, 58 (1951), 89–117; J. Boussard, 'Les destins de la Neustrie du IXe au XIe siècle', *Cahiers de Civilisation Médiévale*, 11 (1968), 15–21; Mitterauer, *Markgrafen*, 180–181.

[87] *Die Urkunden der Karolinger*, i. 251, no. 187: Aio, a Lombard, flees to the Avars; council of Mainz, 852, c. 12, (MGH, Concilia, iii. 248): the case of Albgis, who fled to the Moravians; *Annales Fuldenses*, s.a. 869, pp. 67–8 (Gundachar) and 899, p. 133 (Isanric), both of whom took refuge with the Moravians.

[88] A. C. Sós, *Die slawische Bevölkerung Westungarns im 9. Jahrhundert*, (Munich, 1973), 29–47; H. Wolfram, *Conversio Bagoariorum et Carantanorum*, (Vienna, 1979), 50–57, 129–41.

ning of his reign there, and rather longer in the following year. His stamping-ground was east Francia, and Alemannia in particular.[89] Arnulf's hegemonial position was not simply due to his being the only post-888 *regulus* with obviously Carolingian blood, but reflects the military and political superiority of the east Frankish kingdom: it is a pre-echo of the later Ottonian hegemony. This contrast between economic underdevelopment and political superiority will certainly not sustain any monocausal explanation: but one of the underlying reasons was the fact that the east Frankish kingdom was the only one of the three kingdoms produced by the division of Verdun with an open frontier and the consequent possibilities of plundering and tribute-taking.[90] These emerge very clearly from a reading of the Annals of Fulda, for example, which record Louis the German as being able to put several armies into the field on more than one occasion;[91] and it is in the ninth century that in Germany a new word for slave appears alongside the classical *servus*, *ancillus* and *mancipium*: *sclavus*.[92] Such opportunities were missing in the west. The Spanish frontier, with the consolidation of Islamic power in the ninth century, did not offer the opportunities it had done in the time of Charlemagne and Louis of Aquitaine. Intervention was above all not possible, because Aquitaine itself was only nominally part of Charles the Bald's kingdom for the first twenty years of his reign.[93] Brittany was a poor substitute, and the tribute-payments by Nominöe and Salomon certainly did not compensate in political wealth for the negative balance of payments of the west Frankish kingdom: the Danegeld payments of 845, 853, 860, 862, 865, 877 and 884; the

---

[89] For his itinerary see Böhmer-Mühlbacher, nos. 1577a–1765b.

[90] For a similar point about Austrasia in the sixth century see R. Collins, 'Theudebert I, 'Magnus rex Francorum'', in *Idea and Reality in Frankish and Anglo-Saxon Society. Studies presented to J. M. Wallace-Hadrill*, eds P. Wormald and others (Oxford, 1983), 14–15.

[91] *Annales Fuldenses*, s.a. 858, p. 49; 869, p. 68.

[92] C. Verlinden, 'L'origin de *sclavus*=esclave', *Archivum Latinitatis Medii Aevi*, 17 (1943), 97–128, dates this change in Germany to the tenth and eleventh centuries (elsewhere in Europe not until the thirteenth). But see the diploma of Arnulf for Würzburg, *Die Urkunden der deutschen Karolinger*, ed. P. Kehr, (MGH, Diplomata, Berlin, 1940), iii. 99, no. 66 (889): 'homines ipsius ecclesiae sive accolas vel sclavos': *vel sclavos* is an addition to the text of the *Vorurkunde*, a charter of Louis the Pious' dated 19 December 822 (Böhmer-Mühlbacher, no. 767). The transition can be found in a diploma of Louis the German for Altaich, *Die Urkunden der deutschen Karolinger*, i. 117, no. 80 (857): *servos Sclavos vel accolas*.

[93] L. Auzias, *L'Aquitaine carolingienne (778–987)* (Toulouse, 1937), 176ff. It was only after 864 that Charles the Bald managed a thorough purge of office-holders in Aquitaine: ibid., 328–360. Cf. also P. Classen, 'Die Verträge von Verdun und von Coulaines 843 als politische Grundlagen des Westfränkischen Reiches', *Historische Zeitschrift*, 196 (1963), 1–2, 34.

ransom-payments for important magnates like Louis of Saint-Denis in 858 and Roland of Arles in 869 and for towns.[94] Viewed in this light, Charles the Bald's decision to try for the kingdom of Italy and for the imperial title in 875 may seem more rational than it did to Hincmar and has done to most modern historians: it was not just a chance to dress up in Greek togas.[95] Such differing opportunities helped to determine the political development of what were to become France and Germany. The Ottonian Reich was in this as in so many other ways a continuation of the Carolingian empire by more or less the same means. What did Henry I do after halting the military decline of east Francia and securing a breathing-pause in the fight against the Hungarians, according to Widukind? 'He fell upon the Slavs ... and made them pay tribute.'[96] In the west, the élite turned to other forms of political and military organisation—the principality, the castellany, the beneficed *miles*. These may seem more 'progressive' to us, but they were probably adopted more *faute de mieux* than in a spirit of progress. The old methods could no longer be made to work.

[94] The evidence is comprehensively surveyed by E. Joranson, *The Danegeld in France* (Augustana Library Publications 10, Rock Island, Ill., 1923).

[95] *Annales Fuldenses, s.a.* 876, p. 86; cf. P. E. Schramm, 'Karl der Kahle', in *Kaiser, Könige und Päpste. Gesammelte Aufsätze zur Geschichte des Mittelalters* (Stuttgart, 1968), ii. 133-4. On the treasures, see above, p.78 with n. 17. Hincmar's criticisms are discussed by J. Nelson, 'The 'Annals of St. Bertin'', in *Charles the Bald. Court and Kingdom*, eds M. Gibson and J. Nelson (British Archaeological Reports, International Series, 101, Oxford, 1981), 26.

[96] 'Irruit super Bohemos ... et fecit eos tributarios': Widukind of Corvey, *Rerum gestarum Saxonicarum libri tres* i c. 35 (MGH, SRG, Hannover 1935), 48-51. On the role of tribute-payments in the political economy of the Ottonian Reich see now K. Leyser, 'Ottonian Government', *EHR*, xcvi (1981), 739-41.

RETAINED LEGAL COUNSEL, *c.* 1275–*c.* 1475[*]

The Alexander Prize Essay

By Nigel Ramsay, M.A., Ll.B.

READ 18 MAY 1984

THIS paper is concerned with one aspect of the history of the English legal profession—the annual payment of sums of money to lawyers by institutions and private individuals in medieval England.

The practice of retaining legal officials can be traced back to at least the middle of the twelfth century. As early as *c.* 1150 one Robert de Beauchamp was granted some land by Athelney Abbey, he having promised that he would go to the pleas and business of the abbey whenever requested, as the abbey's friend and brother;[1] a decade later Beauchamp was sheriff of Somerset. If we assume that Beauchamp was still benefitting from the grant during his shrieval years, then this must be one of the earliest instances of an administrator of the law receiving an income from one who might be a party appearing before him. *Ex nihilo nihil fit*: the retention of justices in the later thirteenth and early fourteenth centuries was no innovation but the continuation of a custom of long standing.

It is, however, in the later thirteenth century that the evidence starts to multiply for the retention of lawyers in general—and this is not simply because of any general increase in the survival of the relevant source materials.[2] It is rather because of a changing pattern of law, reflected in, and then strongly reinforced by such Edwardian statutes as *Quia Emptores*: men's lives were coming to be ruled by statute law, and landowners were faced with the need to act in accordance with a more complicated court practice. They could seek to become familiar with these statutes themselves, but there was the

[*] I am grateful to Dr J. H. Baker and Dr Caroline Barron for their kind encouragement.

[1] *Two Cartularies of the Benedictine Abbeys of Muchelney and Athelney*, ed. E. H. Bates (Somerset Record Society, vol. 14, 1899), 152. Beauchamp was sheriff in 1162–3 (or possibly 1161–2), and again in 1175–85: *Somersetshire Archaeological and Natural History Society Proceedings*, vol. 106, 1962, supplement, 5.

[2] For suggestions as to why central financial accounts were kept from about the 1280s in various religious houses, see, for instance, Aelred Watkin's introduction to his edition of a Winchester Cathedral Priory receiver's roll of 1280–1, *EHR*, lxi (1946), 89–105, at 89–90.

further problem that a court might apply not the bald words of a text but rather the judicial interpretation of that text.

Since the king's judges so largely made the law, by both drafting and interpreting the statutes, it was a prudent course to turn for legal advice to the same judges—or to their clerks, for in Edward I's reign it was still sometimes the case that the bench was drawn from among the justices' chief clerks. The practice of feeing the king's judges has been seized upon by enquirers into medieval attitudes towards bribery and corruption,[3] and that the Edwardian bench was certainly not free from this taint is of course shown by the dismissal in disgrace of most of its members in 1289. But why, if a judge was thought to be open to bribery, should a litigant bother to pay him an annual fee? Litigants could, and indeed did make straightforward presents to judges[4]—although even this does not prove corruption. An explanation of annual retention may therefore be sought elsewhere: it is quite simply that the judges and their clerks were the only people who thoroughly knew the law and were felt to be capable of giving sound advice. The men who pleaded before the king's judges—the serjeant-pleaders—were rapidly rising in status, for a time shedding the term serjeant in ordinary usage[5] but they were not generally seen as capable of giving advice until very late in the thirteenth century.

Roughly half a century before the start of Edward I's reign, the courts of the Church had developed into a well established judicial system with sophisticated sets of procedural rules and substantive law.[6] The Church might not be entirely happy about the number of clerks who were keen to develop their knowledge of canon law and of the ecclesiastical courts' practice in order to earn what might be a fairly lucrative living. Was it not the case that *'scientia donum Dei est, unde vendi non potest'*?[7] But from even before the mid-thirteenth

---

[3] G. O. Sayles, 'Medieval Judges as Legal Consultants', *Law Quarterly Review*, 56 (1940), 247-54; reprinted in H. G. Richardson and G. O. Sayles, *The English Parliament in the Middle Ages* (1981); J. R. Maddicott, *Law and Lordship: Royal Justices as Retainers in Thirteenth- and Fourteenth Century England (Past & Present*, Supplement 4, 1978).

[4] For example, in 1285 Bogo de Clare gave silver-gilt cups to three judges, one of whom, Sir John de Metingham, was not found guilty of any corruption in the investigations of 1289-90: 'The Wardrobe and Household Accounts of Bogo de Clare, A. D. 1284-6', ed. M. S. Giuseppi, *Archaeologia*, 70, 1918-20 (1920), 34.

[5] As serjeants at law—servants only of the law—they regained the term in the fourteenth century.

[6] See, for instance, J. E. Sayers, *Papal Judges Delegate in the Province of Canterbury, 1198-1254. A Study in Ecclesiastical Jurisdiction and Administration* (Oxford, 1971) and *Select Cases from the Ecclesiastical Courts of the Province of Canterbury*, eds N. Adams and C. Donahue jr., (Selden Society vol 95, 1978-9 (1981)).

[7] G. Post, K. Giocarinis and R. Kay, 'The Medieval Heritage of a Humanistic Ideal: Scientia donum Dei est, unde vendi non potest', *Traditio*, xi (1955), 195-234.

century English canon lawyers are found in receipt of fees from religious houses and other major landowners. As early as the 1220s, Oseney Abbey was paying two marks a year to *magister* Fulco de Bridport, to serve it in its lawsuits (*causis*), and in each of the next few decades it engaged further *magistri*.[8] At this date Oseney was not an outstandingly rich house, and most of its property was near to it, in or on the perimeter of Oxford, but it does seem to have been precocious in its retaining practices. Even the wealthy Christ Church, Canterbury, only began retaining canon lawyers at the same date,[9] and most houses were much slower to start the practice.

Once a canon lawyer had been enaged by a house, his retention was generally expected to be of a permanent nature. It is exceptional to find anything less, although *master* Gilbert de Middleton, in 1301, was granted a pension of six marks a year for so long as he was an advocate of the Court of Arches.[10] In 1293 master Adam de Freston brought an action against the Prior of Barnwell to regain nine years' arrears of an annuity of 40s. a year which he had been granted in return for being ready to defend the prior and convent in all their actions: the contract had apparently been entered into in about 1263.[11] The canon lawyer was not just an all-purpose pleader, he was also a legal adviser. For example, in the mid thirteenth century, Worcester Cathedral Priory had engaged William de Poywike, a *magister* who was also a royal justice, '*de consilio nostro*',[12] and in 1300 Peter de Dene, Doctor of Civil and Canon Law, was appointed chief legal adviser to St Augustine's, Canterbury.[13] Master Peter de Peckham, who was possibly a Doctor of Civil Law, was retained in the 1280s by Lewes Priory as legal counsel for all cases in London,[14] and at the same time was legal counsel for Christ Church, Canterbury.[15] *Magistri* found employment as counsel with lay magnates too: for instance, among the Earl of Gloucester's counsel at a meeting of the Glamorgan county court in 1299 were four

---

[8] *The Cartulary of Oseney Abbey*, ed. H. E. Salter, vol. iii (Oxford Historical Society, 91, 1931), 47-8

[9] M. McC. Morgan, 'Early Canterbury Administration', *EHR*, lx (1945), 392-9, at 398.

[10] A. B. Emden, *A Biographical Register of the University of Oxford to A.D. 1500*, 3 vols. (Oxford, 1957-9), ii. 1275.

[11] *Liber Memorandorum Ecclesie de Bernewelle*, ed. J. W. Clark (Cambridge, 1907), 185-7; see also A. B. Emden, *A Biographical Register of the University of Cambridge to 1500* (Cambridge, 1963), 243.

[12] Annales Prioratus de Wigornia, in *Annales Monastici*, ed. H. R. Luard, vol. iv (Rolls Series, 1869), 440, 447.

[13] Emden, *B.R.U.O.*, iii. 2168.

[14] Ibid., 1447.

[15] Ibid., ii. 1330.

clerks, of whom two, Thomas de Palisdone and Henry de Lancar-ven, were *magistri*.[16]

In all probability every reasonably well endowed religious house and each bishop was retaining a handful of canon lawyers in the later years of Edward I's reign. Worcester Cathedral Priory was paying for three in the early 1290s[17] and no less than nine in 1313-14;[18] the executors of Richard de Gravesend, bishop of London (died 1303), found themselves burdened with payments to at least six.[19]

Such men were sometimes well rewarded. St Augustine's paid Peter de Dene £10 a year, and Peter de Peckham received 10 marks a year from Lewes Priory, whilst Gilbert de Middleton was granted 10 marks a year by Peterborough Abbey and the same sum by John Drokensford, bishop of Bath and Wells, as well as 6 marks a year by Oseney Abbey.[20] The average retaining fee paid to a canon lawyer in the late thirteenth century was rather less—a range from 20s. to 100s. a year seems to have been more usual—but this was still far more than the mark or half-mark paid to attorneys in either of the London Benches at this time. In some ways Edward I's reign was the heyday of the canon lawyer. It was at this time that he was most widely employed, as a skilled man of affairs no less than as a lawyer, by the Crown as well as by individual magnates and religious houses: some *magistri* were in fact the king's judges, whilst rather more were in influential positions in such parts of the Crown's bureaucracy as the Chancery. Peter de Peckham was a royal clerk[21] whilst Gilbert de Middleton was both an official of the court of Canterbury and a royal councillor.

Royal justices and their clerks were obviously the men who knew the common law best, but there were disadvantages in retaining them. They were primarily at the king's disposal, and, when not sitting in the Common Pleas or King's Bench, might be sent off on

---

[16] N. Denholm-Young, *Seignorial Administration in England* (1937), 28.

[17] *Early Compotus Rolls (1278-1352) of the Priory of Worcester*, eds J. M. Wilson and C. Gordon (Worcestershire Historical Society, 1908), 12, 13, 18, 29; and Emden, *B.R.U.O.*, ii. 1172 (Walter de Ludeford), 1174 (Thomas de Lugoure, D.C.L.), and iii. 1465 (Peter de Periton, later D.Cn.L.).

[18] *Early Compotus Rolls*, ed. Wilson and Gordon, 36-7.

[19] *Account of the Executors of Richard, Bishop of London, 1303 ...*, eds W. H. Hale and H. T. Ellacombe (Camden Society, N.S. 10, 1874), 107.

[20] For Gilbert de Middleton's fees, see Emden, *B.R.U.O.*, ii. 1275; he also received fees of five marks a year from Bishop Walter de Stapledon and Worcester Cathedral Priory. The latter fee was to be paid until he was presented to a benefice, and the two episcopal fees were to be paid until he was given a prebend: the retention of quite a few canon lawyers must be masked as a result of such forms of remuneration, although monetary fees seem to have been much more common.

[21] R. A. L. Smith, *Canterbury Cathedral Priory. A Study in Monastic Administration* (Cambridge, 1943), 71.

a commission to the furthest part of the realm: it was thus far from certain that a lay or ecclesiastical magnate would readily be able to get hold of them for advice. The sacking of so much of the Bench in 1289 must have upset many arrangements—for instance, Leicester Abbey in 1286 is known to have been retaining Sir Thomas of Wayland and his clerk, at 20s. and one mark respectively.[22]

Narrators, or pleaders, were much less commonly retained before 1300, for their emergence as a profession was still in too nascent a state, but the attorney whose term-time life was based on the king's central courts was beginning to enter the fee roll of landowners in the closing years of the thirteenth century, as he emerged as a professional type. At this time he was probably seen as being quite as competent in the handling of lawsuits as was the *narrator*[23]—insofar, indeed, as the two functions were distinguishable. For example, bishop Richard de Gravesend died owing £8 *pro salario suo diversis vicibus* to William of Cotyngham, his attorney and *procurator* in pleas concerning him *in Curia Regia*:[24] it is probable that such a large sum reflects a substantial element of arrears, but that some attorneys were very well paid is shown by the £10 paid to John de Chelmsford in 1307–8 as the attorney *in banco* of the Earl of Gloucester; Chelmsford was also entrusted with £31 for paying the fees of those who were of the earl's counsel.[25] Relatively substantial sums are likewise recorded as paid during two vacancies of the see of Ely—£6 6s. 8d. in the year-and-a-half 1298–9 to one attorney who acted for the see in both Benches and in the Exchequer,[26] and 40s. divided between Benedict de Cambridge and Ralph de Norwich, attorneys who acted similarly in a six months' vacancy in 1310.[27]

[22] Public Record Office, Ministers' Accounts, SC 6/1257/12. Wayland's clerk is named as Robert of Littlebury. The disgraced Richard de Boyland, whose association with Norwich Cathedral Priory went back to at least 1264–5, continued to receive an annual fee of 20s. from the Priory after his dismissal from the bench, until at least 1292–3 and perhaps until his death: Norfolk Record Office, Norwich Cathedral archives, accounts of the prior's camera.

[23] See the discussion of attorneys in J. C. Meier, 'The Beginnings of Professionalism among English Attorneys, 1266–1300', Ph.D. thesis, University of Iowa, 1977, especially at 48ff. At p. 52 she points out that of the 43 *narrators* known from final concords in the Michaelmas terms of 1294, 1296 and 1300, 23 had earlier appeared as attorneys, and she establishes that 15 of these may be termed professional attorneys by virtue of the frequency of their appearance on the membranes recording attorneys' warrants.

[24] *Account of the Executors*, eds Hale and Ellacombe, 107.

[25] Denholm-Young, Seignorial Administration, 42; the date of 1307–8 is suggested by G. A. Holmes, *The Estates of the Higher Nobility in Fourteenth-Century England* (Cambridge, 1957), 74 n.9.

[26] PRO, SC 6/1132/10, mm.4 and 15a; I have included 26s. 8d. for the attorney's robe in the sum.

[27] PRO, SC 6/1132/12.

The scene is thus set for the establishment of the common lawyers as feed retainers and as counsel, and for their displacement, in large measure, of the canon lawyers. Three religious bodies—Lincoln Cathedral, Durham Cathedral Priory, and the Cathedral Priory of Christ Church, Canterbury—have reasonably well preserved early sequences of accounts and related materials that show in exemplary detail the complete change in the pattern of the retention of lawyers that took place between the early years of the reign of Edward II and the later years of Edward III, and this evidence may be supplemented, from later on, by the accounts of other ecclesiastical and lay magnates and town authorities.

Firstly, the retention of separate attorneys in the courts of King's Bench and Common Pleas and in the Exchequer is a practice which a number of religious institutions commenced in about the reign of Edward II. Different sets of men acted in each court, those in the Common Pleas and King's Bench generally having a clientele drawn from one particular county or group of adjacent counties, whilst the local connexions of Exchequer attorneys were more tenuous, if existent at all.[28] Consequently, if one of the religious houses wished to have a representative who was thoroughly *au fait* with each court's practice, it would need to appoint three men.

The Chapter of Lincoln was feeing an attorney in each of the three courts by 1319–20, paying 20s. to their attorney in the Common Pleas, Nicholas de Welton, and 13s. 4d. to *dominus* William de Broclesby, their attorney in the Exchequer (as well as being a clerk of Adam de Lymbergh); the smaller sum of 6s. 8d. paid to their attorney in the King's Bench went to John de Broghton who, unusually for an attorney at this date, was a *magister*.[29] Christ Church, Canterbury, first retained a permanent attorney in the Exchequer in 1325–6, paying him 20s. a year;[30] his successor was only paid 6s. 8d. Smaller religious houses were much slower to retain attorneys in each of the three central courts: St George's Chapel, Windsor, was

---

[28] G. H. Fowler, *Rolls from the Office of the Sheriff of Beds. and Bucks., 1332–1334* (Bedfordshire Historical Record Society, Quarto Memoirs, iii, 1929), 79.

[29] Lincoln, Dean & Chapter Muniments, Bj. 2. 5, fo. 22v. For Broclesby, see Emden, *B.R.U.O.*, i. 273–4. His father was Robert of Welton; he was made a Baron of the Exchequer in 1341, in succession to Robert of Nottingham, whose personal clerk he had previously been: T. F. Tout, *The Place of the Reign of Edward II in English History*, 2nd edn., by Hilda Johnstone (Manchester, 1936), 309 n. 1. No subsequent attorney employed by the Chapter was ever a *magister*.

[30] Canterbury Cathedral Archives, Miscellaneous Accounts, 2 (Treasurer's Accounts, 1307–84), f. 157 (John Evere; Exchequer), f. 193 (William de Waldegrave; King's Bench); D.E. 3 (Day Book of Priors Oxenden and Hathbrand, 1331–43), f. 5ᵛ (Thomas Doyly; Common Pleas). Smith, *Canterbury Cathedral Priory*, 75, is inaccurate.

represented in the Exchequer by 1353–4, but not until 1377 in the Court of Common Pleas, at respective costs of £1 and 6s. 8d.[31]

Religious houses and bishops seem almost always to have found it necessary to retain an attorney in the Exchequer for what was generally non-litigious business; it was less of a priority for them to engage on a regular basis attorneys in the Common Pleas, or, still less, in the King's Bench. For towns, the priorities were different: their need was for someone to act as a writ-purchaser, and on occasion to assist in the defence or extension of their liberties. By the end of the thirteenth century such large towns as Norwich were beginning to find it worth retaining an attorney who was based in Westminster or wherever else the central courts might be, rather than sending someone up to, say, London, as and when it was necessary. The evidence of a Norwich account roll of 1293–4 is valuable as illustrating a transitional stage in the development of its practice of retention.[32] Geoffrey the clerk is sent around on the town's business, including a journey to London in connexion with a plea between the Prior of Norwich and the community of the town, but in this as in subsequent years a fee of 13s. 4d. is paid to Thomas de Framlingham, an attorney in the Common Pleas.[33] The rather larger sum of 20s. is paid—again, as in subsequent years—to John Mutford, a *narrator*, and it is in fact Mutford rather than the attorney Framlingham who is paid the 18s. 1d. expenses that were incurred for the business of the community.

By 1339–40, from when its accounts survive in detail, Exeter was retaining attorneys in both the Common Pleas and the King's Bench.[34] On several occasions in the fourteenth century its legal representatives were also its representatives in parliament, and in 1339–40 its King's Bench attorney, Robert de Bridport, was also paid for concerning himself with the town's interests in the two parliaments held in the course of the year. The attorney was deemed useful as a representative of the town who was in London throughout the legal terms and it was all the better if he could act on its behalf in parliament as well as in his own court.

In the course of the fourteenth century, the attorney declined in importance, in status, and in cost. In the last few years of the thirteenth century he was differentiated from the *narrator* in function

---

[31] A. K. B. Roberts, *St George's Chapel, Windsor Castle, 1348–1416. A Study in Early Collegiate Administration* (Windsor, n.d. [1947]), 146, 147.

[32] Summarised in *Records of the City of Norwich*, ed. W. Hudson and J. C. Tingey, 2 vols. (Norwich, 1906–10), ii. 31–2.

[33] Ibid., 31–4.

[34] Exeter City Archives, Receivers' Account Rolls.

more than in the size of his fee, but each of these differences rapidly sharpened. The *narrator* was commonly retained on a permanent basis, and was thus in a strong position: as was observed in a lawsuit in 1313, a writ of annuity was in the nature of a freehold.[35] The attorney, by contrast, was usually retained on an *ad hoc* yearly basis, for all that his period of service might well be as much as twenty years or more. Fourteenth-century accounts also show a gradual rise in the practice of retaining attorneys in the Common Pleas, as against a relative decline in feeing them in the King's Bench: this reflects the change in relative importance of the two courts. To return to the example of Exeter, when Robert de Bridport ceased to be its attorney in the King's Bench, in about 1356, he was not replaced; the annual fee of the town's attorney in the Common Pleas was reduced from 20s. to one mark from 1349-50, when the town engaged a fresh representative there.[36]

In the first half of the fourteenth century, a few religious houses retained a very modestly feed attorney in a local court,[37] but by and large they preferred to conduct their litigation in the King's central courts. Quite apart from perhaps enjoying a privileged position vis-a-vis the King's Bench, the religious houses, and indeed lay magnates, probably valued the King's courts most because they were courts of record. Any judgement given in the King's courts was enrolled and a copy of it could thus be obtained at any time in the future, to prove a title to property or other right. The King's courts were the landowner's supreme muniment, and as such were to be constantly consulted. Furthermore, once an attorney had been engaged in the Common Pleas or King's Bench, it made sense to conduct all litigation through him: he could easily purchase all the requisite original and judicial writs. The justices of the central courts were also perhaps likely to be more impartial than those who presided in a town court or in the county court. The sheriff who presided over the county court might well be suspected of partiality, and no religious house could have felt happy litigating in a town court that was presided over by the citizens' representative, be he mayor or recorder: cathedral chapters and other religious houses situated in towns were frequently engaged in disputes with their towns.[38]

[35] *Year Books of Edward II. Vol. XV. 6 & 7 Edward II. A.D. 1313*, ed. W. C. Bolland (Selden Society, vol. 36, 1918), 120.

[36] Exeter Archives, Receivers' Rolls.

[37] The Chapter of Lincoln retained John de Thorp as their attorney in the Guildhall at Lincoln from 1331-2 to at least 1339-40, at 6s. 8d. a year; he was the only attorney they ever retained on a yearly basis in this court. Lincoln, Dean & Chapter Muniments, Bj. 2. 5, ff. 127ᵛ, 180ᵛ.

[38] See, for example, the discussion by M. E. Curtis, *Some Disputes between the City and the Cathedral Authorities of Exeter* (Manchester, 1932).

The rise in importance of the Court of Common Pleas and the decline of the attorney form two sides of a triangle that is incomplete without its third, concomitant, part: the gradual ascendancy of the men who alone pleaded in this court—the serjeants at law.[39] The *narrator* or pleader of Edward I's reign was by Edward III's time both the acknowledged expert in pleading in what was now the busiest and foremost court of the land, and was also regarded as the expert in the general understanding and application of the rules of the common law. Where it had once made sense for a landowner to retain canon lawyers, it now was obvious that serjeants at law should be given a *pensio*. Since there were only two or three dozen serjeants practising at any one time—in other words, one for each county of England, on average—and half that number by the 1330s, and since each landowner wished to have the benefit of more than one expert lawyer who lived reasonably nearby, it was equally obviously desirable to retain one or two apprentices at law. Most landowners, in fact, would want to retain more than one serjeant at law, since the quality of their advice and influence was so high and since it was common to use the services of at least two or three as pleaders in a Common Pleas suit. Maitland was not exaggerating when he wrote of up to half 'the practising bar' being retained for a single suit.[40]

It also made good sense to befriend the leading apprentices at law, for these were the serjeants at law of the future just as the serjeants were the king's justices of the future. And the retention of a serjeant was at once both the befriending of one who would probably become a justice of one or other Bench, and also a way round the increasingly dubious and frowned on practice of retaining a royal justice. It may equally be said that most serjeants at law were themselves justices, even before promotion to the Bench, since they were commonly the recipients of commissions of assizes and of gaol delivery.[41]

Even the accounts of religious houses show a gradual replacement of canon lawyers by the common lawyers—both serjeants and apprentices. Durham Cathedral Priory was slower than some to change

---

[39] That the serjeants at law were originally simply the body of narrators who pleaded in the court of Common Pleas is suggested by J. H. Baker, *The Order of Serjeants at Law* (Selden Society, Supplementary Series, vol. 5, 1984), 4–7.

[40] *Year Books of Edward II. Vol. III. A.D. 1309–10*, ed. F. W. Maitland (Selden Society, vol. 20, 1905), p. xi.

[41] Such commissions, where written on the dorses of the patent rolls, have only recently been calendared at the Public Record Office, under the guidance of the late C. A. F. Meekings: *Calendar of the General and Special Assize & General Gaol Delivery Commissions on the Dorses of the Patent Rolls ... (1377–1399)* (Nendeln, Liechtenstein, 1977).

its pattern of retention, but what can be seen in its accounts applies equally to other houses and, *a fortiori*, to lay landowners.[42] In the 1350s Durham's annual pension-list is still headed by up to ten *magistri*, probably all canon lawyers and mostly receiving 40s. a year, but towards the bottom of the list come about eight common lawyers, also mostly receiving 40s. a year, and with the highest paid, Thomas Surtays (the Priory's steward) being paid the same sum as the highest paid canon lawyer—66s. 8d. In 1359–60 Surtays first appears as a knight; in the next year another of the common lawyers, John Moubray, now a Justice of the Common Pleas,[43] is shown as a knight, and for the rest of the fourteenth century one or two of the Priory's pensioned common lawyers were commonly knights. In the 1360s and early 1370s Durham was spending about £40 a year on pensions, of which a little less than half went to common lawyers; it cut back on its pensions in the 1380s, when it was possibly generally hard-pressed for money and was indeed sometimes borrowing from its common lawyers. In the 1390s and 1400s, it was only paying a couple of its common lawyers £2 a year, the other three or four being feed at £1 or 26s. 8d. By 1410, however, its expenditure had recovered to more than former levels: it now spent between £50 and £60 annually on pensions, and, significantly enough, from 1409–10 onwards the common lawyers are always listed before the *magistri* and one or two other ecclesiastical court officials. Into the 1440s, the eight or so common lawyers continue, at £1 or, in perhaps two instances a year, at £2; the sums paid to all the ecclesiastical officials have shrunk and only one or two *magistri* are retained in an advisory (as opposed to proctorial) capacity.

Houses smaller than Durham were quicker to replace their ecclesiastical law advisers with common lawyers, but the same story could be told of the way in which their common lawyers rose up in their esteem. From the mid fourteenth to the mid fifteenth centuries, the practice of retaining serjeants and apprentices[44] was at its most widespread: the fees that these men received were not individually as large as those once received by the leading canon lawyers, but they were paid by a far greater range of religious houses, bishops, lay magnates and gentry, and town authorities. A young apprentice, who pleaded in the county court as much as in the King's Bench, might be retained for as little as one mark, but he could hope to

---

[42] All the material in this paragraph comes from the annual Bursars' Rolls of Durham Cathedral Priory, in the Durham Dean & Chapter Muniments.

[43] Moubray continued to be feed until *c.* 1373, about the time of his death.

[44] Apprentices (at law) took their names from the fact that in the fourteenth century they were deemed to be at the learning stage of their career; there is no evidence to suggest that they were ever articled to anyone.

receive such a sum from large numbers of clients. In 1435 the Buckinghamshire apprentice Edmund Brudenell, of Chalfont, received no more than a mark from half of the dozen local gentry or their ladies who had engaged him, and only two fees of 40s., one of which was from the Dean and Chapter of Windsor, but the total, from 17 clients, was £15 6s. 8d.[45] No full list of the fees of any other lawyer has survived, but some indication of the sorts of fees expected by better known lawyers can be seen from an examination of their clients' account rolls. Robert Tirwhit, created serjeant at law in 1396[46] and a Justice of the King's Bench in 1409, in about 1400 was receiving 40s. from at least three clients—John of Gaunt, Richard de Beauchamp, Earl of Warwick, and the town of Hull—and perhaps from a fourth, the Earl of Norfolk;[47] in addition, he received 26s. 8d. a year from the Dean and Chapter of York, and from Meaux and Selby Abbeys,[48] and £1 from the town of Grimsby and Lincoln Dean and Chapter.[49] It would not be surprising to find that his total income from retaining fees was in excess of £50 a year.[50]

As a lawyer advanced in his career, his circle of clients was drawn from farther and farther afield—as is seen by contrasting Tirwhit's clientele with that of Brudenell. And as his reputation advanced, the lawyer could afford to scorn the retaining fee that he considered inadequate: in 1437-8 John Fortescue, already a well-established apprentice, refused the same fee of 13s. 4d. which he had accepted

---

[45] Westminster Abbey Muniments, no. 6036, m. 6. In 1378 the Corporation of London felt it necessary to pay the Recorder of London (who at this time was always an apprentice) an extra £13 or £14 a year in return for foregoing fees and robes from other clients.

[46] *Calendar of Patent Rolls, 1396-9*, 28.

[47] PRO, DL 28/3/5, f. 10; Hull Chamberlains' accounts, BRF 2/344 *ex inf.* Dr R. Horrox; British Library, Additional Charter 16556. These are accounts for 1396-7, 1406-7 and Easter term 1403.

[48] York, Dean & Chapter Muniments, Chamberlains' Accounts; *Chronica Monasterii de Melsa*, ed. E. A. Bond, vol. iii (Rolls Series, 1868), p. lxvii; Westminster Diocesan Archives, Se/Ac/5. These are accounts for 1402-3 onwards, 1396 and 1398-9.

[49] S. H. Rigby, 'Boston and Grimsby in the Middle Ages', London Ph.D. thesis, 1983, p. 80; Lincoln, D & C Muniments, Bj. 2. 8, f. 118, etc. These are payments made from 1394-5 and from 1395-6 onwards.

[50] William Ayscogh, as a Justice of the Common Pleas and thus as a recipient of a salary of at least £120, petitioned in 1441 asking for a grant on the grounds that he had only been a serjeant for less than two years and, by implication, had lost by his speedy promotion to the Bench the greater winnings and fees that he would have had as a serjeant. *Select Cases in the Court of King's Bench, under Richard II, Henry IV and Henry V, Vol. VII*, ed. G. O. Sayles (Selden Society, vol. 88, 1971), p. xv; S. Lysons, 'Copies of Three Remarkable Petitions to King Henry the Sixth ...', *Archaeologia*, 16 (1812), 4.

the previous year from Exeter, on the ground that it was too modest a reward.[51]

What, it will be asked, were all these fees being paid for? The word used in the accounts that record payments of fees is the Latin *consilium*; the French word *co(u)nseil* is occasionally used, and the lawyers themselves are sometimes referred to as *counsaile* (French), *consiliarii* (Latin) or *counsellors*. How is this to be translated? As J. F. Baldwin observed, quoting Maitland, the problem faced by the medieval clerk was that he was confronted by 'a language too rigid for his thought':[52] he could not make a clear distinction between *concilium* and *consilium* (although he favoured the latter word and its derivatives), partly because he himself found it difficult to distinguish between 'council' and 'counsel'. The consequence has been that modern historians have had to make their own decision whether to translate the Latin *concilium* and *consilium* and all their derivatives, French and English, by the modern 'council' or 'counsel'.

The prevailing fashion for using the word 'council' was no doubt set by Baldwin himself, in his study of *The King's Council in England during the Middle Ages*, published over three quarters of a century ago.[53] He was unquestionably right to prefer the word 'council' to 'counsel' for his subject, since it was a standing body of men with regular functions and responsibilities and, from the reign of Edward III, a building for its own special use.[54] Accordingly, he could easily distinguish between the regular councillors and men such as Lawrence Drew who were retained for law cases only and therefore were not in the full sense members of the council.[55] But the question of translation is far more problematic when the word *consilium* or its equivalent is used in the context of an aristocratic magnate, or a member of the gentry, or a religious house: the archival evidence in such cases is likely to be scanty (whereas hundreds of thousands of

[51] Exeter Archives, Receivers' Rolls. The next two years' rolls do in fact show Fortescue as accepting 13s. 4d. once more, but in 1440-1 (by when he was a serjeant) the sum was increased to £2.

[52] J. F. Baldwin, *The King's Council in England during the Middle Ages* (Oxford, 1913), 104.

[53] Ibid.; also influential were two papers by A. E. Levett: 'The Courts and Court Rolls of St Albans Abbey', *Transactions of the Royal Historical Society*, 4th ser., vol. 7 (1924), 52-76; and 'Baronial Councils and their Relations to Manorial Courts', *Mélanges d'Histoire du Moyen Age, offerts à M. Ferdinand Lot* ... (Paris, 1925), reprinted in *Studies in Manorial History*, by A. E. Levett (Oxford, 1938), 21-40.

[54] Baldwin, *The King's Council*, 354-8. Cf. A. L. Brown 'The King's Councillors in Fifteenth-Century England', *TRHS*, 5th ser., vol. 19 (1969), 95-118.

[55] Ibid., 142, and cf. 166, 205 and 207.

documents remain from the records of the King's council),[56] and it is not even clear how far the fee provider could himself have distinguished between 'council' and 'counsel'. Still, granted that a choice, however anachronistic, must be made between these two words, it may be suggested that the election is too frequently made on the wrong side of the line. A general misconception of how a man's or an institution's affairs were ordered and guided will result from the excessive use of the word 'council', for that word is suggestive of a body of men who meet together on a more or less regular and permanent basis; a 'councillor', besides, will be seen not so much as one who proffers advice but rather as some kind of official or even bureaucrat. And it may be that the words 'council' and 'councillor' are too readily used by modern historians.

It would be unfair to say that this problem of *le mot juste* has gone unappreciated,[57] but there is an unsatisfactory artificiality in the commonly adopted solution which credits a lord or religious house with a council made up of two elements, the administrative and the legal.[58] Whilst this has the merit of making a certain separation between the laymen and the lawyers who were retained of a lord's counsel, it has the misfortune of tending towards an equiparation of the two categories' responsibilities and duties.

The essential point is that when a lawyer was paid a retaining fee of £1 or £2 for his counsel, he was not thereby putting himself under an obligation to attend any regular body of lawyers or bureaucrats, but was simply undertaking to be prepared to offer occasional advice.[59] The sum was, after all, no more than a serjeant at law would expect to receive for one or two mornings' pleading in the Common Pleas. The retained lawyer was not obliged, in return for the sum, either to go anywhere to give his counsel, or to plead in court; for the former he would expect to be paid his expenses, with perhaps a further reward as well, and for the latter he would require to be paid the normal fee. This seemingly constricted view

---

[56] Cf. Holmes, *Estates of the Higher Nobility*, 76–7, for the later fourteenth century: 'Apart from the councils of the king and queen, the only lay councils which have been, and perhaps the only ones which can be, satisfactorily examined are those of the Black Prince and of the Duke of Lancaster'.

[57] See, for instance, R. Somerville, *History of the Duchy of Lancaster*, vol. i, *1265–1603* (1953), 128–9.

[58] E.g., R. Somerville, 'The Duchy of Lancaster Council and Court of Duchy Chamber', *TRHS*, 4th ser., vol. 23 (1941), 159–77, at 170; and C. Rawcliffe, 'Baronial Councils in the Later Middle Ages', *Patronage, Pedigree and Power in Later Medieval England*, ed. C. D. Ross (Gloucester, 1979), 87–108, at 90.

[59] The closest that the accounts get to this is the phrase 'ad essendum de consilio'; e.g. British Library, Egerton Roll 8742 recto (accounts of Roger de Mortimer, Earl of March, 1394).

of the retained lawyer's obligations is fully borne out by contemporary Year Book reports. It was said in 1347, for instance, that a lawyer did not lose his right to an annuity by refusing to travel to court at his client's request, for that would have involved more than giving counsel and the lawyer might have incurred expenditure which he had no claim to recover.[60] How well it was appreciated that the lawyers needed to be remunerated for their advice on particular occasions is graphically illustrated by an account of a meeting between Sir William Beauchamp and his legal counsel in about 1390. While four prominent lawyers were dining with him at his house in London, he came and placed a gold noble before each of them asking them for God''s sake to delay him no more but tell him then and there whether he had the law on his side in his claim to the Hastings inheritance.[61]

A lawyer retained on a yearly basis was really hardly under any greater obligation to his client than was a lawyer who was retained, as was often the case, for his counsel in connexion with just one lawsuit or legal problem. The accounts of Henry of Lancaster, Earl of Derby, for 1391-3 show how for one particular lawsuit, over the manors of Sutton and Potton (Beds.), two serjeants at law, John Woderove and Hugh Huls, were paid a mark each for their counsel, as was an apprentice, Thomas Englys;[62] a total of 66s. 8d. was paid to John Hervy who is described as an apprentice of Bedfordshire, of the lord's counsel.[63] Woderove was subsequently put in receipt of an annual fee of 20s., but Englys and Hervy were local men and were clearly deemed useful solely for this particular case by reason of their local connexions.[64]

It was worth retaining lawyers on a permanent basis both because their skills were highly valued and because such men were worth cultivating for their goodwill. The cost of retention was not high in relation to the total costs of litigation—Henry of Derby spent a total of over £95 on the Sutton and Potton lawsuit, whilst the annual fees that he paid on a permanent basis, to attorneys in each of the three

---

[60] Year Book report, Hil. 21 Edward III, 7, pl. 20; cf. J. H. Baker, 'Counsellors and Barristers. An Historical Study', *Cambridge Law Journal*, 27 (1969), 205-29, at 209.

[61] R. I. Jack, 'Entail and Descent: the Hastings Inheritance, 1370-1436', *Bulletin of the Institute of Historical Research*, 38 (1965), 1-19.

[62] PRO, DL 28/3/3, m. 6; 28/3/4 (i). For the lawsuit, see Somerville, *Duchy of Lancaster*, i. 68 n.6.

[63] PRO, DL 28/3/4 (i).

[64] Ibid., *s.v. Feoda* for Woderove. Englys and Hervy may perhaps be identified with the Engleys and Herny who were stewards of the lordship of Higham Ferrers, in office by 1391; Somerville, *Duchy of Lancaster*, i. 371.

central courts and to apprentices and serjeants of his counsel, came to less than £10.[65]

The lawyers' advice was cheap in relation to, say, the standard sorts of fees incurred in the Chancery in the course of such litigation, whilst it was expensive enough for it to be requested only sparingly. Counsel was sought in connexion with specific problems, particularly where the interpretation of documents such as grants or agreements was at stake. Clear illustration of this can be seen in the remarkably detailed accounts kept for the Dean and Chapter of Lincoln. In 1379–80 they were retaining on an annual basis William Pilet of Scredington (at 26s. 8d) and Thomas Pinchbek (at £1), but they did not seek even once the counsel of Pinchbek, who was at this time a prominent apprentice at law; they twice called upon Pilet for his counsel, once over the imposition of royal taxes within the Cathedral close and apparently also over the actual commission for the tax. In addition to Pilet, they also consulted John de Reppyngale junior (the two being paid 13s. 4d. together), whilst on another occasion Reppyngale came to discuss with the Chapter negotiations with the Princess's own counsel over land in Reepham.[66] Next year, however, Pinchbek, whose fee had now gone up to £2 a year, was called upon for one day's work for the Chapter in connexion with what was evidently the major dispute with the city of Lincoln: he received £1 and his expenses. This dispute, which was over the revocation of the commission of the Peace within the city, reached a head in 1381–2. The Dean and Chapter sent bills, seeking the revocation, to both the King and John of Gaunt, and for one day's counsel and pleading over the revocation paid a whole bevy of lawyers: £2 to Sir Henry Hasty (a Justice of the Common Pleas, of a Lincolnshire background; his role is uncertain), and the same sum to Pinchbek, for his counsel; two sums of 26s. 8d. to Richard de la Launde, for both his counsel and, apparently, pleading; 6s. 8d. for his counsel, and £1, again apparently for pleading, to Pilet; and £1 to John Reppyngale junior.[67] Hasty (or Asty), Justice though he had by now become, had been retained since 1374–5—that is to say, since the financial year before that in which he had become Chief Baron of the Exchequer—and was doubtless regarded as a friend to the Dean and Chapter.[68]

A landowner like Lincoln Dean and Chapter had only a few legal

---

[65] PRO, DL 28/3/4 (i).

[66] Lincoln, D & C Muniments, Bj. 2. 7, ff. 27ᵛ, 28, 29.

[67] Ibid., f. 69ᵛ.

[68] The 1346 ordinance forbidding royal judges to accept fees or robes (*Statutes of the Realm*, i (Record Commission, 1810), 303–6) applied equally to Barons of the Exchequer.

problems each year that merited expert legal advice; the common-place suing of tenants for non-payment of rent and suchlike matters was left in the hands of attorneys and bailiffs. A larger landowner naturally consulted his legal counsel more frequently, and such a leading magnate as the Black Prince or John of Gaunt would also find that tenants and other people who sought his protection or backing, or simply his judgement, brought their own legal and other problems to him. Such a man's counsel were accordingly called upon for their advice so frequently that it is hardly surprising that they are today deemed to have been part of his 'council'. But these two magnates were unusually powerful men with vast estates that were partly outside the ordinary workings of the common law, and they were prepared to pay their lawyers to act at times as advisers to their tenants; other landowners would naturally take a more restricted view of their responsibilities. Likewise, the extent to which baronial councils can be said to have exercised an 'equitable juris-diction' that bypassed the common law risks being exaggerated.[69] It is true that the Court of the Duchy Chamber grew out of the judicial activity of the Duchy of Lancaster council, and that in 1391 it was felt necessary to pass a statute protecting men from being compelled to answer concerning their freehold before the counsel (*conseille*) of any lord or lady,[70] but there is little evidence to show any lord's legal counsel encouraging or taking part in any such activity. In-deed, the increasing resort to the loveday, or arbitration as it came to be called from *c.* 1400, can be seen as an absorption by the com-mon lawyers of a means of settling disputes that had previously been outside the common law, for although the arbitrators' award might be made under the aegis of a baron's legal counsel, the arbitrators' award in the fifteenth century was commonly reinforced by the parties' entry into a bond in a substantial sum of money to accept it. Since a properly bonded award was a bar to common law suits (unless, of course, about land), parties took great care before entering into awards: by the late fourteenth century the arbitrators themselves were commonly lawyers, and the parties themselves were increasingly frequently advised by other lawyers. Arbitrations, it might be said, were becoming agreements between the two parties' legal counsel, binding each party to abide by the decision of other lawyers.

[69] Such suggestions partly represent a building up on the foundations provided by Levett, 'Baronial Councils ...' in her *Studies in Manorial History*. See also J. B. Post, 'Courts, Councils and Arbitrators in the Ladbroke Manor Dispute, 1382–1400', *Medieval Legal Records edited in Memory of C. A. F. Meekings*, eds J. B. Post and R. F. Hunnisett (1978), 290–339.

[70] Stat. 16 Richard II, c. 2; *Statutes of the Realm*, ii. 83.

The formalisation and 'legalisation' of lovedays may be seen as one of the last achievements of retained legal counsel. Retention was founded upon a combination of convenience, utility and need, and although it remained convenient to retain lawyers, the need to do so diminished in the middle years of the fifteenth century. Two principal causes stand out—the rise of the solicitor, and the increase in the number of trained lawyers. The solicitor, as a man with specialist skills in negotiating with lawyers, began to become the chief counsel to institutions,[71] vying for importance not with the serjeants or apprentices but with the attorney, who himself was undergoing the process of metamorphosis into the attorney general.[72] Ultimately the solicitor and the attorney general become distinguishable only by the different locations in which they worked, and then even that distinction disappears. As early as 1410–11, Winchester College had begun to pay a retaining fee to Henry Kesewyk, *sollicitator Collegii in curiis domini Regis*.[73]

The rise of the solicitor and attorney general were matched by a decline in the retention of counsel learned in the law. The growth in numbers of the legal profession meant that legal expertise was now far more readily obtainable, in the country and, especially, in the inns of court in London. From about the middle of the fifteenth century the pension-lists of both religious and secular bodies can be seen to be shortening—gradually, as the various counsel who were in receipt of pensions were promoted to the bench or died. The city of Exeter in 1441–2 was paying fees to eight lawyers, in 1445–6 to six, from 1455–6 to five, from 1458–9 to four, from 1460–1 to three, and from 1463–4 only to the city's attorney, Richard Livermore, who from 1468–9 is styled attorney general.[74] A similar process, usually over a somewhat greater period of time, can be detected in the retention of lawyers by other institutions. At the time when 'good lordship' was coming to assume a non-monetary form, the retention of lawyers was becoming largely redundant.[75] The volume of litigation in the Westminster courts was undiminished, and the

---

[71] For such a reference to a solicitor, Robert Pert, as counsel to the abbot of Winchcombe, see PRO, Early Chancery Proceedings, C1/32/60.

[72] For a discussion of one late fifteenth-century attorney-general and his relations with the feudal magnate who took up most of his time, see E. W. Ives, 'Andrew Dymmock and the Papers of Antony, Earl Rivers, 1482–3', *BIHR*, 41 (1968), 216–29.

[73] H. C[hitty], 'Lawyers employed by Winchester College during the Fifteenth Century', *Notes and Queries*, 12th series, i (1916), 361–3, at 362, no. 22.

[74] Exeter Archives, Receivers' Rolls.

[75] For non-monetary 'good lordship', see W. H. Dunham jr., 'Lord Hastings' Indentured Retainers, 1461–83 …', *Transactions, Connecticut Academy of Arts and Sciences*, 39 (1955), 1–175.

development of the Chancery into a major court of equity was adding yet further complications to the law, but as litigation was coming to be seen less as a haphazard game of chance dependent on the oral skill of pleaders, the lawyers' clients came to approach their litigation in a different manner. They were less concerned to have any personal rapport with the barristers who would plead for them or advise them and saw no need to pay them fees in return for what might be non-existent advice. In the mid fifteenth century Reynold Pecok had praised the clergy for their lavish expenditure 'upon worthi gentil men leerned in lawe for mentenaunces of her rightis',[76] but the need to retain lawyers had previously been very real. When the need passed, the practice of retention faded away, as money that had once seemed so well spent was now felt to be an unnecessary extravagance.

[76] Reginald Pecock, *The Repressor of Over Much Blaming of the Clergy*, ed. C. Babington (Rolls Series, 1860), ii. 370–1.

THE CHURCHILL GOVERNMENT
AND THE BLACK AMERICAN TROOPS IN
BRITAIN DURING WORLD WAR II
By David Reynolds, M.A., Ph.D.

READ 4 JULY 1984

JUST before lunch on Tuesday 13 October 1942 the British War
Cabinet assembled for a hasty meeting in the Prime Minister's room
in the House of Commons. Sandwiched on the agenda between
discussion of the impending visit of the South African premier and
the arrangements for celebrating Armistice Day was a unique item,
one on which no less than six different Cabinet ministers had submitted papers. The subject was the treatment of the black soldiers
who were in Britain as members of the US Army's expeditionary
force. The American policy was to segregate them as much as possible from white troops. The Cabinet had now to make up its mind
about a War Office proposal that British troops should be encouraged to adopt a similar attitude to the black GIs. The issue, bluntly
stated, was whether the British Government should approve a discreet colour bar.[1]

To understand British policy towards the black Americans, we need
to look first at the Government's attitude to British colonial manpower. In World War I the Army had avoided using West Indian
troops in combat, except against non-whites in the Middle East, and
they were mostly employed in labour battalions. Indian troops were,
however, used in action in France, but care was taken to minimise

---

[1] Aspects of this subject have been dealt with in Thomas E. Hachey, 'Jim Crow
with a British accent: Attitudes of London Government officials toward American
negro soldiers in England during World War II', *Journal of Negro History*, 59 (1974),
65-77 (a collection of edited documents); Christopher Thorne, 'Britain and the black
G.I.s: Racial issues and Anglo-American relations in 1942', *New Community*, 3 (1974),
262-71; Graham A. Smith, 'Jim Crow on the home front, 1942-1945', *New Community*,
8 (1980), 317-28; J. E. Flint, 'Scandal at the Bristol Hotel: Some thoughts on racial
discrimination in Britain and West Africa and its relationship to the planning of
decolonisation, 1939-47', *Journal of Imperial and Commonwealth History*, 12 (1983), 74-
93. This article concentrates on the policy of the British government rather than the
wider questions of the race issue in transatlantic diplomacy, colonial policy or wartime
Britain, as discussed by Thorne, Flint and Smith.

their contact with white women and to keep them out of Britain.[2] Similar policies were adopted at the beginning of World War II. Although black pressure groups forced the Government to announce in October 1939 that British citizens 'not of pure European descent' could volunteer for the armed forces and be considered for commissions on the same basis as whites, this was only a temporary measure 'during the present emergency'.[3] And in practice the Cabinet intended that black volunteers should be mainly used in labour units in their home territories.[4] Part of the reason was logistic: the Government lacked the equipment to fit out any additional combat divisions in the foreseeable future. But the Colonial and War Offices also agreed that black West Indians 'would be of doubtful military value for combat service overseas, especially against German troops in Europe', citing the Great War as precedent and evidence. And they also quite explicitly noted that 'for obvious reasons it is not desired to encourage coloured British subjects to come to this country for direct enlistment in the Imperial forces'—whereas that was the approved method for applicants 'of pure European descent.'[5] This policy was enunciated in January 1940. When manpower needs became more acute that summer after the fall of France selective modifications were made in order to secure certain skilled workers. 600 foresters were brought from British Honduras to the Edinburgh area in late summer 1941, followed by another 400 a year later, while some 350 engineering and electrical technicians came to Merseyside between February 1941 and January 1943.[6] These schemes did not, however, represent any fundamental change in policy on non-white immigration. As one Foreign Office official recorded in January 1942, after interdepartmental consultation: 'It became evident that, during discussions on the subject of overseas manpower, the recruitment to the United Kingdom of coloured British subjects, whose remaining in the United Kingdom after the war

[2] C. L. Joseph, 'The British West Indies Regiment, 1914–1918', *Journal of Caribbean History*, 2 (1971), 94–124; Jeffrey Greenhut, 'Race, sex, and war: The impact of race and sex on morale and health services for the Indian Corps on the Western Front, 1914', *Military Affairs*, 45 (1981), 71–4.

[3] House of Commons, *Debates*, 5th series, vol. 352, columns 1083–4, 19 Oct. 1939.

[4] War Cabinet minutes, 25 Jan. 1940, Public Record Office, CAB 65/5, WM 23 (40) 3. (Crown copyright documents are quoted by permission of the Controller of H.M. Stationery Office.)

[5] Malcolm MacDonald, memo, 22 Jan. 1940, War Cabinet papers, PRO, CAB 67/4, WP(G) 4015.

[6] See Colonial Office papers, PRO, CO 876/41–43, and Anthony H. Richmond, *Colour prejudice in Britain: A study of West Indian workers in Liverpool, 1941–1951* (1954). (Place of publication is London unless otherwise stated.)

might create a social problem, was not considered desirable'. This, he said, was 'the accepted view' in Whitehall.[7]

This same desire to minimise the non-white presence in Britain led the Government to oppose the entry of black Americans. Although the USA did not enter the war until December 1941, the issue had first emerged in the middle of that year when Britain was appealing for volunteer doctors from North America to supplement army medical teams in bomb-damaged British cities. Faced with the offer of help from a negro physician in New York the War Office procrastinated until, under pressure from the Foreign Office, it agreed to accept what it termed 'one token negro doctor as evidence of co-operation', but for service in West Africa and not Britain.[8] Two weeks later, however, the War Office was able to reject the volunteer outright when it was discovered that he was over the age-limit for service in the Royal Army Medical Corps.[9] Likewise in 1942 the Government expressed discreet but firm opposition to US plans to send black troops to Britain. The British Chiefs of Staff told Washington in April that they did not favour the use of coloured troops, but, although supported by the US army command in Britain, their preferences were overruled by the US War Department, who decreed that 'in planning for shipment of troops to the British Isles, including Northern Ireland, Colored Troops may be included in reasonable proportion for any type of Service Unit'.[10] In July 1942 the issue was discussed by the War Cabinet, with Anthony Eden, the Foreign Secretary, expressing fears of trouble between GIs and British civilians, particularly 'through certain sections of our people showing more effusiveness to the coloured people than the Americans would readily understand'.[11] The problem was raised with General George C. Marshall, the US Army Chief of Staff, and Harry Hopkins, Roosevelt's confidant, who were both in London at the time, and it seems likely that Churchill personally told Hopkins

---

[7] F. E. Evans, minute, 22 Jan. 1942, PRO, Foreign Office General Political correspondence FO 371/26206, A 10036/257/45.

[8] War Office to Military Attaché, Washington, tel. 78528, 17 July 1941, PRO, War Office papers, WO 193/321.

[9] Col. S. Arnott to V. Cavendish-Bentinck, 2 Aug. 1941, PRO, FO 371/26227, A 8364/538/45.

[10] See Cabinet Office papers, PRO, CAB 79/20, COS 126 (42) 11, 21 April 1942, and CAB 80/62, COS (42) 104 (0); Chaney to War Dept., tel., 25 April 1942, in US War Dept., Operations Div., Diary, copy in Dwight D. Eisenhower Library, Abilene, Kansas, USA; Eisenhower, memo, 25 April 1942, National Archives, Washington, DC, USA, Record Group RG 165, Operations Division, OPD 291.2.

[11] E. Bridges to J. Martin, 21 July 1942, in Franklin D. Roosevelt Library, Hyde Park, New York, USA, Harry Hopkins papers, box 136.

that they did not want any more black GIs.[12] But once again the British were rebuffed. When Marshall returned to Washington he reiterated that the need in Britain for labour units, most of which were black, and the exigencies of US domestic politics necessitated maintenance of the existing policy.[13]

Marshall's last point was the crux of the issue. Ideally the US Army did not want black troops. It ensured that segregation was maintained, that blacks were used mainly as non-combatants and that few negro officers were appointed. But since 1940 President Roosevelt had been obliged to make concessions to the demand of black pressure groups, now increasingly important within the Democratic coalition, for greater participation in the country's war effort. Consequently it was agreed that the percentage of blacks in the American army would be roughly equal to the proportion of blacks in the US population as a whole, namely ten per cent, and that some black troops would be allowed to serve abroad. The first of them landed in Britain in May 1942 and by late summer about 12,000 had arrived.

What alarmed both the British and US authorities was the generally welcoming attitude of British civilians to the black troops. This is not to say that Britain was devoid of race prejudice. On the contrary. One anecdote going the rounds in London in the summer of 1942 concerned a grand English lady who decided to do her bit for the war effort by writing to the local American commander and inviting him to send half-a-dozen of his men to join her for Sunday lunch. But, she added on the invitation, 'No Jews, please'. At Sunday lunchtime there was a knock at the door. She opened it and discovered six huge black GIs standing outside. Horrified, she exclaimed that there must be some mistake. 'Oh no, ma'am', one of them replied, 'Colonel Cohen no make any mistakes.'[14] This story may be apocryphal, but racial discrimination was definitely evident in parts of Britain. In port cities, such as Cardiff, Liverpool and London, the black communities had grown steadily after World War I, when many colonial seamen who had served in the wartime Merchant Navy decided to settle in Britain. Racial clashes had occurred in 1919, notably in Liverpool, and the Depression had aggravated the high unemployment of these areas, where pioneering sociological

---

[12] Cf. Angus Malcolm, minute, 28 Dec. 1942, PRO, FO 371/30680, A 11903/990/45.

[13] Sir Ronald Campbell to FO, tel. 4086, 12 Aug. 1942, PRO, FO 954/30A, f. 151. On US policy see Ulysses Lee, *The employment of negro troops* (Washington, 1966) in the series 'US Army in World War II: Special studies'; and Morris J. MacGregor, Jr., *Integration of the Armed Forces, 1940–1965* (Washington, 1981).

[14] Cf. *New Statesman and Nation*, 26 Sept. 1942, p. 202.

studies revealed established patterns of discrimination in housing, employment and social relationships.[15]

But Britain's black community was minute at this time—probably no more than seven or eight thousand in 1939[16]—and most British people, particularly in rural areas, had never met a non-white. Moreover, the black GI was a temporary visitor. He did not pose the same 'threat' to jobs, housing and womenfolk as the black Britons were felt to do. Consequently, British people on the whole treated him well, as reports from all sources concur. Frequently the black GI's courtesy was contrasted favourably with the brashness of the whites. There was little sense of a colour bar: blacks were often invited into British homes and were popular with many British women, particularly mid-teenagers. Yet this kind of inter-racial contact, especially across the sexes, was anathema to white GIs from the South, where a clear code of 'racial etiquette' kept the races apart and the blacks 'in their place'. They vented their fury on blacks, vilified British women who associated with them, and tried to persuade hoteliers and publicans to exclude black customers. Again the reports concur that British people, though disliking black-white contact across the sexes, generally repudiated this kind of overt discrimination and often took the blacks' side in fracas with whites and even with US military police.[17]

The US army command in Britain did its best to limit these incidents. Basic policy was laid down by General Dwight D. Eisenhower, the Commander of the European Theater of Operations (ETO) from June 1942.[18] On arrival in Britain troops were to be warned against making any racial slurs. Instructions were also given about the lack of a colour bar in Britain and the need to respect this custom. But as far as possible black and white troops were kept apart, both on bases and in leave accommodation. In an attempt to eliminate contact in local towns the principle of 'rotating passes' was

[15] See James Walvin, *Black and white: The negro and English society, 1555-1945* (1973), esp. chap. 13; Roy May and Robin Cohen, 'The interaction between race and colonialism: A case study of the Liverpool race riots of 1919', *Race and Class*, 16 (1974), 111-126; K. L. Little, *Negroes in Britain: A study of racial relations in English society* (1947), based on research done in Cardiff in 1941.

[16] See Colonial Office memo, Aug. 1942, PRO, CO 876/14, f. 4. Harold A. Moody, *The Colour Bar* (1944), 8, suggests a figure of at least 10,000 for 1939, which is probably too high.

[17] E. g., James Warburg to Elmer Davis, 1 Sept. 1942, National Archives, Washington, RG 107/47, box 124, ASW 291.2; extracts from Regional Commissioners' reports, Jul.-Nov. 1942, PRO, FO 371/34123, A 866/33/45.

[18] See Eisenhower's directives of 16 July and 5 Sept. 1942, National Archives, Washington, RG 332: European Theater of Operations, US Army (ETOUSA), Adjutant General records, (AG), Classified General Correspondence (CGC) 291.2.

used, whereby blacks used the town, or selected pubs and dancehalls, on one night and whites on another. (To avoid imputations of racial discrimination the passes were ostensibly allocated by unit, but since units were racially homogeneous the result was the same.) Eisenhower also tried to restrict black troops to certain defined areas of the country, particularly around the western ports where the black British population was concentrated.

Although the British Cabinet was still unhappy about the influx of black GIs,[19] it was well pleased with Eisenhower's policy of segregation. This promised to reduce contacts between black GIs and British civilians. However, the Government was at pains to distance itself officially from the US Army's policy. The Home Office issued a circular to all Chief Constables on 4 September 1942. This stated that:

> It is not the policy of His Majesty's Government that any discrimination as regards the treatment of coloured troops should be made by the British authorities. The Secretary of State, therefore, would be glad if you would be good enough to take steps to ensure that the police do not make any approach to the proprietors of public houses, restaurants, cinemas or other places of entertainment with a view to discriminating against coloured troops.

Should the US Army wish to put certain places out of bounds to coloured troops, the circular stressed, this was their own decision and was to be implemented by them. British police 'should not make themselves in any way responsible for the enforcement of such orders'.[20]

Not everyone in Whitehall, however, was content to leave the matter in the hands of the US Army. It was agreed at a conference in the War Office on 5 August that British officers should explain the American attitude so that their own troops, especially women of the Auxiliary Territorial Service (ATS), might avoid contact with the black GIs. The War Office injunction was to use only oral instructions because of the delicacy of the subject, but two days later the senior administrative officer in Southern Command, where most of the black troops were stationed, issued his own written advice to district commanders and civilian regional commissioners. This document depicted the history of American blacks in a roseate hue, following the presentation by a US officer at the 5 August meeting. Blacks were portrayed as inherently the intellectual and moral inferiors of whites, having 'a simple mental outlook' and lacking 'the

---

[19] Cf. War Cabinet minutes, 10 and 31 Aug. 1942, PRO, CAB 65/27, WM (42) 109/6 and 119/6.
[20] Home Office circular, 4 Sept. 1942, annex to PRO, CAB 66/29, WP (42) 456.

white man's ability to think and act to a plan'. In the USA, particularly in the South, they lived their own separate lives but, according to the paper, 'they are sympathetically treated by the white man' who 'feels his moral duty to them as it were to a child'. After this disingenuous, not to say inaccurate, account of race relations in the American South, the paper suggested ways for British men and women soldiers 'to adjust their attitude so that it conforms to that of the white American citizen'. While showing sympathy for blacks, 'soldiers should not make intimate friends with them, taking them to cinemas or bars'. And 'white women should not associate with coloured men'. This meant that 'they should not walk out, dance, or drink with them'. Any attempt by 'political extremists' to stir up trouble on the race question must be ignored, and British troops should scotch all inflammatory stories and rumours of racial friction.[21]

This document was intended for the guidance of British soldiers. But some local military commanders and their civilian counterparts wanted to 'guide' civilian behaviour as well. In July the GOC of Western Command complained to the city authorities of Chester that black GI truck drivers stationed near the city had been walking around with white women. He pointed out 'that this sort of thing is not customary in America and that we do not want to infringe American customs'. (The Lord Mayor of Chester replied that Indians and West Indians could be described as coloured and asked what was to be done about them.)[22] At an inter-departmental meeting in Whitehall on 12 August it was proposed that British women might be warned off association with black GIs 'by an open statement on the danger of venereal disease'. That idea, and a related one for 'a whispering campaign on the same lines', were blocked by the Foreign Office.[23] But whispering campaigns of a less pointed character were undoubtedly fostered. On the same day, the Ministry of Information's advisory committee for the West Region, centred on Bristol, discussed with concern the association of black GIs and British girls. The suggestion of an admonitory broadcast was rejected because the problem was 'dynamite', but the BBC's regional director recorded:

> Probably the best means of approach is that individual and unofficial warnings should be spread about by members of such

[21] 'Notes on relations with coloured troops', annex to PRO, CAB 66/29, WP (42) 441.
[22] Quoted in report by Regional Information Officer, Manchester, 23 July 1942, in PRO, CAB 123/176.
[23] Minutes of BC (L) (42) Misc. 3, 1st mtg., 12 Aug. 1942, in PRO, CO 876/14.

services as the A.R.P. [Air Raid Precautions Service], W.V.S. [Womens' Voluntary Service], and Housewives Committees. This, I know, is the view of the Regional Commissioner here.[24]

This discussion presumably explains the action of the wife of the vicar of Worle in Somerset, who the *Sunday Pictorial* reported on 6 September, had proposed to local women a six-point code of behaviour. This included crossing to the other side of a street if a black soldier was coming towards her, moving immediately to another seat in a cinema if he sat next to her and leaving a shop as quickly as possible if he entered. On no account were coloured troops to be invited into the homes of white women or to have a 'relationship' with any of them.[25]

It is unlikely that the vicar's wife was acting off her own bat. One may assume that her homily was an example of the characteristic MOI policy of using the right sort of people to foster discreetly the right sort of attitudes among the general public. But, inevitably on such a contentious issue, word about the official policy leaked out in late summer. Not only did the *Sunday Pictorial* publicise the story of the vicar's wife, the *New Statesman* reported a British soldier's account of his unit's guidance about non-fraternisation with black GIs and also noted 'on fairly good authority that the ruling in one area is that if an A.T.S. girl is seen walking with a coloured soldier "she should be removed to another district for another reason" '.[26] The issue was also raised by backbench MPs in the House of Commons on 29 September. Responding, Churchill regretted the 'unfortunate question' and expressed the hope 'that without any action on my part the points of view of all concerned will be mutually understood and respected.'[27] Most significantly, the Southern Command memo fell into the hands of the Colonial Office who took the matter up with the Army. According to the Ministry of Defence, the War Office's papers on the subject have been destroyed (no doubt an unfortunate mistake!),[28] but from documents that have survived in the Colonial Office files it would seem that the War Office had previously hoped to handle the problem in its own way without official fuss. Forced out into the open, the Secretary of State for War, Sir James Grigg, apparently decided to request Cabinet sanction for the policy he and his officials had been following. By 8

[24] BBC West Regional Director, memo, 14 Aug. 1942, in BBC Written Archives, Caversham Park, Reading, R 34/912/1. Quoted by permission.

[25] *Sunday Pictorial*, 6 Sept. 1942, p. 3.

[26] *New Statesman and Nation*, 22 Aug. 1942, p. 121, and 19 Sept. 1942, p. 184.

[27] *H. C. Debs.*, 5s, 383: 670, 29 Sept. 1942.

[28] Letters to author from Mrs J. C. North, Ministry of Defence, 29 July 1983, and Dr M. J. Jubb, PRO, 7 June 1982 (on relevant FO papers also destroyed).

September a draft War Office paper for the Cabinet was circulating in Whitehall.[29]

In this paper, Grigg presented himself as 'on a razor's edge' between US racial practices and British public resentment of them. He argued that as far as possible the Government should rely on the US Army to keep white and black GIs apart, but that where its fiat did not apply, for example in British railway canteens, there should be no discrimination against black GIs. In addition Grigg wanted to give British soldiers information about 'the facts and history of the colour question' in the USA and the American army. To this end he proposed a special article in 'Current Affairs', the organ of ABCA (the Army Bureau of Current Affairs) which used weekly pamphlets as the basis for officer-led group discussion. In addition, Grigg wanted Army officers, 'without the issue of overt or written instructions', to 'interpret these facts to the personnel of the Army including the A.T.S. and so educate them to adopt towards the U.S.A. coloured troops the attitude of the U.S.A. Army authorities'.[30]

Over the next month the question was debated intensively around Whitehall. Papers were submitted by the Home and Colonial Offices, the Ministry of Information, the Lord Chancellor and the Lord Privy Seal. But the final discussion in Cabinet proved something of an anti-climax. Not only were ministers in a rush to get away for lunch, but Churchill had just returned from Scotland and had not read the relevant papers. While he did so the debate ebbed and flowed around him in turbulent fashion, which, as so often, is artfully concealed in the orderly minutes distilled by the Cabinet Secretary.[31] (One is reminded of the anonymous verse by one harried civil servant:[32]

> And so while the great ones depart to their dinner
> The secretary stays, growing thinner and thinner,
> Racking his brains to record and report
> What he thinks that they think that they ought to have thought.)

The main opposition to the War Office paper had come, not surprisingly, from the Colonial Office. John Keith, head of the CO's Student Department, called the Southern Command memo 'puerile and prejudiced stuff' and condemned Grigg's paper as 'full of special

[29] This account reconstructed from the draft WO paper in PRO, CO 876/14, esp. para. 12.

[30] PRO, CAB 66/29, WP (42) 441.

[31] PRO, CAB 65/28, WM 140 (42) 4, 13 Oct. 1942; cf. *The Diaries of Sir Alexander Cadogan, 1938-1945*, ed. David Dilks (1971), 483.

[32] Sir Arthur Bryant, *The Turn of the Tide, 1939-1943* (1957), 320.

pleading'.[33] His superiors were less incensed, but all agreed that the interests of black British subjects in Britain had to be safeguarded and that an overt colour bar against black GIs would arouse deep resentment at home and in the colonies. The Colonial Secretary, Viscount Cranborne, therefore put up a Cabinet paper arguing that while information should be provided to British troops about the US race problem, they should be left to draw their own conclusions about how to behave towards black GIs. Equally, the different British attitude to race relations should be explained to the Americans and the US Army must be asked to respect the rights of black Britons.[34] Cranborne was supported by the Lord Chancellor, Viscount Simon. Although usually stigmatised as an amoral appeaser, Simon was a veteran Liberal with a long record as an advocate of civil liberties, who had resigned from the Asquith Cabinet in 1916 over conscription. Unlike some of his colleagues, he knew the USA, made no secret of his distaste for the 'Jim Crow' South, and argued that Grigg's proposals could be the thin end of the wedge towards a general colour bar.[35] Cranborne raised these concerns about black British subjects in the Cabinet meeting on 13 October. He instanced one of his own black officials who had been recently barred from his habitual restaurant at the instigation of the US officers who now frequented it. The Prime Minister, however, was unsympathetic. 'That's all right', he said. 'If he takes a banjo with him they'll think he's one of the band.'[36]

As Churchill's flippancy suggests, Cranborne's concerns were not taken all that seriously by the War Cabinet. In fact, on the major issues Grigg got his way. Ministers accepted that the US Army's attitude 'was a factor of great importance' when determining British policy towards black GIs, and, in the words of the Cabinet minutes, 'it was generally agreed that it was desirable that the people of this country should avoid becoming too friendly with coloured American troops'. On specifics, there was no objection, even from the Colonial Office, to the double-standard policy of covertly supporting US Army segregation as long as the British authorities were not involved in enforcing it, and the War Cabinet also agreed that information on US race policies should be provided to British troops through

---

[33] Minute, 12 Sept. 1942, PRO, CO 876/14.

[34] Memo of 2 Oct. 1942, PRO, CAB 66/29, WP (42) 442.

[35] Memo of 9 Oct. 1942, ibid., WP (42) 455. Back in 1934 Simon's wife had greatly angered the US Ambassador by interrogating him at an official luncheon as to 'when you southern people are going to stop your hideous, horrible lynching of negroes.' Robert W. Bingham, diary, 30 Oct. 1934, Library of Congress, Washington, DC, U.S.A.

[36] Cadogan, *Diaries*, 483.

ABCA. On Cranborne's request that the flow of information should be two-way, the Cabinet minutes did note the feeling that 'it was equally important that the Americans should recognise that we had a different problem as regards our coloured people and that a modus vivendi between the two points of view should be found'.[37] But no specific action on this point was recommended in the Cabinet conclusions, and this fact was used by the War Office to justify their failure to make any approach to Eisenhower and his staff. Keith's consequent remonstrances within the Colonial Office were not supported by his superiors who felt that any pressure to have the British attitude explained to GIs would get them 'into very deep water indeed'.[38]

The main modification to Grigg's proposals was on the question of whether troops should not merely be informed but 'educated' into adopting US Army attitudes to black troops. Some ministers outside the War Office supported this view. Richard Law, son of the former Conservative prime minister and Parliamentary Under Secretary at the Foreign Office, approved of the WO paper and the Southern Command memo, arguing that 'the really important thing is that we should not have avoidable friction between the two armies, and that the American troops should not go back to their homes with the view that we are a decadent and unspeakable race'. But Anthony Eden, the Foreign Secretary, thought that Grigg's proposal went 'much too far'[39] and most of his Cabinet colleagues agreed that it should be toned down. Many liked the amendments proposed by Sir Stafford Cripps and he was invited, in consultation with Grigg and Herbert Morrison, the Home Secretary, to prepare a revised memo to guide senior officers. This was approved by the Cabinet on 20 October.[40] Presentation of the US racial situation was somewhat more complex than in the original Southern Command version, and the patronising appraisal of negro character was omitted. But the account of race relations in the South was still partial and disingenuous—on Churchill's instructions the revised document had been shown by Cripps to Eisenhower before the Cabinet discussed it[41]—and although British troops were to be told that there was no reason for them to 'adopt the American attitude ... they should respect it and avoid making it a subject for argument and dispute'. The drift of the specific advice was to avoid contact with black GIs

[37] PRO, WM 140 (42) 4.
[38] See Keith, min., 24 Oct. 1942, min. by Sir Arthur Dawe (quotation) and letter from Col. Rolleston, 31 Oct. 1942, PRO, CO 876/14.
[39] Law, min., 5 Oct. 1942, Eden, notes, PRO, FO 371/30680, A 9731/990/45.
[40] PRO, CAB 65/28, WM 143 (42) 3, and CAB 66/30, WP (42) 473.
[41] Cf. Prime Minister's papers, PRO, PREM 4, 26/9, f. 864.

as far as possible, whether in a bar or particularly in the company of white women, because this would lead to 'controversy and ill-feeling'.

The guidance memo and the related ABCA article were issued in early December 1942, and their contents widely but cautiously disseminated among troops. That caution is one reason for the lack of public fuss on the matter during the winter of 1942–3. Another is the influence probably exerted on the press. To forestall embarrassing publicity the memo had been framed in deliberately blander terms than either the Southern Command's original or Cripps' first revision. And the Cabinet agreed that, in the best British lobby tradition of press management, the Minister of Information should give copies of the memo and the ABCA article 'to such editors as he thought appropriate, for their confidential information'. Probably they were advised, as Cripps suggested, that they should not 'feature' the ABCA article or make any reference to the guidance memo.[42] I have not been able to discover direct evidence of these briefings—the War Office files have been destroyed and in any case the whole emphasis of Government policy was now on the avoidance of written instructions—but such cosy briefings, encouraging a sense of special privilege and appealing to editors' public spiritedness, were characteristic MOI techniques for promoting press self-censorship. An extant example of what was done is the record of a briefing of editors in Belfast in August 1942. After a US officer had explained American racial attitudes, the editors were asked to help in 'playing down' racial incidents on the grounds that publicity might be exploited by enemy propaganda. The editors offered assurances that they would handle such stories 'with great discretion' and do 'everything possible to encourage a better understanding' between GIs, British troops and civilians.[43]

A further reason for the lack of fuss in 1942–3 was the tailing-off of the US influx into Britain. Plans for an invasion of the continent in 1943 or even late 1942 were abandoned in favour of the Anglo-American assault on North Africa. This began a prolonged diversion of US manpower into the Mediterranean, while, at the same time, the Pacific theatre received far more troops and supplies in 1942–3 than envisaged in original Allied plans. The casualty in all this was

---

[42] PRO, WM 143 (42) 3, and Cripps, memo, WP (42) 473. My interpretation differs somewhat from that of Ian McLaine, *Ministry of Morale: Home front morale and the Ministry of Information in World War II* (1979), 271–3, who suggests that little was done to guide opinion.

[43] C. L. Frankland, memo, 21 Aug. 1942, in Public Record Office, Belfast, Northern Ireland, Cabinet Secretariat files, CAB 9CD/225/19. (Quoted by permission of the Deputy Keeper.)

operation BOLERO—the projected build-up in Britain.[44] By early 1943 there were little more than 100,000 US troops in Britain, only 7,000 of whom were black.[45] Not until mid-1943, with the go-ahead for operation OVERLORD in spring 1944, did the build-up resume.

This new wave of GIs gave rise to further racial friction, as white and black troops unfamiliar with the situation in Britain came into contact with each other and with a larger number of British civilians. On the whole the British and US army authorities were happy with their mutual collaboration and with the guidance given to British troops. But in the autumn of 1943 renewed thought was given to an issue skirted the previous year, namely what if any 'advice' should be offered to British civilians. The Commander of the Southern Base Section of ETO was concerned at the number of incidents in which British civilians took the side of black GIs abused by whites, and his British counterpart, the GOC Southern Command, suggested to the War Office in September that guidance should be given to civilians along the lines of the army memo of the previous year. A possible method was through the informal network of influence available to the MOI through the civil defence services, the WVS and other voluntary organisations who met regularly with MOI staff. The whole idea was rejected as impractical by the Home Office's Southern Regional Commissioner, who pointed out that most of the incidents stemmed fundamentally not from British civilians' ignorance about the American colour problem but from resentment at 'what they regard as unfair and bullying treatment'.[46] But Churchill's roving eye had, temporarily, lighted on the papers, directed there in part by his cousin, the Duke of Marlborough, who was a liaison officer with ETO. And Sir James Grigg in the War Office took advantage of the prime minister's attention to argue the case for wider civilian education: 'I expect that the British soldier [abroad] who fears for the safety or faithfulness of his women-folk at home would not feel so keenly as the B.B.C. and the public at home appear to do in favour of a policy of no colour bar and complete

[44] Because of the diminishing number of incidents and the desire to avoid Anglo-American controversy at the time of the North African invasion, by late Oct. 1942 Grigg wanted to postpone issuing the guidance memo until further trouble occurred. It would seem that he was trying to return to the covert and more extreme guidance policy that the WO had been following until drawn out into the open by the Colonial Office. But the Cabinet Office was aware of Grigg's foot-dragging, and Cripps successfully argued that the papers should be issued to avert renewed incidents rather than in the wake of them. (See papers in PRO, CAB 120/727 and CAB 127/62.)

[45] See Roland G. Ruppenthal, *Logistical support of the armies*, vol. I (Washington, 1953), 100, 129; Lee, *Negro troops*, 433; statistical summaries in National Archives, Washington, RG 332: ETOUSA, Admin. 424.

[46] Sir Harry Haig, memo, 6 Sept. 1943, PRO, FO 371/34126, A 10199/33/45.

equality of treatment of negro troops'. And he warned that 'there is a danger that grave mischief will be done to Anglo-American relations unless we realise that before the problem can be solved we may have to face the question of changing our attitude to the colour question'.[47]

Grigg's concern for good relations with the USA was echoed in the Foreign Office. In fact the FO's attitude to this whole question is worthy of particular comment. In July 1941, when the War Office attempted to bar the volunteer black doctor from New York, the FO wished 'a fuss to be made', telling the War Office: 'on political grounds we urge that this negro doctor should be accepted as the effect of insisting on a colour bar in this matter might well have serious repercussions in the United States at the moment'.[48] The FO presumably had in mind the 'March on Washington' threatened by American black leaders and only recently headed off when Roosevelt ordered an end to discrimination among defence contractors. With this illustration of black muscle, at a time when the USA was not in the war and much of the pro-allied pressure came from American liberals, the FO evidently felt it unwise to affront black aspirations. By 1942-3, however, the balance of power in Washington had shifted. Conservative Democrats from the South, whose underlying sympathy for Britain had previously been held in check by antagonism to Roosevelt's New Deal, now rallied around the President's war policies and constituted the most reliable supporters of Britain in Congress. Nevile Butler, head of the FO's North American Department from late summer 1941, was a cautious career diplomat whose previous post had been at the Washington Embassy. He was therefore well aware of the importance of the Southern Democrats and also of their intense racism. Butler feared an anti-British backlash in Southern states if Britain was accused of 'undue kindness to the negroes' or of arousing black expectations which then led to trouble in post-war America, and he argued that there were consequently 'strong incentives for trying to do something' to educate British civilians 'and for letting the Americans know we have tried to do something, even if our action is ineffective'.[49] For the FO, the primary concern was the maintenance of Anglo-American amity and its continuance in to the post-war world. What Butler called 'our Southern friends'[50] would have far more say about

[47] Grigg to Churchill, 2 Dec. 1943, PRO, PREM 4, 26/9, ff. 804-10.

[48] Quotations from Evans, min., 21 July 1941, and Cavendish-Bentinck to Brigadier P. G. Whitefoorde, 11 July 1941, PRO, FO 371/26227, A 8364/538/45.

[49] Quotations from Butler, min., 12 Feb. 1944, PRO, FO 371/38623, f. 120 ('kindness'), and mins. of 24 Nov. 1943, FO 371/34126,, ff. 231, 236. Butler's juniors in the North American Dept. disagreed with him about 'educating' civilians.

[50] Butler to Michael Wright, 14 Mar. 1944, PRO, FO 371/38609, AN 587/159/45.

that than American blacks, and the FO determined its policy on race relations accordingly.

In the event nothing resulted officially from this debate about guidance for British civilians. Churchill's interest reverted to grand strategy—as Lord Halifax once observed, the Prime Minister was generally 'pretty bored with anything except the actual war'.[51] Furthermore, the record of black GIs began to improve perceptibly in late 1943, as the US Army commanders in Britain, shaken by several serious incidents that summer, took positive measures to ameliorate the blacks' lot through better recreational facilities and proper health education. Recognising that incompetent, racist white officers were often at the root of the problem, ETO and the Eighth Air Force also selected many new unit commanders who combined strict discipline with genuine sympathy for their men. Following these and other reforms (such as the increasing use of joint black–white military police patrols) there was a distinct improvement in black performance, conduct and morale, and Churchill and the War Office decided to drop the idea of further guidance for British civilians.

It would be wrong, however, to treat the decisions taken or not taken in Whitehall as definitive guides to what British officials actually did. For it is clear that local army and police authorities frequently exceeded their written instructions. For instance, there is considerable evidence to suggest that, as the *New Statesman* reported in August 1942, ATS women soldiers continued to be disciplined for associating with black GIs. The guidance memo approved by the Cabinet that October simply advised that 'for a white woman to go about in the company of a negro American is likely to lead to controversy and ill-feeling'. But the original Southern Command memo had firmly instructed soldiers that 'white women should not associate with coloured men',[52] and it would seem that this bore closer relationship to the line actually adopted. For local police forces seem to have routinely reported women soldiers found in the company of black GIs, and in January 1944 William Leach, the Labour MP for Bradford Central, asked Grigg in the House of Commons 'who is responsible for a recent issue of an order to the A.T.S. forbidding its members to speak with coloured American soldiers except in the presence of a white'. When Grigg professed no knowledge of such an order, Leach responded with the inevitable supplementary: 'If I send the right hon. gentleman a copy of this order, will he go further into the matter?' A furious Grigg replied:

[51] Halifax to Eden, 5 Jan. 1942, Churchill College, Cambridge, Hickleton papers, A4.410.4.15.
[52] PRO, CAB 66/29, WP (42) 441, annex.

'Yes, and I shall be very grateful if the hon. Member will tell me how he got hold of it too'. Nowhere in the exchange or in the Foreign and War Office minutes on the question was there any denial that such an order had been issued.[53]

It is also clear that British officials were more involved in enforcing segregation than Government policy statements permitted. In the summer of 1942, for instance, the US Army lacked sufficient hospital space of its own and would have had to use British facilities in the event of an early invasion of the continent. Officials of the BOLERO committee handling US requirements agreed in principle that, although black GIs should be transferred as quickly as possible to American army hospitals, if they had to be treated in British hospitals 'separate lavatory accommodation should be provided for them, even though it might not be possible to provide treatment in separate wards'.[54] This policy never had to be implemented and it was enunciated before the War Cabinet's discussions in autumn 1942. But in June 1943, when the BOLERO committee agreed to billet GIs in British homes to ease the accommodation shortage, it was 'definitely agreed with the U.S. authorities that no coloured troops should be billeted'.[55] Likewise, black troops were excluded from the exchanges between British and US units which were arranged on a large scale in the winter of 1943-4.[56] And there is also evidence that the British police infringed Home Office instructions that they should in no way help to enforce US segregation policy. For instance, the Dorothy Dance Hall in Cambridge was out of bounds to black troops in 1943-4. The proprietor's stated reason was that his floor would not stand the strain of jitterbugging, but in fact he was acting on verbal advice from the Chief Constable of Cambridge who had apparently reached an informal understanding with the local US Provost Marshal about how to divide the city's recreational facilities between black and white GIs.[57]

Local police and magistrates in some areas also found legal pretext to come down very hard on British civilian women found in the company of black GIs. In June 1943 the Derbyshire county police reported: 'The association of U.S.A. coloured troops with British

[53] H. C. Debs, 5s, 397: 3-4, 15 Feb. 1944; PRO, FO 371/38623, AN 738/275/45.

[54] PRO, CAB 81/48, BC(L) 15 (42) 6, 29 July 1942.

[55] QMC 10 (43) 6, 11 June 1943, copy in PRO, FO 371/34117, A 5706/32/45.

[56] AAR/M 2 (44) 10, 16 Feb. 1944, PRO, WO 163/222. See also David Reynolds, 'GI and Tommy in Wartime Britain: The Army "Inter-Attachment" Scheme of 1943-1944', Journal of Strategic Studies, 7 (1984), 413.

[57] National Archives, Washington, RG 332, ETOUSA, AG, CGC, 291.2, 'Report of Investigation', esp. exhibit G; Hq ETO to CG, ETO, 27 Feb. 1944, copy in Library of Congress, Washington, National Association for the Advancement of Colored People papers, II/A, box 587: 'White's European tour'.

women is still continuing at Hilton. Prosecutions under the Defence (General) Regulations are pending in this connection, with a view to stopping this practice'. The Foreign Office and Ministry of Home Security privately admitted that they could not understand how the wartime Defence Regulations could be invoked in this way. Nevertheless the Derbyshire police continued to do so. The following month they were prosecuting racially mixed couples on account of the damage they caused to growing crops. And in Melton Mowbray in Leicestershire five young women were imprisoned in June for one month 'for trespassing on premises in the occupation of coloured troops'. The police report noted: 'There is no doubt that the young women were on these premises for an immoral purpose, undoubtedly attracted by the amount of money these troops can either give them or spend on them'.[58] The following January, in the city of Leicester two young women of 20 and 22, cotton hands from Preston, were found sleeping in a hut on a US Army camp where black GIs were stationed. According to the police report:

> They alleged that they had been taken there by soldiers. They were charged under Regulations 15 (1) and 104A of the Defence (General) Regulations, 1939, with trespassing on a Military Camp, the said premises then being used in H.M. Service. They were sentenced to 3 months Hard Labour.[59]

It is therefore apparent, despite the destruction of much of the official archival evidence, that the British authorities during World War II did try to regulate the behaviour not merely of soldiers but also civilians towards the black GIs.[60] In part, the Cabinet determined policy, but frequently Whitehall departments and local officials went farther than it decreed, and, as Grigg's conduct in 1942 suggests, Cabinet 'decisions' could be used to throw a seemly but loose veil of authority over departmental actions. Thus efforts to influence civilian mores continued, even though the Cabinet had

---

[58] All quotations from reports in PRO, FO 371/34126, A 6556/33/45.

[59] Police report, Leicester city, 15 Jan. 1944, PRO, FO 371/38624, AN 2089/275/45. ' "Hard labour" at this time meant that the prisoner performed whatever labour he or she was medically fit to do, and also went without a mattress during the first fourteen days of the sentence'. Edward Smithies, *Crime in wartime: A social history of crime in World War II* (1982), 7.

[60] It is interesting to note that when US units were moved to Britain again in large numbers during the Korean War, the Foreign Office once more did its best to discourage the sending of black troops. Among the reasons given were the likelihood of 'numerous black babies', the danger that discrimination by white GIs against blacks would arouse anti-American feeling among the British public, and the opportunities thereby provided for communist propaganda. PRO, FO 371/90966, esp. AU 1194/20, J. N. O. Curle, min., 7 Nov. 1951.

officially declined to 'educate' public opinion, as shown by the evidence of 'whispering campaigns' in 1942 and the activities of Derbyshire and Leicester police in 1943–4. Likewise, within the British army, where a general non-fraternisation policy was approved by the Cabinet, far more rigid controls were imposed by the Army on the conduct of women soldiers. On occasions when infractions of the Cabinet guidelines were discovered, Whitehall departments were frequently ready to turn a blind eye, assisted by the lack of media fuss thanks to effective government management of the press.

Official British policy towards the black American troops was determined by three principal considerations. First, and not always consciously recognised, were certain basic assumptions about nonwhites. The British Government wanted neither black colonials nor black Americans in Britain. Their own manpower policies could control the influx of British colonial subjects, but, unable to dissuade the Roosevelt Administration from sending black GIs, the Government was happy to connive at the US Army's policy of de facto segregation in order to minimise black–white contacts. Unlike the Americans, the British did not deny privately that this was racial discrimination. Their particular legal fiction was to claim that segregation was purely an American matter, though in fact they approved of it and local British officials often helped covertly to enforce it. Underpinning British policy was a set of racial stereotypes, formed in the late nineteenth century as the development of anthropology, comparative anatomy and other fields of post-Darwinian scholarship fostered pseudo-scientific justifications for the belief that there were definable 'races' with fixed, inherited differences of moral and intellectual capacity.[61] In particular, the assumption of aggressive black sexuality was deeply ingrained. Fears about this lay at the root of official efforts to keep black GIs away from British civilians, efforts which far outstripped their concern for the consequences of white GI indiscretions and which reflected an abhorrence of interracial sexual contact. This was frankly admitted, for example in the ABCA memo of December 1942 where soldiers were told that 'in our present society such unions are not desirable, since the children resulting from them are neither one thing nor the other and are thus badly handicapped in the struggle for life'.[62] In fact the number of illegitimate children fathered by black GIs proved to be considerably less than the authorities feared or sensationalist press reports of 10,000–20,000 suggested. Authoritative estimates placed the total at 1,200 to 1,700, a proportion comparable with what seem to be

---

[61] Cf. Douglas A. Lorimer, *Colour, class and the Victorians: English attitudes to the negro in the mid-nineteenth century* (Leicester, 1978).

[62] *Current Affairs*, 32 (5 Dec. 1942), 11.

reliable figures of 22,000 children born out of wedlock to white GIs in Britain.[63]

In addition to a basic prejudice against non-whites, the British Government was motivated by a concern for public order. Racial friction was almost inevitable when white and black GIs were transported to a freer social milieu, and, in a compact island with British women the (often eager) object of competition, the local populace was naturally drawn in. Even General Benjamin O. Davis, Roosevelt's token black general who took a keen interest in the situation in Britain, did not seriously contest the need to keep black and white GIs apart as much as possible.[64] Nor did the Colonial Office, despite its concern for the consequences of segregation on British and colonial race relations. It should also be noted that much of the debate took place in a fraught atmosphere. This was in part due to the intense emotions raised by white–black contact: many reports of black GIs' sexual exploits were little more than gossip and evaporated under investigation. One US diplomat in London in late summer 1942 found the city 'filled with stories of the black and white problem, many of which are exaggerated'.[65] What added to the frenzy in 1942 was the erroneous British conviction that by April 1943 100,000 black GIs would be in Britain. This figure, which recurred in official discussions, was an extrapolation from the BOLERO plan, with its target of one million GIs in Britain by April 1943, and from the US Government's principle of ten per cent black representation. The fear that a totally unprepared country would have to deal in six months with that size of racial minority helps to account for something of the panicky atmosphere of autumn 1942. In fact, thanks to the invasion of North Africa, the dreaded 100,000 mark was not reached until a year later, in the spring of 1944, by which time official policies had been developed and the US Army in Britain had begun to reform itself, thereby helping ensure that the anticipated disasters did not happen.

The third main consideration defining British official attitudes was the importance of good relations with the USA. It was vital in

---

[63] George Padmore to Walter White, 29 April 1947 and enclosed memo of 24 April, in NAACP papers, II/A, box 631: 'US Army–brown babies'; *Ebony*, 4 (Mar. 1949), p. 22; *Life*, 23 Aug. 1948, p. 41 (22,000). To give some sense of proportion: about three million US servicemen passed through Britain in the years 1942–5 (cf. TSFET, Transportation Corps, Progress report, 30 Sept. 1945, Table I, in RG 332, ETOUSA, Admin. 452.)

[64] E.g. Davis, memo, 24 Dec. 1942, National Archives, Washington, RG 107/47, box 123, ASW 291.2.

[65] William Phillips, diary, vol. 28, 28 Aug. and 18 Sept. 1942 (quotation), Houghton Library, Harvard University, Cambridge, Mass, U.S.A. Cf. *The War Diaries of Oliver Harvey*, ed. John Harvey (1978), 21 July 1942, p. 141.

the short term to maintain harmony between the British and US armies who would have to fight together in the Mediterranean and continental Europe. But, as we have seen, the Foreign Office, and the British Government as a whole, also considered it essential that the wartime alliance be perpetuated into the post-war world as one of the foundations of British foreign policy. Churchill called it 'my deepest conviction that unless Britain and the United States are joined in a special relationship ... another destructive war will come to pass.'[66] Moreover, British leaders did not take that post-war relationship for granted—rightly, as events later proved—and there were protracted official debates about the possibility of renewed US isolationism once the war was over. Convinced that 'public opinion' largely determined US foreign policy, the British Government spent a huge amount of time, money and effort in welcoming and entertaining the GIs—far more than they did on less important allies such as the very numerous Canadian troops—and it was hoped that this hospitality would pay dividends when the GIs returned home. Likewise it was important to conciliate the power brokers in Congress, notably the Southern Democrats who would help decide whether the alliance would persist and whether Britain would receive essential financial aid after the war. In both cases the British Government deemed it vital not to offend American racial sensitivities. By comparison, solicitude for colonial feelings or the civil rights of black Britons was far less salient. The Colonial Office did articulate these concerns, but its achievements were limited to toning down the official statements of guidance for troops and ensuring that British policy operated more circumspectly than might otherwise have been the case.[67]

Racial prejudice, a panicky concern for public order, and a determination not to upset the USA—these were the underlying reasons for British policy, both as stated and as implemented. What is striking throughout the debate is the lack of reference to any fundamental moral issues, or the dismissal of these as tangential.[68] In part that is because the treatment of the black GIs was an American matter. But the Government could have refused to co-operate with

---

[66] Churchill to Law, 16 Feb. 1944, PRO, PREM 4, 27/10, f. 1261.

[67] Throughout the war, Colonial Office staff continued to protest against what they called the 'blimpish' attitude of other departments on race questions, especially that of the War Office. E.g., A. H. Poynton, min., 17 Mar. 1944, PRO, CO 537/1223.

[68] Cf. this comment by a junior FO official on 'educating' civilians to shun black GIs: 'Apart altogether from the ethical aspect, even to attempt to proceed as the Americans suggested would obviously be political dynamite for ourselves in most parts of the Colonial Empire.' J. Donnelly, min., 16 Nov. 1943, PRO, FO 371/34126, A 10199/33/45.

segregation, or requested, as the Colonial Office wished, that British views of race relations be explained more directly to the GIs. It chose not to do so, for reasons that I have just tried to elucidate. This was not the only occasion in World War II on which the Churchill government ignored what we would now consider fundamental moral principles. Two others—of a different order of magnitude—are the repressive restriction of Jewish immigration into Palestine, despite mounting evidence of the Holocaust, and the repatriation to the Soviet Union against their will of ethnic Russians such as the Cossacks.[69] In their consequences these two latter cases were obviously far more appalling than the treatment of black GIs, but there are underlying similarities. Bureaucratic insulation was one common factor. Cocooned in Whitehall, it was all too easy to reduce the human realities to numbers and letters on a page. A sense of racial superiority also played its part. Blacks, Cossacks and Jews were not regarded as on a par with Western European whites. And diplomatic exigencies were often decisive. Keeping in with America, Russia or the Arab oil states was seen as essential for winning a victory and securing a peace that would benefit *all* peoples in their search for justice. For harassed British officials, faced with a multitude of simultaneous problems at a time of declining national power and influence, victory was the ultimate morality.[70]

[69] Cf. Bernard Wasserstein, *Britain and the Jews of Europe, 1939-1945* (Oxford, 1979); Nicholas Bethell, *The Last Secret* (1974); J. E. Hare and Carey B. Joynt, *Ethics and International Affairs* (1982), 80-87.

[70] Research for this article was generously supported by the American Council of Learned Societies, the British Association for American Studies, the British Academy, the Mellon fund, the Master and Fellows of Gonville and Caius College, Cambridge, and the US Army Military History Institute. The author is also grateful to Professor J. E. Flint (Dalhousie University) and Dr J. A. Thompson (Cambridge University) for helpful comments on a draft version.

THE PROBLEM OF 'ATHEISM' IN EARLY MODERN ENGLAND

By Michael Hunter, M.A., D.Phil., F.S.A.

READ 12 OCTOBER 1984

TO speak of 'atheism' in the context of early modern England immediately invites confusion, and it is for this reason that I shall place the word in inverted commas throughout this paper.[1] On the one hand, I intend to deal with what a twentieth-century reader might expect 'atheism' to imply, namely overt hostility to religion. On the other, I want to consider at some length the profuse writings on 'atheism' that survive from the period: in these, as we shall see, the word if often used to describe a much broader range of phenomena, in a manner typical of a genre which often appears frustratingly heightened and rhetorical. Some might argue that this juxtaposition displays—and will encourage—muddled thought. But, on the contrary, I think that it is precisely from such a combination that we stand to learn most. Not only are we likely to discover how contemporaries experienced and responded to the threat of irreligion in the society of their day. In addition, by re-examining the relationship between the real and the exaggerated in their perceptions of such heterodoxy, we may be able to draw broader conclusions about early modern thought.

I intend to limit myself to the period before the Civil War, largely for the sake of clarity: an attempt to generalise about the whole period from the 1580s to the 1690s, say, would create more problems than it would solve. Much of what I shall be saying is, however, equally applicable to the late seventeenth century,[2] while there is arguably also something to be learnt about how we should interpret the contemporary views of Interregnum radicalism that have come down to posterity.[3]

---

[1] For comments on an earlier draft of this paper I am indebted to various seminar audiences and to Stuart Clark, Patrick Collinson, Margaret Spufford and Keith Thomas.

[2] See Michael Hunter, 'Science and Heterodoxy: An Early Modern Problem Reconsidered', in *Reappraisals of the Scientific Revolution*, eds. D. C. Lindberg and R. S. Westman (forthcoming).

[3] For example, the characterisation of 'The Ranters' in Ephraim Pagitt, *Heresiography* (5th edn, 1654), 143-4, has many echoes of the stock figure of the 'atheist' outlined in this paper, and Pagitt's book shares other features with the anti-atheist literature.

At the outset, I should define what it is that I wish to consider in the context of contemporary perceptions of it, and this is irreligion in the sense of a more or less extreme attack on orthodox Christianity from a cynical or Deistic viewpoint. This cynical, iconoclastic attitude towards religion represents a genuine historical phenomenon which was consistently described at the time as 'atheism'. Moreover it can be distinguished from sectarian heresy—as it was, for instance, by Francis Bacon, who devoted separate essays to 'Atheisme' and 'Superstition'[4]—although some views might be shared by heretics and infidels, and despite the fact that there was a suspicion at the time that sectarianism could encourage outright disbelief.[5]

Undoubtedly the best-known case of such heterodoxy in England in the period we are considering is that of Christopher Marlowe, whose fertile speculations were retailed in depositions by Thomas Kyd and Richard Baines, besides being reported by godly authors like Thomas Beard and William Vaughan.[6] The context of the official investigation of Marlowe seems to have been a broader heresy hunt which took place in 1593, since the depositions concerning him are preserved among the papers of Sir John Puckering, Lord Keeper of the Great Seal, alongside examinations of sectaries and recusants carried out at the same time, a juxtaposition not hitherto noted.[7] In the same context—and therefore probably inspired by the same concern—survives a record of the only known official enquiry into 'Atheisme; or Apostacye' in the period, the special commission held at Cerne Abbas in Dorset in 1594 to investigate the supposed heterodoxy of Sir Walter Ralegh and his circle: this brought to light

[4] Bacon's Essays, ed. W. A. Wright (3rd edn., Cambridge and London, 1865), 64–70.

[5] For shared opinions, see Thomas Rogers, The Catholic Doctrine of the Church of England, ed. J. J. S. Perowne (Parker Society, Cambridge, 1854), 78, 147–8, 246. On heresy as a route to 'atheism', e.g. Thomas Heywood, A True Discourse of the Two Infamous Upstart Prophets (1636), 7.

[6] Thomas Beard, The Theatre of Gods Iudgements (1597), 147–8; William Vaughan, The Golden-groue, moralized in three books (1600), sigs. C4v–5. The relevant papers from British Library, Harleian MSS 6848, 6849 and 6853, are printed in F. C. Danchin, 'Etudes Critiques sur Christopher Marlowe', Revue Germanique, 9 (1913), 566–87 (with commentary in ibid., 10 (1914), 52–68), and C. F. Tucker Brooke, The Life of Christopher Marlowe and the Tragedy of Dido Queen of Carthage (1930) (each has some material not included by the other). On the context of the accusations, see, in addition to these works, John Bakeless, The Tragicall History of Christopher Marlowe (2 vols., Harvard, 1942), chap. 5, and P. H. Kocher, Christopher Marlowe (Chapel Hill, 1946), chaps. 2–3.

[7] This juxtaposition is made particularly plain by the transcripts and abstracts of the material by the antiquary Thomas Baker, from whom Harley acquired the documents, in British Library, Harleian MS 7042, ff. 193–236. For the material relating to the sectaries, see The Writings of John Greenwood and Henry Barrow, 1591–3, ed. L. H. Carlson (Elizabethan Nonconformist Texts, vi, 1970).

various more or less extreme irreligious utterances which would evidently normally have gone unrecorded.[8]

Apart from this, we know of isolated cases of anti-religious talk, as with a man who said to Richard Bancroft, then Bishop of London, at the London sessions in 1599: 'My Lord, if any heere can proove there is a God, I will beleeue it', or one John Baldwin, a witness in a 1595 Star Chamber case, 'who questioned whether there were a god; if there were, howe he showld be knowne; if by his worde, who wrote the same; if the prophetes & the Apostles, they were but men, *et humanum est errare*; & such like most damnable doubtes, & not suffered to be reade in the hearinge of this Courte'.[9] A scattering of cases of more or less extreme utterances of a clearly sceptical rather than sectarian variety have also come to light in local ecclesiastical records.[10]

But, even allowing for the disappearance of relevant records that would have dealt with such matters, such as those of the High Commission based in London, not many instances of this kind ever seem to have come before the courts. Moreover, aside from the exceptional episode in 1593 when irreligion became peripherally involved in the government's general clamp-down on religious extremism, it is also telling how often cases came to light by accident, arising only in connection with assessing the character of witnesses or of defendants who were primarily in trouble on other charges. And it goes almost without saying that nearly all the accusations were based on hearsay evidence: only in the case of Marlowe was it claimed that he wrote an irreligious treatise, and the uniqueness of this is plain from the almost incredulous tone of Thomas Beard's report of the fact.[11]

What makes this the more surprising is the unanimity of contemporary commentators on the seriousness of the threat that 'atheism' presented, and the need for rigour in dealing with this 'sinne of all sinnes'[12]. As will become apparent from my citations in the course of this paper, this was a topic in which there was considerable

---

[8] BL, Harl. MS 6849, ff. 183–90, printed in Danchin, 'Etudes Critiques', 578–87, and *Willobie His Avisa*, ed. G. B. Harrison (1926), 255–71. See also E. A. Strathmann, *Sir Walter Ralegh: A Study in Elizabethan Skepticism* (New York, 1951), 46–52, and Pierre Lefranc, *Sir Walter Ralegh, Ecrivain* (Paris, 1968), 379–93 (who stresses the local context of the enquiry).

[9] *The Triall of Maist. Dorrell* (1599), 88; John Hawarde, *Les Reportes del Cases in Camera Stellata, 1593–1609*, ed. W. P. Baildon (1894), 17.

[10] A selection of such cases will be noted in the course of this paper. See also Keith Thomas, *Religion and the Decline of Magic* (1971), 168–72.

[11] Beard, *Theatre*, 148. For the hypothesis that the Baines note is based on a written text by Marlowe, see Kocher, *Marlowe*, chap. 3.

[12] Adam Hill, *The Crie of England* (1595), 32.

consensus among figures covering a spectrum of affiliations and status: churchmen who wrote on the subject ranged from Richard Hooker and Joseph Hall through Thomas Fuller to 'puritans' like Richard Greenham, William Perkins and Thomas Adams, while lay authors included both the godly country gentleman, Sir George More of Loseley, and the incendiary *littérateur*, Thomas Nashe. Fuller's paraphrase of Greenham's claim—'That Atheisme in England is more to be feared then Popery'—is not so different from Nashe's sentiment: 'There is no Sect now in *England* so scattered as Atheisme'.[13] Similarly, Hooker's view that his contemporaries should follow Nebuchadnezzar in their treatment of these infidels was echoed by William Perkins' opinion that they deserved the death penalty or Thomas Adams' conviction that they should be branded.[14]

What are the reasons for this disparity? One might be that the authorities were too lax, a view certainly held by the divine, John Dove, who would have liked his countrymen to emulate the rigour of the Spanish Inquisition[15]. It is revealing that the case of the 1599 London 'atheist' is known only because the author who recorded it shared Dove's view,[16] and this is a point to the implications of which we will return. More pertinent, however, is a question of terminology. Was what contemporaries described as 'atheism' and said was common anything that we would recognise as irreligion according to the criteria so far outlined?

In fact, from the time of its introduction into English in the middle years of the sixteenth century onwards, the word 'atheist' was frequently used to mean 'godless' in a rather broad and loose sense.[17]

---

[13] Thomas Fuller, *The Holy State and the Profane State* (Cambridge, 1642), 383 (cf. Richard Greenham, *Workes*, ed. H. Holland (3rd edn, 1601), 3); Thomas Nashe, *Works*, ed. R. B. McKerrow (2nd edn, 5 vols., Oxford, 1958), ii. 121-2.

[14] Richard Hooker, *Works*, ed. John Keble (3 vols., Oxford, 1836), ii. 26 (cf. *Daniel*, iii. 29); William Perkins, *Workes* (3 vols., Cambridge, 1608-9), i, 130, ii. 527; Thomas Adams, *A Commentary or, Exposition Upon the Divine Second Epistle Generall, [of] St. Peter* (1633), 1179. On More's views, see below.

[15] John Dove, *A Confutation of Atheisme* (1605), 14.

[16] *The Triall of Maist. Dorrell*, 88.

[17] For early examples of the use of the word, see, e.g., John Veron, *A Fruteful treatise of predestination* ([1561]) (where it is used as a synonym for 'anabaptists') or H. S. Bennett, *English Books and Readers, 1558-1603* (Cambridge, 1965), 148. Other early instances of usage are included in Friedrich Brie, 'Deismus und Atheismus in der Englischen Renaissance', *Anglia*, 48, (1924), 54-98, 105-68, and G. T. Buckley, *Atheism in the English Renaissance* (Chicago, 1932; repr. New York, 1965). See also *Oxford English Dictionary*, s.v. 'atheism', 'atheist', and, on the continental background, Henri Busson, 'Les Noms des Incrédules au XVIᵉ siècle', *Bibliotheque d'Humanisme et Renaissance*, 16 (1954), 273-83, and Concetta Bianca, 'Per la Storia del Termine "Atheus" nel Cinquecento: Fonti et Traduzioni Greco-Latine', *Studi Filosofici*, 3 (1980), 71-104 (I owe this reference to Charles Schmitt).

Thus the word was commonly employed to describe a failure to espouse the new Protestant creed in a positive as against a merely negative way, and in this connection lack of enthusiasm for the new religion was often conflated with a continued attachment to the old. 'Papistes, Atheistes, and all wicked enemies of the Ghospell' was Josias Nichols' inclusive formula, while another godly divine, Samuel Smith, saw as 'atheists' those 'that thinke it lost labour to bee Religious, and that there is no good got by hearing Sermons, and leading of a godly life'.[18] From this, it is easy to see how the word's currency could be extended to imply a lack of commitment in the eyes of the beholder even in those ostensibly devoted to pursuing the good of the national church, as when Elizabeth I was accused of being 'an atheist, and a maintainer of atheism'.[19] By a similar process of elision, Roman Catholicism could also be condemned as—if no worse—'the high way to Atheisme'.[20]

Broader still was the usage of the word to describe godlessness in the sense of evil living, as expounded by the religious writer, Thomas Palfreyman, in a helpful lexicographical note on 'the accurssed': 'whome the *Hebricians* doe call *Reshaim*: that is to say, *Sinners*: the Latine menne *Impios*, that is, Wicked: the Grecians, *Atheos*, which is, Ungodlie or without God'.[21] This appropriation of the word to describe 'the generall prophannesse of mens liues' is perhaps particularly to be found in sermons and the like, though it is also in evidence in accusations against certain individuals.[22] 'Many that shall read this title', wrote the preacher John Wingfield in his book, *Atheisme Close and open, Anatomized* (1634), 'will be ready to say, Is there any such? that dare say, or dare think, that there is no God?' 'Let me tell you', he continued, '& tel you that it is truth, and let these few lines witnesse against you: the hypocrite is a close Atheist: the loose wicked man is an open Atheist, the secure, bold, and proud transgressour is an Atheist: he that will not be taught & reformed, is an Atheist'.[23]

Such inclusive rhetoric has led some to dismiss 'atheism' as an empty term of abuse, but the difficulty is that this co-existed with the use of the word to signify overt irreligion of the kind manifested

---

[18] Josias Nichols, *The Plea of the Innocent* (1602), 221 (bis); Samuel Smith, *The Great Assize* (3rd impression, 1618), 263. Cf. Patrick Collinson, *The Religion of Protestants* (Oxford, 1982), 200.

[19] *Calendar of State Papers Domestic, 1601-3*, 23.

[20] John Hull, *The Unmasking of the Politike Atheist* (2nd edn, 1602), 42 and *passim*.

[21] Thomas Palfreyman, *The Treatise of Heauenly Philosophie* (1578), 83.

[22] Pierre de la Primaudaye, *The Second Part of the French Academie*, trans. Thomas Bowes (1594), sig. b3v. For accusations against individuals, e.g. C. T. Prouty, *George Gascoigne* (New York, 1942), 61.

[23] John Wingfield, *Atheisme Close and open, Anatomized* (2 pts, 1634), ii. 20-1.

by Marlowe and others. Such descriptions of 'atheism' go back to the years around 1570, and perhaps particularly to Roger Ascham's tirade in *The Scholemaster* against Machiavellian, Italianate Englishmen, 'Epicures in liuing, and 'άθεοι in doctrine', who 'counte as Fables, the holie misteries of Christian Religion. They make Christ and his Gospell, onelie serue Ciuill pollicie'.[24] An equally well-known early specimen is John Lyly's dialogue between Euphues and Atheos of 1578, while, more unexpectedly, the State Papers have filed among them under the year 1571 a 'confutation of the atheists opynyon as Aristotle etc: who foleshely doeth affyrme the world to be wythout begynnyng'.[25]

If the latter, particularly, is rather crude in its evocation of an 'atheist' threat, a series of works from the 1580s onwards deal at length with 'atheism' in the sense of overt hostility to Christianity, elaborating a godless view of the world which is then duly refuted. This is seen, for instance, in sections of Robert Parsons' *Christian Directorie* or Sir Philip Sidney's *Arcadia*, while in chapter 2 of book 5 of Hooker's *Laws of Ecclesiastical Polity*, 'atheism' appears in polarisation to superstition in a passage which should be pondered by all inclined to dismiss Elizabethan writings about 'atheism' as unworthy of serious attention.[26]

By the early seventeenth century, England could boast a number of books devoted exclusively to the subject, such as John Dove's *A Confutation of Atheisme* (1605) or the unfinished *Atheomastix* (1622) of Martin Fotherby, Bishop of Salisbury.[27] Somewhat livelier than these solemn treatises is Jeremy Corderoy's dialogue, *A Warning for Worldlings, or, a comfort to the godly and a terror to the wicked* (1608), which presents a disarmingly vivid portrait of a Traveller who not only states at one point, 'I am fully perswaded, that there is no God', but also divulges a whole series of hererodox opinions and attitudes in discussion with a godly Scholar who has been taken to

[24] Roger Ascham, *English Works*, ed. W. A. Wright (Cambridge, 1904), 228–36.

[25] John Lyly, *Euphues: The Anatomy of Wit and Euphues & his England*, ed. M.W. Croll and H. Clemons (1916), 147–62; Public Record Office, SP 12/83, ff. 114–5.

[26] Robert Parsons, *A Christian Directorie Guiding Men to their Salvation* ([Louvain], 1585), chaps. 2, 4 (these chapters do not appear in the 1582 edition; they recur in the 1598 edition but are omitted from that of 1607); cf. Ernest Strathmann, 'Robert Parsons' Essay on Atheism', in *Joseph Quincy Adams Memorial Studies*, eds. J. G. McManaway, G. E. Dawson and E. E. Willoughby (Washington, D.C., 1948), 665–81. Sir Philip Sidney, *The Countess of Pembroke's Arcadia*, ed. Maurice Evans (Harmondsworth, 1977), 487–92; cf. D. P. Walker, 'Atheism, the Ancient Theology and Sidney's *Arcadia*', in *The Ancient Theology* (1972), 132–63. Hooker, *Works*, ii. 24–30.

[27] For an account of various of these books, see Strathmann, *Ralegh*, chap. 3. See also G. E. Aylmer, 'Unbelief in Seventeenth-century England', in *Puritans and Revolutionaries*, eds. Donald Pennington and Keith Thomas (Oxford, 1978), 22–46.

represent Corderoy—chaplain of Merton College, Oxford—himself.[28]

In these and other books, a profile emerges of the 'atheist' as the kind of free-thinker we might expect, denying the existence of God and supporting this position with a fairly standard battery of arguments. Prominent was the questioning of the authority of the scriptures and drawing attention to inconsistencies within them: indeed, Corderoy's Traveller averred that 'the Scripture was it, that first draue me to these opinions. For I find in it so many falshoods and vntruthes, so many absurdities, so many vnreasonable things, that he is a sencelesse man that perceaueth it not, and a foole that beleeueth it'.[29] Equally central, it was believed, was a preference for natural as against supernatural explanations, the view that 'all things come to passe by nature, or fortune'.[30] Hence God's active supervision of the world came under challenge, while it was also axiomatic that 'atheists' questioned the doctrine of the creation on the basis of a view of the world as eternal derived 'from Aristotle his schoole'.[31]

A denial of the immortality of the soul was seen as a further common trait of 'atheists'; this was thought to lead to a dismissal of the Last Judgment as 'ridiculous and fabulous', and to the belief 'that vertue, innocence, and craftie dealing be alike rewarded', while an overriding worldliness was also presumed to be quintessential.[32] Lastly, 'atheists' were supposed to hold a cynical view of religion itself as 'nothing else but a certaine humane inuention and politike rule of mans wit', intended 'to keepe men within the compasse of humane lawes', a view that was frequently associated with Machiavelli, of whose ideas 'atheists' were habitually seen as devotees.[33]

There is also consensus on the milieu and characteristics of 'atheists'. That Corderoy's was a traveller was symptomatic—since Ascham's time, Italy had been seen as the source of heterodoxy of this kind—while it was also a commonplace that such free-thought was associated with education and with verbal agility in the form of 'wit'. Martin Fotherby thought that the doubts that he refuted in his *Atheomastix* 'neuer creepe into the heads of simpler and vnlearned persons', while Thomas Nashe averred that 'it is the superabound-

---

[28] Jeremy Corderoy, *A Warning for Worldlings* (1608), 37 and *passim*; C. M. Dent, *Protestant Reformers in Elizabethan Oxford* (Oxford, 1983), 159.

[29] Corderoy, *Warning*, 202–3.

[30] Perkins, *Workes*, ii. 451.

[31] Henry Cuffe, *The Differences of the Ages of Mans Life* (1607), 24.

[32] Samuel Gardiner, *Doomes-day Booke* (1606), 1; John Stephens, *Satyrical Essayes Characters and Others* (1615), 212.

[33] John Carpenter, *A Preparatiue to Contentation* (1597), 233; Corderoy, *Warning*, 12.

ance of witte that makes Atheists'.[34] In manner, 'atheists' were thought to be 'always confident beyond reformation', speaking their ideas 'openly & boldly', promoting their ideas with almost missionary zeal in the oral milieux in which they were thought to express them, appealing to 'sense, reason and experience', and having recourse to 'vnsauourie scorne' in propounding their opinions.[35] Indeed, 'scoffing' was seen as a typical irreligious trait, its apparently increased incidence being seen by Hooker as confirming St Peter's prophecy about the latter days.[36]

I have separated this recognisably modern concept of 'atheism' from the broader usage of the word to mean in effect godlessness, and contemporaries themselves recognised that this was a word 'of a very large extent', being employed to describe more things than one.[37] This is shown by a series of more or less convoluted attempts to classify different types of 'atheist', and to distinguish 'atheists' proper from such other classes of person as hypocrites, temporisers, Epicures and 'Common Profane persons'[38]—in other words, the uncommitted Protestants and evil-doers whom we have already seen the word being used to describe.

It would be possible to write at length about the varying definitions used by different authors and the inconsistencies between them, and sometimes even within the works of a single author, as to what should or should not be described as 'atheism'—whether hypocrisy was to be seen as part of it or as a separate phenomenon, for instance[39]—and as to what terminology should be used to convey the degrees of seriousness of irreligion. A certain consensus emerges in distinguishing between 'inward' and 'outward atheism'—irreligious views openly expressed and those that their holders kept to themselves—and between 'atheism in judgment' and 'practical atheism', heterodoxy expressed through immoral actions.

But though differing degrees of infidelity were distinguished, there was a constant tendency to conflate them and to argue that in fact they inevitably led to one another. In particular, a kind of circular connection was presumed between theoretical irreligion and bad behaviour. As the divine, William Ames, put it: 'such wicked opinions or imaginations do let loose the raines of all concupiscence, and

[34] Martin Fotherby, *Atheomastix* (1622), sig. A2v; Nashe, *Works*, ii. 124.

[35] Stephens, *Satyrical Essayes*, 216; Robert Burton, *The Anatomy of Melancholy* (3rd edn, Oxford, 1628), 618; Corderoy, *Warning*, 38; Cuffe, *Differences*, 20. On 'atheists' as proselytizers, see *Bacon's Essays*, 65.

[36] Hooker, *Works*, ii. 26. Cf. *2 Peter* iii. 3.

[37] Fuller, *Holy State*, 378.

[38] Thomas Adams, *Workes* (1630), 16.

[39] E.g. compare Perkins, *Workes*, i. 479, with ibid., ii. 526.

therefore are the cause of increasing that wickednesse, whereof at the first they were the effect'.[40] Moreover free-thought was itself seen as progressive, with mild positions inexorably giving way to more extreme ones. In his portrait of an 'atheist' in *The Profane State* (1642), Thomas Fuller considered that articulate irreligion grew from quarrelling and scoffing at sacred things, which 'by degrees abates the reverence of religion, and ulcers mens hearts with profanenesse', a view expressed more rhetorically by Thomas Adams: 'The Chayre of the Scorner, is the seate of Sathan, the lowest staire and very threshold of Hell'.[41]

In addition, Fuller saw anti-providentialism as a preliminary step to outright 'atheism', and it was doubtless because they thought the same that others simply elided the difference between the two, like the Catholic writer, Thomas Fitzherbert, who pointed out 'that I take Atheists, not only for those, who deny that there is a God, but also for such, as deny the particuler prouidence of God in the affaires of men: who are no lesse to be counted Atheists, then the other'.[42] It is similarly symptomatic that the word 'Epicure' was used as a label both for 'A lover of pleasure, more then of God' and also for the man 'which denieth his prouidence'.[43]

Hence, though our inclination might be to try to separate the two, there is an overlap between the portrayal of 'philosophical atheism' and the attack on godlessness. Authors like John Wingfield or Josias Nichols whose main thrust is an attack on sinfulness or lack of commitment also allude to the phenomenon of philosophical doubt.[44] More serious, it is apparent that even some of those who portrayed and attacked articulate irreligion were really concerned about 'practical atheism'. Thus, for all the apparent verisimilitude of Jeremy Corderoy's portrait of an 'atheist' in his *A Warning for Worldlings*, in his 'To the Reader' he paradoxically claimed that 'fewe or none there are, who now in words deny God', continuing: 'But the Scripture forewarneth vs of a more dangerous kind of Atheist, who wil not in words deny God, but by their deeds'.[45]

Indeed, though all agreed on the menace presented by 'practical atheism', there is a frustrating lack of consensus among contempor-

[40] William Ames, *An Analyticall Exposition of both the Epistles of the Apostle Peter* (1641), 237–8.
[41] Fuller, *Holy State*, 379; Adams, *Workes*, 14.
[42] Fuller, *Holy State*, 380; Thomas Fitzherbert, *The Second Part of a Treatise Concerning Policy, and Religion* ([Douai], 1610), 69–70.
[43] Adams, *Workes*, 498; John Spicer, *The Sale of Salt* (1611), 32. See also W. R. Elton, *King Lear and the Gods* (San Marino, 1966), chap. 2.
[44] Wingfield, *Atheisme*, esp. i. 66–7; Nicholas, *Plea*, 208–9 (bis).
[45] Corderoy, *Warning*, sig. A6v.

aries as to whether 'philosophical atheists' were common to all. To some extent this depends on what 'common' is taken to mean, and matters are further complicated by contemporaries' fastidiousness in their definition of true 'atheism'. Thomas Fuller, for instance, thought that 'to give an instance of a speculative Atheist, is both hard and dangerous'—a view similar to that of Francis Bacon—but this was partly because 'we cannot see mens speculations otherwise then as they cloth themselves visible in their actions, some Atheisticall speeches being not sufficient evidence to convict the speaker an Atheist'.[46] Moreover, while some asserted that 'I can assure you of my owne experience, that there are such, that denie not onely the prouidence, but euen the very nature and existence of God', other writers were simply vague or inconsistent, like Sir George More, who alternated between expressing amazement that anyone should disbelieve in God and asserting that open 'atheists' actually existed.[47]

But he was not thereby prevented from entering into a refutation of irreligious views, which might appear to suggest that what orthodox writers attacked was not necessarily very closely related to any phenomenon in contemporary life, despite the existence in England at this time of occasional cases of outright infidelity of the kind already noted.

Certainly the anti-atheist literature displays a number of features which suggest artificiality. In these books as a whole there is a disquieting shortage of instances of native 'atheists', and instead a reliance on examples from classical antiquity or Renaissance Europe. The names of Diagoras, Epicurus, Lucian, Lucretius, Pliny, Protagoras and Theodorus recur again and again, and more recent specimens are equally standard, the commonest being Machiavelli and—perhaps more surprisingly—Pope Leo X. Even when native instances are given, there is often a distinctly folklorish quality about them, as with the 'gentleman of Barkshire, whose name I forebeare to expresse, a man of great possessions', who figures in Thomas Beard's *Theatre of God's Judgements*. This person was said to be an open 'atheist', given over to swearing and to 'all sensualitie of the flesh', who wanted the name 'Beelzebub' to be given to a child whose christening he attended. He was struck dead while out hunting and 'discoursing of many vaine matters', 'and because a terrible example to all wicked Atheists, of God's justice'.[48]

Equally disturbing is the derivative and clichéd nature of the

---

[46] Fuller, *Holy State*, 383; *Bacon's Essays*, 66.

[47] Thomas Morton, *A Treatise of the Nature of God* (1599), 30 (a statement by the Gentleman who acts as an interlocutor in the dialogue); Sir George More, *A Demonstration of God in his workes* (1597), sig. A2v, pp. 20, 25-6 and *passim*.

[48] Thomas Beard, *The Theatre of God's Judgements* (3rd edn, 1631), 150-1.

argument with 'atheists' in which orthodox polemicists engaged. To some extent their sources lay in recent continental writings, and especially French ones, including such works as Phillippe Duplessis Mornay's *De la Verité de la Religion Chrestienne*, of which an English translation by Sir Philip Sidney and Arthur Golding appeared in 1587. Perhaps more significant, however, were classical, patristic and Biblical texts, as is clear from the frequency with which passages from the Bible and the names of the Fathers and of classical authors like Cicero are cited. As Thomas Nashe put it as he ended his breathless summary of the design argument in *Christs Teares over Ierusalem* (1593): 'O why should I but squintingly glance at these matters, when they are so admirably expatiated by auncient Writers?'[49] Even within the literature itself, there is a substantial derivative element. Roger Ascham's 'atheist' profile was quoted verbatim by Thomas Palfreyman in his *Treatise of Heauenly Philosophie* (1578) and was repeatedly paraphrased thereafter.[50] More surprisingly, Nashe's evocation of 'atheism' in *Christs Teares* was cited as an authority in Thomas Rogers' *Catholic Doctrine of the Church of England* (1607), apart from being reworked by Thomas Adams along with other existing accounts of infidelity.[51] In addition, folklorish accounts of 'atheism' were borrowed by one author from another.[52]

The element of cliché emerges perhaps particularly in the views that 'atheists' were supposed to hold. John Hull's summary of the presumed arguments of infidels in his *Saint Peters Prophesie of these Last Daies* (1610)—'making *Christ* an imposter, *Moyses* a deceiuer, the Gospell a tale, and the Law a fable'[53]—recites formulae that had been used time and time again, in particular the notion of all or part either of the scriptures or the Christian religion being a 'fable', and the accusation that Moses and Christ were cozenors, which in fact echoes the views of Celsus as refuted by Origen.[54] This also applies to such aspects of the profile of the 'atheist' already outlined as the naturalism, or the view of religion as a device of policy.

[49] Nashe, *Works*, ii. 121.

[50] Palfreyman, *The Treatise*, 702-4, and see, e.g., Primaudaye, *Second Part*, sig. b4v; John Hull, *Saint Peters Prophesie of these Last Daies* (1610), 127; Thomas Jackson, *Londons New-Yeeres Gift* (1609), f. 18.

[51] Rogers, *Catholic Doctrine*, 78, 148; Adams, *Commentary*, 1159-66: other sources include Bacon.

[52] For instance, Richard Greenham's account of an 'atheist' (*Workes*, 3) was reused in Miles Mosse, *Ivstifying and Saving Faith distinguished from the faith of the Deuils* (Cambridge and London, 1614), 17-18, and in Adams, *Commentary*, 16.

[53] Hull, *Saint Peters Prophesie*, 8.

[54] *Origen: Contra Celsum*, trans. Henry Chadwick (Cambridge, 1953), 22, 28, 37, 297 and *passim*. For an instance of a typical formulaic description of 'atheism', see Daniel Price, *Sauls Prohibition Staide* (1609), sig. E3.

Moreover, the arguments used to 'refute' infidels are markedly lacking in originality, though some expositions are more ingenious than others. We hear again and again the design argument, rehearsed in greater or lesser detail, or the argument from man's conscience, or the 'consent of nations', the innate religiosity of mankind. Equally frequent is the argument that 'atheists' come a bad end, a theme epitomised by the relevant section of Beard's *Theatre of God's Judgements*.

All this artificiality is compounded by a distinctly complacent and self-congratulatory tone about the literature. It was a commonplace that 'atheists' were unreasonable, that true rationality could only underwrite an orthodox religious outlook. As John Lyly's Euphues put it in his dialogue with Atheos: 'But why go I about in a thing so manifest to use proofs so manifold? If thou deny the truth who can prove it; if thou deny that black is black, who can by reason reprove thee when thou opposest thyself against reason?' It goes almost without saying that the dialogue ends with Atheos in a state of gushing repentance, and there was a widespread tendency to presume that those who resisted theistic arguments could not be so much men as 'brute beasts'.[55]

To a large extent these books were clearly aimed at the godly rather than the ungodly, as is shown by their effusive dedications or by passages where authors break off from their anti-atheist polemic to include asides for the orthodox.[56] Quite apart from the actual existence of 'atheism', the spectre of it undoubtedly allowed authors to rehearse arguments on matters 'most needefull to be beleeued; yet least laboured in by *Diuines*'.[57] By visualising unbelievers who 'must be refuted by the principles of nature onely, for all other arguments they scorne', writers were given an excuse to expound the principles of natural theology, while the Gentleman who acts as interlocutor in Thomas Morton's *Treatise of the Nature of God* (1599) sought comfort even in matters 'which are most certaine, manifest, and without all question ... that I may knowe and hold that more firmly, which I doo alreadie both beleeue, and also know in part'.[58]

The notion of 'atheism' served other intellectual functions which it is important for us to understand. In part, it stemmed from an a priori assumption that anti-Christian behaviour must be linked to anti-Christian belief, that there must be as articulate a rationale for evil as for good. And, both for this reason and more generally,

---

[55] Lyly, *Euphues*, 150, 161–2; More, *Demonstration*, 34.
[56] E.g. Dove, *Confutation*, 70.
[57] Fotherby, *Atheomastix*, sig. A2.
[58] John Weemes, *A Treatise of the Foure Degenerate Sonnes* (1636), 7; Morton, *Treatise*, 7.

the evocation and elaboration of an image of irreligion played an important part in a world percolated by Aristotelian contraries, rather comparable to the significance of statements about witchcraft which has been demonstrated by Stuart Clark.[59] Hooker saw 'affected atheism' as 'the most extreme opposite to true religion', and others used the concept of 'Antipodes'.[60]

The sense of contrariety is confirmed by the overlap between the attacks on 'atheism' and the Theophrastan character literature which was so popular in early seventeenth-century England.[61] 'The Atheist' is one of the stock characters of these books, and, in the typical moralistic manner of the genre, he is presented as an ideal type of the 'most badde man', to quote the synonym for 'An Atheist' in Nicholas Breton's *The Good and the Badde, or Descriptions of the Worthies, and Vnworthies of this Age* (1616).[62] The function of polarities of this kind was explained by a divine who himself wrote a character-book, Bishop Joseph Hall, who claimed that 'this light contraries give to each other in the midst of their enmity, that one makes the other seem more good or ill'.[63] Josias Nichols had earlier pointed out the value, in expounding Christian doctrine, of noting 'errors which are contrarie to these trueths ... and so it wil much further them; euen as by all contraries, euery good thing is the more perceiued, felt and esteemed'.[64]

It would be quite possible, therefore, to argue that 'atheism' would have had to be invented in the early modern period even if it had not existed, that the anti-atheist literature served purposes in its own right to which the actual incidence of articulate irreligion was barely relevant. Undoubtedly there is an element of truth in this, but the question to which we must address ourselves is whether this is the whole of the story, or whether there was in fact more interconnection between fiction and the actual phenomenon of infidelity than has so far been apparent.

For one thing, we must be careful not to impose modern standards on our early modern forebears. The fact that their categorisation may seem to us rather artificial does not mean that they were not trying to make sense of real phenomena in such terms, while the

[59] Stuart Clark, 'Inversion, Misrule and the Meaning of Witchcraft', *Past & Present*, 87 (1980), 98–127.

[60] Hooker, *Works*, ii. 24; Burton, *Anatomy*, 614; Weemes, *Treatise*, 6.

[61] See Benjamin Boyce, *The Theophrastan Character in England to 1642* (Cambridge, Mass., 1947), and C. N. Greenough, *A Bibliography of the Theophrastan Character in English* (Cambridge, Mass., 1947).

[62] Nicholas Breton, *The Good and the Badde* (1616), 20.

[63] Joseph Hall, *Works*, new edn., ed. Philip Wynter (10 vols., Oxford, 1863), vi. 106.

[64] Josias Nichols, *An Order of Houshold Instruction* (1596), sig. E5.

dependence on written sources for 'atheist' instances is equally easily misconstrued. Though we may find the most recent and local examples the most telling, for them classical ones offered at the same time authority and an established typology of unbelief. The proclivity to cite antique instances was encouraged by the sense of virtual contemporaneity with the classics and the Fathers shown by these writers, so that it seemed quite natural to cite opinions and statements from such sources as if they were of universal validity and hence to conflate 'all Atheistes of olde, and of our tyme'.[65]

There is also the nature of the genre to consider, for an envenomed tirade against free-thought would have been weakened by pausing to name nonentities, particularly when the commonness of the phenomenon was all along being asserted. Even concerning God's vengeance, where individual cases were most relevant, there was a premium on spectacular examples rather than ordinary ones. Hence most of the specimens in Beard's *Theatre of God's Judgements* came from books rather than experience—even when he extended the work with extra material—and Marlowe's case was virtually the only local one which seemed to Beard 'not inferior to any of the former in Atheisme & impiety, and equall to all in maner of punishment'.[66]

But, as the instancing of Marlowe by Beard and by William Vaughan in his *Golden-groue* reveals, these authors were concerned to document a connection between their stock 'atheist' figure and real phenomena in the society of their day, and it would be wrong to see the erudition of such writers as in any way precluding empirical experience. In Nicholas Gibbens' *Questions and Disputations Concerning the Holy Scripture* (1601), for instance, the margins are mainly filled with learned patristic citations, but among these appears at one point the rather incongruous note, 'My selfe hath bin an eye and an eare witnes', to document the fact that 'there are of this our age, which will demaunde, more curious then wise, where these skins were had so sodainelie, which made *Adam* clothing ... yea they will be so madde as to demaund, where *Adam* had a thred to sew his figge leaues'.[67]

Moreover when one returns to the actual instances of irreligion recorded in contemporary documents after soaking oneself in the anti-atheist literature, one finds in the descriptions of those accused echoes of the 'atheist' stereotype which, because of its pedigree and

[65] Parsons, *Christian Directorie*, 25.

[66] Beard, *Theatre* (1597), 147. For Beard's additions, see the 1631 edition, esp. 548–9.

[67] Nicholas Gibbens, *Questions and Disputations Concerning the Holy Scripture* (1601), 168–9.

presentation, one might otherwise have been tempted to dismiss. This suggests a more complex relationship between the imaginary and the real than has so far been allowed for.

Thus in one of the instances of heterodox talk that came up at Star Chamber, the 'heretical and execrable words' which one Robert Fisher was accused of uttering—'that Christe was no savioure & the gospell a fable'—repeat almost verbatim one of the commonplaces of anti-atheist writings.[68] The same is true of some of what was said in our best-documented case, that of Marlowe. Even parts of the informers' reports about him fall into this category—for instance, the view retailed by Richard Baines, 'That the first beginning of Religioun was only to keep men in awe'—while there is a strong element of cliché in Thomas Beard's account of Marlowe's supposed writings, 'affirming our Sauiour to be but a deceiuer, and *Moses* to be but a coniurer and seducer of the people, and the holy Bible to be but vaine and idle stories, and all religion but a deuice of pollicie'.[69]

This might be taken to suggest that the accusations merely represented an attempt at character assassination by projecting conventional expectations onto those suspected of irreligion, though the originality of some of the opinions attributed to Marlowe suggests that this cannot be the whole truth.[70] It might show that the orthodox tended to perceive the heterodoxy they heard in hackneyed terms, as is certainly suggested by Beard's description, which—though bearing sufficient relationship to the more detailed informers' reports on Marlowe not to be dismissed—nevertheless ignores Marlowe's more ingenious speculations.

But it is surely no less likely that the vocabulary of irreligion itself comprised commonplaces of heterodoxy picked up from orthodox sources. Paul H. Kocher has painstakingly demonstrated how many of the views said to have been expressed by Marlowe can be paralleled in writings against 'atheism',[71] and such books may well have helped to create the very phenomenon which they sought to refute. There are hints of this in our sources, and it is certainly revealing that anti-atheist authors felt the need to defend themselves

---

[68] Hawarde, *Reportes*, 41.

[69] Brooke, *Life*, 98; Beard, *Theatre* (1597), 148. Compare Robert Parsons' accusation against Ralegh (Lefranc, *Ralegh*, 356), or the allegations against the Earl of Oxford in 1581, in which appear such clichés as 'The trinity a fable' and 'Scriptures for pollicye': see ibid., 340-1, and PRO, SP 12/151, ff. 102, 109, 118.

[70] For such a suggestion in a comparable context, see David Wootton, *Paolo Sarpi: between Renaissance and Enlightenment* (Cambridge, 1983), 143. On Marlowe's originality, see Kocher, *Marlowe*, chap. 3.

[71] Ibid., 30n and chap. 3 *passim*.

against those 'more scrupulous, then rightly zealous; who thinke it not conuenient, that any question should be made, whether there be any God or no, (because as they say) there are very fewe, who doubt of it, and the very calling of it in question, breedeth scruples in the mindes of those, who made no question of it before'.[72]

Whichever of these things is true—or whether they all are to some extent—we nevertheless have to visualise a kind of symbiotic relationship between 'atheism' as imagined and irreligion as it existed. It is therefore hardly surprising to find that the cases of irreligious talk that came to light duplicate in piecemeal form elements of the stock atheist figure that I have already outlined.

Thus one finds doubts about the scope of God's providential intervention in the world, as reported of 'Mr Thinn' at the Cerne Abbas enquiry of 1594—probably Charles Thynne, Ralegh's nephew, though it might have been John Thynne of Longleat—who spoke 'as though godes providence did not reach ouer all creatures or to like effecte'.[73] Similarly, William Gardiner, a Surrey landowner and JP, was accused in the 1580s of claiming—if not 'that there was no God'—'that He had no government in the world'.[74] Antiscripturalism was spectacularly manifested by Marlowe, who was said to have denounced Moses, Christ and St Paul, questioned the Biblical age of the world, jested at the scriptures and compiled a collection of 'Contrarieties' in them.[75] But at a humbler level comparable sentiments were also attributed to one Robert Blagden of Keevil in Wiltshire, who was alleged in 1619 to have 'made doubt . . . whether the prophetts and Appostles writings were true or not'.[76]

The denial of the immortality of the soul from an atheistic standpoint was imputed to Thomas Allen, Lieutenant of Portland Castle, and his servant Oliver at the Cerne Abbas hearing, to Marlowe's

---

[72] Corderoy, Warning, sig. A6. For examples—though more of heretical than atheistic ideas—see the manuscript owned by Kyd in which an anti-Arian work was eviscerated for heretical opinions (Danchin, 'Etudes Critiques', 568-70, and W. D. Briggs, 'On a Document concerning Christopher Marlowe', Studies in Philology, 20 (1923), 153-9) or the claim of the Sherborne shoemaker, Robert Hyde, at the Cerne Abbas hearing, to have derived his notions from reports of a local priest's sermon attacking sectarian views: Willobie his Avisa, 264, 269-70.

[73] Ibid., 259. For the possibility that this was Charles Thynne, see Lefranc, Ralegh, 387; on John Thynne, to whom Carew Ralegh was gentleman of horse and whose widow Carew married, see DNB s.v. 'Sir Walter Ralegh'. Thynne's view was possibly heretical rather than atheistic: see the different positions distinguished in Stephen Gosson, The Trumpet of Warre (1598), 52-4.

[74] Leslie Hotson, Shakespeare versus Shallow (1931), 54-8, 198, 202, 228-9.

[75] Brooke, Life, 98-100, 107. According to Simon Aldrich, Marlowe's 'booke' was 'against the Scriptur': Bakeless, Tragicall History, i. 120.

[76] PRO, STA 8/59/11, memb. 2. For the reference, I am indebted to M. J. Ingram, 'Eccclesiastical Justice in Wiltshire, 1600-1640' (Oxford D.Phil. thesis, 1977), 103-4.

protegé, Thomas Fineoux or Finis of Dover, and also to a Wiltshire gentleman, John Derpier, who was accused in 1607 of maintaining the 'most hereticall & damnable opinion (that there was noe god & noe resurrection, & that men died a death like beastes)'.[77] With this might go a cynicism about the function of religion and the motives of the clergy, expressed not only by Marlowe but also by a Yorkshire gentleman, Peter Vavasour, who was accused before the York High Commission in 1637 of having 'held, uttered and vented diverse and sundrye hereticall and damnable opinions and sayings touchinge the mysteries of faith, and especiallye ... beinge talkeinge of the Resurrection of the dead, said in a most impious and hereticall manner tush tush. that is but a tricke of the clergye, to cause the people to beleeve that to gett money and to catch fooles withall, and that prayers weere noe better then the barkeinge of doggs'.[78]

In manner, too, there is evidence of that confidence, that sense almost of proselytising, which anti-atheist authors stress. The 'atheist' who challenged Bancroft at the London sessions in 1599 did so, we are told, 'openly and impudently', while Richard Baines reported of Marlowe that 'almost into every Company he Cometh he perswades men to Atheism'.[79] It is perhaps also in this light that one should interpret the case of John Derpier, since the deposition against him reveals that it was only after he affirmed his views 'in disputation' with a local vicar in front of his scholars in church that Derpier was presented by the churchwardens. In addition, the sarcastic wit imputed to 'atheists' is borne out by some of these instances, while the orthodox would hardly have been surprised by the view of another alleged 'atheist', Brian Walker of Bishop Auckland, County Durham: 'neyther will I beleive anie thinge but what I see'.[80]

More significant still, these cases substantiate what might otherwise seem perhaps the most frustrating feature of the literature, that

[77] *Willobie his Avisa*, 262–3; Bakeless, *Tragicall History*, i. 120, 122–3; Wiltshire Record Office, Diocese of Salisbury Dean's Presentments, 1607–9 (10), f. 66: this is another case to which I was alerted by Ingram, 'Ecclesiastical Justice', 81; he does not, however, note the circumstances in which Derpier was accused of uttering these words, as referred to below. Such cases seem to me distinct from the non-atheistic mortalism dealt with in N. T. Burns, *Christian Mortalism from Tyndale to Milton* (Cambridge, Mass., 1972).

[78] Borthwick Institute, York, HC CP 1637/3: I am indebted to Bill Sheils for his help with this case. Cf Brooke, *Life*, 98–9, 107.

[79] *The Triall of Maist. Dorrell*, 88; Brooke, *Life*, 99.

[80] *The Acts of the High Commission Court within the Diocese of Durham*, ed. W. H. D. Longstaffe (Surtees Society, xxxiv, Durham, 1858), 116: I am indebted to Pete Rushton for his advice on this case. On wit, see Kocher, *Marlowe*, 48, 56–7, and *Willobie his Avisa*, esp. 266–8.

conviction of the progressive nature of infidelity, the difficulty of distinguishing between mild and extreme irreligious traits. The very manner in which such opinions came to light was prone to confirm presumptions about the link between theoretical and practical 'atheism'. As already noted, it was often only because people had been accused of other misdemeanours that their irreligious views were disclosed—in Vavasour's case, of interfering sexually with a servant, for instance, or in Gardiner's of trying to defraud his son-in-law. This kind of presumption was made explicit in the case of Robert Fisher, another figure whose 'blasphemous heresy' was recorded in conjunction with other offences at the Court of Star Chamber, who was condemned 'by his outrage and impudence' despite there being 'not much testimony', Lord Treasurer Burghley observing: 'He who is once evil in the highest degree is always presumed to be evil, and [Fisher's] previous acts and subsequent life declare his impiety'.[81]

These instances also bear out the idea of a spectrum from mild to graver irreligion. The way in which horse-play could merge into something more serious is illustrated by the case of Robert Blagden, who was accused not only of antiscripturalism but also of having 'procured one Francis the Tapster of the George in Warminster to stand on a stoole and preache', 'in disgrace of gods worde & the ministrie',[82] and the same kind of juxtaposition is in evidence from the Cerne Abbas hearing. Against Thomas Allen, for instance, the allegations ranged from the serious claim that he had denied the immortality of the soul to such matters as his tearing two leaves out of a Bible to dry tobacco on, or expostulating when it rained while he was out hawking: 'if there be a god A poxe on that god which sendeth such weather to marr our sporte'.[83]

With Sir Walter Ralegh's brother, Carew, we again have a spectrum from mild anticlericalism to more serious heresy, from facetiously telling a local priest that his horse could preach as well as he could to maintaining the heterodox position that 'there was a god in nature', and arguing about the godhead in a manner said to be 'as like a pagan as euer you harde anye'. Ralegh was also said to have admitted 'that he had in deade sinned in manye thinges but what hurte had come vnto him for it?', asserting that death came to

---

[81] Hawarde, *Reportes*, 42. See above, p. 149.

[82] PRO, STA 8/59/11, memb. 2.

[83] *Willobie his Avisa*, 262–3, 256 (these, like other words cited in the 'Interrogatories', are clearly based on hearsay reports of those accused: cf. ibid., 264, for a slightly different version of the same story about Allen).

sinners and righteous alike and thus giving expression to exactly the kind of cynical attitude which caused concern at the time.[84]

None of this casual talk may seem very significant or dangerous, and it is perhaps not surprising that such cases were rarely pursued very far. It must have been hard to obtain a conviction on hearsay reports of table-talk, particularly when—as happened even in some of these instances—those accused denied that they had uttered the words imputed to them, and particularly with people of high status. Indeed, it is worth noting parenthetically here that, though the survival of accusations is far too random for any serious conclusions to be drawn concerning the social affiliations of articulate irreligion, gentlemen are disproportionately represented, even in cases from local ecclesiastical records. In addition, this random element makes it difficult to be sure how common such heterodoxy was, while, in the bulk of instances, we do not know how systematically thought-out even extreme-sounding statements were: one could easily believe that the most outspoken of these men were not outright 'atheists' in a modern sense.

But here we must again beware of being too literal-minded in searching for 'real' phenomena and return to an attempt to understand how anxiety about irreligion actually functioned. Allowance must be made for the ease with which oral evidence can be misconstrued, for the conviction that mild and extreme atheistic traits were inextricably linked, and for the intellectualist character of early modern thought, its tendency to extrapolate directly from premises to conclusions, from piecemeal evidence to a complete 'atheist' stereotype.[85] In these circumstances—and particularly in the light of the overlap of characteristics between real and imaginary 'atheists'—it is easy to see how scattered cases of irreligion like those I have surveyed fed a belief in a serious threat of the kind depicted in the literature.

Moreover the juxtaposition of an exaggerated 'atheist' stereotype with the sense of an inexorable continuum from mild to extreme infidelity had a wider significance. For it may be argued that through the concept of 'atheism' it was possible to express disquiet about tendencies in contemporary ideas and attitudes which were commonplace and which ultimately had irreligious implications, but

[84] Ibid., 258, 260, 261, 262, 266. It is interesting that Ralegh's opinion on the godhead had been uttered on an earlier occasion, but was 'shutt up' till brought to light by the enquiry (ibid., 258).

[85] Cf. the suggestive remarks in Lucien Febvre, *The Problem of Unbelief in the Sixteenth Century: the Religion of Rabelais*, trans. Beatrice Gottlieb (Cambridge, Mass., 1982), 142 f., though my disagreement with the general thrust of Febvre's argument should have become apparent in the course of this paper.

which were rarely found in so extreme a form. It is thus possible to see a certain rationale even in the broad usage of 'atheism' to mean godlessness that I alluded to earlier in this paper, if due allowance is made for the preacherly exaggeration to which its exponents were prone.

The threat of 'atheism' sensationalised the religious doubt which was widely experienced by the devout, which, it was feared, could all too easily develop into articulate irreligion if not kept in check. Many, like the politician and antiquary Sir Simonds D'Ewes, were attacked by 'unruly thoughts of atheism',[86] and one important function of the anti-atheist literature was to act 'as a stablishment to such as any way eyther by their owne infirmitie or through the wilinesse of wicked persons are made to wauer and hang in suspense'.[87]

To some extent, the seeds of 'atheism' were seen as the inheritance of natural man, and it is not surprising to find the appearance of 'atheism' as a symptom of melancholy in Robert Burton's treatise on that subject.[88] But 'atheism' also illustrated the new situation inaugurated by the Reformation, epitomising in extreme form the fuller awareness of alternatives in religious outlook between which, for the first time, people had to choose. It was a commonplace of anti-atheist writings that unbelief had been encouraged by religious schism, something which Richard Greenham illustrated by a story of a man who moved from Catholicism, through Protestantism, to the Family of Love, before throwing religion over altogether.[89] In addition, recorded cases of heterodoxy reveal an open-minded attitude towards different religions of precisely the kind deprecated by the devout.[90]

More serious—in view of the intellectual character of the stock 'atheist' figure—was the ambivalence that the fear of infidelity induced in the educated, particularly on topics which overlapped with elements in the stereotype, where usage of the word could express anxiety about even mild instances of the secularist tendencies which 'atheism' exemplified in exaggerated form. Here the fear of 'atheism' arguably had a negative effect, inhibiting heterodoxy and underwriting orthodoxy: many would have shared Thomas Kyd's

---

[86] Sir Simonds D'Ewes, *Autobiography and Correspondence*, ed. J. O. Halliwell (2 vols., 1845), i. 253. Cf. Thomas, *Religion and the Decline of Magic*, 167–8, 474–5.

[87] Phillippe Duplessis Mornay, *A Woorke concerning the trewnesse of the Christian Religion*, trans. Sir Philip Sidney and Arthur Golding (1587), sig. *3.

[88] Burton, *Anatomy*, 614–21 (pt 3, sect. 4, memb. 2, subsect. 1).

[89] Greenham, *Workes*, 3.

[90] E.g. the case of Richard Barker in W. H. Hale, *A Series of Precedents and Proceedings in Criminal Causes* (1847), 176.

anxiety, writing to Sir John Puckering in 1593, 'to cleere my selfe of being thought an Atheist . . . a deadlie thing'.[91]

Wit itself could be seen to have its dangers—'impiety doth infect the wisest wit, if it be giuen to idlenes', Francis Meres averred in his *Palladis Tamia* (1598)—while the perils of speculation in areas where the boundary between correct and incorrect opinion was ill-defined, such as the doctrine of the soul, were noted by John Woolton, Bishop of Exeter, in his book on that subject.[92] Such problems were perhaps borne out in the case of Sir Walter Ralegh, for, though views differ on his orthodoxy in religious matters, the evidence of the Cerne Abbas enquiry illustrates the imprudence of venting sceptical opinions on fundamental doctrinal issues at dinner parties.[93]

Anxiety focused on two areas, both of them well-known, where a challenge was presented to the providentialist and moralistic worldview of the day. One was a secular attitude to politics of the kind habitually associated with Machiavelli, whose centrality to the 'atheist' stereotype has been indicated. Much has been written about anti-Machiavellianism, but here we may note the good evidence that exists of concern on the part of those interested in Machiavellian writings to try to devise a Christian version of 'policy' to avoid finding themselves on the highroad to irreligion.[94] In addition, naturalism and systems of scientific explanation seen as implicitly atheistic caused misgivings: 'Young Naturalists oft Atheists old doe proue', as Sir William Alexander put it in a dedicatory poem to a work by John Abernethy in which 'atheism' bulked large.[95] It is against the background of such orthodox presumptions that one should see the almost unreasonably touchy attitude of a man like Thomas Harriot, arguably as much under suspicion for the character of his interests as for anything he actually said.[96]

---

[91] Brooke, *Life*, 103, 104.

[92] Francis Meres, *Palladis Tamia. Wits Treasury* (1598), f. 303v; John Woolton, *A Treatise of the Immortalitie of the Soule* (1576), Ep. Ded., f. 26.

[93] Strathmann, *Ralegh, passim*; Lefranc, *Ralegh*, chap. 12; S. J. Greenblatt, *Sir Walter Ralegh: the Renaissance Man and his Roles* (New Haven, 1973), 99–101; *Willobie his Avisa*, 266–8.

[94] E.g. Stuart Clark, 'Wisdom Literature of the Seventeenth century: a Guide to the Contents of the "Bacon-Tottel" Commonplace Books', *Transactions of the Cambridge Bibliographical Society*, 6 (1976), 300. See also particularly G. L. Mosse, *The Holy Pretence* (Oxford, 1957) and Felix Raab, *The English Face of Machiavelli* (1964), chap. 3.

[95] John Abernethy, *A Christian and Heavenly Treatise Containing Physicke for the Soule* (3rd edn, 1630), sig. A7v. On this theme see also P. H. Kocher, *Science and Religion in Elizabethan England* (San Marino, 1953), esp. chap. 5.

[96] See particularly D. B. Quinn and J. W. Shirley, 'A Contemporary List of Hariot References', *Renaissance Quarterly*, 22 (1969), esp. 18f. But see also Jean Jacquot, 'Thomas Harriot's Reputation for Impiety', *Notes and Records of the Royal Society*, 9

Moreover, since naturalistic views had been set out most fully by classical authors like Pliny, it is hardly surprising that the orthodox should experience particular anxiety in connection with these, as epitomising the milder tendencies that they observed in contemporaries. It is thus symptomatic that when Philemon Holland translated Pliny's *Natural History* into English he felt concern about the possible danger of Pliny's 'attributing so much unto Nature', which might derogate from the power of God. 'Farre be it from me, that I should publish any thing to corrupt mens manners, and much lesse to prejudice Christian religion', he wrote, and, after conferring with 'sundrie divines' on the subject, he actually appended a letter from one of them to his preface, to 'settle the minds of the weake, and free my labours from the taint of irreligion'.[97]

It would, of course, be naive to conflate secularism and naturalism with outright 'atheism', though it did not help that ideas of a secularist and naturalistic kind were expressed by outspoken free-thinkers like Marlowe, who also specifically alluded to Harriot.[98] What is significant, in reconstructing contemporary anxieties, is to see how such incipiently irreligious tendencies appeared in the light of contemporaries' conviction of the progressive nature of 'atheism' and their proclivity to conflate mild manifestations into an extreme image. It is worthy of note that at this time no alternative word like 'Deist' caught on to describe such milder heterodoxy, despite the existence of this word in English at an earlier date than has hitherto been suspected.[99] Instead, in a manner typical of the thought of the day, people preferred to use the inclusive concept of 'atheism' to encapsulate a range of phenomena that were believed to present a threat to religion by sensationalising them in a single, pervasive stereotype.

Indeed, 'atheism' is by no means the only example of this. One can draw a parallel with other genres in which real and exaggerated components were brought together into an idealised whole that we find distastefully artificial but which clearly served significant

---

(1952), 164-87, and Stephen Greenblatt, 'Invisible Bullets: Renaissance Authority and its Subversion', *Glyph: Johns Hopkins Textual Studies*, 8 (1981), 40-61 (a reference I owe to Moti Feingold): Harriot almost certainly had Deistic tendencies.

[97] *The Historie of the World. Commonly called, The Naturall Historie of C. Plinius Secundus*, trans. Philemon Holland (1601), 'The Preface to the Reader'.

[98] See Brooke, *Life*, 98-9, 107; Kocher, *Marlowe*, 61-3 and *passim*. On this aspect of Marlowe's ideas see, for instance, D. J. Palmer, 'Marlowe's Naturalism', in *Christopher Marlowe*, ed. Brian Morris (1968), 151-75.

[99] The word is used by Josias Nichols in his *Order of Houshold Instruction* (1596), sig. E7, although the earliest usage given in *OED* is Burton's of 1621; it is symptomatic, however, that Nichols uses the word as a synonym for 'atheist'. On its (rare) use in sixteenth-century France, see Busson, 'Les Noms', 278-9.

descriptive and prescriptive functions at the time, and coloured contemporary perceptions of reality. There are the writings on witchcraft and on sodomy; the Protestant onslaught on Roman Catholicism and the attack on the radical sects from the mid-Tudor period onwards; the vexed questions of Puritanism and Arminianism; even ideas about enclosers, or about Court and Country. In each case, as with 'atheism', though it would be quite wrong to take the contemporary concept completely seriously, it would be equally mistaken to write it off altogether. Some of these genres have received sympathetic attention in which this has been illustrated, as in Carol Z. Wiener's stress on the element of projection in anti-Catholicism, or Patrick Collinson's note of the overlap between the literature on Puritanism and the Theophrastan character tradition.[100] Others, however, deserve more scrutiny than they have yet received, from a standpoint similar to that which I have adopted here.

As with more recent 'moral panics',[101] hostility to a specific stock figure could encapsulate a wider range of anxieties, and only a sensitive appraisal can do justice to the mixture of real and exaggerated phenomena involved. As historians we have to be able to handle contemporary statements in which the imaginary and the real have a kind of symbiotic relationship, understanding the meaning of constructs that seem to us fantastic. Such heightened effusions may provide us with important information about anxieties of the day which is not available from more direct statements, while their mode of presentation throws significant light on contemporary thought.

[100] C. Z. Wiener, 'The Beleaguered Isle. A Study of Elizabethan and Early Stuart Anti-Catholicism', *Past & Present*, 51 (1971), 27-62; Patrick Collinson, 'A Comment: Concerning the Name Puritan', *Journal of Ecclesiastical History*, 31 (1980), 483-88, and *English Puritanism* (Historical Association, 1983), 7-11.

[101] Cf. Stanley Cohen, *Folk Devils and Moral Panics: the Creation of the Mods and Rockers* (1972). See also K. T. Erikson, *Wayward Puritans: a Study in the Sociology of Deviance* (New York, 1966).

THE HISPANIC-*CONVERSO* PREDICAMENT

By Angus MacKay, M.A., Ph.D., F.R. Hist.S.

READ 14 DECEMBER 1984

The hispanic-*converso* predicament developed over a considerable period of time and was the consequence of intolerance. It affected both Jews and Muslims who converted to Christianity, frequently under extreme pressure. The former are generally known as *conversos* and the latter as *moriscos*. The rise of intolerance involved a reclassification of notions of purity and danger, most notably during the reign of Henry IV of Castile. It also eventually entailed the establishment of an Inquisition. But intolerance was not simply a matter of religion, for both *conversos* and *moriscos* found that their habits, customs, and styles of life were viewed with suspicion and hostility. This, then, was their predicament. This paper will consider the predicament in the light of developing intolerance, and brief attention will also be devoted to the possibility that *conversos* encoded secret predicament messages in literary works. The emphasis is on the kingdom of Castile but, where apposite, examples have been used relating to Portugal, the Crown of Aragon, and Italy.

The causes of the rising tide of intolerance and hate during the later medieval period, as evidenced by such pogroms as those of 1391, 1467 and 1473, were manifold.[1] Economic factors played a particularly important role. When faced with rampant inflation, arbitrary reductions of billon coins, rising taxation, bad harvests, famine, and plague, the urban populace tended to turn on the Jews and *conversos*.[2] The climatic and harvest disasters from 1471 to 1473 in Andalusia, for example, can hardly be discounted as a causative element in the horrific Andalusian pogroms of 1473. Sometimes the sources make the point directly. Descriptions of the pogrom in Lisbon in 1506, for example, tell us that people believed that God was punish-

---

[1] For a recent survey of this subject, see R. Highfield, 'Christians, Jews and Muslims in the same Society: The Fall of *Convivencia* in Medieval Spain', *Studies in Church History 15*, ed. D. Baker (Oxford, 1978), 121–46.

[2] A. MacKay, 'Popular Movements and Pogroms in Fifteenth-Century Castile', *Past & Present*, 55 (1972), 33–67; and 'Climate and Popular Unrest in Late Medieval Castile' in *Climate and History: Studies in Past Climates and Their Impact on Man*, eds.T. M. L. Wigley, M.J. Ingram, G. Farmer (Cambridge, 1981), 356–76; and *Money, Prices and Politics in Fifteenth-Century Castile* (1981), 101–2.

ing the kingdom with plague because of the presence of crypto-Jews, and that at the start of the trouble women had shouted at the *conversos*: '¡Por vosotros, perros, vienen esas pestilencias y males!'[3]

Nevertheless, as in the case just cited, people tended to explain natural and economic disasters, as well as socio-political defects, in terms of a malfunction in the relationship between Man and God. Sin, which could arouse God's anger, required individual confession and penitence. But sin also had a social dimension, for it might not simply be a matter of the sins of an individual but those of society in general or of particular groups within that society. In the ominous and prophetic poem of the *Coplas de Mingo Revulgo*, written at the height of the appalling anarchy of Henry IV's reign in Castile, Mingo Revulgo, representing the *república*, blames all the evils and disasters on the sins and inadequacies of one man, the king. But the prophet Gil Arribato, believing that the sins of the *república* are the cause of the troubles, argues that once society has purged itself of its wickedness, God will provide a remedy.[4] The example illustrates the possibility of choice—in this case between putting all the blame on one individual or blaming society in general. And faced with a choice, what could be more logical than that Christians, like those in Lisbon in 1506, should tend to pick on Jews or crypto-Jews as the obvious culprits?

Yet in dealing with this question the profound changes in attitudes to Jews and *conversos* which took place during the later medieval period must be taken into account. Most historians would accept, with qualifications, that thirteenth-century Spain enjoyed a period of relative tolerance and *convivencia*.[5] The *Cantigas de Santa María* provide a good example of the nature of this 'tolerance'.[6] Several of the standard medieval themes relating to Jews are treated in the *Cantigas*. The Jew as Devil's disciple, for example, is an essential element in the well-known story of Theophilus who, with the aid of a Jew, sold his soul to the Devil. And in the miniatures which accompany this particular *cantiga* the Jew can be seen as a satanic intermediary at the anti-court of the Devil.[7] Other *cantigas* illustrate

---

[3] Alonso de Santa Cruz, *Crónica de los reyes católicos*, ed. J. de Mata Carriazo (2 Vols., Seville, 1951), *II*. 85–8: 'It is because of you, you dogs, that these pestilences and evils have come'.

[4] *Le 'Coplas de Mingo Revulgo'*, ed. Marcella Ciceri in *Cultura Neolatina*, XXXVII (1977), 75–266.

[5] For what follows, see V. Hatton and A. MacKay, 'Anti-Semitism in the *Cantigas de Santa María*', *Bulletin of Hispanic Studies*, LXI (1983), 189–99.

[6] The texts of the poems are in Alfonso X, O Sabio, *Cantigas de Santa María*, ed. W. Mettmann (4 Vols., Coimbra, 1959–72). The miniatures which correspond to the poems are reproduced in J. Guerrero Lovillo, *Las Cántigas. Estudio arqueológico de sus minaturas* (Madrid, 1949). Subsequent references will be to *cantiga* numbers.

[7] *Cantiga* 3.

the themes of the Jew as traitor, the Jew as child murderer, and the Jews as re-enactors of the crucifixion, albeit in this case using a wax image and not a Christian child.[8] Despite the absence of some of the more extreme views to be found elsewhere in Europe, therefore, it might be supposed that the Jews in the *Cantigas* are irremediably evil and satanic. But in fact this is not the case. In comparison to later attitudes, both the *Cantigas* and the *Siete Partidas* demonstrate the existence of a religious attitude which may be termed 'optimistic'. If the Jew was satanic this was because of his religion, not because of his race. The Jew as potential convert, therefore, was not irremediably wicked, and baptism, which changed the Jew into a Christian, was the crucial rite of transition which altered everything. There is even the implication that Jews were the unwitting accomplices of the Devil. In *cantiga* 109, for example, a Jew asks some devils why they never harm Jews, and when he is told that this is because they do not bear the sign of baptism and serve the Devil, he is clearly frightened by this revelation. Seen as souls to be saved for Christ, therefore, it is hardly surprising that numerous *cantigas* emphasise peaceful methods of converting Jews.[9] This 'optimistic' attitude is also enshrined in the laws of the *Siete Partidas*:

> Fuerça, nin premia non deuen fazer en ninguna manera a ningund Judio, porque se torna Christiano; mas por buenos exemplos, e con los dichos de las Santas Escripturas, e con falagos los deuen los Christianos convertir a la Fe de Nuestro Señor Jesu Christo; ca el non quiere, nin ama seruicio, que le sea fecho por premia.[10]

Successful persuasion, of course, meant that the converted Jew was like any other Christian. This 'optimistic' attitude was echoed by the fifteenth-century *converso* and royal secretary, Fernán Díaz de Toledo, when he argued that baptism made the baptised a new person, cancelled any obligation of atonement, and eliminated previous blame and sin.[11] But by the time that Fernán Díaz was writing attitudes had changed considerably.

---

[8] For example *cantigas* 4, 6, 12, 348.

[9] For example *cantigas* 85, 89, 107, 108.

[10] *Siete Partidas*, Part VII, Tit. XXIV, Ley VI, in *Los códigos españoles concordados y anotados* (12 Vols., Madrid, 1847-8), IV. 430-1: 'Force and violence should not in any way be used on any Jew in order to convert him to Christianity. On the contrary Christians should convert them to the faith of our Lord Jesus Christ by good example, quotations from the Holy Scriptures, and friendly persuasion. For Christ does not want or love any service which is done on his behalf by force'.

[11] See the text of the *Instrucción del Relator* which is reproduced in Alonso de Cartagena, *Defensorium Unitatis Christianae*, ed. P. Manuel Alonso (Madrid, 1943), 345.

Peaceful conversion was not easily achieved. If there was no constraint or if, as seems to have been the case with Nachmanides in
the disputation at Barcelona in 1263, Jews were allowed a relative
freedom of speech,[12] then persuasion failed because of the very nature of the arguments used. For, in order to persuade Jews that
Christ was the Messiah, the Christians had increasingly to resort to
allegory in order to prove, as best they could, that the New Testament was the logical fulfilment of the Old. But by doing so they ran
directly counter to Jewish insistence on the *peshat*—that is, the literal
meaning of the Old Testament. In contrast, Christian attempts at
literal interpretations of Talmudic *aggadah* were rejected by Jews
who insisted on allegorical interpretations of the same texts.[13] There
were of course isolated cases of conversion, but in general terms the
context within which peaceful persuasion was attempted failed
because, quite simply, the Jews regarded Christian arguments as
illogical, not to say absurd.

It was quite another matter, however, when peaceful persuasion
turned into attempts at conversion under pressure—a change that
was facilitated by the intransigent zeal of the mendicant orders and
the eschatalogical belief that all infidels would be converted to Christianity before the last days.[14] The Jew as potential convert was not
irremediably evil. But what about the obstinate Jew who refused to
let himself be converted? Already in the 1240s in Aragon Jews and
Muslims were compelled to attend the sermons of mendicant friars,[15]
and from this point on successive waves of evangelisation by pressure
occurred. Writing in the early sixteenth-century the chronicler
Bernáldez commented naively, with reference to the fifteenth-century
evangelisation campaigns of Vicente Ferrer, that many Jews
'veníanse a las iglesias ellos mismos a se baptizar.'[16] But he revealed
the true state of affairs when dealing with the last attempts at conversion on the eve of the expulsion:

> ... los judíos ... aunque ante los ojos vían el destierro e perdición

[12] Y. Baer, *A History of the Jews in Christian Spain* (2 vols., Philadelphia, 1978), I.
152–3.
[13] For the difficulties in general, see A. P. Hayman, 'Judaism and the Christian
Predicament', *The Modern Churchman*, XX (1979), 86–100.
[14] M. Kriegel, *Les Juifs à la fin du Moyen Age dans l'Europe méditerraneenne* (Paris, 1979),
182–3, 196, 218–20. On problems relating to the phenomenon of conversion, see J. H.
Edwards, 'Religious Belief and Social Conformity: The 'Converso' Problem in Late-
Medieval Córdoba', *Transactions of the Royal Historical Society*, 5th Series, 31 (1981),
115–28.
[15] Baer, *History of the Jews*, I, 151–2.
[16] Andrés Bernáldez, *Memorias del reinado de los reyes católicos*, eds. M. Gómez-Moreno
and J. de Mata Carriazo (Madrid, 1962), 95: '... they themselves came to the
churches to have themselves baptised'.

suya, aunque requeridos fueron e amonestados por las dichas ped-
ricaciones e amonestamientos, sienpre pertinasces e incrédulos que-
daron, e aunque de fuerça dieron el oído nunca de grado recogeron
en el coraçon cosa que les aprovechasse . . .[17]

But in fact worse problems were posed by those Jews who did
convert, and in large numbers, during and after the pogrom of 1391,
during the campaign of Vicente Ferrer, and during and after the
expulsion. There was firstly a social problem. The Jews were de-
barred from holding offices in Church and State but, having
accepted baptism, the same did not apply to *conversos*. Thus during
the late fourteenth and the first half of the fifteenth centuries a
substantial number of *converso* families succeeded in obtaining important offices in the Church, the royal administration, and the
urban oligarchies.[18] Many of these *conversos* also married into Old
Christian families. Indeed if the royal secretary Fernán Díaz de Toledo is to be believed, almost all the noble families of Castile had
acquired *converso* relatives by the mid fifteenth century.[19] Inevitably,
the rapid social advancement of certain *converso* families provoked
resentment and even hate. It was alleged that *conversos* bought urban
offices and that, as oligarchs, they acted in a manner which was
insufferable to Old Christians.[20] When, during the uprising in Toledo in 1449, Pedro Sarmiento, the rebel leader, promulgated a
'sentencia-estatuto' in which he named all the *conversos* who were to
be expelled from the town's offices, the first step had been taken in
the formulation of the doctrine of *limpieza de sangre*.[21]

The second problem was religious. Among the *conversos* there were,
no doubt, genuine Christians, but many who had converted under
duress remained crypto-Jews. Still others, the so-called 'Averroists',
appear to have been basically irreligious, and statements such as 'No
vos fagan entender que ay parayso nin ynfierno nin vos fagan creer
otra cosa syno nasçer e morir e tener onbre lo que ha menester' or

---

[17] Ibid., 253: '. . . although they could see exile and ruin in front of their eyes, and
although they were pressurised and admonished by the said sermons and admoni-
tions, the Jews continued to remain obstinate and unbelieving. And although they
were forced to listen, they never willingly took to heart anything that would benefit
them . . .'.
[18] MacKay, 'Popular Movements', 46–8; F. Márquez Villanueva, 'Conversos y car-
gos concejiles en el siglo XV', *Revista de archivos, bibliotecas y museos*, LXIII (1975),
503–40.
[19] *Instrucción del relator*, 342–3
[20] See, for example, Mosén Diego de Valera, *Memorial de diversas hazañas*, ed. J. de
Mata Carriazo (Madrid, 1941), 240
[21] E. Benito Ruano, *Toledo en el siglo XV* (Madrid, 1961), 191–6. 'Limpieza de
sangre' means 'Cleanliness of blood'.

'No cures, en este mundo no me veays padeçer que en el otro no me vereys arder' became almost clichés.[22] Finally, a large number of *conversos*, and later *moriscos*, can only have had the haziest of notions about the doctrines of the religion to which they had now, in theory, converted. It is hardly surprising, therefore, that historians have failed to agree on the religious characteristics of the *conversos*, some identifying them as crypto-Jews and others insisting on their Christianity. The same confusion reigned at the time. When Diego de Susán, a rich and prominent citizen of Seville, was burned by the Inquisition, Bernáldez remarked that 'era gran rabí, e según pareció murió como cristiano'.[23]

Faced with this confusion, there were demands for a relocation of social and religious boundaries. Not surprisingly, the efficacy of baptism was called into question. Bernáldez, himself a priest, described a mass baptism by 'sprinkling' which was later 'supplemented' by priests, presumably by additional baptisms. Yet elsewhere he bluntly states that the baptisms of *conversos* were invalidated because of '*nulidad*' and because of judaizing.[24] By the time he was writing, however, the opposite was the official view—the religious distinction between Jews and Christians remained but, precisely because of baptism, it was possible for the Inquisition to try *conversos* as Christian heretics. But, earlier, those who had called for the establishment of an Inquisition had not been immediately successful. For right at the centre of power in Castile there were powerful men who were allegedly trying to undermine the moral and religious values of Christian society. Before the establishment of the Inquisition the volume of real and imaginary deviance was to increase dramatically.

Late in 1463 several Franciscans, led by Alonso de Espina and Fernando de la Plaza, appeared at the royal court and asked Henry IV to carry out an '*inquisición*' into the activities of *converso* heretics. In fact the friars preached on the subject, and in one sermon Fernando de la Plaza claimed that he had in his possession the foreskins of boys circumcised by their *converso* parents. Henry IV reacted by telling the friars that their allegations were very serious, that he,

---

[22] The examples cited are taken from a recent study which suggests that such attitudes were more widespread than has been thought: M. Monsalvo Antón, 'Herejía conversa y contestación religiosa a fines de la edad media: Las denuncias a la Inquisición en el obispado de Osma', *Studia Historica*, II (1984), 109–38: 'Do not let them persuade you that there is a heaven or a hell, and do not let them make you believe in anything else save being born and dying and having what is necessary', or 'Do not worry, you do not see me suffer in this world, and you will not see me burning in the next'.

[23] Bernáldez, *Memorias*, 99–100: 'he was a famous Rabbi, and it seems that he died like a Christian'.

[24] Ibid., 97, 260.

as king, would deal with this danger to the Catholic faith, and that they should give him the foreskins and the names of the guilty parties. Fray Fernando, who of course had no foreskins in his possession, replied that everything he had stated had been testified to by 'persons of authority'. The king asked for their names, but once again the friar failed to provide the evidence.[25]

This was no mere isolated incident. By 1460 Alonso de Espina, who participated in the events just described, had completed his *Fortalitium Fidei*, which not only covered a host of real and imagined enemies, such as Jews, Moors, heretics, and demons, but also constituted 'a ready-made manual' for the establishment of an Inquisition.[26] In fact the very next year Espina persuaded the less fanatical Jeronymites, led by Alfonso de Oropesa, to join the Franciscans in demanding an inquisition, and Henry IV actually agreed to a limited operation in the Toledan region under the more moderate Oropesa.[27] To the fanatical Espina, however, only radical measures could be acceptable. Significantly, his *Fortalitium Fidei* not only reveals his obsession with blood-libel stories and the practice of circumcision, but it also contains allegations that the royal government and its judges deliberately impeded the execution of justice and protected the evil-doers.[28]

That the royal government protected the wicked and that the king himself should have refused to accept Fernando de la Plaza's accusations about circumcision at face value was hardly surprising. Were not the king, his courtiers and officials sodomites or heretics as well? The anonymous and ferocious dialogues of the *Coplas del Provincial* named names. In them, Henry IV named his homosexual lovers. In them Diego Arias, the royal *contador*, was asked how, having no foreskin, he acquired a cross among his heraldic arms, and replied that he had been present at the crucifixion and had put Christ on the cross. These are only examples from a vast catalogue of names and alleged types of deviance.[29] The moderate and sophisticated *Coplas de Mingo Revulgo* likewise accepted the allegations of sodomy and the crisis of religious identity at the Castilian court.[30] Nor were the accusations confined to poetry. The chronicler Alonso

---

[25] Diego Enríquez del Castillo, *Crónica del rey don Enrique el cuarto de este nombre* (*Biblioteca de autores españoles*, Vol. LXX, Madrid, 1953), 130.

[26] Baer, *A History of the Jews*, II. 283-4; H. Beinart, *Conversos on Trial: The Inquisition in Ciudad Real* (Jerusalem, 1981), 9-20.

[27] Baer, *A History of the Jews*, II. 289-91.

[28] Ibid., II. 283, 287; Beinart, *Conversos on Trial*, 12.

[29] For the text of the *Coplas del Provincial*, see J. Rodríguez Puértolas, *Poesía crítica y satírica del siglo XV* (Madrid, 1981), 233-62.

[30] For the text of the *Coplas de Mingo Revulgo*, see above, note 4.

de Palencia linked the phenomenon of sodomy to the presence of *moros infieles* at court, and from this it was but a short step to allege that, when the king's enemies dethroned Henry IV in effigy at Avila in 1465, they had considered accusing him of heresy:

> ... fundar la acusación en el crimen de herejía, así por ser manifiestos sus muchos delitos contra la religión perpetrados, o mejor dicho, por no verse en él vestigio alguno de la fe católica, como por otros más secretos testimonios, aducidos por el marqués de Villena allí presente, y por el maestre de Calatrava, ausente, según los cuales, habíales inducido secretamente a abrazar el culto mahometano, con promesas de mayor engrandecimiento.[31]

And when, after the dethronement, the boy Alfonso had been raised up as king, letters of propaganda were sent out in his name expressing the hope that 'seran por mi estirpados e derribados de mis regnos los pecados de heregia sodomia e blasfemia que en tiempo de mi antecesor don Enrique tanto se ha contynuado quanto es notorio ...'.[32] Castile, a Christian realm, had been corrupted by a demonic king: 'sosteniendo los moros enemigos de nuestra santa fe catolica e trayendolos consigo e teniendolos en su casa e palacio e dandoles el sueldo doblado ... e cometiendo e continuando por sy mismo e mandando faser e cometer en su casa e corte e palacio los enormes pecados que corrompen los aires e destruyen la natura humana ... e por ello se espera la perdicion e destruycion de aquestos reynos.'[33]

Obviously, according to the king's enemies, a fundamental religious and moral reform, including the establishment of a proper Inquisition, was desperately needed. And when it came, in the reign of the Catholic Kings, it was portrayed as being something beyond

---

[31] Alonso de Palencia, *Crónica de Enrique IV*, trans. and ed. A. Paz y Melia (3 Vols., Madrid, 1973-5), I. 68, 167: '... to base their accusation on the crime of heresy. Not only were his many misdeeds committed against religion well known or, rather, not only was it impossible to detect in him any sign of the Catholic Faith, but there were other more secret testimonies. These were provided by the Marquis of Villena, who was present, and by the Master of Calatrava, who was absent. According to them, the king had secretly tried to persuade them to embrace the Muslim religion, with promises of greater riches and status'.

[32] Archivo Municipal de Burgos, Actas Capitulares of 1465, ff. 71R-71V: 'the sins of heresy, sodomy, and blasphemy, which were as prevalent as they were notorious in the reign of my predecessor Henry, will be uprooted and destroyed by me from my kingdoms ...'.

[33] Ibid., ff. 81V-82V: 'sustaining the Moors, enemies of our Holy Catholic Faith, and bringing them in his company and having them in his house and palace and giving them double pay ... and continuing to commit with his own person and ordering to do and commit in his house and court and palace the enormous sins which corrupt the air and destroy human nature ... with the result that the loss and destruction of these kingdoms is nigh'.

human capability—in fact the work of God. Nothing, according to Fernando del Pulgar, could have remedied matters except God, using his chosen instrument Isabella.[34] Bernáldez, on describing the death of this 'tan cathólica y neçesaria reina', even drew a deliberate parallel with the portents which, according to Einhard, marked the approach of Charlemagne's death.[35]

But what did the transition from darkness to light imply? In the first place a growing awareness of a 'cluster' of associated dangers and, by extension, a reclassification of notions of purity and impurity. In the attacks on Henry IV and his supporters the terminology linked together heresy, sodomy, and blasphemy as if they constituted a single phenomenon of some sort.[36] Just as Henry IV's abominable homosexuality, which was probably linked to sodomitical Muslims, whose religion the king had probably embraced, 'corrupted' the very air that people breathed, so too had the Jews 'corrupted' the wells and streams of medieval Europe. Corruption, contamination, and filth were almost tangible phenomena. That Jews gave off a foul smell, for example, was a medieval commonplace,[37] so it is not surprising to find someone like Bernáldez referring to the 'hedionda sinagoga' and the 'hediondos judíos'.[38] It is this sense of impurity and contamination which gathered strength in the fifteenth century, as can be seen in the famous constitutional demands, known as the *Sentencia de Medina del Campo*, which the rebel nobles presented to Henry IV in 1465.[39] It appears from this lengthy project of reform

---

[34] Fernando del Pulgar, *Letras. Glosa a las Coplas de Mingo Revulgo*, ed. J. Domínguez Bordona (Madrid, 1958), 210.

[35] Bernáldez, *Memorias*, 487-8. 'such a Catholic and indispensable queen'.

[36] In this, of course, Spain was not exceptional. See, for example, M. Barber, 'Lepers, Jews and Moslems: The Plot to Overthrow Christendom in 1321', *History*, 66 (1981), 1-17. Forms of punishment may have helped to group 'deviants' together. A thirteenth-century Castilian law stipulated that sodomites be hung upside down by the legs until dead: J. Boswell, *Christianity, Social Tolerance, and Homosexuality* (Chicago and London, 1980), 288. Jews condemned to death suffered the same fate, and Kriegel has noted that, during the 1449 uprising in Toledo, 'la foule massacra des Nouveaux Chrétiens, traîna leurs cadavres jusqu'à la grande-place de la ville, et pour bien manifester la véritable identité religieuse de ses victimes, les pendit à la manière des Juifs': Kriegel, *Les Juifs*, 32. The same fate awaited the *conversos* who fell victim to the Toledan massacres of 1467. Indeed in this case the cry of the *pregonero* explained the punishment: 'Esta es la justicia que manda facer la comunidad de Toledo a estos traidores, capitanes de los conversos hereges; por cuanto fueron contra la Iglesia, mándalos colgar de los pies cabeza abajo: quien tal face, que tal pague'. See Benito Ruano, *Toledo en el siglo XV*, 98.

[37] L. K. Little, *Religious Poverty and the Profit Economy in Medieval Europe* (1978), 52-3.

[38] Bernáldez, *Memorias*, 94, 96: 'the foul-smelling synagogue'; 'the foul-smelling Jews'.

[39] For the full text of the *sentencia*, see *Memorias de don Enrique IV de Castilla* (2 Vols., Madrid, 1835-1913), II. 355-479.

that Jews and Moors tried to convert and circumcise Christians; that they entered churches to abuse representations of Christ, the Virgin, and the saints; that they committed 'great and enormous' sins with Christian virgins and wives; that their guile was so great that they succeeded in obtaining any offices they asked for; and that they had tried to obtain consecrated hosts, break altars, and take chrism, holy oil and other consecrated objects in order to commit wicked deeds against Christ, the Church, and the Faith. Even the very touch of Jews and Moors could contaminate, and so food and medicine prepared by them could not be sold or given to Christians. Was it not natural, then, that the Conquest of Granada by the Catholic Kings should be seen by some as cleansing the country of a 'sucia lepra'?[40]

But what about the converts to Christianity? Traditionally, for example, it was thought that at the critical point of baptism the foul smell of the Jews disappeared because of the purifying effects of the baptismal water.[41] Not so, according to Bernaldez: 'E puesto caso que algunos fueron baptizados, mortificado el carácter del baptismo en ellos por la nulidad e por judaizar, hedían como judios'. And, in referring to 'esta erética pravedad', Bernáldez equated it with 'lepra'.[42] In cataloguing their misdeeds, he also seems to have been almost repeating the contents of the *Sentencia de Medina del Campo*. Like the Jews and Moors, the *conversos* set little store by virginity and chastity; they concentrated on multiplying their own numbers; they profaned nuns in order to insult Christ and the Church; and they attempted, with success, to obtain the best offices and easiest jobs at the expense of the Old Christians.[43] But the reclassification process did not stop here. Filth and impurity became a characteristic of blood and could not be lost at conversion; *limpieza*, on the other hand, was the term used to describe the blood of Old Christians. The *converso* could still 'ensuciar y mancillar la sangre limpia.'[44] The same was to be the case with the *moriscos*. For the Old Christians Muhammad was 'puto, suzio y bellaco', and the *moriscos'* lack of *limpieza de sangre* was due to the fact that they descended from the bastard lineage of Ismael,

---

[40] Garci Rodríguez de Montalvo, *Las sergas del muy esforzado caballero Esplandián* (*Biblioteca de autores españoles*, Vol. XL, Madrid, 1953), 505: 'dirty leprosy'.

[41] Little, *Religious Poverty*, 53.

[42] Bernáldez, *Memorias*, 97, 102–3: 'And even if some of them were baptised, the nature of this baptism being cancelled by nullity and by judaizing, they still smelt foully like Jews'. 'This depraved heresy'; 'leprosy'.

[43] Ibid., 97–8.

[44] This view, which became widespread, might have been current as early as the reign of John II. See the alleged 'carta de privilegio que el rey don Juan II dio a un Hijo dalgo' in N. López Martínez, *Los Judaizantes castellanos y la Inquisición en tiempo de Isabel la Católica* (Burgos, 1954), 385: 'dirty and stain clean blood'.

whereas the Christians belonged to the noble lineage of Isaac.[45] At the same time, however, there was a curious inversion of 'cleanliness' and 'dirt'. Cleanliness became a sign of religious impurity. The *morisco* fondness for washing was something that scandalised the Old Christians, and they interpreted it as a ritual act denoting heresy. Even if it was accepted in a particular instance that washing was not a rite, it was still believed that the intention was religious.[46]

Secondly, the transition involved the establishment of the Inquisition, and this in turn brought about fundamental changes. The Inquisition monopolised persecution and, by working within a framework of rules and procedures, it substituted a rule of law, whatever one thinks of it, for mob violence. On the other hand, before the Inquisition, persecution and violence had been decentralised and illegal. The monarchy, for example, condemned the pogroms of 1391, the uprising and killings in Toledo in 1449 constituted a 'rebellion', and even literary insults against *conversos* tended to be anonymous. But with the Inquisition this persecution was transferred, as it were, from the private to the public sector, the sanctions became legal, and the individuals accused were confronted by a hierarchy of state officials who sought them out and then determined their innocence or guilt. The guilty, for their part, had to bear the full weight of public and legal sanctions—they were ritually punished, their errors were formally recorded, and their future conduct subjected to control. Many *conversos* and *moriscos*, of course, were never directly affected by the Inquisition, but it should be remembered that fear itself acted as a sanction against anti-social conduct.

The use of the term 'anti-social conduct' might seem odd in this context, but in fact it can be justified. Of course the Inquisition preoccupied itself with properly religious issues and, since all three religions were strongly ritualistic, the performance of rituals acquired a particular importance.[47] Since baptism was a sacrament, for example, *conversos* and *moriscos* could hardly avoid it. But, safe within their houses, they tried to 'dechristianize' their children immediately after baptism with an 'anti-ritual' which would efface the effects of the Christian sacrament.[48] Confession presented similar

[45] L. Cardaillac, *Morisques et chrétiens: Un affrontement polémique (1492-1640)* (Paris, 1977), 20, 44-6: A 'vile, dirty, sodomite'.

[46] M. García-Arenal, *Inquisición y moriscos: Los procesos del Tribunal de Cuenca* (Madrid, 1978), 50-1.

[47] Edwards, 'Religious Belief', 126-7.

[48] Beinart, *Conversos on Trial*, 279-80, 290; Beinart, 'The Spanish Inquisition and a *Converso* Community in Extremadura', *Medieval Studies*, XLIII (1981), 460; Cardaillac, *Morisques et chrétiens*, 27-8; García-Arenal, *Inquisición y moriscos*, 56-7.

problems. A deaf confessor at Miravete was beseiged by *moriscos*, and elsewhere *conversos* and *moriscos* were rapidly despatched because they had nothing to confess.[49] According to Bernáldez one priest cut a piece of clothing from a *converso*, saying: 'Pues nunca pecaste, quiero que me quede de vuestra ropa reliquia para sanar los enfermos'.[50] How, too, could these suspects avoid crossing themselves in Church? Inés López, it was alleged at her trial, 'non haze señal de Cruz, syno de la frente tira hasta el honbro, en manera que no haze señal de Cruz' and 'desya "en Nombre del Padre" e nunca desya "en Nombre del Hijo" ni mas'.[51]

It is also clear, however, that mundane activities, such as the way people ate or dressed, carried a ceremonial or ritual significance indicating religious deviance or conformity. The willingness or refusal to eat pork was the classic case, but it was by no means the only one as far as food was concerned. In the trial of Juan González Pintado, formerly royal secretary to both John II and Henry IV, the defence was forced to go to extraordinary lengths to try and prove that the accused 'de todo comia como otro qualquier christiano viejo comia e devia comer, sin enpacho alguno'.[52] Similarly, in 1538 the *morisco* Juan de Burgos was put on trial because he had organised *fiestas* in which those invited ate *alcuzcuz*, danced *zambras*, talked in arabic, and used their Muslim rather than their Christian names—'y esto se presume, que lo fazían por guarda de la seta de Mahoma'. Even sitting on the floor and not eating at table were regarded as *cerimonias* 'de la dicha secta de Mahoma'.[53] It was not, therefore, simply a matter of doctrinal or theological divergence, but of pressure towards social conformity. Fray Hernando de Talavera explained it in the following manner to the inhabitants of the Albaicín:

> Mas para que vuestra conversión sea sin escándalo de los cristianos de nación y no piensen que aún teneis la secta de Mahoma en el coraçon, es menester que os conformeis en todo y por todo a la buena y honesta conversación de los buenos y honestos cristianos

[49] Cardaillac, *Morisques et chrétiens*, 31.

[50] Bernáldez, *Memorias*, 97: 'Since you have never sinned, I want a bit of your clothing as a relic to cure the ill'.

[51] *Records of the Trials of the Spanish Inquisition in Ciudad Real*, ed. H. Beinart (3 Vols., Jerusalem, 1974–81), II. 78, 80, 84, 88, 96, 104, 119–20: 'does not make the sign of the cross; instead she only motions from the forehead to the shoulder, so that she does not make the sign of the cross'; 'she said "in the name of the Father" and never said "in the name of the Son" or anything else'.

[52] Ibid., I. 92–132: 'ate everything that any other Old Christian ate or should have eaten, without exception'.

[53] Cardaillac, *Morisques et chrétiens*, 19, 27: 'and it is assumed that they did this in order to observe the sect of Muhammad'; 'of the said sect of Muhammad'.

y cristianas, en vestir y calçar y afeitar y en comer y en mesas y en viandas guisadas como comunmente las guisan ...[54]

Bernáldez, referring to other *moriscos*, put it more bluntly—'y nunca fueron leales'.[55]

In practice, then, the predicament of the *conversos* and *moriscos* meant that a chance remark or an inappropriate action, even if uttered or performed by a child, might have the most serious consequences. And it does not take much imagination to comprehend the possibility that tensions existed between the outward or public performance of meaningless Christian rituals and the inward adherence to beliefs and customs which could not be expressed openly. It is this situation which has led scholars to posit the existence of what may be termed 'predicament messages' in literary works. If, for example, *conversos* could not express themselves openly, they may well have used literature as a vehicle in which to encode attacks on the prevailing religious and social values which they despised. Alternatively if, say, an anonymous work can be interpreted as containing such an attack, might not its author have been a *converso*?

This whole problem has, I believe, been complicated by the recent twentieth-century predicament in Spain. During and after the Civil War liberal and left-wing intellectuals, like the fifteenth-century Jews, had to choose between going into exile or paying lip service to the values of the new regime. Within Spain authors had to submit their work for 'democratic orientation and consultation' to the Department of Popular Culture, a process which was simply political censorship and had nothing to do with either 'democracy' or 'popular culture'. Meanwhile, in the schools and universities, there was a tendency to teach a kind of 'national' history which has been described, with some exaggeration, by the novelist Juan Goytisolo.[56] As children they were taught that the primitive inhabitants of the peninsula had the same eternal, almost racial, characteristics as those possessed by their twentieth-century descendents. There was,

---

[54] See M. Espadas Burgos, 'Aspectos sociorreligiosos de la alimentación española', *Hispania*, no. 131 (1975), 547: 'But in order that your conversion should not scandalise the national Christians and make them feel that you still have the sect of Muhammad in your hearts, it is necessary that you conform completely to the good and honest conversation of the good and honest Christian men and women, and this is also necessary in your clothes and shoes, and in shaving, and in your food, and in eating at tables, and in cooking food in the way that it is normally cooked ...'.

[55] Bernáldez, *Memorias*, 399: 'and they were never loyal'.

[56] For what follows, see Juan Goytisolo, 'Supervivencias tribales en el medio intelectual español', in *Estudios sobre la obra de Américo Castro* ed. P. Laín Entralgo (Madrid, 1971), 141–56.

in other words, a direct line of connection which, starting with Pelayo, passed through the Cid and Isabella the Catholic, and reached down to Franco. This eternal and Christian Spain had survived throughout the centuries because of a kind of biological war against antibodies—that is, Jews, Muslims, Protestants, Encyclopaedists, Liberals, Masons, Anarchists, and of course Marxists and Communists. Such a view, of course, produced some curious results. For example St Isidore, according to the historian Fray Justo Pérez de Urbel, was a Spanish nationalist,[57] in the introduction to Ballesteros Gaibrois' biography of Isabella the Catholic both Isabella and Franco are identified as the exemplary leaders of Spain's 'manifest destiny',[58] and as late as the 1960s reputable historians collaborated in a rather hilarious periodical which was started up with the specific objective of securing the beatification of Isabella.[59] Meanwhile, however, students who were aware of censorship and the poverty of university intellectual life busied themselves in reading precisely those books which were frowned upon or banned. Their 'predicament' has been well described by Márquez Villanueva, and he also relates the effects which Américo Castro's *España en su historia* had on his generation.[60] For Castro in effect invited the Jews, Moors, and *conversos* back into Spain's history and stressed their contributions to Spanish civilisation. An insight into this interpretative trend can be obtained from the text of a public lecture, very reminiscent of Andrei Sinyavsky's essay 'The Literary Process in Russia',[61] which

---

[57] See P. Linehan, 'Religion, Nationalism and National Identity in Medieval Spain and Portugal', in *Studies in Church History 18*, ed. S. Mews (Oxford, 1982), 163-4.

[58] M. Ballesteros Gaibrois, *La obra de Isabel la Católica* (Segovia, 1953). The introduction was by the *Gobernador Civil* and *Jefe Provincial del Movimiento de Segovia*. In it Ballesteros Gaibrois, Professor at the University of Madrid, is lavishly praised for his falangist historical interpretation, and Franco, identifying his 'mission' with that of the Catholic Kings, is quoted at length. Ballesteros, for his part, indulges in a shoddy manipulation of history. Referring to the case of the Santo Niño de La Guardia, for example, he states that 'hoy no cabe la menor duda acerca de su certeza' (p. 157), and José Antonio Primo de Rivera is approvingly quoted with respect to Isabella's great legacy of the 'criterio supremo de unidad' (p. 307).

[59] See *Reina Católica. Boletín de la causa de beatificación de la reina Isabel I de Castilla*, no. 1 (1964).

[60] F. Márquez Villanueva, 'El encuentro con la obra de Américo Castro', in *Estudios sobre la obra de Américo Castro*, ed. P. Laín Entralgo (Madrid, 1971), 157-69; Américo Castro, *España en su historia (Cristianos, moros y judíos)* (Buenos Aires, 1948). Lack of space prevents me from discussing the polemic to which Castro's publications gave rise, but it should be noted that its most bitter manifestations involved historians in exile. For a succinct survey and bibliography, see T. F. Glick, *Islamic and Christian Spain in the Early Middle Ages* (Princeton, 1979), 314-16.

[61] Andrei Sinyavsky, 'The Literary Process in Russia', in *Kontinent: The Alternative Voice of Russia and Eastern Europe*, ed. V. Maximov and I. Golomshtok (1977), 73-110.

Goytisolo gave after Franco's death.[62] In a situation where the State monopolises truth and the way in which language is used, the writer, unless he is an official time-server in which case his writings have little interest, can literally be a criminal. Thus just as Christophorovich, the Soviet prosecutor, told Mandelstam that his famous poem was a 'terrorist act', so Goytisolo was solemnly informed that he was a 'gangster de la pluma'.[63] But in his lecture Goytisolo also drew parallels with the past. Beginning precisely with the Catholic Kings and the Inquisition, no other European literature, save that of Russia, could match that of Spain for its tension between official persecution and truly creative writing:

> Rojas y Fray Luis, Huarte de San Juan y Cervantes cumplieron su obra a sabiendas del eventual delito en que incurrían, de su aleatoria condición de criminales. Habiendo secuestrado el poder la totalidad del lenguaje, no les cabía otro recurso que expresarse, que buscar huecos, agujeros, rendijas por donde colar una realidad no mixtificada por la ideología a través del muro alienador del discurso oficial ... Jugaban literalmente con fuego y lo sabían: las hogueras del Santo Oficio estaban allí para recordárselo.[64]

Clearly, in such circumstances, the notion of a *converso* predicament takes on added dimensions. Yet it should be emphasised that in most cases the object of attention is 'great literature', written by a few individual geniuses, and that the historian is likely to be more interested in wider aspects of the *converso* predicament. There is, too, another obvious problem. To avoid retribution, the encoding of a 'predicament message' would have to be virtually undetectable. The detection of it by modern scholarship, therefore, frequently turns out to be only one possible reading of a text, and one for which it is usually difficult to marshal enough evidence.

Rojas' *La Celestina* is a case in point. Although the author was a *converso*, he does not hint that the reader should look for a hidden meaning, and the plot is basically about love or lust. Now it may be

---

[62] For what follows, see Juan Goytisolo, 'De la literatura considerada como una delincuencia', in the newspaper *El País*, published on 29 April 1979, 'Arte y Pensamiento' section, pp. IV–V.

[63] Nadezhda Mandelstam, *Hope against Hope* (Harmondsworth, 1975), 97; Goytisolo, 'De la literatura', p. IV: 'a pen-wielding gangster'.

[64] Ibid., IV–V: 'Rojas and Fray Luis, Huarte de San Juan and Cervantes fulfilled their work aware of the future guilt which they incurred, aware of their possible status as criminals. Since state power monopolised language, the only way they had of expressing themselves was by looking for holes, pin-pricks, and cracks in the hostile wall of official discourse through which they could sieve a reality which was not contaminated by official ideology ... They were literally playing with fire, and they knew it: the pyres of the Holy Office were there to remind them of the fact'.

that, by identifying the author with some of his characters, it is more than possible to arrive at a Rojas who was sceptical and cynical about prevailing religious and social values, and it may be that this scepticism and cynicism derived from his status as a *converso*. But we cannot be sure.[65] In contrast, the Portuguese 'chivalrous' or 'sentimental' novel, *Menina e Moça*, does invite a search for a hidden meaning. Although very little is known about its author, Bernardim Ribeiro, such evidence as there is strongly suggests that he was a *converso*.[66] So, too, perhaps, does the content of his novel. The author does hint that his audience should read between the lines.[67] And the effect of these warnings is heightened not only by the events as they unfold but by the curious names given to the characters—names which seem to cry out for decipherment. Who, for example, is Bimnarder? He appears at first as an anonymous knight. He falls in love and decides to change his name anagrammatically. There then follows a curious sequence in which a man, who is burned by fire, says 'Bim'n'arder' ('I saw myself burn'). At this point the knight, who knows that he too will burn, decides to call himself Bimnarder.[68] But Bimnarder is also an anagram of the author's name, Bernardim. And is the knight simply aware that he will be consumed by the fire of love, or is there a more sinister implication? In fact Bimnarder is deserting his previous lady, the vengeful Aquelisia, whose odd name appears to be a thinly disguised approximation of *Ecclesia*, the Church.[69] By changing his name and style of life the knight Bimnarder, or perhaps the author Bernardim, hopes in vain to escape the retribution of Aquelisia, or perhaps the Church. Is Bimnarder, therefore, a knightly protagonist in a very odd romance of chivalry, or is he a *converso* who has decided to return to Judaism despite the inevitable retribution that he foresees? In fact he is deserting Aquelisia and turning to his oddly-named new love, Aónia ('to the strength of God').[70] Since ambiguities of this sort abound in the text, it is

---

[65] The leading exponent of the *converso* interpretation is S. Gilman, *The Spain of Fernando de Rojas: The Intellectual and Social Landscape of 'La Celestina'* (Princeton, 1972). For a sceptical reaction to this interpretation, see the important review article by P. E. Russell in *Comparative Literature*, XXVII (1975), 59-74.

[66] See H. Macedo, *Do significado oculto da Menina e Moça* (Lisbon, 1977). B. Pullan, *The Jews of Europe and the Inquisition of Venice, 1550-1670* (Oxford, 1983), 229-41 provides a great deal of information on the Portuguese *converso* family of the Ribeiros to which Bernardim Ribeiro might well have belonged.

[67] Macedo, *Do significado*, 14.

[68] Bernardim Ribeiro, *Menina e Moça*, eds. Aquilino Ribeiro and M. Marques Braga (Lisbon, 1972), 58-9.

[69] Macedo, *Do significado*, 84.

[70] I would like to thank Mr Philip Hersch for suggesting this hebraic interpretation of the name to me.

hardly surprising that the admonition to read between the lines has been taken seriously. Macedo, for example, finds the key to the novel in the kabbalistic and redemptive female figure of the Shekkinah, who was not only seen as a mystical attribute of God, but as the Community of Israel.[71] In his view *Menina e Moça* can be read as 'uma obra de resistência, escrita do ponto de vista de uma minoria perseguida'.[72] And, curiously, when from the mid fifteenth century *conversos* thought of returning to the faith of their fathers, many of them did express their desire in terms of leaving Spain and going abroad to dwell under the shelter of the Shekkinah.[73]

Despite the intrinsic interest of such interpretations, however, the interest for the historian is marginal. Given their existence, what kind of minority audience would be capable of picking up such sophisticated predicament messages? Is there nothing more tangible, more down-to-earth, and more representative which can be used to illustrate the predicament? Fortunately two *converso* writers, Fernando del Pulgar and Francisco Delicado, did concern themselves in a direct and specific way with the fate of that generation of Andalusian *conversos*, especially the females, who first suffered from the activities of the Inquisition.

When the first inquisitors began their work in Seville in 1481 Pulgar openly attacked their policies in a letter to Cardinal Pedro González de Mendoza. The letter marked the beginning of a bitter polemic between Pulgar and an anonymous opponent which took the form of a pamphlet-war carried out in public.[74] In Pulgar's view the *conversos* of Andalusia were not deliberately wicked but simply ignorant and confused, and he went on to calculate that 'mozas donzellas de diez a veinte años hay en el Andaluçía diez mill niñas, que dende que naçieron nunca de sus cassas salieron, ni oyeron ni supieron otra dotrina sino la que vieron hazer a sus padres de sus puertas adentro'.[75] Such people, Pulgar argued, should be brought to the truth by Christian example and religious instruction and, making some bitter allusions to the shortcomings of the Old Christians, he

---

[71] Macedo, *Do significado*, especially chaps. VI and VII.

[72] Ibid., 83: 'a work of resistance, written from the point of view of a persecuted minority'.

[73] H. Beinart, 'The *Converso* Community in 15th Century Spain', in *The Sephardi Heritage: Essays on the History and Cultural Contribution of the Jews of Spain and Portugal*, ed. R. D. Barnett (2 Vols., 1971), I. 438.

[74] F. Cantera Burgos, 'Fernando de Pulgar y los conversos', *Sefarad*, IV (1944), 295-348 not only gives the texts of the letters but provides an exhaustive commentary.

[75] Ibid., 308: 'there are in Andalusia ten thousand girls, between ten and twenty years of age, who, from birth, have never left their homes and have never heard or learned of any doctrine save that which they have seen their parents perform inside their homes'.

drew unfavourable comparisons between the inquisitors, appointed by the royal chancellor, and earlier *converso* bishops who, chosen by Christ, had produced better Christians with the water of baptism than the inquisitors would do with fire.[76] His prediction of the results of the inquisitors' actions in this case was simple and accurate: 'Quemar todos éstos sería cossa crudelíssima y aun difiçile de hazer, porque se avsentarían con desesperaçión a lugares donde no se esperase dellos correptión jamás. También sé cierto que hay algunos que vyen más de la enemiga de los juezes que del miedo de sus consçiençias'.[77] Although the rest of the polemic is of great interest, all that need be emphasised here is its public nature and the obvious fact that this last attempt to urge a policy of moderation in dealing with the *converso* problem failed. In terms of Pulgar's prediction, one of the places where no 'correction' could ever be expected and to which the young Andalusians fled was, ironically, Rome itself.

Francisco Delicado's *La Lozana Andaluza*, published in Venice in 1528, provides, as it were, the next episode of the drama of this lost generation and picks up the story where Pulgar had left off.[78] Delicado, Andalusian *converso*, priest, and author of a treatise on syphilis, from which he himself suffered, lived most of his life in Rome and was intimately acquainted with its low life.[79] His book, in which he participated as both author and character, is regarded as a masterpiece of realistic literature. It is almost as if Delicado had equipped himself with a tape-recorder and video-camera and plunged in to film life.[80] Yet despite the realism, the intervention of the author in his book is evident. Not only did he decide what to 'record' and 'film', but he was by no means above judging the actions of his protagonists.[81]

---

[76] Ibid., 309.

[77] Ibid., 308–9: 'To burn all these people would be an enormously cruel thing to do and also very difficult, because they would in desperation flee to places where no hope of correcting them could ever be expected. I also know for certain that some of them have fled because of the hate of the judges rather than because of their consciences'.

[78] Francisco Delicado, *La Lozana Andaluza*, ed. Bruno M. Damiani (Madrid, 1969).

[79] For further details, see Bruno M. Damiani, *Francisco Delicado* (New York, 1974).

[80] For examples of scholars' views on Delicado's realism, including comparisons with cinematographic techniques, Ibid., 9, 21, 42, 45, 121; A. E. Foley, *La Lozana Andaluza* (1977), 26–7, 29.

[81] Indeed Delicado went out of his way to stress that the low life and corruption of Rome set the scene for the Divine Judgement which took the form of the Sack of Rome in 1527. However the book was written between 1513 and 1527, and the 'Divine Judgement' interpretation of it could not possibly constitute an explanation for Delicado's original aims and intentions. What happened was that Delicado revised his text before publication: a text which described low life was now endowed with characters who cunningly foresaw the disaster of 1527, and the epilogue of the book confirmed the prophecies.

To an overwhelming extent the characters in *La Lozana* are Andalusians, they are humble in wealth and social status, and they are
conversas.[82] Indeed the young *conversa* girls whom Pulgar defended
appear in Delicado's book. For when Lozana asks her *conversa* friends
how long they have been in Rome, they reply: 'Señora mía, desde el
año que se puso la Inquisición'.[83] These are women, too, who are
aware of the practical dilemma of being *conversas*. When Lozana, a
stranger, first appears in their midst they want to know if she is a
conversa as well, so that they can speak freely. But, of course, Lozana
too is on her guard and, if challenged directly, will make herself out
to be a 'cristiana linda'. The solution to this problem once again lies
in the preparation of food. The *conversas* decide to ask Lozana, cas-
ually, to prepare a dish of *hormigos* for them—the point being that
if she prepares the pastry with olive oil, instead of water, this will
indicate that she too is a *conversa*.[84] Lozana passes the test and is
immediately accepted, with all manner of advice and help, into the
converso sub-world of Rome.

But what kind of *conversas* are these women? While, on the one
hand, they are certainly not Christian, it is equally clear that they
are not crypto-Jews. The best summary of their religious attitude is
Teresa of Cordoba's assessment of Lozana as a woman who is a
Christian among Christians, a Jew among Jews, and a Muslim
among Muslims.[85] Clearly, as the text demonstrates again and again,
this attitude does not arise out of a deep knowledge of these religions
but is a matter of low-life expediency, a picaresque-type ability to
behave like others. Although Delicado stresses Lozana's intelligence
and cunning, this is not the same as religious knowledge. Indeed
Delicado, as author and priest, emphasises the difference between
audacia and *sapienzia*. *Audacia* or boldness allows someone like Lozana
to survive—as a prostitute, procuress, and pedlar of curative charms
and other dubious magical practices. *Sapienzia* is the very quality
which these women might have possessed if Pulgar's policy, rather
than that of the Inquisition, had been put into effect. Delicado
defines it as 'temer al Señor' ('fear of the Lord'), and his view derives
directly from Job XXVIII, particularly verse 28: 'Et dixit homini:
Ecce timor Domini, ipsa est sapientia; et recedere a malo, intelligen-
tia'. Women who are *audaces* pander to the sexual desires of men,
do not possess *sapienzia*, and are most vile. Women who possess

[82] See F. Márquez Villanueva, 'El mundo converso de La Lozana Andaluza', *Archivo Hispalense*, LVI (1973), 87–97.

[83] Delicado, *La Lozana Andaluza*, 54–5: 'My lady, we have been here since the year in which the Inquisition began its work'.

[84] Ibid., 51–3.

[85] Ibid., 56.

sapienzia are more precious than any diamond.[86] Clearly Lozana, prostitute and bawd, lacks *sapienzia* and is most vile. Yet, astonishingly, Delicado reaches the opposite conclusion and refuses to condemn her. This priestly absolution is based on two grounds. Firstly Lozana's use of *audacia* was a necessary strategy for survival.[87] And secondly, Lozana does in the end manage to acquire a kind of *sapienzia*, and she leaves Rome to live on the island of Lípari. But this *sapienzia* is not the result of Christian or Jewish religious instruction—it is an instinctive knowledge arising from Lozana's perception of the vanity of life.[88] When Lozana departs for Lípari she is still not a Christian or a crypto-Jew—she is an Andalusia *conversa*.

Was Delicado, an Andalusian *converso* priest, aware of the pamphlet-war which Pulgar had publicly waged against the inquisitors? Certainly we can recognise Pulgar's girls in Delicado's book—older, living by their wits, and religiously indifferent. And it is surely remarkable that, at the beginning of his work, Delicado actually quoted Pulgar in part explanation of his purpose: 'Y como dice el coronista Fernando del Pulgar, 'así daré olvido al dolor'' '.[89] Yet even if Delicado was not aware of Pulgar's attack on the inquisitors, the conclusion is equally impressive because the former corroborated the accuracy of the latter's prediction. These young *conversas* were not given a chance, they did flee in desperation to foreign places, and their fate was miserable.

The predicament of the *conversos* and *moriscos* in the late medieval and early modern period was not simply a religious one but one that involved all manner of habits and customs. The tendency to detect religious differences in terms of such habits and customs implied an alternative of either total integration or rejection. In Talavera's words: '... es menester que os conformeis en todo y por todo ...'. Yet this tendency was not confined to the Old Christians. The *conversas* in Rome accepted Lozana as one of them because she prepared her pastry with olive oil. The more astute could even try and confuse matters by adopting 'positive' habits. Some *moriscos* cultivated vineyards to demonstrate their 'Christianity'. One *morisco*, who had been heard proclaiming the goodness of Mohammad, claimed that he was drunk at the time—an essentially Christian character-

[86] Ibid., 247–8.
[87] Ibid., 45, 248.
[88] See the curious mixture of elements—astrology and a dream involving *Plutón, Mercurio*, and the *árbor de la vanidad*—which precedes Lozana's decision to leave Rome and gives rise to Delicado's judgement that Lozana 'se apartó con tiempo': Ibid., 243–5, 248.
[89] Ibid., 34: 'And as the chronicler Fernando del Pulgar says, "In this way I will forget my grief" '.

istic.[90] No doubt many of those who were caught up in this predicament were either genuine converts or remained steadfast in their Jewish or Muslim faiths. A few, perhaps, encoded their own predicaments in literary works. But it is extremely fortunate that two *converso* intellectuals, Pulgar and Delicado, should have recorded the predicament of those *conversos*, perhaps the majority, who were uninstructed and perhaps indifferent to all organised religions.

[90] Cardaillac, *Morisques et chrétiens*, 24-5.

THE ROYAL HISTORICAL SOCIETY
REPORT OF COUNCIL, SESSION 1984-1985

THE Council of the Royal Historical Society has the honour to present the following report to the Anniversary Meeting.

Grave threats to historical scholarship have arisen as a result of government policies during the past year and given Council cause for deep concern. Pre-eminent has been the effect of the Local Government Act on record offices and archive services in all the metropolitan county areas, and on the *Survey of London* and the Historic Buildings Division in London. Much time and effort was devoted, in company with the Society of Antiquaries and the professional archivists' organisations, to endeavouring to secure the future of, at the very least, joint or unified archive services where they exist, and prevent the extension of 'archive powers' to all the metropolitan districts. The joint campaign was successful only in obtaining very small improvements in the act, but Council is grateful to all those members of both Houses of Parliament who supported its efforts. The campaign has now to move to the localities.

Much alarm was aroused by widely-disseminated rumours that the government would extend VAT to books and periodicals, and Council supported the strong campaign that was waged against the proposal. In the event, no action was taken by the government. Unfortunately, however, its policy of restricting public spending has had a serious effect on the resources of the British Library, though the reduction of services has been so far kept to a minimum. Council is continuing its efforts to make the government aware of the short-sightedness of reducing its funding for the British Library.

Difficulties about remodelling accommodation within University College London have caused the postponement of the proposed move of the Society's rooms, now expected to take place late in 1986.

The Society's offspring STUDIES IN HISTORY has given cause for concern during the year. The original publishers of the series, Swifts, were taken over by Messrs Watmoughs, a change that has not proved advantageous to the publishing of new titles or the marketing of the series. Council in co-operation with the Editorial Board, chaired by Professor Elton, has the problem currently under consideration.

During the year Council voted financial support for the History at the Universities Defence Group and for the forthcoming international colloquium to be held at Oxford as part of academic events marking the bicentenary of the French Revolution. Final arrangements were made for the Society's own conference, in collaboration with the Institute of British Geographers, to mark the novocentenary of Domesday Book, to be held at Winchester, 14–18 July 1986.

The age at which reduced subscriptions become payable by Fellows who have retired was reduced from 67 to 65 to accord with the arrangements under the current universities' superannuation scheme.

Professor J. C. Holt retired from the Presidency of the Society at the Anniversary Meeting on 23 November 1984. Council wishes to record its gratitude to him for the excellent and dedicated service he gave to the Society, and, in particular, for conducting crucial negotiations with the Provost of University College London on the issue of the Society's proposed move to alternative accommodation in University College London.

Council is pleased to report that Professor David Palliser has kindly agreed to succeed Professor G. R. Elton as editor of the *Annual Bibliography of British and Irish History*.

An evening party was held for members and guests at University College London on Wednesday 4 July 1984 for which 152 acceptances were received.

The representation of the Society upon various bodies was as follows: Professor F. M. L. Thompson and Mr A. T. Milne on the Joint Anglo-American Committee exercising a general supervision over the production of the *Bibliographies of British History*; Professor G. W. S. Barrow, Dr P. Chaplais, Mr M. Roper and Professor P. H. Sawyer on the Joint Committee of the Society and the British Academy established to prepare an edition of Anglo-Saxon charters; Professor E. B. Fryde on a committee to regulate British co-operation in the preparation of a new repertory of medieval sources to replace Potthast's *Bibliotheca Historica Medii Aevi*; Professor H. R. Loyn on a committee to promote the publication of photographic records of the more significant collections of British coins; Professor P. Lasko on the Reviewing Committee of the Advisory Council on the Export of Works of Art; Professor J. C. Holt and Professor J. J. Scarisbrick on the British National Committee of the International Historical Congress; Dr G. H. Martin on the Council of the British Records Association; Mr M. R. D. Foot on the Committee to advise the publishers of *The Annual Register*; Professor K. Cameron on the Trust for Lincolnshire Archaeology; Professor C. J. Holdsworth on History at the Universities Defence Group. Council received reports from its representatives.

Professor W. N. Medlicott represents the Society on the Court of the University of Exeter, Professor J. A. S. Grenville on the Court of the University of Birmingham, Professor Glanmor Williams on the Court of the University College of Swansea, Professor A. L. Brown on the University Conference of Stirling University; Professor C. N. L. Brooke on the British Sub-Commission of the Commission Internationale d'Histoire Ecclésiastique Comparée, and Dr A. I. Doyle on the Anthony Panizzi Foundation.

At the Anniversary Meeting on 23 November 1984 at which the President, Professor J. C. Holt, retired under By-law XV, Dr G. E. Aylmer was elected to replace him. The Vice-Presidents retiring under By-law XVI were Professor P. H. Sawyer and Mr K. V. Thomas. Dr G. H. Martin, Professor K. G. Robbins and Professor P. Smith were elected to replace them and to fill the vacancy left by the elevation of Dr Aylmer to the presidency. The members of Council retiring under By-law XIX were Mr U. P. Burke, Professor R. B. Dobson, Professor G. S. Holmes and Professor D. E. Luscombe. Professor D. E. D. Beales, Professor R. C. Floud, Mr G. C. F. Forster and Professor W. A. Speck were elected to fill the vacancies. Professor J. C. Holt was elected an Honorary Vice-President. Messrs Beeby, Harmar and Co. were appointed auditors for the year 1984–85 under By-law XXXVIII.

Publications and Papers read

Transactions, Fifth Series, volume 35, *Handbook of Medieval Exchange,* and *Handbook of British Chronology,* 3rd edition went to press during the session and are due to be published in November 1985. The following works were published during the session: the *Annual Bibliography of British and Irish History* (1983 publications); and one volume in the STUDIES IN HISTORY series: *The Parlement of Poitiers: War, Government and Politics in France 1418–1436,* by R. G. Little (volume 42).

At the ordinary meetings of the Society the following papers were read:

'The Problem of "Atheism" in Early Modern England', by Dr M. C. W. Hunter (12 October 1984).

'The Hispanic *Converso* Predicament', by Dr A. I. K. MacKay (14 December 1984).

'Perceptions of Imperial Decline in Twentieth-Century Britain', by Dr G. J. Darwin (1 February 1985).

'"A king over the sea": Alfred in Continental perspective', by Dr Janet L. Nelson (15 March 1985).

'Plebeian Marriage in Stuart England: some Evidence from Popular Literature', by Dr J. A. Sharpe (19 April 1985).

'The survival of the monarchy in modern Britain', by Professor J. A. Cannon (3 July 1985: Prothero Lecture).

At the Anniversary Meeting on 23 November 1984, the President, Professor J. C. Holt, delivered an address on 'Feudal Society and the Family in early medieval England: IV. The heiress and the alien'.

The Alexander Prize was awarded to Mr George Garnett for his essay 'Coronation and Propaganda: Some Implications of the Norman Claim to the Throne of England in 1066', which was read on 17 May 1985.

The Whitfield Prize for 1984 was awarded to Dr David Hempton for his book *Methodism and Politics in British Society 1750–1850*.

Membership

Council records with regret the death of Professor Walther Hubatsch, a Corresponding Fellow, and of 18 Fellows and 2 Associates. The resignations of 12 Fellows, 7 Associates and 8 Subscribing Libraries were received. 64 Fellows and 6 Associates were elected and 2 libraries were admitted. One Fellow was reinstated. 5 Fellows and 1 Associate were removed from the roll for non-payment of subscriptions. The membership of the Society on 30 June 1985 comprised 1,524 Fellows (including 76 Life Fellows and 111 Retired Fellows), 39 Corresponding Fellows, 154 Associates and 727 Subscribing Libraries (1,494, 37, 158, 733 respectively on 30 June 1984). Professor Monsignor L. E. Boyle, Dr Giles Constable and Professor Edmund Morgan were elected Corresponding Fellows. The Society exchanged publications with 12 Societies, British and foreign.

Finance

A determined drive to recover arrears of subscriptions helped income to rise slightly compared with the previous year. Provision for a computer data base for the *Handbook of British Chronology*, and for contribution towards the Domesday Book Conference 1986, caused expenditure to rise more steeply. In the circumstances, it is pleasing to report a modest surplus on the year's account.

Council heard with deep regret of the death in May of the Society's auditor, Mr Alan Harmar. It warmly welcomed the news that his son Martin, also of Messrs Beeby, Harmar & Co., would continue to audit the Society's accounts.

ROYAL HISTORICAL SOCIETY

Balance Sheet as at 30 June 1985

£	£	£	ACCUMULATED FUNDS		£	£
			General Funds			
	108,605		As at 1 July 1984	.	123,924	
	14,201		*Add* Excess of Income over Expenditure . . .		7,682	
3,924	1,118		*Add* Profit on sale of Investments	.	81	131,687
			Sir George Prothero Bequest			
5,894			As at 1 July 1984			15,894
			Reddaway Fund			
5,000			As at 1 July 1984			5,000
			Andrew Browning Fund			
0,162			As at 1 July 1984			80,162
			Sinking Fund			
	110,923		As at 1 July 1984	.	121,007	
	8,091		*Add* Interest, Dividends and Tax recoverable .	.	9,525	
			Transfer from Miss E. M. Robinson Bequest—			
	1,993		Income for the year	.	1,956	
			Transfer from Mrs W. M. Frampton Bequest—			
	—		Accumulated Fund		22,444	
	121,007				154,932	
			Less Expenditure in the year—			
1,007	—		A-level Prizes		500	154,432
			Miss E. M. Robinson Bequest			
	21,463		As at 1 July 1984	.	21,463	
	1,993		*Add* Interest, Dividends and Tax recoverable .	.	1,956	
	23,456				23,419	
1,463	1,993		*Less* Transfer to Sinking Fund	.	1,956	21,463
			A. S. Whitfield Prize Fund			
	10,172		As at 1 July 1984	.	10,426	
	854		*Add* Interest, Dividends and Tax recoverable .	.	979	
	11,026				11,405	
		600	*Less* Prize awarded	600		
0,426	600	—	Advertisement	126	726	10,679
			Studies in History Account			
	13,538		As at 1 July 1984	.	13,431	
	2,050		*Add* Contributions received in the year . .	.	538	
	—		Royalties received in the year . .		—	
	1,065		Interest received	.	1,197	
	16,653				15,166	
3,431	3,222		*Less* Expenditure	.	3,375	11,791
			Mrs W. M. Frampton Bequest			
	22,444		As at 1 July 1984	.	22,444	
2,444	—		*Less* Transfer to Sinking Fund	.	22,444	—
3,751						£431,108

ROYAL HISTORICAL SOCIETY

BALANCE SHEET AS AT 30 JUNE 1985

30.6.84 £	£	£	REPRESENTED BY:	£	£	£
			INVESTMENTS			
	339,989		Quoted Securities at cost		362,186	
			Market Value £663,852 (1984: £570,076)			
	41,500		Money at Call		37,500	
	30,000		Short Term Deposits		30,000	
412,866	1,377		Due from Stockbrokers		892	430,57
			CURRENT ASSETS			
			Balances at Bank:			
		10,275	Current Accounts	. 8,714		
		21,709	Deposit Accounts	. 39,707		
		31,984		48,421		
		18	Cash in Hand	—		
		1,870	Income Tax repayable	. 5,680		
		1,078	Payments and Accruals in advance . .	. 2,052		
		503	Sundry Debtors	—		
	40,450	4,997	Stock of paper in hand	. 7,240	63,393	
			LESS CURRENT LIABILITIES			
		3,308	Subscriptions received in advance . .	. 6,146		
		2,007	Sundry Creditors	. 2,067		
885	39,565	34,250	Provision for Publications in hand . .	. 54,650	62,863	
£413,751						£431,

Note The Society's Library and Archives and its Furniture, Fittings and Equipment are written off in the respective years of purchase.

ROYAL HISTORICAL SOCIETY

INCOME AND EXPENDITURE ACCOUNT FOR THE YEAR ENDED 30 JUNE 1985

£	£	£	INCOME	£	£	£
	907		Subscriptions for 1984/85: Associates . . .		872	
	14,807		Libraries . .		14,083	
35,059	19,345		Fellows		19,649	34,
			Note The Society also had 76 Life Fellows at 30 June 1985)			
1,188			Tax recovered on Covenanted Subscriptions .			1,
555			Arrears of Subscriptions received in the year .			1,
28,158			Interest, Dividends and Tax recoverable . .			28,
403			Royalties and Reproduction Fees . . .			
2,276			Donations and Sundry Receipts . . .			2,
£67,639			TOTAL INCOME		£	69,
			EXPENDITURE			
			SECRETARIAL AND ADMINISTRATIVE EXPENSES			
	14,621		Salaries, Pension contributions and National Insurance		15,432	
	2,176		General Printing and Stationery . . .		1,667	
	1,867		Postage, Telephone and Sundry Expenses . .		1,700	
	1,171		Accountancy and Audit		1,265	
	232		Insurance		252	
21,434	1,367		Meetings		1,452	21,

£	£	£		£	£	£
1,434	12,308		Brought forward			21,768
			PUBLICATIONS			
	500		Directors' Expenses		500	
			Publishing costs in the year:			
			Transactions, Fifth Series, Vol. 34 . . .	9,487		
			Camden, Fourth Series, Vol. 30 . . .	11,516		
				21,003		
	11,808		Less Provision made 30 June 1984 . . .	19,400	1,603	
			Provision for Publications in progress:			
			Transactions, Fifth Series, Vol. 35 . . .	9,600		
			Guides and Handbooks No. 10. Vol. 2 . .	14,850		
			Guides and Handbooks No. 13—			
			Medieval Exchange	9,600		
			Guides and Handbooks No. 2—			
			British Chronology	15,600		
			Domesday Book Conference	5,000		
				54,650		
	19,400		Less Provision made 30 June 1984 . . .	14,850	39,800	
			Other Publicaton costs:			
			Guide to Provincial Directories	539		
			Handbook of Dates	655		
	693		Texts and Calendars II	46	1,240	
		1,198	Preparation of Annual Bibliography . . .	1,561		
	809	389	Less Royalties received in the year . . .	1,509	52	
	400		Storage and Insurance of Stock		400	
	33,610				43,595	
9,685	3,925		Less Sales of Publications in the year . . .		5,379	38,216
			LIBRARY AND ARCHIVES			
	1,054		Purchase of Books and Publications . . .		945	
1,054	—		Library Assistance		51	996
			OTHER CHARGES			
	328		Alexander Prize and Medal		306	
	37		Subscription to other bodies		186	
	250		Prothero Lecture fee		—	
	400		Grant—Sutton Hoo		200	
1,265	250		A-Level Prizes		—	692
3,438			**TOTAL EXPENDITURE**			61,672
			EXCESS OF INCOME OVER EXPENDITURE FOR THE			
4,201			**YEAR**			£7,682

. AYLMER, *President.*

. KITCHING, *Treasurer.*

e have examined the foregoing Balance Sheet and Income and Expenditure Account, which have been
ared under the historical cost convention, with the books, vouchers and records of the Society.
e have verified the Investments and Bank Balances appearing in the Balance Sheet.
our opinion the foregoing Balance Sheet and Income and Expenditure Account have been properly drawn
as to exhibit a true and fair view of the state of affairs of the Society as at 30th June 1985.

LEONARD STREET,
DON EC2A 4QS
July 1985

BEEBY, HARMAR & CO.,
Chartered Accountants
Auditors

THE DAVID BERRY TRUST

Receipts and Payments Account for the Year Ended 30 June 1985

RECEIPTS

£	£		£
		BALANCES IN HAND 1 July 1984:	
		Cash at Bank:	
	3	Current Account	3
	1,073	Deposit Account	1,299
	1,076		1,302
	530	483.63 Shares Charities Official Investment Fund	530
	1,606		1,832
1,591	15	*Less* Due to Royal Historical Society	15
	160	DIVIDENDS ON INVESTMENT PER CHARITY COMMISSIONERS	183
226	66	DEPOSIT INTEREST	113
£1,817			

PAYMENTS

£	£		£
		BALANCES IN HAND 30 June 1985:	
		Cash at Bank:	
	3	Current Account	3
	1,299	Deposit Account	1,580
	1,302		1,583
	530	483.63 Shares Charities Official Investment Fund—at cost (Market Value 30.06.85—£1,401)	530
	1,832		2,113
£1,817	15	*Less* Due to Royal Historical Society	—

We have examined the above account with the books and vouchers of the Trust and find it to be in accorda
therewith.

79 LEONARD STREET,   BEEBY, HARMAR & C
LONDON, EC2A 4QS   *Chartered Account*
20th July 1985   *Aud.*

The late David Berry, by his Will dated 23rd April 1926, left £1,000 to provide in every three years a
medal and prize money for the best essay on the Earl of Bothwell or, at the discretion of the Trustees, on Sco
History of the James Stuarts I to VI, in memory of his father, the late Rev. David Berry.

The Trust is regulated by a scheme sanctioned by the Chancery Division of the High Court of Justice da
23rd January 1930, and made in an action 1927 A1233 David Anderson Berry deceased, Hunter and anoth
Robertson and another and since modified by an order of the Charity Commissioners made on 11th Janu
1978, removing the necessity to provide a medal.

The Royal Historical Society is now the Trustee. The Investment held on Capital Account consists of
Charities Official Investment Fund Shares (Market Value £1,836).

The Trustee will in every second year of the three-year period advertise inviting essays.

ALEXANDER PRIZE

The Alexander Prize was established in 1897 by L. C. Alexander, F.R.Hist.S. It consists of a silver medal and £100 awarded annually for an essay upon some historical subject. Candidates may select their own subject provided such subject has been previously submitted to and approved by the Literary Director. The essay must be a genuine work of original research, not hitherto published, and one which has not been awarded any other prize. It must not exceed 6,000 words in length and must be sent in on or before 1 November of any year. The detailed regulations should be obtained in advance from the Secretary.

LIST OF ALEXANDER PRIZE ESSAYISTS (1898-1985)[1]

1898. F. Hermia Durham ('The relations of the Crown to trade under James I').
1899. W. F. Lord, BA ('The development of political parties during the reign of Queen Anne').
1901. Laura M. Roberts ('The Peace of Lunéville').
1902. V. B. Redstone ('The social condition of England during the Wars of the Roses').
1903. Rose Graham ('The intellectual influence of English monasticism between the tenth and the twelfth centuries').
1904. Enid W. G. Routh ('The balance of power in the seventeenth century').
1905. W. A. P. Mason, MA ('The beginnings of the Cistercian Order').
1906. Rachel R. Reid, MA ('The Rebellion of the Earls, 1569').
1908. Kate Hotblack ('The Peace of Paris, 1763').
1909. Nellie Nield, MA ('The social and economic condition of the unfree classes in England in the twelfth and thirteenth centuries').
1912. H. G. Richardson ('The parish clergy of the thirteenth and fourteenth centuries').
1917. Isobel D. Thornely, BA ('The treason legislation of 1531-1534').
1918. T. F. T. Plucknett, BA ('The place of the Council in the fifteenth century').
1919. Edna F. White, MA ('The jurisdiction of the Privy Council under the Tudors').
1920. J. E. Neale, MA ('The Commons Journals of the Tudor Period').
1922 Eveline C. Martin ('The English establishments on the Gold Coast in the second half of the eighteenth century').
1923. E. W. Hensman, MA ('The Civil War of 1648 in the east midlands').
1924. Grace Stretton, BA ('Some aspects of mediæval travel').

[1] No award was made in 1900, 1907, 1910, 1911, 1913, 1914, 1921, 1946, 1948, 1956, 1969, 1975, and 1977. The Prize Essays for 1909 and 1919 were not published in the *Transactions*. No Essays were submitted in 1915, 1916 and 1943.

1925. F. A. Mace, MA ('Devonshire ports in the fourteenth and fifteenth centuries').

1926. Marian J. Tooley, MA ('The authorship of the *Defensor Pacis*').

1927. W. A. Pantin, BA ('Chapters of the English Black Monks, 1215–1540').

1928. Gladys A. Thornton, BA, PhD ('A study in the history of Clare, Suffolk, with special reference to its development as a borough').

1929. F. S. Rodkey, AM, PhD ('Lord Palmerston's policy for the rejuvenation of Turkey, 1839–47').

1930. A. A. Ettinger, DPhil ('The proposed Anglo-Franco-American Treaty of 1852 to guarantee Cuba to Spain').

1931. Kathleen A. Walpole, MA ('The humanitarian movement of the early nineteenth century to remedy abuses on emigrant vessels to America').

1932. Dorothy M. Brodie, BA ('Edmund Dudley, minister of Henry VII').

1933. R. W. Southern, BA ('Ranulf Flambard and early Anglo-Norman administration').

1934. S. B. Chrimes, MA, PhD ('Sir John Fortescue and his theory of dominion').

1935. S. T. Bindoff, MA ('The unreformed diplomatic service, 1812–60').

1936. Rosamund J. Mitchell, MA, BLitt ('English students at Padua, 1460–1475').

1937. C. H. Philips, BA ('The East India Company "Interest", and the English Government, 1783–4').

1938. H. E. I. Philips, BA ('The last years of the Court of Star Chamber, 1630–41').

1939. Hilda P. Grieve, BA ('The deprived married clergy in Essex, 1553–61').

1940. R. Somerville, MA ('The Duchy of Lancaster Council and Court of Duchy Chamber').

1941. R. A. L. Smith, MA, PhD ('The *Regimen Scaccarii* in English monasteries').

1942. F. L. Carsten, DPhil ('Medieval democracy in the Brandenburg towns and its defeat in the fifteenth century').

1944. Rev. E. W. Kemp, BD ('Pope Alexander III and the canonization of saints').

1945. Helen Suggett, BLitt ('The use of French in England in the later middle ages').

1947. June Milne, BA ('The diplomacy of John Robinson at the court of Charles XII of Sweden, 1697–1709').

1949. Ethel Drus, MA ('The attitude of the Colonial Office to the annexation of Fiji').

1950. Doreen J. Milne, MA, PhD ('The results of the Rye House Plot, and their influence upon the Revolution of 1688').

1951. R. G. Davies, BA ('The origins of the commission system in the West India trade').

1952. G. W. S. Barrow, BLitt ('Scottish rulers and the religious orders, 1070–1153').

1953. W. E. Minchinton, BSc(Econ) ('Bristol—metropolis of the west in the eighteenth century').

1954. Rev. L. Boyle, OP ('The *Oculus Sacerdotis* and some other works of William of Pagula').

1955. G. F. E. Rudé, MA, PhD ('The Gordon riots: a study of the rioters and their victims').

1957. R. F. Hunnisett, MA, DPhil ('The origins of the office of Coroner').
1958. Thomas G. Barnes, AB, DPhil ('County politics and a puritan *cause célèbre*: Somerset churchales, 1633').
1959. Alan Harding, BLitt ('The origins and early history of the Keeper of the Peace').
1960. Gwyn A. Williams, MA, PhD ('London and Edward I').
1961. M. H. Keen, BA ('Treason trials under the law of arms').
1962. G. W. Monger, MA, PhD ('The end of isolation: Britain, Germany and Japan, 1900-1902').
1963. J. S. Moore, BA ('The Domesday teamland: a reconsideration').
1964. M. Kelly, PhD ('The submission of the clergy').
1965. J. J. N. Palmer, BLitt ('Anglo-French negotiations, 1390-1396').
1966. M. T. Clanchy, MA, PhD ('The Franchise of Return of Writs').
1967. R. Lovatt, MA, DPhil, PhD ('The *Imitation of Christ* in late medieval England').
1968. M. G. A. Vale, MA, DPhil ('The last years of English Gascony, 1451-1453').
1970. Mrs Margaret Bowker, MA, BLitt ('The Commons Supplication against the Ordinaries in the light of some Archidiaconal Acta').
1971. C. Thompson, MA ('The origins of the politics of the Parliamentary middle groups, 1625-1629').
1972. I. d'Alton, BA ('Southern Irish Unionism: A study of Cork City and County Unionists, 1884-1914').
1973. C. J. Kitching, BA, PhD ('The quest for concealed lands in the reign of Elizabeth I').
1974. H. Tomlinson, BA ('Place and Profit: an Examination of the Ordnance Office, 1660-1714').
1976. B. Bradshaw, MA, BD ('Cromwellian reform and the origins of the Kildare rebellion, 1533-34').
1978. C. J. Ford, BA ('Piracy or Policy: The Crisis in the Channel, 1400-1403').
1979. P. Dewey, BA, PhD ('Food Production and Policy in the United Kingdom, 1914-1918').
1980. Ann L. Hughes, BA, PhD ('Militancy and Localism: Warwickshire Politics and Westminster Politics, 1643-1647').
1981. C. J. Tyerman, MA ('Marino Sanudo Torsello and the Lost Crusade. Lobbying in the Fourteenth Century').
1982. E. Powell, BA, DPhil ('Arbitration and the Law in England in the Late Middle Ages').
1983. A. G. Rosser, MA ('The essence of medieval urban communities: the vill of Westminster 1200-1540').
1984. N. L. Ramsay, MA, LLB ('Retained Legal Counsel, c. 1275-1475').
1985. Georges S. Garnett, MA ('Coronation and Propaganda: Some Implications of the Norman Claim to the Throne of England in 1066').

DAVID BERRY PRIZE

The David Berry Prize was established in 1929 by David Anderson-Berry in memory of his father, the Reverend David Berry. It consists of a money prize awarded every three years for Scottish history. Candidates may select any subject dealing with Scottish history within the reigns of James I to James VI inclusive, provided such subject has been previously submitted to and approved by the Council of the Royal Historical Society. The essay must be a genuine work of original research not hitherto published, and one which has not been awarded any other prize. The essay should be between 6,000 and 10,000 words, excluding footnotes and appendices. It must be sent in on or before 31 October 1988.

LIST OF DAVID BERRY PRIZE ESSAYISTS (1937-76)[1]

1937. G. Donaldson, MA ('The polity of the Scottish Reformed Church *c.* 1460-1580, and the rise of the Presbyterian movement').

1943. Rev. Prof. A. F. Scott Pearson, DTh, DTh, DLitt ('Anglo-Scottish religious relations, 1400-1600').

1949. T. Bedford Franklin, MA, FRSE ('Monastic agriculture in Scotland, 1440-1600').

1955. W. A. McNeill, MA ('"Estaytt" of the king's rents and pensions, 1621').

1958. Prof Maurice Lee, PhD ('Maitland of Thirlestane and the foundation of the Stewart despotism in Scotland').

1964. M. H. Merriman ('Scottish collaborators with England during the Anglo-Scottish war, 1543-1550').

1967. Miss M. H. B. Sanderson ('Catholic recusancy in Scotland in the sixteenth century').

1970. Athol Murray, MA, LLB, PhD ('The Comptroller, 1425-1610').

1973. J. Kirk, MA, PhD ('Who were the Melvillians: A study in the Personnel and Background of the Presbyterian Movement in late Sixteenth-century Scotland').

1976. A Grant, BA, DPhil ('The Development of the Scottish Peerage').

[1] No essays were submitted in 1940 and 1979. No award was made in 1946, 1952, 1961 and 1982.

WHITFIELD PRIZE

The Whitfield Prize was established by Council in 1976 as a money prize of £400 out of the bequest of the late Professor Archibald Stenton Whitfield: in May 1981 Council increased the prize to £600. Until 1982 the prize was awarded annually to the STUDIES IN HISTORY series. From 1983 the prize, value £600, will be awarded annually to the best work of English or Welsh history by an author under 40 years of age, published in the United Kingdom. The award will be made by Council in the Spring of each year in respect of works published in the preceding calendar year. Authors or publishers should send two copies (non-returnable) of a book eligible for the competition to the Society to arrive not later than 31 December of the year of publication.

LIST OF WHITFIELD PRIZE WINNERS (1977-1984)

1977. K. D. Brown, MA, PhD (*John Burns*).
1978. Marie Axton, MA, PhD (*The Queen's Two Bodies: Drama and the Elizabethan Succession*).
1979. Patricia Crawford, MA, PhD (*Denzil Holles, 1598-1680: A study of his Political Career*).
1980. D. L. Rydz (*The Parliamentary Agents: A History*).
1981. Scott M. Harrison (*The Pilgrimage of Grace in the Lake Counties 1536-7*).
1982. Norman L. Jones (*Faith by Statute: Parliament and the Settlement of Religion 1559*).
1983. Peter Clark (*The English Alehouse: A social history 1200-1830*).
1984. David Hempton, BA, PhD (*Methodism and Politics in British Society 1750-1850*).

THE ROYAL HISTORICAL SOCIETY

(INCORPORATED BY ROYAL CHARTER)

OFFICERS AND COUNCIL— 1985

STANDING COMMITTEES 1985

Finance Committee

Miss V. CROMWELL
P. J. C. FIRTH, Esq
PROFESSOR R. C. FLOUD
PROFESSOR H. R. LOYN
PROFESSOR B. E. SUPPLE, PhD, MA
And the Officers

Publications Committee

P. BURKE, Esq, MA
PROFESSOR P. COLLINSON
C. R. ELRINGTON, Esq, MA, FSA
PROFESSOR A. HARDING
PROFESSOR M. A. JONES, MA, DPhil
Dr. K. O. MORGAN
PROFESSOR W. A. SPECK
PROFESSOR W. R. WARD
And the Officers

Library Committee

PROFESSOR J. H. BURNS, MA, PhD
PROFESSOR P. J. MARSHALL
Miss S. M. G. REYNOLDS
PROFESSOR P. SMITH
And the Officers

LIST OF FELLOWS OF THE
ROYAL HISTORICAL SOCIETY

Names of Officers and Honorary Vice-Presidents are printed in capitals.
Those marked* have compounded for their annual subscriptions.

Abbott, A. W., CMG, CBE, Frithys Orchard, West Clandon, Surrey.
Abramsky, Professor Chimen A., MA, Dept of Hebrew and Jewish Studies, University College London, Gower Street, London WC1E 6BT.
Abulafia, D. S. H., MA, PhD, Gonville and Caius College, Cambridge CB2 1TA.
Acton, E. D. J., PhD, School of History, The University, P.O. Box 147, Liverpool L69 3BX.
Adair, Professor J. E., MA, PhD, Newlands Cottage, 41 Pewley Hill, Guildford, Surrey.
Adam, Professor R. J., MA, Easter Wayside, Hepburn Gardens, St Andrews KY16 9LP.
Adams, Professor Ralph J. Q., PhD, Dept of History, Texas A & M University, College Station, Texas 77843-4236, U.S.A.
Adams, S. L., MA, DPhil, 4 North East Circus Place, Edinburgh EH3 6SP.
Adamthwaite, Professor A.P., BA, PhD, Dept of History, The University, Loughborough LE11 3TU.
Addison, P., MA, DPhil, Dept of History, The University, William Robertson Building, George Square, Edinburgh EH8 9JY.
Ailes, A., MA, 24 Donnington Gardens, Reading, Berkshire RG1 5LY.
Akrigg, Professor G. P. V., BA, PhD, FRSC, 4633 West 8th Avenue, Vancouver, B.C., V6R 2A6, Canada.
Alcock, Professor L., MA, FSA, 29 Hamilton Drive, Glasgow G12 8DN.
Alder, G. J., BA, PhD, Dept of History, The University, Whiteknights, Reading RG6 2AA.
Alderman, G., MA, DPhil, 172 Colindeep Lane, London NW9 6EA.
Allan, D. G. C., MSc(Econ), PhD, c/o Royal Society of Arts, John Adam Street, London WC2N 6EZ.
Allen, D. F., BA, PhD, School of History, The University, P.O. Box 363, Birmingham B15 2TT.
Allen, D. H., BA, PhD, 105 Tuddenham Avenue, Ipswich, Suffolk IP4 2HG.
Allmand, C. T., MA, DPhil, FSA, 111 Menlove Avenue, Liverpool L18 3HP.
Alsop, J. D., MA, PhD, Dept of History, McMaster University, 1280 Main Street West, Hamilton, Ontario, Canada L8S 4L9.
Altholz, Professor J., PhD, Dept of History, University of Minnesota, 614 Social Science Building, Minneapolis, Minn. 55455, U.S.A.
Altschul, Professor M., PhD, Case Western Reserve University, Cleveland, Ohio 44106, U.S.A.
Anderson, Professor M. S., MA, PhD, London School of Economics, Houghton Street, London WC2A 2AE.
Anderson, Mrs O. R., MA, BLitt, Westfield College, London NW3 7ST.

Anderson, Miss S. P., MA, BLitt, 17–19 Chilworth Street, London W2 3QU.

Andrew, C. M., MA, PhD, Corpus Christi College, Cambridge CB2 1RH.

Anglesey, The Most Hon., The Marquess of, FSA, FRSL, Plas-Newydd, Llanfairpwll, Anglesey LL61 6DZ.

Anglo, Professor S., BA, PhD, FSA, 59 Green Ridge, Withdean, Brighton BN1 5LU.

Annan, Lord, OBE, MA, DLitt, DUniv, 16 St John's Wood Road, London NW8 8RE.

Annis, P. G. W., BA, 65 Longlands Road, Sidcup, Kent DA15 7LQ.

Appleby, J. S., Little Pitchbury, Brick Kiln Lane, Great Horkesley, Colchester, Essex CO6 4EU.

Armstrong, Miss A. M., BA, 7 Vale Court, Mallord Street, London SW3.

Armstrong, C. A. J., MA, FSA, Gayhurst, Lincombe Lane, Boars Hill, Oxford OX1 5DZ.

Armstrong, Professor F. H., PhD, University of Western Ontario, London 72, Ontario, Canada.

Armstrong, W. A., BA, PhD, Eliot College, The University, Canterbury, Kent CT2 7NS.

Arnstein, Professor W. L., PhD, Dept of History, University of Illinois at Urbana-Champaign, 309 Gregory Hall, Urbana, Ill. 61801, U.S.A.

Artibise, Professor Alan F. J., Inst. of Urban Studies, University of Winnipeg, 515 Portage Avenue, Winnipeg, Canada R3B 2E9.

Ash, Marinell, BA, MA, PhD, 42 Woodburn Terrace, Edinburgh EH10 4ST.

Ashton, Professor R., PhD, The Manor House, Brundall, near Norwich NOR 86Z.

Ashworth, J., MLitt, DPhil, School of English and American Studies, University of East Anglia, Norwich NR4 7TJ.

Ashworth, Professor W., BSc(Econ), PhD, Flat 14, Wells Court, Wells Road, Ilkley, W. Yorks. LS29 9LG.

Aston, Margaret, MA, DPhil, Castle House, Chipping Ongar, Essex.

Aston, T. H., MA, FSA, Corpus Christi College, Oxford OX1 4JF.

Austin, M. R. BD, MA, PhD, The Glead, 2a Louvain Road, Derby DE3 6BZ.

Axelson, Professor E. V., DLitt, Box 15, Constantia, 7848, S. Africa.

*Aydelotte, Professor W. O., PhD, State University of Iowa, Iowa City, U.S.A.

AYLMER, G. E., MA, DPhil, FBA, (*President*), St Peter's College, Oxford OX1 2DL.

Bahlman, Professor Dudley W. R., PhD, Dept of History, Williams College, Williamstown, Mass. 01267, U.S.A.

Bailie, The Rev. W. D., MA, BD, PhD, DD, Kilmore Manse, 100 Ballynahinch Road, Crossgar, Downpatrick, N. Ireland BT30 9HT.

Bailyn, Professor B., MA, PhD, LittD, LHD, Widener J., Harvard University, Cambridge, Mass. 02138, U.S.A.

Baker, D., BSc, PhD, Dept of History, Christ Church College, Canterbury, Kent CT1 1QU.

Baker, J. H., LLD, FBA, St Catharine's College, Cambridge CB2 1RL.

Baker, L. G. D., MA, BLitt, Christ's Hospital, Horsham, West Sussex.

Baker, T. F. T., BA, Camden Lodge, 50 Hastings Road, Pembury, Kent.

Ball, A. W., BA, 71 Cassiobury Park Avenue, Watford, Herts. WD1 7LD.

Ballhatchet, Professor K. A., MA, PhD, 11 The Mead, Ealing, London W13.

Banks, Professor J. A., MA, Dept of Sociology, The University, Leicester LE1 7RH.
Barber, M. C., BA, PhD, Dept of History, The University, Whiteknights, Reading, Berks. RG6 2AA.
Barber, R. W., MA, PhD, FSA, Stangrove Hall, Alderton, near Woodbridge, Suffolk IP12 3BL.
Barker, E. E., MA, PhD, FSA, 60 Marina Road, Little Altcar, Formby, Merseyside L37 6BP.
Barker, Professor T. C., MA, PhD, Minsen Dane, Brogdale Road, Faversham, Kent.
Barkley, Professor the Rev. J. M., MA, DD, 2 College Park, Belfast, N. Ireland.
*Barlow, Professor F., MA, DPhil, FBA, Middle Court Hall, Kenton, Exeter.
Barnard, T. C., MA, DPhil, Hertford College, Oxford OX1 3BW.
Barnes, Miss P. M., PhD, Public Record Office, Chancery Lane, London WC2 1LR.
Barnett, Correlli, MA, Churchill College, Cambridge CB3 0DS.
Barratt, Miss D. M., DPhil, The Corner House, Hampton Poyle, Kidlington, Oxford.
Barratt, Professor G. R. de V., PhD, 197 Belmont Avenue, Ottawa, Canada K1S 0V7.
Barron, Mrs C. M., MA, PhD, 35 Rochester Road, London NW1.
Barrow, Professor G. W. S., MA, BLitt, DLitt, FBA, FRSE, 12a Lauder Road, Edinburgh EH9 2EL.
Bartlett, Professor C. J., PhD, Dept of Modern History, The University, Dundee DD1 4HN.
Bates, D., PhD, Dept of History, University College, P.O. Box 78, Cardiff CF1 1XL.
Batho, Professor G. R., MA, Dept of Education, The University, 48 Old Elvet, Durham DH1 3JH.
Baugh, Professor Daniel A., PhD, Dept of History, McGraw Hill, Cornell University, Ithaca, N.Y. 14853, U.S.A.
Baxter, Professor S. B., PhD, 608 Morgan Creek Road, Chapel Hill, N.C. 27514, U.S.A.
Baylen, Professor J. O., MA, PhD, 38 Dean Court Road, Brighton, E. Sussex BN2 7DJ.
Beachey, Professor R. W., BA, PhD, 1 Rookwood, De La Warr Road, Milford-on-Sea, Hampshire.
Beales, Professor D. E. D., MA, PhD, Sidney Sussex College, Cambridge CB2 3HU.
Bealey, Professor F., BSc(Econ), Dept of Politics, The University, Taylor Building, Old Aberdeen AB9 2UB.
Bean, Professor, J. M. W., MA, DPhil, 622 Fayerweather Hall, Columbia University, New York, N.Y. 10027, U.S.A.
Beardwood, Miss Alice, BA, BLitt, DPhil, 415 Miller's Lane, Wynnewood, Pa, U.S.A.
Beasley, Professor W. G., PhD, FBA, 172 Hampton Road, Twickenham, Middlesex TW2 5NJ.
Beattie, Professor J. M., PhD, Dept of History, University of Toronto, Toronto M5S 1A1, Canada.
Beaumont, H., MA, Silverdale, Severn Bank, Shrewsbury.
Beckerman, John S., PhD, 225 Washington Avenue, Hamden, Ct. 06518, U.S.A.

Beckett, I. F. W., BA, PhD, 11 Tolpuddle Way, Yateley, Camberley, Surrey GU17 7BH.
Beckett, Professor J. C., MA, 19 Wellington Park Terrace, Belfast 9, N. Ireland.
Beckett, J. V., BA, PhD, Dept of History, The University, Nottingham NG7 2RD.
Bedarida, Professor F., 13 rue Jacob, 75006 Paris, France.
Beddard, R. A., MA, DPhil, Oriel College, Oxford OX1 4EW.
Beeler, Professor J. H., PhD, 1302 New Garden Road, Greensboro, N.C. 27410, U.S.A.
*Beer, E. S. de, CBE, MA, DLitt, FBA, FSA, 65 Century Court, Grove End Road, London NW8 9LD.
Beer, Professor Samuel H., PhD, Faculty of Arts & Sciences, Harvard University, Littauer Center G-15, Cambridge, Mass. 02138, U.S.A.
Behrens, Miss C. B. A., MA, Dales Barn, Barton, Cambridge CB3 7BA.
Bell, P. M. H., BA, BLitt, School of History, The University, P.O. Box 147, Liverpool L69 3BX.
Beloff, Lord, DLitt, FBA, Flat No. 9, 22 Lewes Crescent, Brighton BN2 1GB.
Benedikz, B. S., MA, PhD, Main Library, University of Birmingham, P.O. Box 363, Birmingham B15 2TT.
Bennett, Rev. G. V., MA, DPhil, FSA, New College, Oxford OX1 3BN.
Bennett, M. J., BA, PhD, History Dept, University of Tasmania, Box 252C, G.P.O., Hobart, Tasmania 7001, Australia.
Bennett, R. F., MA, Magdalene College, Cambridge CB3 0AG.
Benson, J., BA, MA, PhD, The Polytechnic, Wolverhampton WV1 1LY.
Bentley, M., BA, PhD, Dept of History, The University, Sheffield S10 2TN.
Bernard, G. W., MA, DPhil, 92 Bassett Green Village, Southampton.
Bhila, Professor H. H. K., BA, MA, PhD, Dept of History, University of Zimbabwe, P.O. Box MP 167, Mount Pleasant, Harare, Zimbabwe.
Biddiss, Professor M. D., MA, PhD, Dept of History, The University, Whiteknights, Reading RG6 2AA.
Biddle, M., MA, FSA, Christ Church, Oxford OX1 1DP.
Bidwell, Brigadier R. G. S., OBE, 8 Chapel Lane, Wickham Market, Woodbridge, Suffolk IP13 0SD.
Bill, E. G. W., MA, DLitt, Lambeth Palace Library, London SE1.
Binfield, J. C. G., MA, PhD, 22 Whiteley Wood Road, Sheffield S11 7FE.
Birch, A., MA, PhD, University of Hong Kong, Hong Kong.
Bishop, A. S., BA, PhD, 44 North Acre, Banstead, Surrey SM7 2EG.
Bishop, T. A. M., MA, 16 Highbury Road, London SW19 7PR.
Black, Professor Eugene C., PhD, Dept of History, Brandeis University, Waltham, Mass. 02154, U.S.A.
Blake, E. O., MA, PhD, Roselands, Moorhill Road, Westend, Southampton SO3 3AW.
Blake, Professor J. W., CBE, MA, DLitt, Splashy Mill, Lower Modershall, Stone, Staffordshire.
Blake, Lord, MA, FBA, The Queen's College, Oxford OX1 4AW.
Blakemore, H., PhD, 43 Fitzjohn Avenue, Barnet, Herts.
*Blakey, Professor R. G., PhD, c/o Mr Raymond Shove, Order Dept, Library, University of Minnesota, Minneapolis, Minn., U.S.A.
Blanning, T. W. C., MA, PhD, Sidney Sussex College, Cambridge CB2 3HU.
Blaxland, Major W. G., Lower Heppington, Street End, Canterbury, Kent CT4 7AN.

Blewett, Hon Dr N., BA, DipEd, MA, DPhil, 68 Barnard Street, North Adelaide, South Australia 5006.

Blomfield, Mrs K., 8 Elmdene Court, Constitution Hill, Woking, Surrey GU22 7SA.

Blunt, C. E., OBE, FBA, FSA, Ramsbury Hill, Ramsbury, Marlborough, Wilts.

*Bolsover, G. H., OBE, MA, PhD, 7 Devonshire Road, Hatch End, Middlesex HA5 4LY.

Bolton, Miss Brenda, BA, Dept of History, Westfield College, London NW3 7ST.

Bolton, Professor G. C., MA, DPhil, Australian Studies Centre, 27 Russell Square, London WC1B 5DS.

Bond, B. J., BA, MA, Dept of War Studies, King's College, London WC2R 2LS.

Bonney, Professor R. J., MA. DPhil, Dept of History, The University, Leicester LE1 7RH.

Booker, J. M. L., BA, MLitt, Braxted Place, Little Braxted, Witham, Essex CM8 3LD.

Boon, G. C., BA, FSA, FRNS, National Museum of Wales, Cardiff CF1 3NP.

Borrie, M. A. F., BA, 142 Culford Road, London N1.

Bossy, Professor J. A., MA, PhD, Dept of History, University of York, York YO1 5DD.

Bottigheimer, Professor Karl S., Dept of History, State University of New York at Stony Brook, Long Island, N.Y., U.S.A.

Bourne, Professor K., BA, PhD, London School of Economics, Houghton Street, London WC2A 2AE.

Bowker, Mrs M., MA, BLitt, The Cottage, Bailrigg Lane, Lancaster.

Bowyer, M. J. F., 32 Netherhall Way, Cambridge.

*Boxer, Professor C. R., DLitt, FBA, Ringshall End, Little Gaddesden, Berkhamsted, Herts.

Boyce, D. G., BA, PhD, Dept of Political Theory and Government, University College of Swansea, Swansea SA2 8PP.

Boyle, T., Cert.Ed, BA, MPhil, Jersey Cottage, Mark Beech, Edenbridge, Kent TN8 5NS.

Boynton, L. O. J., MA, DPhil, FSA, Dept of History, Westfield College, London NW3 7ST.

Brading, D. A., MA, PhD, 28 Storey Way, Cambridge.

Bradshaw, Rev. B., MA, BD, PhD, Queens' College, Cambridge CB3 9ET.

Brake, Rev. G. Thompson, 19 Bethell Avenue, Ilford, Essex.

Brand, P. A., MA, DPhil, 155 Kennington Road, London SE11.

Brandon, P. F., BA, PhD, Greensleeves, 8 St Julian's Lane, Shoreham-by-Sea, Sussex BN4 6YS.

Bray, Jennifer R., MA, PhD, 99 Benthall Road, London N16.

Breck, Professor A. D., MA, PhD, LHD, DLitt, University of Denver, Denver, Colorado 80210, U.S.A.

Brentano, Professor R., DPhil, University of California, Berkeley 4, Calif., U.S.A.

Brett, M., MA, DPhil, 7 Bardwell Road, Oxford OX2 6SU.

Breuilly, J. J., BA, DPhil, Dept of History, The University, Manchester M13 9PL.

Bridge, F. R., PhD, The Poplars, Rodley Lane, Rodley, Leeds.

Bridges, R. C., BA, PhD, Dept of History, University of Aberdeen, King's College, Aberdeen AB9 2UB.

Briggs, Lord, BSc(Econ), MA, DLitt, FBA, Worcester College, Oxford OX1 2HB.
Briggs, J. H. Y., MA, Dept of History, University of Keele, Staffs. ST5 5BG.
Briggs, R., MA, All Souls College, Oxford OX1 4AL.
Broad, J., BA, DPhil, Dept of History, Polytechnic of North London, Prince of Wales Road, London NW5 3LB.
Brock, M. G., MA, Nuffield College, Oxford OX1 1NF.
Brock, Professor W. R., MA, PhD, 49 Barton Road, Cambridge CB3 9LG.
Brocklesby, R., BA, The Elms, North Eastern Road, Thorne, Doncaster, S. Yorks. DN8 4AS.
Brogan, D. H. V., MA, Dept of History, University of Essex, Colchester CO4 3SQ.
*Bromley, Professor J. S., MA, Merrow, Dene Close, Chilworth, Southampton SO1 7HL.
*Brooke, Professor C. N. L., MA, LittD, FBA, FSA, Faculty of History, West Road, Cambridge CB3 9EF.
Brooke, J., BA, 63 Hurst Avenue, Chingford, London E4 8DL.
Brooke, Mrs R. B., MA, PhD, c/o Faculty of History, West Road, Cambridge CB3 9EF.
Brooks, N. P., MA, DPhil, The University, St Andrews, Fife KY16 9AJ.
Brown, Mrs Alison M., MA, 25 Rosemont Road, Richmond, Surrey TW10 6QN.
Brown, Professor A. L., MA, DPhil, Dept of History, The University, Glasgow G12 8QQ.
Brown, G. S., PhD, 1720 Hanover Road, Ann Arbor, Mich. 48103, U.S.A.
Brown, Judith M., MA, PhD, 8 The Downs, Cheadle, Cheshire SK8 1JL.
Brown, K. D., BA, MA, PhD, Dept of Economic and Social History, The Queen's University, Belfast BT7 1NN, N. Ireland.
Brown, Miss L. M., MA, PhD, 93 Church Road, Hanwell, London W7.
Brown, Professor M. J., MA, PhD, 350 South Candler Street, Decatur, Georgia 30030, U.S.A.
Brown, P. D., MA, 18 Davenant Road, Oxford OX2 8BX.
Brown, P. R. L., MA, FBA, Hillslope, Pullen's Lane, Oxford.
Brown, R. A., MA, DPhil, DLitt, FSA, King's College, London WC2R 2LS.
Bruce, J. M., ISO, MA, FRAeS, 51 Chiltern Drive, Barton-on-Sea, New Milton, Hants. BH25 7JZ.
Brundage, Professor J. A., Dept of History, University of Wisconsin at Milwaukee, Milwaukee, Wisconsin, U.S.A.
Bryson, Professor W. Hamilton, School of Law, University of Richmond, Richmond, Va. 23173, U.S.A.
Buchanan, R. A., MA, PhD, School of Humanities and Social Sciences, The University, Claverton Down, Bath BA2 7AY.
Buckland, P. J., MA, PhD, 6 Rosefield Road, Liverpool L25 8TF.
Bueno de Mesquita, D. M., MA, PhD, 283 Woodstock Road, Oxford OX2 7NY.
Buisseret, Professor D. J., MA, PhD, The Newberry Library, 60 West Walton Street, Chicago, Ill. 60610, U.S.A.
Bullock, Lord, MA, DLitt, FBA, St Catherine's College, Oxford OX1 3UJ.
Bullock-Davies, Constance, BA, PhD, Dept of Classics, University College of North Wales, Bangor, Gwynedd LL57 2DG.
Bullough, Professor D. A., MA, FSA, Dept of Mediaeval History, 71 South Street, St Andrews, Fife KY16 9AJ.

Burke, U. P., MA, Emmanuel College, Cambridge CB2 3AP.
Burns, Professor J. H., MA, PhD, 39 Amherst Road, London W13.
Burroughs, P., PhD, Dalhousie University, Halifax, Nova Scotia, Canada B3H 3J5.
Burrow, J. W., MA., PhD, Sussex University, Falmer, Brighton BN1 9QX.
Butler, R. D'O., CMG, MA, All Souls College, Oxford OX1 4AL.
Byerly, Professor B. F., BA, MA, PhD, Dept of History, University of Northern Colorado, Greeley, Colorado 80631, U.S.A.
Bythell, D., MA, DPhil, Dept of Economic History, University of Durham, 23-26 Old Elvet, Durham City DH1 3HY.

Cabaniss, Professor J. A., PhD, University of Mississippi, Box No. 253, University, Mississippi 38677, U.S.A.
Callahan, Professor Raymond, PhD, Dept of History, University of Delaware, Newark, Delaware 19716, U.S.A.
Callahan, Professor Thomas, Jr., PhD, Dept of History, Rider College, Lawrenceville, N.J. 08648, U.S.A.
Calvert, Brigadier J. M. (ret.), DSO, MA, 33a Mill Hill Close, Haywards Heath, Sussex.
Calvert, P. A. R., MA, PhD, AM, Dept of Politics, University of Southampton, Highfield, Southampton SO9 5NH.
Cameron, A., BA, 35 Trevor Road, West Bridgford, Nottingham.
Cameron, Professor J. K., MA, BD, PhD, St Mary's College, University of St Andrews, Fife KY16 9JU.
Cameron, Professor K., PhD, FBA, Dept of English, The University, Nottingham NG7 2RD.
Campbell, Professor A. E., MA, PhD, School of History, University of Birmingham, P.O. Box 363, Birmingham B15 2TT.
Campbell, J., MA, FBA, Worcester College, Oxford OX1 2HB.
*Campbell, Professor Mildred L., PhD, Vassar College, Poughkeepsie, N.Y., U.S.A.
Campbell, Professor R. H., MA, PhD, University of Stirling, Stirling FK9 4LA.
Cannadine, D. N., BA, DPhil, Christ's College, Cambridge CB2 3BU.
Canning, J. P., MA, PhD, Dept of History, University College of North Wales, Bangor, Gwynedd LL57 2DG.
Cannon, Professor J. A., CBE, MA, PhD, Dept of History, The University, Newcastle upon Tyne NE1 7RU.
Canny, Professor N. P., MA, PhD, Dept of History, University College, Galway, Ireland.
Cant, R. G., MA, DLitt, 2 Kinburn Place, St Andrews, Fife KY16 9DT.
Cantor, Professor N. F., PhD, New York University, Dept of History, 19 University Place, New York, N.Y. 10003, U.S.A.
Capp, B. S., MA, DPhil, Dept of History, University of Warwick, Coventry, Warwickshire CV4 7AL.
Carey, P. B. R., DPhil, Trinity College, Oxford OX1 3BH.
*Carlson, Leland H., PhD, Huntington Library, San Marino, California 91108, U.S.A.
Carlton, Professor Charles, Dept of History, North Carolina State University, Raleigh, N.C. 27607, U.S.A.
Carman, W. Y., FSA, 94 Mulgrave Road, Sutton, Surrey.
Carpenter, M. Christine, MA, PhD, New Hall, Cambridge CB3 0DF.
Carr, A. D., MA, PhD, Dept of Welsh History, University College of North Wales, Bangor, Gwynedd LL57 2DG.

Carr, A. R. M., MA, FBA, St Antony's College, Oxford OX2 6JF.

Carr, W., PhD, 22 Southbourne Road, Sheffield S10 2QN.

Carrington, Miss Dorothy, 3 Rue Emmanuel Arene, 20 Ajaccio, Corsica.

Carter, Mrs A. C., MA, 12 Garbrand Walk, Ewell, Epsom, Surrey.

Carter, Jennifer J., BA, PhD, The Old Schoolhouse, Glenbuchat, Strathdon, Aberdeenshire AB3 8TT.

Carwardine, R. J., MA, DPhil, Dept of History, The University, Sheffield S10 2TN.

Casey, J., BA, PhD, School of Modern Languages and European History, University of East Anglia, Norwich NR4 7TJ.

Cassels, Professor Alan, Dept of History, McMaster University, Hamilton, Ontario L8S 4L9.

Catto, R. J. A. I., MA, Oriel College, Oxford OX1 4EW.

Cazel, Professor Fred A., Jr., Dept of History, University of Connecticut, Storrs, Conn. 06268, U.S.A.

Chadwick, Professor W. O., OM, KBE, DD, DLitt, FBA, Selwyn Lodge, Cambridge CB3 9DQ.

Challis, C. E., MA, PhD, 14 Ashwood Villas, Headingley, Leeds 6.

Chalmers, C. D., Public Record Office, Kew, Richmond, Surrey TW9 4DU.

Chambers, D. S., MA, DPhil, Warburg Institute, Woburn Square, London WC1H 0AB.

Chandaman, Professor C. D., BA, PhD, 23 Bellamy Close, Ickenham, Uxbridge UB10 8SJ.

Chandler, D. G., MA, Hindford, Monteagle Lane, Yately, Camberley, Surrey.

Chaplais, P., PhD, FBA, FSA, Lew Lodge, Mount Owen Road, Bampton, Oxford.

Charles-Edwards, T. M., DPhil, Corpus Christi College, Oxford OX1 4JF.

*CHENEY, Professor C. R., MA, DLitt, LittD, FBA, 17 Westberry Court, Grange Road, Cambridge CB3 9BG.

Cheney, Mrs Mary, MA, 17 Westbury Court, Grange Road, Cambridge CB3 9BG.

Cherry, John, MA, 58 Lancaster Road, London N4.

Chibnall, Mrs Marjorie, MA, D Phil, FBA, 6 Millington Road, Cambridge CB3 9HP.

Child, C. J., OBE, MA, PhM, 94 Westhall Road, Warlingham, Surrey CR3 9HB.

Childs, J. C. R., BA, PhD, School of History, The University, Leeds LS2 9JT.

Childs, Wendy R., MA, PhD, School of History, The University, Leeds LS2 9JT.

Christianson, Assoc. Professor P. K., PhD, Dept of History, Queen's University, Kingston, Ontario K7L 3N6, Canada.

Christie, Professor I. R., MA, FBA, 10 Green Lane, Croxley Green, Herts. WD3 3HR.

Church, Professor R. A., BA, PhD, School of Social Studies, University of East Anglia, Norwich NOR 88C.

Cirket, A. F., 71 Curlew Crescent, Bedford.

Clanchy, M. T., MA, PhD, FSA, Medieval History Dept, The University, Glasgow G12 8QQ.

Clark, A. E., MA, 32 Durham Avenue, Thornton Cleveleys, Blackpool FY5 2DP.

Clark, D. S. T., BA, PhD, History Dept, University College, Swansea SA2 8PP.

Clark, Professor Dora Mae, PhD, Menno Village, 510d, Chambersburg, Pa. 17201, U.S.A.

Clark, P. A., MA, Dept of Economic and Social History, The University, Leicester LE1 7RH.

Clarke, Howard B., BA, PhD, Room K104, Arts-Commerce-Law Building, University College, Dublin 4, Ireland.

Clarke, P. F., MA, PhD, St John's College, Cambridge CB2 1TP.

Clementi, Miss D., MA, DPhil, Flat 7, 43 Rutland Gate, London SW7 1BP.

Clemoes, Professor P. A. M., BA, PhD, Emmanuel College, Cambridge CB2 3AP.

Cliffe, J. T., BA, PhD, 263 Staines Road, Twickenham, Middx. TW2 5AY.

Clive, Professor J. L., PhD, 38 Fernald Drive, Cambridge, Mass. 02138, U.S.A.

Clough, C. H., MA, DPhil, FSA, School of History, The University, P.O. Box 147, Liverpool L69 3BX.

Cobb, H. S., MA, FSA, 1 Child's Way, London NW11.

Cobban, A. B., MA, PhD, School of History, The University, P.O. Box 147, Liverpool L69 3BX.

Cockburn, Professor J. S., LLB, LLM, PhD, History Dept, University of Maryland, College Park, Maryland 20742, U.S.A.

Cocks, E. J., MA, Middle Lodge, Ardingly, Haywards Heath, Sussex RH17 6TS.

Cohn, H. J., MA, DPhil, University of Warwick, Coventry CV4 7AL.

Cohn, Professor N., MA, DLitt, FBA, 61 New End, London NW3.

Coleman, B. I., MA, PhD, Dept of History, The University, Exeter EX4 4QH.

Coleman, Professor D. C., BSc(Econ.), PhD, LittD, FBA, Over Hall, Cavendish, Sudbury, Suffolk.

Coleman, Professor F. L., MA, PhD, Dept of Economics & Economic History, Rhodes University, P.O. Box 94, Grahamstown 6140, S. Africa.

Collier, W. O., MA, FSA, 34 Berwyn Road, Richmond, Surrey.

Collinge, J. M., BA, Institute of Historical Research, Senate House, Malet Street, London WC1E 7HU.

Collini, S. A., MA, PhD, Dept of History, The University, Falmer, Brighton, Sussex BN1 9QX.

Collins, B. W., MA, PhD, Dept of Modern History, The University, Glasgow G12 8QQ.

Collins, Mrs I., MA, BLitt, School of History, The University, P.O. Box 147, Liverpool L69 3BX.

Collinson, Professor P., MA, PhD, FBA, Dept of History, The University, Sheffield ST10 2TN.

Colvin, H. M., CBE, MA, FBA, St John's College, Oxford OX1 3JP.

Colyer, R. J., BSc, PhD, Inst. of Rural Sciences, University College of Wales, Aberystwyth, Dyfed.

Congreve, A. L., MA, FSA, Galleons Lap, Sissinghurst, Kent TN17 2JG.

Connell-Smith, Professor G. E., PhD, 7 Braids Walk, Kirkella, Hull, Yorks. HU10 7PA.

Contamine, Professor P., DèsL., 12 Villa Croix-Nivert, 75015 Paris, France.

Conway, Professor A. A., MA, University of Canterbury, Christchurch 1, New Zealand.

Cook, A. E., MA, PhD, 20 Nicholas Road, Hunter's Ride, Henley-on-Thames, Oxon.

Cook, C. P., MA, DPhil, Dept of History, The Polytechnic of North London, Prince of Wales Road, London NW5 3LB.

Cooke, Professor, J. J., PhD., Dept of History, College of Liberal Arts, University of Mississippi, University, Miss. 38677, U.S.A.

Coolidge, Professor R. T., MA, BLitt, History Dept, Loyola Campus, Concordia University, 7141 Sherbrooke Street West, Montreal, Quebec H4B 1R6, Canada.

Cope, Professor Esther S., PhD, Dept of History, Univ. of Nebraska, Lincoln, Neb. 68508, U.S.A.

Copley, A. R.H., MA, MPhil, Rutherford College, The University, Canterbury, Kent CT2 7NX.

Corfield, Penelope J., MA, PhD, 99 Salcott Road, London SW11 6DF.

Cornell, Professor Paul G., PhD, Dept of History, University of Waterloo, Waterloo, Ontario, Canada N2L 3G1.

Corner, D. J., BA, Dept of History, St Salvator's College, The University, St Andrews, Fife KY16 9AJ.

Cornford, Professor J. P., MA, The Brick House, Wicken Bonhunt, Saffron Walden, Essex CB11 3UG.

Cornwall, J. C. K., MA, 1 Orchard Close, Copford Green, Colchester, Essex.

Corson, J. C., MA, PhD, Mossrig, Lilliesleaf, Melrose, Roxburghshire.

Cosgrove, A. J., BA, PhD, Dept of Medieval History, University College, Dublin 4, Ireland.

Coss, P. R., BA, PhD, 20 Whitebridge Close, Whitebridge Grove, Gosforth, Newcastle upon Tyne NE3 2DN.

Costeloe, Professor M. P., BA, PhD, Dept of Hispanic and Latin American Studies, The University, 83 Woodland Road, Bristol BS8 1RJ.

Cowan, I. B., MA, PhD, University of Glasgow, Glasgow G12 8QQ.

Coward, B., BA, PhD, Dept of History, Birkbeck College, Malet Street, London WC1E 7HX.

Cowdrey, Rev. H. E. J., MA, St Edmund Hall, Oxford OX1 4AR.

Cowie, Rev. L. W., MA, PhD, 38 Stratton Road, Merton Park, London SW19 3JG.

Cowley, F. G., PhD, 17 Brookvale Road, West Cross, Swansea, W. Glam.

Cox, D. C., BA, PhD, 12 Oakfield Road, Copthorne, Shrewsbury SY3 8AA.

Craig, R. S., BSc(Econ), The Anchorage, Bay Hill, St Margarets Bay, nr Dover, Kent CT15 6DU.

Cramp, Professor Rosemary, MA, BLitt, FSA, Department of Archaeology, The Old Fulling Mill, The Banks, Durham.

Crampton, R. J., BA, PhD, Rutherford College, The University, Canterbury, Kent CT2 7NP.

Craton, Professor M. J., BA, MA, PhD, Dept of History, University of Waterloo, Waterloo, Ontario, Canada N2L 3G1.

Crawford, Patricia M., BA, MA, PhD, Dept of History, University of Western Australia, Nedlands, Western Australia 6009.

*Crawley, C. W., MA, 1 Madingley Road, Cambridge.

Cremona, His Hon Chief Justice Professor J. J., KM, DLitt, PhD, LLD, DrJur, 5 Victoria Gardens, Sliema, Malta.

Cressy, D. A., 231 West Sixth Street, Claremont, Calif. 91711, U.S.A.

Crimmin, Patricia K., MPhil, BA, Dept of History, Royal Holloway College, Englefield Green, Surrey TW20 0EX.

Crisp, Olga, BA, PhD, 'Zarya', 1 Millbrook, Esher, Surrey.

Croft, Pauline, MA, DPhil, Dept of History, Royal Holloway College, Englefield Green, Surrey TW20 0EX.

Crombie, A. C., BSc, MA, PhD, Trinity College, Oxford OX1 3BH.

Cromwell, Miss V., MA, University of Sussex, Falmer, Brighton, Sussex BN1 9QX.

Crook, D., MA, PhD, Public Record Office, Chancery Lane, London WC2A 1LR.
Cross, Miss M. C., MA, PhD, Dept of History, University of York, York YO1 5DD.
Crowder, Professor C. M. D., DPhil, Queen's University, Kingston, Ontario, Canada K7L 3N6.
Crowder, Professor M., MA, Dept of History, University of Botswana, P.B. 0022, Gaborone, Botswana.
Crowe, Miss S. E., MA, PhD, 112 Staunton Road, Headington, Oxford.
Cruickshank, C. G., MA, DPhil, 15 McKay Road, Wimbledon Common, London SW20.
Cruickshanks, Eveline G., PhD, 46 Goodwood Court, Devonshire Street, London W1N 1SL.
Cumming, Professor A., MA, DipMA, PGCE, PhD, Centre for Education Studies, University of New England, Armidale, Australia 2351.
Cumming, I., MEd, PhD, 672A South Titirangi Road, Titirangi, Auckland, New Zealand.
Cummins, Professor J. S., PhD, University College London, Gower Street, London WC1E 6BT.
Cumpston, Miss I. M., MA, DPhil, Birkbeck College, Malet Street, London WC1E 7HX.
Cunliffe, Professor M. F., MA, BLitt, DHL, Room 102, T Building, George Washington University, 2110 G. Street N.W., Washington, D.C., 20052, U.S.A.
Cunningham, Professor A. B., MA, PhD, Simon Fraser University, Burnaby 2, B.C., Canada.
Currie, C. R. J., MA, DPhil, Institute of Historical Research, Senate House, Malet Street, London WC1E 7HU.
Curry, Anne E., BA, MA, PhD, 12 Melrose Avenue, Reading, Berkshire RG6 2BN.
Curtis, Professor L. Perry, PhD, Dept of History, Brown University, Providence, R.I. 02912, U.S.A.
Curtis, Timothy C., PhD, School of Combined Studies, The Polytechnic, Corporation Street, Preston PR1 2TQ.
*Cuttino, Professor G. P., DPhil, FSA, Department of History, Emory University, Atlanta, Ga., 30322, U.S.A.
Cuttler, S. H., BPhil, DPhil, 5051 Clanranald #302, Montreal, Quebec, Canada H3X 2S3.

*Dacre, Lord, MA, FBA, Peterhouse, Cambridge CB2 1RD.
Dakin, Professor D., MA, PhD, 20 School Road, Apperley, Gloucester GL19 4DJ.
D'Arcy, F. A., BA, MA, PhD, Dept of Modern History, University College, Belfield, Dublin 4, Ireland.
Daunton, M. J., BA, PhD, Dept of History, University College London, Gower Street, London WC1E 6BT.
Davenport, Professor T. R. H., MA, PhD, Dept of History, Rhodes University, P.O. Box 94, Grahamstown 6140, South Africa.
Davenport-Hines, R. P. T., PhD, BA, 51 Elsham Road, London W14 8HD.
Davidson, R., MA, PhD, Dept of Economic and Social History, The University, 50 George Square, Edinburgh EH8 9JY.
Davies, C. S. L., MA, DPhil, Wadham College, Oxford OX1 3PN.
Davies, Canon E. T., BA, MA, 11 Tŷ Brith Gardens, Usk, Gwent.

Davies, I. N. R., MA, DPhil, 22 Rowland Close, Wolvercote, Oxford.
Davies, P. N., MA, PhD, Cmar, Croft Drive, Caldy, Wirral, Merseyside.
Davies, R. G., MA, PhD, Dept of History, The University, Manchester M13 9PL.
Davies, Professor R. R., BA, DPhil, University College of Wales, Dept of History, 1 Laura Place, Aberystwyth SY23 2AU.
Davies Wendy, BA, PhD, Dept of History, University College London, Gower Street, London WC1E 6BT.
*Davis, G. R. C., CBE, MA, DPhil, FSA, 214 Somerset Road, London SW19 5JE.
Davis, Professor J. C., Dept of History, Massey University, Palmerston North, New Zealand.
Davis, Professor R. H. C., MA, FBA, FSA, 349 Banbury Road, Oxford OX2 7PL.
Davis, Professor Richard W., Dept of History, Washington University, St Louis, Missouri 63130, U.S.A.
*Dawe, D. A., 46 Green Lane, Purley, Surrey.
Deane, Professor Phyllis M., MA, 4 Stukeley Close, Cambridge CB3 9LT.
*Deeley, Miss A. P., MA, 41 Linden Road, Bicester, Oxford.
de la Mare, Miss A. C., MA, PhD, Bodleian Library, Oxford.
Denham, E. W., MA, 27 The Drive, Northwood, Middx. HA6 1HW.
Dennis, P. J., MA, PhD, Dept of History, Royal Military College, Duntroon, A.C.T. 2600, Australia.
Denton, J. H., BA, PhD, Dept of History, The University, Manchester M13 9PL.
Devine, T. M., BA, Viewfield Cottage, 55 Burnbank Road, Hamilton, Strathclyde Region.
Dewey, P. E., BA, PhD, Dept of History, Royal Holloway College, Englefield Green, Surrey TW20 0EX.
DICKENS, Professor A. G., CMG, MA, DLit, DLitt, LittD, FBA, FSA, Institute of Historical Research, University of London, Senate House, London WC1E 7HU.
Dickinson, H. T., MA, PhD, Dept of Modern History, The University, Edinburgh EH8 9YL.
Dickinson, Rev. J. C., MA, DLitt, FSA, Yew Tree Cottage, Barngarth, Cartmel, South Cumbria.
Dickson, P. G. M., MA, DPhil, St Catherine's College, Oxford, OX1 3UJ.
Dilks, Professor D. N., BA, Dept of International History, The University, Leeds LS2 9JT.
Dilworth, Rev. G. M., OSB, MA, PhD, Columba House, 16 Drummond Place, Edinburgh EH3 6PL.
Dinwiddy, J. R., PhD, Dept of History, Royal Holloway College, Englefield Green, Surrey TW20 0EX.
Ditchfield, G. McC, BA, PhD, Darwin College, University of Kent, Canterbury, Kent CT2 7NY.
Dobson, Professor R. B., MA, DPhil, Dept of History, The University, York YO1 5DD.
Dockrill, M. L., MA, BSc(Econ), PhD, King's College, Strand, London WC2R 2LS.
*Dodwell, Miss B., MA, The University, Reading RG6 2AH.
Dodwell, Professor C. R., MA, PhD, FSA, History of Art Department, The University, Manchester M13 9PL.
Don Peter, The Rt. Revd. Monsignor W. L. A., MA, PhD, Aquinas University College, Colombo 8, Sri Lanka.

*DONALDSON, Professor G., MA, PhD, DLitt, FRSE, FBA, 6 Pan Ha', Dysart, Fife KY1 2TL.

Donaldson, Professor P. S., MA, PhD, Dept of Humanities, 14n-422, Massachusetts Institute of Technology, Cambridge, Mass. 02139, U.S.A.

*Donaldson-Hudson, Miss R., BA, (address unknown).

Donoughue, Lord, MA, DPhil, 7 Brookfield Park, London NW5 1ES.

Dore, R. N., MA, Holmrook, 19 Chapel Lane, Hale Barns, Altrincham, Cheshire WA15 0AB.

Downer, L. J., MA, LLB, Dept of Medieval Studies, Australian National University, Box 4, P.O., Canberra, ACT 2601, Australia.

Doyle, A. I., MA, PhD, University College, The Castle, Durham.

Doyle, Professor W., MA, DPhil, Dept of History, The University, Nottingham NG7 2RD.

Driver, J. T., MA, BLitt, PhD, 25 Abbot's Grange, Chester CH2 1AJ.

*Drus, Miss E., MA, 18 Brampton Tower, Bassett Avenue, Southampton SO1 7FB.

Duckham, Professor B. F., MA, Dept of History, St David's University College, Lampeter, Dyfed SA48 7ED.

Duffy, Michael, MA, DPhil, Dept of History and Archaeology, The University, Exeter EX4 4QH.

Duggan, Anne J., BA, PhD, Dept of History, Queen Mary College, Mile End Road, London E1 4NS.

Duggan, C., PhD, King's College, Strand, London WC2R 2LS.

Dugmore, The Rev. Professor C. W., DD, Thame Cottage, The Street, Puttenham, Guildford, Surrey GU3 1AT.

Duke, A. C., MA, Dept of History, The University, Southampton SO9 5NH.

Dumville, D. N., MA, PhD, Dept of Anglo-Saxon, Norse and Celtic, 9 West Road, Cambridge CB3 9DP.

Dunbabin, J. P. D., MA, St Edmund Hall, Oxford OX1 4AR.

Duncan, Professor A. A. M., MA, The University, Dept of History, Glasgow G12 8QQ.

Dunn, Professor R. S., PhD, Dept of History, The College, University of Pennsylvania, Philadelphia, Pa. 19104, U.S.A.

Dunning, R. W., BA, PhD, FSA, Musgrove Manor East, Barton Close, Taunton TA1 4RU.

Durack, Mrs I. A., MA, PhD, University of Western Australia, Nedlands, Western Australia 6009.

Durey, M. J., BA, DPhil, School of Social Inquiry, Murdoch University, Perth 6150, Western Australia.

Durie, A. J., MA, PhD, Dept of Economic History, Edward Wright Building, The University, Aberdeen AB9 2TY.

Dutton, D. J., BA, PhD, School of History, The University, P.O. Box 147, Liverpool L69 3BX.

Dykes, D. W., MA, Cherry Grove, Welsh St Donats, nr Cowbridge, Glam. CF7 7SS.

Dyson, Professor K. H. F., BSc(Econ), MSc(Econ), PhD, Undergraduate School of European Studies, The University, Bradford BD7 1DP.

Earle, P., BSc(Econ), PhD, Dept of Economic History, London School of Economics, Houghton Street, London WC2A 2AE.

Eastwood, Rev. C. C., PhD, Heathview, Monks Lane, Audlem, Cheshire CW3 0HP.

Eckles, Professor R. B., PhD, Apt 2, 251 Brahan Blvd., San Antonio, Texas 78215, U.S.A.

Edbury, P. W., MA, PhD, Dept of History, University College, P.O. Box 78, Cardiff CF1 1XL.

Ede, J. R., CB, MA, Palfreys, East Street, Drayton, Langport, Somerset TA10 0JZ.

Edmonds, Professor E. L., MA, PhD, University of Prince Edward Island, Charlottetown, Prince Edward Island, Canada.

Edwards, F. O., SJ, BA, FSA, 114 Mount Street, London W1Y 6AH.

Edwards, O. D., BA, Dept of History, William Robertson Building, The University, George Square, Edinburgh EH8 9YL.

Edwards, Professor R. W. D., MA, PhD, DLitt, 21 Brendan Road, Donnybrook, Dublin 4, Ireland.

Ehrman, J. P. W., MA, FBA, FSA, The Mead Barns, Taynton, Nr Burford, Oxfordshire OX8 5UH.

Eisenstein, Professor Elizabeth L., PhD, 82 Kalorama Circle N.W., Washington D.C. 20008, U.S.A.

Eldridge, C. C., PhD, Dept of History, Saint David's University College, Lampeter, Dyfed SA48 7ED.

Eley, G. H., BA, DPhil, MA, Dept of History, University of Michigan, Ann Arbor, Michigan 48109, U.S.A.

Elliott, Professor J. H., MA, PhD, FBA, The Institute for Advanced Studies, Princeton, New Jersey 08540, U.S.A.

Ellis, R. H., MA, FSA, Cloth Hill, 6 The Mount, London NW3.

Ellis, S. G., BA, MA, PhD, Dept of History, University College, Galway, Ireland.

Ellsworth, Professor Edward W., AB, AM, PhD, 27 Englewood Avenue, Brookling, Mass. 02146, U.S.A.

Ellul, M., BArch, DipArch, 'Pauline', 55 Old Railway Road, Birkirkara, Malta.

Elrington, C. R., MA, FSA, Institute of Historical Research, Senate House, London WC1E 7HU.

ELTON, Professor G. R., MA, PhD, LittD, DLitt, DLitt, DLit, FBA, 30 Millington Road, Cambridge CB3 9HP.

Elvin, L., FSA, FRSA, 10 Almond Avenue, Swanport, Lincoln LN6 0HB.

*Emmison, F. G., MBE, PhD, DUniv, FSA, 8 Coppins Close, Chelmsford, Essex CM2 6AY.

Emsley, C., BA, MLitt, Arts Faculty, The Open University, Walton Hall, Milton Keynes MK7 6AA.

d'Entrèves, Professor A. P., DPhil, Strada Ai Ronchi 48, Cavoretto 10133, Torino, Italy.

Erickson, Charlotte, J., PhD, 8 High Street, Chesterton, Cambridge CB4 1NG.

*Erith, E. J., Shurlock House, Shurlock Row, Berkshire.

Erskine, Mrs A. M., MA, BLitt, FSA, 44 Birchy Barton Hill, Exeter EX1 3EX.

Evans, Mrs A. K. B., PhD, FSA, White Lodge, 25 Knighton Grange Road, Leicester LE2 2LF.

Evans, Sir David (L.), OBE, BA, DLitt, Whitegates, Stratton-on-the-Fosse, Somerset.

Evans, E. J., MA, PhD, Dept of History, Furness College, University of Lancaster, Bailrigg, Lancaster LA1 4YG.

Evans, Gillian R., PhD, Sidney Sussex College, Cambridge CB2 3HU.

Evans, R. J., MA, DPhil, School of European Studies, University of East Anglia, Norwich NR4 7TJ.

Evans, R. J. W., MA, PhD, Brasenose College, Oxford OX1 4AJ.
Everitt, Professor A. M., MA, PhD, The University, Leicester LE1 7RH.
Eyck, Professor U. F. J., MA, BLitt, Dept of History, University of Calgary, Alberta T2N IN4, Canada.

Fage, Professor J. D., MA, PhD, Centre of West African Studies, The University, Birmingham B15 2TT.
Fairs, G. L., MA, Thornton House, Bear Street, Hay-on-Wye, Hereford HR3 5AN.
Falkus, M. E., BSc(Econ), Dept of History, London School of Economics, Houghton Street, London WC2A 2AE.
Farmer, D. F. H., BLitt, FSA, The University, Reading RG6 2AH.
Farr, M. W., MA, FSA, 12 Emscote Road, Warwick.
Fell, Professor C. E., MA, Dept of English, The University, Nottingham NG7 2RD.
Fenlon, Revd. D. B., BA, PhD, St Edmunds, 21 Westgate Street, Bury St Edmunds, Suffolk IP33 1QG.
Fenn, Rev. R. W. D., MA, BD, FSAScot, The Ditch, Bradnor View, Kington, Herefordshire.
Fennell, Professor J., MA, PhD, 8 Canterbury Road, Oxford OX2 6LU.
Ferguson, Professor A. B., PhD, Dept of History, 6727 College Station, Duke University, Durham, N.C. 27708, U.S.A.
Fernandez-Armesto, F. F. R., DPhil, River View, Headington Hill, Oxford.
Feuchtwanger, E. J., MA, PhD, Highfield House, Dean Sparsholt, nr Winchester, Hants.
Fieldhouse, D. K., MA, Jesus College, Cambridge CB5 8BL.
Finer, Professor S. E., MA, All Souls College, Oxford OX1 4AL.
Fines, J., MA, PhD, 119 Parklands Road, Chichester.
Finlayson, G. B. A. M., MA, BLitt, 11 Burnhead Road, Glasgow G43 2SU.
Finley, Professor Sir Moses, MA, PhD, DLitt, FBA, 12 Adams Road, Cambridge CB3 9AD.
Fisher, Professor Alan W., PhD, Dept of History, Michigan State University, East Lansing, Michigan 48824, U.S.A.
Fisher, D. J. V., MA, Jesus College, Cambridge CB3 9AD.
Fisher, Professor F. J., MA, London School of Economics, Houghton Street, London WC2A 2AE.
Fisher, F. N., Holmelea, Cromford Road, Wirksworth, Derby DE4 4FR.
Fisher, H. E. Stephen, BSc, PhD, Dept of History, The University, Exeter EX4 4RJ.
Fisher, J. R., BA, MPhil, PhD, School of History, The University, P.O. Box 147, Liverpool L69 3BX.
Fisher, R. M., MA, PhD, Dept of History, University of Queensland, St Lucia, Queensland, Australia 4067.
Fisher, Professor S. N., PhD, 221 St Antoine, Worthington, Ohio 43085, U.S.A.
Fitch, Dr M. F. B., FSA, 37 Avenue de Montoie, 1007 Lausanne, Switzerland.
Fletcher, A. J., MA, 16 Southbourne Road, Sheffield S10 2QN.
*Fletcher, The Rt Hon The Lord, PC, BA, LLD, FSA, The Barn, The Green, Sarratt, Rickmansworth, Herts. WD3 6BP.
Fletcher, R. A., MA, Dept of History, The University, York YO1 5DD.
Flint, Professor J. E., MA, PhD, Dalhousie University, Halifax, Nova Scotia B3H 3J5, Canada.

Flint, Valerie I. J., MA, DPhil, Dept of History, The University, Private Bag, Auckland, New Zealand.
Floud, Professor R. C., MA, DPhil, Dept of History, Birkbeck College, Malet Street, London WC1E 7HX.
Fogel, Professor Robert W., PhD, Center for Population Economics, University of Chicago, 1101 East 58th Street, Chicago, Illinois 60637, U.S.A.
Foot, M. R. D., MA, BLitt, 45 Countess Road, London NW5 2XH.
Forbes, D., MA, 89 Gilbert Road, Cambridge.
Forbes, Thomas R., BA, PhD, FSA, 86 Ford Street, Hamden, Conn. 06517, U.S.A.
Ford, W. K., BA, 48 Harlands Road, Haywards Heath, West Sussex RH16 1LS.
Forster, G. C. F., BA, FSA, The University, Leeds LS2 9JT.
Foster, Professor Elizabeth R., AM, PhD, 205 Strafford Avenue, Wayne, Pa. 19087, U.S.A.
Foster, R. F., MA, PhD, Dept of History, Birkbeck College, Malet Street, London WC1E 7HX.
Fowler, Professor K. A., BA, PhD, 2 Nelson Street, Edinburgh 3.
Fowler, P. J., MA, PhD, 1a Althorp Road, St Albans, Herts. AL1 3AH.
Fox, J. P., BSc(Econ), MSc(Econ), PhD, 98 Baring Road, London SE12 0PT.
Fox, L., OBE, DL, LHD, MA, FSA, FRSL, Silver Birches, 27 Welcombe Road, Stratford-upon-Avon.
Fox, R., MA, DPhil, The University, Bailrigg, Lancaster LA1 4YG.
Frame, R. F., MA, PhD, Dept of History, The University, 43 North Bailey, Durham DH1 3HP.
Franklin, R. M., BA, Baldwins End, Eton College, Windsor, Berks.
Fraser, Lady Antonia, 52 Campden Hill Square, London W8.
*Fraser, Miss C. M., PhD, 39 King Edward Road, Tynemouth, Tyne and Wear NE30 2RW.
Fraser, D., BA, MA, PhD, 117 Alwoodley Lane, Leeds, LS17 7PN.
Fraser, Professor Peter, MA, PhD, The Priory, Old Mill Lane, Marnhull, Dorset DT10 1JX.
Freeden, M. S., DPhil, Mansfield College, Oxford OX1 3TF.
French, D. W., Dept of History, University College London, Gower Street, London WC1E 6BT.
Frend, Professor W. H. C., MA, DPhil, DD, FRSE, FSA, The Rectory, Barnwell, nr. Peterborough, Northants. PE8 5PG.
Fritz, Professor Paul S., BA, MA, PhD, Dept of History, McMaster University, Hamilton, Ontario, Canada.
Fryde, Professor E. B., DPhil, Preswylfa, Trinity Road, Aberystwyth, Dyfed.
Fryde, Natalie M., BA, DrPhil, Schloss Grünsberg, D-8503 Altdorf, Germany.
*Fryer, Professor C. E., MA, PhD (address unknown).
Fryer, Professor W. R., BLitt, MA, 68 Grove Avenue, Chilwell, Beeston, Notts, NG9 4DX.
Frykenberg, Professor R. E., MA, PhD, 1840 Chadbourne Avenue, Madison, Wis. 53705, U.S.A.
Fuidge, Miss N. M., 13 Havercourt, Haverstock Hill, London NW3.
*Furber, Professor H., MA, PhD, c/o History Department, University of Pennsylvania, Philadelphia, Pa., U.S.A.
Fussell, G. E., DLitt, 45 Beech Road, Horsham, W. Sussex RH12 4DX.
Fyrth, H. J., BSc(Econ), 72 College Road, Dulwich, London SE21.

Gabriel, Professor A. L., PhD, FMAA, CFIF, CFBA, P.O. Box 578, University of Notre Dame, Notre Dame, Indiana 46556, U.S.A.

*Galbraith, Professor J. S., BS, MA, PhD, University of California, Los Angeles, Calif. 90024, U.S.A.

Gale, Professor H. P. P., OBE, PhD, 38 Brookwood Avenue, London SW13.

Gale, W. K. V., 19 Ednam Road, Goldthorn Park, Wolverhampton WV4 5BL.

Gann, L. H., MA, BLitt, DPhil, Hoover Institution, Stanford University, Stanford, Calif. 94305, U.S.A.

Gash, Professor N., MA, BLitt, FBA, Old Gatehouse, Portway, Langport, Somerset TA10 0NQ.

Gee, E. A., MA, DPhil, FSA, 28 Trentholme Drive, The Mount, York YO2 2DG.

Geggus, D. P., MA, DPhil, Dept of History, University of Florida, Gainesville, Florida 32611, U.S.A.

Genet, J., Ph., Agrégé d'Histoire, 147 Avenue Parmentier, Paris 75010, France.

Gentles, Professor I., BA, MA, PhD, Dept of History, Glendon College, 2275 Bayview Avenue, Toronto M4N 3M6, Canada.

Gerlach, Professor D. R., MA, PhD, University of Akron, Akron, Ohio 44325, U.S.A.

Gibbs, G. C., MA, Birkbeck College, Malet Street, London WC1E 7HX.

Gibbs, Professor N. H., MA, DPhil, All Souls College, Oxford OX1 4AL.

Gibson, J. S. W., FSA, Harts Cottage, Church Hanborough, Oxford OX7 2AB.

Gibson, Margaret T., MA, DPhil, School of History, The University, P.O. Box 147, Liverpool L69 3 BX.

Gifford, Miss D. H., PhD, FSA, Public Record Office, Chancery Lane, London WC2A 1LR.

Gilbert, Professor Bentley B., PhD, Dept of History, University of Illinois at Chicago Circle, Box 4348, Chicago, Ill. 60680, U.S.A.

Gilley, S. W., BA, DPhil, Dept of Theology, University of Durham, Abbey House, Palace Green, Durham DH1 3RS.

Gillingham, J. B., MA, London School of Economics, Houghton Street, London WC2A 2AE.

Ginter, Professor D. E., AM, PhD, Dept of History, Sir George Williams University, Montreal 107, Canada.

Girtin, T., MA, Butter Field House, Church Street, Old Isleworth, Middx.

Gleave, Group Capt. T. P., CBE, RAF (ret.), Willow Bank, River Gardens. Bray-on-Thames, Berks.

*Glover, Professor R. G., MA, PhD, 2937 Tudor Avenue, Victoria, B.C. V8N IM2.

*Godber, Miss A. J., MA, FSA, Mill Lane Cottage, Willington, Bedford.

*Godfrey, Professor J. L., MA, PhD, 231 Hillcrest Circle Hill, N.C., U.S.A.

Goldie, Mark, MA, PhD, Churchill College, Cambridge CB3 0DF.

Golding, B. J., MA, DPhil, Dept of History, The University, Southampton SO9 5NH.

Goldsmith, Professor M. H., PhD, Dept of Politics, University of Exeter, Exeter EX4 4RJ.

Gollin, Professor A., DLitt, University of California, Dept of History, Santa Barbara, Calif. 93106, U.S.A.

Gooch, John, BA, PhD, Dept of History, The University, Bailrigg, Lancaster LA1 4YG.

Goodman, A. E., MA, BLitt, Dept of Medieval History, The University, Edinburgh EH8 9YL.

Goodspeed, Professor D. J., BA, 164 Victoria Street, Niagara-on-the-Lake, Ontario, Canada.

*Gopal, Professor S., MA, DPhil, 30 Edward Elliot Road, Mylapore, Madras, India.

Gordon, Professor P., BSc(Econ), MSc(Econ), PhD, 241 Kenton Road, Kenton, Harrow HA3 0HJ.

Gordon-Brown, A., Flat 7, Whitehall Court, Main Street, Rondebosch, South Africa 7700.

Goring, J. J., MA, PhD, Little Iwood, Rushlake Green, Heathfield, East Sussex TN21 9QS.

Gorton, L. J., MA, 41 West Hill Avenue, Epsom, Surrey.

Gosden, P. H. J. H. MA, PhD, School of Education, The University, Leeds LS2 9JT.

Gough, Professor Barry M., PhD, History Dept, Wilfrid Laurier University, Waterloo, Ontario, Canada N2L 3C5.

Gowing, Professor Margaret, CBE, MA, DLitt, BSc(Econ), FBA, Linacre College, Oxford OX1 1SY.

*Graham, Professor G.S., MA, PhD, DLitt, LLD, Hobbs Cottage, Beckley, Rye, Sussex.

Gransden, Mrs A., MA, PhD, DLitt, FSA, Dept of History, The University, Nottingham NG7 2RD.

Grant, A., BA, DPhil, Dept of Modern History, The University, Bailrigg, Lancaster LA1 4YG.

Grattan-Kane, P., 12 St John's Close, Helston, Cornwall.

Graves, Professor Edgar B., PhD, LLD, LHD, 318 College Hill Road, Clinton, New York 13323, USA.

Gray, Professor J. R., MA, PhD, School of Oriental and African Studies, University of London, London WC1E 7HP.

Gray, J. W., MA, Dept of Modern History, The Queen's University of Belfast, Belfast BT7 1NN, N. Ireland.

Gray, Miss M., MA, BLitt, 68 Dorchester Road, Garstang, Preston PR3 1HH.

Greaves, Professor Richard L., PhD, 910 Shadowlawn Drive, Tallahassee, Florida 32312, U.S.A.

Greaves, Mrs R. L., PhD, 1920 Hillview Road, Lawrence, Kansas 66044, U.S.A.

Green, I. M., MA, DPhil, Dept of Modern History, The Queen's University of Belfast, Belfast BT7 1NN, N. Ireland.

Green, Judith A., BA, DPhil, Dept of Modern History, The Queen's University of Belfast, Belfast BT7 1NN, N. Ireland.

Green, Professor Thomas A., BA, PhD, JD, Legal Research Building, University of Michigan Law School, Ann Arbor, Michigan 48109, U.S.A.

Green, Rev. V. H. H., MA, DD, Lincoln College, Oxford OX1 3DR.

Greene, Professor Jack P., Dept of History, Johns Hopkins University, Baltimore, Md. 21218, U.S.A.

Greengrass, M., MA, DPhil, Dept of History, The University, Sheffield S10 2TN.

Greenhill, B. J., CMG, DPh, FSA, National Maritime Museum, Greenwich, London SE10 9FN.

Greenleaf, Professor W. H., BSc(Econ), PhD, 57 Westport Avenue, Mayels, Swansea SA3 5EQ.

Greenslade, M. W., JP, MA, FSA, 20 Garth Road, Stafford ST17 9JD.

GREENWAY, D. E., MA, PhD (*Assistant Literary Director*), Institute of Historical Research, Senate House, Malet Street, London WC1E 7HU.

Gregg, E., MA, PhD, Dept of History, University of South Carolina, Columbia, S.C. 29208, U.S.A.

Grenville, Professor J. A. S., PhD, University of Birmingham, P.O. Box 363, Birmingham B15 2TT.

Gresham, C. A., BA, DLitt, FSA, Bryn-y-deryn, Criccieth, Gwynedd, LL52 0HR.

GRIERSON, Professor P., MA, LittD, FBA, FSA, Gonville and Caius College, Cambridge CB2 1TA.

Grieve, Miss H. E. P., BA, 153 New London Road, Chelmsford, Essex.

Griffiths, Professor R. A., PhD, University College, Singleton Park, Swansea SA2 8PP.

Grimble, I. A. M., PhD, 10 Cumberland Road, London SW13.

Grisbrooke, W. J., MA, Jokers, Bailey Street, Castle Acre, King's Lynn, Norfolk PE21 2AG.

*Griscom, Rev. Acton, MA (address unknown).

Gruner, Professor Wolf D., DrPhil, DrPhil. Habil, Pralleweg 7, 2000 Hamburg 67 (Volksdorf), West Germany.

Gum, Professor E. J., PhD, 2043 N.55th Street, Omaha, Nebraska 68104, U.S.A.

Guth, Professor D. J., Faculty of Law, University of British Columbia, Vancouver, B.C., Canada V6T 1Y1.

Guy, J. A., PhD, Dept of History, The University, Wills Memorial Building, Queens Road, Bristol BS8 1RJ.

HABAKKUK, Sir John (H.), MA, FBA, Jesus College, Oxford OX1, 3DW.

Haber, Professor F. C., PhD, 3926 2R Street NW, Washington, D.C. 20007, U.S.A.

Hackett, Rev. M. B., OSA, BA, PhD, Curia Generalizia Agostiniana, Via del S. Uffizio 25, 00193 Rome, Italy.

Haffenden, P. S., PhD, 36 The Parkway, Bassett, Southampton.

Haigh, C. A., MA, PhD, Christ Church, Oxford OX1 1DP.

Haight, Mrs M. Jackson, PhD, 3 Wolger Road, Mosman, N.S.W. 2088, Australia.

Haines, R. M., MA, MLitt, DPhil, FSA, 20 Luttrell Avenue, London SW15 6PF.

Hainsworth, D. R., MA, PhD, University of Adelaide, Dept of History, North Terrace, Adelaide, South Australia 5001.

Hair, Professor P. E. H., MA, DPhil, School of History, The University, P.O. Box 147, Liverpool L69 3BX.

Hale, Professor J. R., MA, FBA, FSA, University College London, Gower Street, London WC1E 6BT.

Haley, Professor K. H. D., MA, BLitt, 15 Haugh Lane, Sheffield S11 9SA.

Hall, Professor A. R., MA, PhD, DLitt, FBA, 14 Ball Lane, Tackley, Oxford OX5 3AG.

Hall, B., MA, PhD, FSA, DD, 2 Newton House, Newton St Cyres, Devon EX5 5BL.

Hallam, Elizabeth M., BA, PhD, Public Record Office, Chancery Lane, London WC2A 1LR.

Hallam, Professor H. E., MA, PhD, University of Western Australia, Nedlands 6009, Western Australia.

Hamer, Professor D. A., MA, DPhil, History Dept, Victoria University of Wellington, Private Bag, Wellington, New Zealand.

Hamilton, B., BA, PhD, The University, Nottingham NG7 2RD.

Hammersley, G. F., BA, PhD, University of Edinburgh, William Robertson Building, George Square, Edinburgh EH8 9JY.

Hampson, Professor N., MA, Ddel'U, 305 Hull Road, York YO1 3LB.

Hand, Professor G. J., MA, DPhil, Faculty of Law, University of Birmingham, P.O. Box 363, Birmingham B15 2TT.

Handford, M. A., MA, MSc, 6 Spa Lane, Hinckley, Leicester LE10 1JB.

Hanham, Dean H. J., MA, PhD, School of Humanities and Social Science, Massachusetts Institute of Technology, Cambridge, Mass. 02139, U.S.A.

Harcourt, Freda, PhD, Dept of History, Queen Mary College, Mile End Road, London E1 4NS.

Harding, Professor A., MA, BLitt, School of History, The University, P.O. Box 147, Liverpool L69 3BX.

Harding, The Hon Mr Justice H. W., BA, LLD, FSA, 39 Annunciation Street, Sliema, Malta.

Haren, M. J., DPhil, 5 Marley Lawn, Dublin 16, Ireland.

Harfield, Major A. G., Little Beechwood, Childe Okeford, Dorset DT11 8EH.

Hargreaves, Professor J. D., MA, 'Balcluain', Raemoir Road, Banchory, Kincardineshire.

Harkness, Professor D. W., MA, PhD, Dept of Irish History, The Queen's University, Belfast BT7 1NN, N. Ireland.

Harman, Rev. L. W., 72 Westmount Road, London SE9.

Harper-Bill, C., BA, PhD, 15 Cusack Close, Strawberry Hill, Twickenham, Middlesex.

Harris, B. E., MA, PhD, 25 Platts Lane, Tarvin, Chester CH3 8LH.

Harris, G., MA, 4 Lancaster Drive, London NW3.

Harris, Mrs J. F., BA, PhD, 30 Charlbury Road, Oxford OX1 3UJ.

Harris, Professor J. R., MA, PhD, The University, P.O. Box 363, Birmingham B15 2TT.

Harrison, B. H., MA, DPhil, Corpus Christi College, Oxford OX1 4JF.

Harrison, C. J., BA, PhD, The University, Keele, Staffs. ST5 5BG.

Harrison, Professor Royden, MA, DPhil, 4 Wilton Place, Sheffield S10 2BT.

Harriss, G. L., MA, DPhil, FSA, Magdalen College, Oxford OX1 4AU.

Hart, C. J. R., MA, MB, DLitt, Goldthorns, Stilton, Peterborough PE7 3RH.

Harte, N. B., BSc(Econ), Dept of History, University College London, Gower Street, London WC1E 6BT.

Hartley, T. E., BA, PhD, Dept of History, The University, Leicester LE1 7RH.

Harvey, Miss B. F., MA, BLitt, FBA, Somerville College, Oxford OX2 6HD.

Harvey, Margaret M., MA, DPhil, St Aidan's College, Durham DH1 3LJ.

Harvey, Professor P. D. A., MA, DPhil, FSA, Dept of History, The University, Durham DH1 3EX.

Harvey, Sally P. J., MA, PhD, Sint Hubertuslaan 7, 1980 Tervuren, Brussels, Belgium.

Haskell, Professor F. J., MA, FBA, Trinity College, Oxford OX1 3BH.

Haskins, Professor G. L., AB, LLB, JD, MA, University of Pennsylvania, The Law School, 3400 Chestnut Street, Philadelphia, Pa. 19104 U.S.A.

Haslam, Group Captain E. B., MA, RAF (retd), 27 Denton Road, Wokingham, Berks. RG11 2DX.

Haslam, Jonathan G., BSc(Econ), MLitt, PhD, 1610 c Beekman Place NW, Washington, D.C., 20009, U.S.A.

Hassall, W. O., MA, DPhil, FSA, The Manor House, 26 High Street, Wheatley, Oxford OX9 1XX.

Hast, Adele, PhD, Marquis Who's Who, Inc., 200 E. Ohio Street, Chicago, Ill. 60611, U.S.A.

Hatcher, M. J., BSc(Econ), PhD, Corpus Christi College, Cambridge CB2 1RH.

Hatley, V. A., BA, ALA, 6 The Crescent, Northampton NN1 4SB.

Hatton, Professor Ragnhild M., PhD, 49 Campden Street, London W8.

Havighurst, Professor A. F., MA, PhD, 11 Blake Field, Amherst, Mass. 01002, U.S.A.

Havinden, M. A., MA, BLitt, Dept of Economic History, Amory Building, The University, Exeter EX4 4QH.

Havran, Professor M. J., MA, Corcoran Dept of History, Randall Hall, University of Virginia, Charlottesville, Va. 22903, U.S.A.

HAY, Professor D., MA, DLitt, FBA, FRSE, Dr. h.c. Tours, Dept of History, The University, Edinburgh EH8 9JY.

Hayes, P. M., MA, DPhil, Keble College, Oxford OX1 3PG.

Hayter, A. J., BA, PhD, Chase House, Mursley, N. Bucks. MK17 0RT.

Hayton, D. W., BA, DPhil, 8 Baker Street, Ampthill, Bedford MK45 2QE.

Hazlehurst, Cameron, BA, DPhil, FRSL, 8 Hunter Street, Yarralumla, A.C.T. 2600, Australia.

Hearder, Professor H., BA, PhD, University College, P.O. Box 78, Cardiff CF1 1XL.

Heath, P., MA, Dept of History, The University Hull HU6 7RX.

Heathcote, T. A., BA, PhD, Cheyne Cottage, Birch Drive, Hawley, Camberley, Surrey.

Helmholz, R. H., PhD, LLB, The Law School, University of Chicago, 1111 East 60th Street, Chicago, Ill. 60637, U.S.A.

Hembry, Mrs P. M., BA, PhD, Pleasant Cottage, Crockerton, Warminster, Wilts. BA12 8AJ.

Hempton, D. N., BA, PhD, 57 Gilnahirk Park, Belfast, N. Ireland BT5 7DY.

Hendy, M. F., MA, Dept of History, The University, P.O. Box 363, Birmingham B15 2TT.

Henning, Professor B. D., PhD, History of Parliament, 34 Tavistock Square, London WC1H 9EZ.

Hennock, Professor E. P., MA, PhD, School of History, University of Liverpool, P.O. Box 147, Liverpool L69 3BX.

Heppell, Muriel, BA, MA, PhD, 97 Eton Place, Eton College Road, London NW3 2DB.

Herde, Professor Peter, PhD, Cranachstr. 7, 8755 Alzenau, F.R. of Germany.

Hexter, Professor J. H., PhD, Dept of History, Washington University, St Louis, Missouri, U.S.A.

Highfield, J. R. L., MA, DPhil, Merton College, Oxford OX1 4JD.

Hill, B. W., BA, PhD, School of English and American Studies, University of East Anglia, Norwich NR4 7TJ.

Hill, J. E. C., MA, DLitt, FBA, Woodway, Sibford Ferris, nr. Banbury, Oxfordshire OX15 5RA.

Hill, Professor L. M., AB, MA, PhD, 5066 Berean Lane, Irvine, Calif. 92664, U.S.A.

*Hill, Miss M. C., MA, Crab End, Brevel Terrace, Charlton Kings, Cheltenham, Glos.

*Hill, Professor Rosalind M. T., MA, BLitt, FSA, Westfield College, Kidderpore Avenue, London NW3 7ST.

Hilton, A. J. Boyd, MA, DPhil, 1 Carlyle Road, Cambridge CB4 3DN.

Hilton, Professor R. H., DPhil, FBA, University of Birmingham, P.O. Box 363, Birmingham B15 2TT.

Himmelfarb, Professor Gertrude, PhD, The City University of New York, Graduate Center, 33 West 42 St, New York, N.Y. 10036, U.S.A.

Hind, R. J., BA, PhD, Dept of History, University of Sydney, Sydney, N.S.W. 2006, Australia.

*Hinsley, Professor F. H., OBE, MA, St John's College, Cambridge CB2 1TP.

Hirst, Professor D. M., PhD, Dept of History, Washington University, St Louis, Missouri, U.S.A.

Hoak, Professor Dale E., PhD, Dept of History, College of William and Mary, Williamsburg, Virginia 23185, U.S.A.

Hockey, The Rev. S. F., BA, Quarr Abbey, Ryde, Isle of Wight PO33 4ES.

*Hodgett, G. A. J., MA, FSA, King's College, Strand, London WC2R 2LS.

Holderness, B. A., MA, PhD, School of Economic and Social Studies, University of East Anglia, Norwich NR4 7TJ.

Holdsworth, Professor C. J., MA, PhD, FSA, 5 Pennsylvania Park, Exeter EX4 6HD.

Hollaender, A. E. J., PhD, FSA, 119 Narbonne Avenue, South Side, Clapham Common, London SW4 9LQ.

Hollis, Patricia, MA. DPhil, 30 Park Lane, Norwich NOR 47F.

Hollister, Professor C. Warren, MA, PhD, University of California, Santa Barbara, Calif. 93106, U.S.A.

Holmes, Professor Clive A., MA, PhD, Dept of History, McGraw Hill, Cornell University, N.Y. 14853, U.S.A.

Holmes, G. A., MA, PhD, Highmoor House, Weald, Bampton, Oxon. OX8 2HY.

Holmes, Professor G. S., MA, DLitt, FBA, Tatham House, Burton-in-Lonsdale, Carnforth, Lancs.

Holyroyd, M. de C. F., 85 St Mark's Road, London W10.

HOLT, Professor J. C., MA, DPhil, DLitt, FBA, FSA, Fitzwilliam College, Cambridge CB3 0DG.

Holt, Professor P. M., MA, DLitt, FBA, School of Oriental and African Studies, Malet Street, London WC1E 7HP.

Holt, The Rev. T. G., SJ, MA, FSA, 114 Mount Street, London W1Y 6AH.

Honey, Professor, J. R. de S., MA, DPhil, 5 Woods Close, Oadby, Leicester LE2 4FJ.

Hopkins, E., MA, PhD, 77 Stevens Road, Stourbridge, West Midlands DY9 0XW.

Hoppen, K. T., MA, PhD, Dept of History, The University, Hull HU6 7RX.

Horrox, Rosemary E., MA, PhD, 61-3 High Street, Cottenham, Cambridge CB4 3SA.

Horwitz, Professor H. G., BA, DPhil, Dept of History, University of Iowa, Iowa City, Iowa 52242, U.S.A.

Houlbrooke, R. A., MA, DPhil, Faculty of Letters and Social Sciences, The University, Reading RG6 2AH.

Housley, N. J., MA, PhD, Dept of History, The University, Leicester, LE1 7RH.

*Howard, C. H. D., MA, 15 Sunnydale Gardens, London NW7 3PD.

*Howard, Professor M. E., CBE, MC, DLitt, FBA, Oriel College, Oxford OX1 4EW.

Howarth, Mrs J. H., MA, St Hilda's College, Oxford OX4 1DY.

Howat, G. M. D., MA, MLitt, Old School House, North Moreton, Didcot, Oxfordshire OX11 9BA.

Howell, Miss M. E., MA, PhD, 10 Blenheim Drive, Oxford OX2 8DG.

Howell, Professor R., MA, DPhil, Dept of History, Bowdoin College, Brunswick, Maine 04011, U.S.A.

Howells, B. E., MA, Whitehill, Cwm Ann, Lampeter, Dyfed.

Hudson, Miss A., MA, DPhil, Lady Margaret Hall, Oxford OX2 6QA.

Hufton, Professor Olwen H., BA, PhD, 40 Shinfield Road, Reading, Berks.

Hughes, J. Q., BArch, PhD, 10a Fulwood Park, Liverpool L17 5AH.

Hull, F., BA, PhD, Roundwell Cottage, Bearsted, Maidstone, Kent ME14 4EU.

HUMPHREYS, Professor R. A., OBE, MA, PhD, DLitt, LittD, DLitt, DUniv, 5 St James's Close, Prince Albert Road, London NW8 7LG.

Hunnisett, R. F., MA, DPhil, 23 Byron Gardens, Sutton, Surrey SM1 3QG.

Hunt, Professor K. S., PhD, MA, Dept of History, Rhodes University Grahamstown 6140, South Africa.

Hurst, M. C., MA, St John's College, Oxford OX1 3JP.

Hurt, J. S., BA, BSc(Econ), PhD, 66 Oxford Road, Moseley, Birmingham B13 9SQ.

*Hussey, Professor Joan M., MA, BLitt, PhD, FSA, Royal Holloway College, Englefield Green, Surrey TW20 0EX.

Hutton, R. E., BA, DPhil, Dept of History, The University, Queen's Road, Bristol BS8 1RJ.

Hyams, P. R., MA, DPhil, Pembroke College, Oxford OX1 1DW.

*Hyde, H. Montgomery, MA, DLit, Westwell House, Tenterden, Kent.

Hyde, Professor J. K., MA, PhD, The University, Manchester M13 9PL.

Ingham, Professor K., OBE, MA, DPhil, The Woodlands, 94 West Town Lane, Bristol BS4 5DZ.

Ingram Ellis, Professor E. R., MA, PhD, Dept of History, Simon Fraser University, Burnaby, B.C, VSA IS6, Canada.

Inkster, Ian, PhD, Dept of Economic History, University of New South Wales, P.O. Box 1, Kensington, N.S.W., Australia 2033.

Ives, E. W., PhD, 214 Myton Road, Warwick.

Jack, Professor R. I., MA, PhD, University of Sydney, Sydney, N.S.W., Australia.

Jack, Mrs S. M., MA, BLitt, University of Sydney, Sydney, N.S.W., Australia.

Jackman, Professor S. W., PhD, FSA, 1065 Deal Street, Victoria, British Columbia, Canada.

Jacob, Professor Margaret C., Eugene Lang College, New School for Social Research, 66 West 12th Street, New York, N.Y. 10011, U.S.A.

Jagger, Rev. P. J., MA, MPhil, St Deiniol's Library, Hawarden, Deeside, Clwyd CH5 3DF.

Jalland, Patricia, PhD, MA, BA, Dept of History, School of Social Sciences, Western Australian Institute of Technology, South Bentley, Western Australia 6102.

James, Edward, MA, DPhil, Dept of History, The University, York YO1 5DD.

James, M. E., MA, Middlecote, Stonesfield, Oxon. OX7 2PU.

James, R. Rhodes, MP, MA, FRSL, The Stone House, Great Gransden, nr Sandy, Beds.

Jeffery, K. J., MA, PhD, Dept of History, University of Ulster, Shire Road, Newtownabbey, Co. Antrim, N. Ireland BT37 0QB.

Jeffs, R. M., MA, DPhil, FSA, 6a Gladstone Road, Sheffield S10 3GT.

Jenkins, Professor B. A., PhD, 133 Lorne, Lennoxville, Quebec, Canada.

Jenkins, Professor D., MA, LLM, LittD, Adeilad Hugh Owen, Penglais, Aberystwyth SY23 3DY.

Jeremy, D. J., BA, MLitt, PhD, 16 Britannia Gardens, Westcliff-on-Sea, Essex SS0 8BN.

Jewell, Miss H. M., MA, PhD, School of History, The University, P.O. Box 147, Liverpool L69 3BX.

Johnson, D. J., BA, 41 Cranes Park Avenue, Surbiton, Surrey.

Johnson, Professor D. W. J., BA, BLitt, University College London, Gower Street, London WC1E 6BT.

*Johnson, J. H., MA, Whitehorns, Cedar Avenue, Chelmsford, Essex.

Johnston, Professor Edith M., MA, PhD, Dept of History, Macquarie Univ., North Ryde, N.S.W. 2113, Australia.

Johnston, Professor S. H. F., MA, Fronhyfryd, Llanbadarn Road, Aberystwyth, Dyfed.

Jones, C. D. H., BA, DPhil, Dept of History and Archaeology, The University, Exeter EX4 4QH.

Jones, Clyve, MA, DLitt, 41 St Catherines Court, London W4 1LB.

Jones, D. J. V., BA, PhD, Dept of History, University College of Swansea, Singleton Park, Swansea SA2 8PP.

Jones, Dwyryd W., MA, DPhil, Dept of History, The University, York YO1 5DD.

Jones, Revd. F., BA, MSc, PhD, 4a Castlemain Avenue, Southbourne, Bournemouth BH6 5EH.

Jones, G. A., MA, PhD, Dept of History, University of Reading, Whiteknights, Reading, Berks. RG6 2AH.

Jones, G. E., MA, PhD, MEd, 130 Pennard Drive, Pennard, Gower, West Glamorgan.

Jones, Professor G. Hilton, PhD, Dept of History, Eastern Illinois University, Charleston, Ill. 61920, U.S.A.

Jones, G. J., MPhil, The Croft, Litchard Bungalows, Bridgend, Glam.

Jones, Professor G. W., BA, MA, DPhil, Dept of Government, London School of Economics, Houghton Street, London WC2A 2AE.

Jones, H. E., MA, DPhil, Flat 3, 115-117 Highlever Road, London W10 6PW.

Jones, Professor I.G., MA, DLitt, 12 Laura Place, Aberystwyth, Dyfed SY23 3DY.

Jones, J. D., MA, PhD, Woodlands Cottage, Marvel Lane, Newport, Isle of Wight PO30 3DT.

Jones, Professor J. R., MA, PhD, School of English and American Studies, University of East Anglia, Norwich NOR 30A.

Jones, Professor M. A., MA, DPhil, Dept of History, University College London, Gower Street, London WC1E 6BT.

Jones, Mrs Marian H., MA, Glwysgoed, Caradog Road, Aberystwyth, Dyfed.

Jones, M. C. E., MA, DPhil, FSA, Dept of History, The University, Nottingham NG7 2 RD.

Jones, The Venerable O. W., MA, 10 Camden Crescent, Brecon, Powys LD3 7BY.

Jones, P. J., DPhil, FBA, Brasenose College, Oxford OX1 4AJ.
Jones, Professor W. J., PhD, Dept of History, The University of Alberta, Edmonton T6G 2E1, Canada.
Jones-Parry, Sir Ernest, MA, PhD, Flat 3, 34 Sussex Square, Brighton, Sussex BN2 5AD.
Judd, D., BA, PhD, Dept of History and Philosophy, Polytechnic of North London, Prince of Wales Road, London NW6.
Judson, Professor Margaret A., PhD, 8 Redcliffe Avenue, Highland Park, N.J. 08904, U.S.A.
Jukes, Rev. H. A. Ll., MA, STh, 1 St Mary's Court, Ely, Cambs. CB7 4HQ.

Kaeuper, Professor R. W., MA, PhD, 151 Village Lane, Rochester, New York 14610, U.S.A.
Kamen, H. A. F., MA, DPhil, The University, Warwick, Coventry CV4 7AL.
Kanya-Forstner, A. S., PhD, Dept of History, York University, 4700 Keele Street, Downsview, Ontario M3J 1P3, Canada.
Kapelle, Asst. Professor, William E., History Department, Brandeis University, Waltham, Mass. 02254, U.S.A.
*Kay, H., MA, 68 Alwoodley Lane, Leeds LS17 7PT.
Kealey, Professor Gregory S., Dept of History, Memorial University of Newfoundland, St John's, Newfoundland. A1C 5S7, Canada.
Kedward, H. R., MA, MPhil, 137 Waldegrave Road, Brighton BN1 6GJ.
Keeler, Mrs Mary F., PhD, 302 West 12th Street, Frederick, Maryland 21701, U.S.A.
Keen, L. J., MPhil, Dip Archaeol, FSA, 7 Church Street, Dorchester, Dorset.
Keen, M. H. MA, Balliol College, Oxford OX1 3BJ.
Keene, D. J., MA, DPhil, Long Park, Crawley, Winchester, Hants.
Kellas, J. G., MA, PhD, Dept of Politics, Glasgow University, Adam Smith Building, Glasgow G12 8RT.
Kellaway, C. W., MA, FSA, 18 Canonbury Square, London N1.
Kelly, Professor T., MA, PhD, FLA, Oak Leaf House, Ambleside Road, Keswick, Cumbria CA12 4DL.
Kemp, Miss B., MA, FSA, St Hugh's College, Oxford OX2 6LE.
Kemp, B. R., BA, PhD, 12 Redhatch Drive, Earley, Reading, Berks.
Kemp, The Right Rev. E. W., DD, The Lord Bishop of Chichester, The Palace, Chichester, Sussex PO19 1PY.
Kemp, Lt-Commander P. K., RN, Malcolm's, 51 Market Hill, Maldon, Essex.
Kennedy, J., MA, 14 Poolfield Avenue, Newcastle-under-Lyme ST5 2NL.
Kennedy, Professor P. M., BA, DPhil, School of English and American Studies, University of East Anglia, Norwich NOR 88C.
Kent, Professor C. A., DPhil, Dept of History, University of Saskatchewan, Saskatoon, Sask. S7N 0WO, Canada.
Kent, Professor J. H. S., MA, PhD, Dept of Theology, University of Bristol, Senate House, Bristol BS8 1TH.
Kent, Miss M. R., PhD, BA, School of Social Sciences, Deakin University, Geelong, Victoria, Australia 3217.
Kenyon, Professor J. P., PhD, Dept of Modern History, St Salvator's College, St Andrews, Fife KY16 9AL.
Kerridge, E. W. J., PhD, 6 Llys Tudur, Myddleton Park, Denbigh LL16 4AL.

Kettle, Miss A. J., MA, FSA, Dept of Mediaeval History, 71 South Street, St Andrews, Fife.

Keynes, S. D., MA, PhD, Trinity College, Cambridge CB2 1TQ.

Kiernan, Professor V. G., MA, 27 Nelson Street, Edinburgh EH3 6LJ.

*Kimball, Miss E. G., BLitt, PhD, 200 Leeder Hill Drive, Apt 640, Hamden, Conn. 06517, U.S.A.

King, E. J., MA, PhD, Dept of History, The University, Sheffield S10 2TN.

King, P. D., BA, PhD, Furness College, The University, Bailrigg, Lancaster LA1 4YG.

Kirby, D. P., MA, PhD, Manoraven, Llanon, Dyfed.

Kirby, J. L., MA, FSA, 209 Covington Way, Streatham, London SW16 3BY.

Kirby, M. W., BA, PhD, Dept of Economics, Gillow House, The University, Lancaster LA1 4YX.

Kirk, J., MA, PhD, Dept of Scottish History, University of Glasgow, Glasgow G12 8QQ.

Kishlansky, Professor Mark, Dept of History, University of Chicago, 1126 East 59th Street, Chicago, Illinois 60637, U.S.A.

Kitchen, Professor Martin, BA, PhD, Dept of History, Simon Fraser University, Burnaby, B.C. V5A 1S6, Canada.

KITCHING, C. J., BA, PhD, FSA (Hon. Treasurer), 11 Creighton Road, London NW6 6EE.

Klibansky, Professor R., MA, PhD, DPhil, FRSC, 608 Leacock Building, McGill University, P.O. Box 6070, Station A, Montreal H3C 3G1, Canada.

Knafla, Professor L. A., BA, MA, PhD, Dept of History, University of Calgary, Alberta, Canada.

Knecht, R. J., MA, DLitt, 22 Warwick New Road, Leamington Spa, Warwickshire.

Knowles, C. H., PhD, University College, P.O. Box 78, Cardiff CF1 1XL.

Koch, H. W., BA, Dept of History, University of York, York YO1 5DD.

Kochan, L. E., MA, PhD, 237 Woodstock Road, Oxford OX2 7AD.

Koenigsberger, Dorothy M. M., BA, PhD, 41a Lancaster Avenue, London NW3.

Koenigsberger, Professor H. G., MA, PhD, Dept of History, King's College, Strand, London WC2R 2LS.

Kohl, Professor Benjamin G., AB, MA, PhD, Dept of History, Vassar College, Poughkeepsie, New York, 12601, U.S.A.

Korr, Charles P., MA, PhD, College of Arts and Sciences, Dept of History, University of Missouri, 8001 Natural Bridge Road, St Louis, Missouri 63121, U.S.A.

Kossmann, Professor E. H., DLitt, Rijksuniversiteit te Groningen, Groningen, The Netherlands.

Kouri, E. I., PhD, Institut für Neuere Geschichte, Franz-Joseph-Strasse 10, D-8000 München, W. Germany.

Lake, P., BA, PhD, Dept of History, Royal Holloway and Bedford Colleges, Egham Hill, Surrey TW20 0EX.

Lambert, The Hon. Margaret, CMG, PhD. 39 Thornhill Road, Barnsbury Square, London N1 1JS.

Lambert, W. R., BA, PhD, 36 Five Mile Drive, Oxford OX2 8HR.

Lamont, W. M., PhD, Manor House, Keighton Road, Denton, Newhaven, Sussex BN9 0AB.

Lander, J. R., MA, MLitt, 5 Canonbury Place, London N1 2NQ.

Landes, Professor D. S., PhD, Widener U, Harvard University, Cambridge, Mass. 02138, U.S.A.

Landon, Professor M. de L., MA, PhD, Dept of History, The University, Mississippi 38667 U.S.A.

Langford, P., MA, DPhil, Lincoln College, Oxford OX1 3DR.

Langhorne, R. T. B., MA, 15 Madingley Road, Cambridge.

Lapridge, M., BA, MA, PhD, Dept of Anglo-Saxon, Norse and Celtic, 9 West Road, Cambridge CB3 9DP.

Larkin, Rev J. F., CSV, PhD, 1212 East Euclid Street, Arlington Heights, Illinois 60004, U.S.A.

Larner, J. P., MA, The University, Glasgow G12 8QQ.

Lasko, Professor P. E., BA, FSA, Courtauld Institute of Art, 20 Portman Square, London W1H 0BE.

Latham, R. C., CBE, MA, FBA, Magdalene College, Cambridge CB3 0AG.

Law, J. E., MA, DPhil, Dept of History, University College, Swansea SA2 8PP.

Lawrence, Professor C. H., MA, DPhil, Royal Holloway and Bedford Colleges, Egham Hill, Surrey TW20 0EX.

Laws, Captain W. F., BA, MLitt, 23 Marlborough Road, St. Leonards, Exeter EX2 4TJ.

Lead, P., BA, 3 Montrose Court, Holmes Chapel, Cheshire, CW4 7JJ.

Le Cordeur, Professor Basil A., MA, PhD, Dept of History, University of Cape Town, Rondebosch 7700, Republic of South Africa.

Leddy, J. F., MA, BLitt, DPhil, University of Windsor, Windsor, Ontario, Canada.

Lee, Professor J. M., MA, BLitt, Dept of Politics, University of Bristol, 77/79 Woodland Road, Bristol BS8 1UT.

Legge, Professor M. Dominica, MA, DLitt, FBA, 191a Woodstock Road, Oxford OX2 7AB.

Lehmann, Professor J. H., PhD, De Paul University, 25e Jackson Blvd., Chicago, Illinois 60604, U.S.A.

Lehmberg, Professor S. E., PhD, Dept of History, University of Minnesota, Minneapolis, Minn. 55455, U.S.A.

Leinster-Mackay, D. P., MA, MEd, PhD, Dept of Education, University of Western Australia, Nedlands, Western Australia 6009.

Lenman, B. P., MA, MLitt, FSA(Scot), 'Cromalt', 50 Lade Braes, St Andrews, Fife KY16 9DA.

Lentin, A., MA, PhD, 57 Maids Causeway, Cambridge CB5 8DE.

Leslie, Professor R. F., BA, PhD, Market House, Church Street, Charlbury, Oxford OX7 3PP.

Lester, Professor M., PhD, Dept of History, Davidson College, Davidson, N.C. 28036, U.S.A.

Levine, Professor Joseph M., Dept of History, Syracuse University, Syracuse, New York 13210, U.S.A.

Levine, Professor Mortimer, PhD, 529 Woodhaven Drive, Morgantown, West Va. 26505, U.S.A.

Levy, Professor F. J., PhD, University of Washington, Seattle, Wash. 98195, U.S.A.

Lewis, Professor A. R., MA, PhD, History Dept, University of Massachusetts, Amherst, Mass. 01003, U.S.A.

Lewis, Professor B., PhD, FBA, Near Eastern Studies Dept, Jones Hall, The University, Princeton, N.J. 08540, U.S.A.

Lewis, C. W., BA, FSA, University College, P.O. Box 78, Cardiff CF1 1XL.

Lewis, P. S., MA, All Souls College, Oxford OX1 4AL.

Lewis, R. A., PhD, University College of North Wales, Bangor, Gwynedd LL57 2DG.

Leyser, Professor K., MA, All Souls College, Oxford OX1 4AL.

Liddell, W. H., MA, Dept of Extra-Mural Studies, University of London, 26 Russell Square London WX1B 5DG.

Liddle, Peter H., BA, MLitt, 'Dipity Cottage', 20 Lime Street, Waldridge Fell, Nr. Chester-le-Street, Co Durham.

Lieu, Samuel N. C., BA, MA, DPhil, 2a Dickinson Square, Croxley Green, Rickmansworth, Herts. WD3 3EZ.

Lindley, K. J., MA, PhD, Dept of History, New University of Ulster, Coleraine, N. Ireland BT52 1SA.

*Lindsay, Mrs H., MA, PhD (address unknown).

Lindsay, Lt.-Col. Oliver, MBIM, Brookwood House, Brookwood, nr Woking, Surrey.

Linehan, P. A., MA, PhD, St John's College, Cambridge CB2 1TP.

Lipman, V. D., CVO, MA, DPhil, FSA, 9 Rotherwick Road, London NW11 9DG.

Livermore, Professor H. V., MA, Sandycombe Lodge, Sandycombe Road, St Margarets, Twickenham, Middx.

Lloyd, H. A., BA, DPhil, The University, Cottingham Road, Hull HU6 7RX.

Loach, Mrs J., MA, Somerville College, Oxford OX2 6HD.

Loades, Professor D. M., MA, PhD, University College of North Wales, Bangor, Gwynedd LL57 2DG.

Lobel, Mrs M. D., BA, FSA, 16 Merton Street, Oxford.

Lockie, D. McN., MA, 25 Chemin de la Panouche, Saint-Anne, 06130 Grasse, France.

Lockyer, R. W., MA, Dept of History, Royal Holloway College, Englefield Green, Surrey TW20 0EX.

Logan, F. D., MA, MSD, Emmanuel College, 400 The Fenway, Boston, Mass. 02115, U.S.A.

Logan, O. M. T., MA, PhD, 18 Clarendon Road, Norwich NR2 2PW.

London, Miss Vera C. M., MA, 55 Churchill Road, Church Stretton, Shropshire SY6 6EP.

Longley, D. A., MA, PhD, Dept of History, King's College, The University, Old Aberdeen AB9 2UB.

Longmate, N. R., MA, 30 Clydesdale Gardens, Richmond, Surrey.

Loomie, Rev. A. J., SJ, MA, PhD, Fordham University, New York, N.Y. 10458, U.S.A.

Loud, G. A., DPhil, School of History, The University, Leeds LS2 9JT.

Louis, Professor William R., BA, MA, DPhil, Dept of History, University of Texas, Austin, Texas 78712, U.S.A.

Lourie, Elena, MA, DPhil, Dept of History, University of The Negev, P.O. Box 4653, Beer Sheva, Israel.

Lovatt, R. W., MA, DPhil, Peterhouse, Cambridge CB2 1RD.

Lovell, J. C., BA, PhD, Eliot College, University of Kent, Canterbury CT2 7NS.

Lovett, A. W., MA, PhD, 26 Coney Hill Road, West Wickham, Kent BR4 9BX.

Lowe, P. C., BA, PhD, The University, Manchester M13 9PL.

Lowerson, J. R., BA, MA, Centre for Continuing Education, University of Sussex, Brighton.

Loyn, Professor H. R., MA, FBA, FSA, Westfield College, Kidderpore Avenue, London NW3 7ST.

Lucas, C. R., MA, DPhil, Balliol College, Oxford OX1 3BJ.

Lucas, P. J., MA, PhD, University College, Belfield, Dublin 4, Ireland.

Luft, Rev. Canon H. M., MA, MLitt, Highfurlong, 44 St Michael's Road, Blundellsands, Liverpool L23 7UN.

*Lumb, Miss S. V., MA, Torr-Colin House, 106 Ridgway, Wimbledon, London SW19.

Lunn, D. C., STL, MA, PhD, 25 Cornwallis Avenue, Clifton, Bristol BS8 4PP.

Lunt, Major-General J. D., MA, Hilltop House, Little Milton, Oxfordshire OX9 7PU.

Luscombe, Professor D. E., MA, PhD, FSA, 4 Caxton Road, Broomhill, Sheffield S10 3DE.

Luttrell, A. T., MA, DPhil, 14 Perfect View, Bath BA1 5JY.

Lyman, Professor Richard W., PhD, 350 East 57th Street, Apt 14-B, New York, N.Y. 10022, U.S.A.

Lynch, Professor J., MA, PhD, Inst. of Latin American Studies, 31 Tavistock Square, London WC1H 9HA.

Lynch, M., MA, PhD, Dept of Scottish History, The University, 50 George Square, Edinburgh EH8 9YW.

Lyttelton, The Hon. N. A. O., BA, 30 Paulton's Square, London SW3.

Mabbs, A. W., 14 Acorn Lane, Cuffley, Hertfordshire.

Macaulay, J. H., MA, PhD, 6 Hamilton Drive, Hillhead, Glasgow G12 8DR.

McBriar, Professor A. M., BA, DPhil, FASSA, Dept of History, Monash University, Clayton, Victoria 3168, Australia.

MacCaffrey, Professor W. T., PhD, 745 Hollyoke Center, Harvard University, Cambridge, Mass. 02138, U.S.A.

McCann, W. P., BA, PhD, 41 Stanhope Gardens, Highgate, London N6.

McCaughan, Professor R. E. M., MA, BArch, Hon DSc, FSA, FRAnthl, FRIBA, 'Rowan Bank', Kingsley Green, Fernhurst, West Sussex GU27 3LL.

McConica, Professor J. K., CSB, MA, DPhil, University of St Michael's College, 81 St Mary's Street, Toronto, Ontario, M5S 1J4, Canada.

McCord, Professor N., PhD, 7 Hatherton Avenue, Cullercoats, North Shields, Northumberland.

McCracken, Professor J. L., MA, PhD, 31 Cross Street Grahamstown 6140, South Africa.

MacCulloch, D. N. J., Wesley College, Henbury Road, Westbury-on-Trym, Bristol BS10 7QD.

MacCurtain, Margaret B., MA, PhD, Dept of History, University College, Belfield, Dublin 4, Ireland.

McCusker, J. J., MA, PhD, Dept of History, University of Maryland, College Park, Maryland 20742, U.S.A.

MacDonagh, Professor O., MA, PhD, Research School of Social Sciences, Institute of Advanced Studies, Australian National University, P.O. Box 4, Canberra, A.C.T. 2600, Australia.

Macdonald, Professor D. F., MA, DPhil, 11 Arnhall Drive, Dundee.

McDonald, Professor T. H., MA, PhD, R. R. 1, Site 1A, Peachland, BC., VOH 1XO, Canada.

McDowell, Professor R. B., PhD, LittD, Trinity College, Dublin, Ireland.

Macfarlane, A., MA, DPhil, PhD, King's College, Cambridge CB2 1ST.

Macfarlane, L. J., PhD, FSA, King's College, University of Aberdeen, Aberdeen AB9 1FX.

McGrath, Professor P. V., MA, University of Bristol, Bristol BS8 1RJ.
MacGregor, D. R., MA, ARIBA, FSA, 99 Lonsdale Road, London SW13 9DA.
McGurk, J. J. N., BA, MPhil, PhD, Conway House, 10 Stanley Avenue, Birkdale, Southport, Merseyside PR8 4RU.
McGurk, P. M., PhD, Birkbeck College, Malet Street, London WC1E 7HX.
Machin, G. I. T., MA, DPhil, Dept of Modern History, University of Dundee, Dundee DD1 4HN.
MacIntyre, A. D., MA, DPhil, Magdalen College, Oxford OX1 4AU.
McKendrick, N., MA, Gonville and Caius College, Cambridge CB2 1TA.
McKenna, Professor J. W., MA, PhD, Orchard Hill Farm, Sandown Road, P.O. Box 343, N. Danville, N.H. 03819, U.S.A.
MacKenzie, J. MacD., MA, PhD, Dept of History, The University, Bailrigg, Lancaster LA1 4YG.
Mackesy, P. G., MA, DPhil, DLitt, Pembroke College, Oxford OX1 1DW.
McKibbin, R. I., MA, DPhil, St John's College, Oxford OX1 3JP.
McKinley, R. A., MA, 42 Boyers Walk, Leicester Forest East, Leicester.
McKitterick, Rosamond D., MA, PhD, Newnham College, Cambridge CB3 9DF.
Maclagan, M., MA, FSA, Trinity College, Oxford OX1 3BH.
MacLeod, Professor R. M., AB, PhD, Dept of History, The University of Sydney, Sydney, N.S.W., Australia 2006.
*McManners, Professor J., MA, DLitt, FBA, Christ Church, Oxford OX1 1DP.
MacMichael, N. H., FSA, 2b Little Cloister, Westminster Abbey, London SW1.
McMillan, J. F., MA, DPhil, Dept of History, The University, York YO1 5DD.
MacNiocaill, Professor G., PhD, DLitt, Dept of History, University College, Galway, Ireland.
McNulty, Miss P. A., BA, 84b Eastern Avenue, Reading RG1 5SF.
Macpherson, Professor C. B., BA, MSc(Econ), DSc(Econ), DLitt, LLD, FRSC, 32 Boswell Avenue, Toronto M5R 1M4, Canada.
Madariaga, Professor Isabel de, PhD, 25 Southwood Lawn Road, London N6.
Madden, A. F., DPhil, Nuffield College, Oxford OX1 1NF.
Maddicott, J. R., MA, DPhil, Exeter College, Oxford OX1 3DP.
Maehl, Professor W. H., PhD, College of Liberal Studies, Office of the Dean, 1700 Asp Avenue, Suite 226, Norman, Oklahoma 73037, U.S.A.
Maffei, Professor Domenico, MLL, DrJur, Via delle Cerchia 19, 53100 Siena, Italy.
Magnus-Allcroft, Sir Phillip, Bt., CBE, FRSL, Stokesay Court, Craven Arms, Shropshire SY7 9BD.
Maguire, W. A., MA, PhD, 18 Harberton Park, Belfast, N. Ireland BT9 6TS.
Mahoney, Professor T. H. D., AM, PhD, MPA, Massachusetts Institute of Technology, Cambridge, Mass. 02138, U.S.A.
*MAJOR, Miss K., MA, BLitt, LittD, FBA, FSA, 21 Queensway, Lincoln LN2 4AJ.
Malcolm, Joyce L., 1264 Beacon Street, Brookline, Mass. 02146, U.S.A.
Mallett, Professor M. E., MA, DPhil, Dept of History, The University, Coventry CV4 7AL.
Mallia-Milanes, V., BA, MA, PhD, 135 Zabbar Road, Paola, Malta.
Malone, Professor J. J., PhD, 2022 Wyoming Avenue N.W., Apt 602, Washington, D.C. 20009, U.S.A.

Mangan, James A., BA, PhD, PGGE, 39 Abercorn Drive, Hamilton, Scotland.

Manning, Professor A. F., Bosweg 27, Berg en Dal, The Netherlands.

Manning, Professor B. S., MA, DPhil, New University of Ulster, Coleraine, Co Londonderry, Northern Ireland BT52 1SA.

Manning, Professor R. B., PhD, 2848 Coleridge Road, Cleveland Heights, Ohio 44118, U.S.A.

Mansergh, Professor P. N. S., OBE, MA, DPhil, DLitt, LittD, FBA, The Master's Lodge, St John's College, Cambridge.

Maprayil, C., BD, LD, DD, MA, PhD, c/o Institute of Historical Research, Senate House, London WC1E 7HU.

Marchant, The Rev Canon R. A., PhD, BD, Laxfield Vicarage, Woodbridge, Suffolk IP13 8DT.

Marett, W. P., BSc(Econ), BCom, MA, PhD, 20 Barrington Road, Stoneygate, Leicester LE2 2RA.

Margetts, J., MA, DipEd, DrPhil, 5 Glenluce Road, Liverpool L19 9BX.

Markus, Professor R. A., MA, PhD, The University, Nottingham NG7 2RD.

Marriner, Sheila, MA, PhD, Dept of Economic History, P.O. Box 147, Liverpool L69 3BX.

Marsh, Professor Peter T., PhD, Dept of History, Syracuse University, Syracuse, New York 13210, U.S.A.

Marshall, J. D., PhD, Brynthwaite, Charney Road, Grange-over-Sands, Cumbria LA11 6BP.

Marshall, Professor P. J., MA, DPhil, King's College, Strand, London WC2R 2LS.

Martin, E. W., Crossways, 41 West Avenue, Exeter EX4 4SD.

Martin, G. H., MA, DPhil, Public Record Office, Chancery Lane, London WC2A 2LR.

Martin, Professor Miguel, P.O. Box 1696, Zone 1, Panama, Republic of Panama.

Martindale, Jane M., MA, DPhil, School of English and American Studies, University of East Anglia, Norwich NR4 7TJ.

Marwick, Professor A. J. B., MA, BLitt, Dept of History, The Open University, Walton Hall, Milton Keynes, Bucks MK7 6AA.

Mason, E. Emma, BA, PhD, Dept of History, Birkbeck College, Malet Street, London WC1E 7HX.

Mason, F. K., Beechwood, Watton, Norfolk IP25 6AB.

Mason, J. F. A., MA, DPhil, FSA, Christ Church, Oxford OX1 1DP.

Mather, Professor F. C., MA, 69 Ethelburt Avenue, Swaythling, Southampton.

Mathew, W. M., MA, PhD, School of English and American Studies, University of East Anglia, University Plain, Norwich NR4 7TJ.

Mathias, Professor P., MA, FBA, All Souls College, Oxford OX1 4AL.

*Mathur-Sherry, Tikait Narain, BA, LLB, 3/193 4 Prem-Nagar, Dayalbagh, Agra-282005 (U.P.), India.

Matthew, Professor D. J. A., MA, DPhil, Dept of History, The University, Reading RG6 2AA.

Matthew, H. C. G., MA, DPhil, St Hugh's College, Oxford OX2 6LE.

Mattingly, Professor H. B., MA, Dept of Ancient History, The University, Leeds LS2 9JT.

Mayr-Harting, H. M. R. E., MA, DPhil, St Peter's College, Oxford OX1 2DL.

Mbaeyi, P. M., BA, DPhil, Alvan Ikoku College of Education, Dept of History, PMB 1033, Owerri, Imo State, Nigeria.

Medlicott, Professor W. N., CBE, MA, DLit, DLitt, LittD, 172 Watchfield Court, Sutton Court Road, Chiswick, London W4 4NE.

Meek, Christine E., MA, DPhil, 3145 Arts Building, Trinity College, Dublin 2, Ireland.

Meek, D. E., MA, BA, Dept of Celtic, University of Edinburgh, George Square, Edinburgh EH8 9JX.

Meller, Miss Helen E., BA, PhD, 2 Copenhagen Court, Denmark Grove, Alexandra Park, Nottingham NG3 4LF.

Merson, A. L., MA, Flat 12, Northerwood House, Swan Green, Lyndhurst SI4 17DT.

Mettam, R. C., BA, MA, PhD, Dept of History, Queen Mary College, Mile End Road, London E1 4NS.

Mews, Stuart, PhD, Dept of Religious Studies, Cartmel College, Bailrigg, Lancaster.

Micklewright, F. H. A., MA, PhD, 228 South Norwood Hill, London SE25.

Middlebrook, Norman M., 48 Linden Way, Boston, Lincs. PE21 9DS.

Midgley, Miss L. M., MA, 84 Wolverhampton Road, Stafford ST17 4AW.

Miller, Professor A., BA, MA, PhD, Dept of History, University of Texas, Houston, Texas, U.S.A.

Miller, E., MA, LittD, 36 Almoners Avenue, Cambridge CB1 4PA.

Miller, Miss H., MA, University College of North Wales, Bangor, Gwynedd LL57 2DG.

Miller, J., MA, PhD, Dept of History, Queen Mary College, Mile End Road, London E1 4NS.

Milne, A. T., MA, 9 Frank Dixon Close, London SE21 7BD.

Milne, Miss D. J., MA, PhD, King's College, Aberdeen.

Milsom, Professor S. F. C., MA, FBA, 113 Grantchester Meadows, Cambridge CB3 9JN.

Minchinton, Professor W. E., BSc(Econ), The University, Exeter EX4 4PU.

Mingay, Professor G. E., PhD, Mill Field House, Selling Court, Selling, nr Faversham, Kent.

Mitchell, C., MA, BLitt, LittD, Woodhouse Farmhouse, Fyfield, Abingdon, Berks.

Mitchell, L. G., MA, DPhil, University College, Oxford OX1 4BH.

Mitchison, Professor Rosalind, MA, Great Yew, Ormiston, East Lothian EH35 5NJ.

Momigliano, Professor A. D., DLitt, FBA, University College London, Gower Street, London WC1E 6BT.

Mommsen, Professor Dr W. J., German Historical Institute, 17 Bloomsbury Square, London WC1.

Mondey, D. C., 175 Raeburn Avenue, Surbiton, Surrey KT5 9DE.

Money, Professor J., PhD, 912 St Patrick Street, Victoria, B.C., Canada V8S 4X5.

Moore, B. J. S., BA, University of Bristol, 67 Woodland Road, Bristol BS8 1UL.

Moore, Professor Cresap, 935 Memorial Drive, Cambridge, Mass. 02138, U.S.A.

Moore, R. I., MA, Dept of History, The University Sheffield S10 2TN.

*Moorman, Mrs M. MA, 22 Springwell Road, Durham DH1 4LR.

Morey, Rev. Dom R. Adrian, OSB, MA, DPhil, LittD, Benet House, Mount Pleasant, Cambridge CB3 0BL.

Morgan, B. G., BArch, PhD, Tan-y-Fron, 43 Church Walks, Llandudno, Gwynedd.

Morgan, David R., MA, PhD, Dept of Politics, The University, P.O. Box 147, Liverpool L69 3BX.
Morgan, K. O., MA, DPhil, FBA, The Queen's College, Oxford OX1 4AW.
Morgan, Miss P. E., 1a The Cloisters, Hereford HR1 2NG.
Morgan, Victor, BA, School of English and American Studies, University of East Anglia, Norwich NR4 7TJ.
Morrell, J. B., BSc., MA, Dept of Social Sciences, The University, Richmond Road, Bradford BD7 1DP.
*Morrell, Professor W. P., CBE, MA, DPhil, 20 Bedford Street, St Clair, Dunedin SW1, New Zealand.
Morrill, J. S., MA, DPhil, Selwyn College, Cambridge CB3 9DQ.
Morris, The Rev. Professor C., MA, 53 Cobbett Road, Bitterne Park, Southampton SO2 4HJ.
Morris, G. C., MA, King's College, Cambridge CB2 1ST.
Morris, L. P., BA, PhD, Dept of History and Archaeology, The University, Exeter EX4 4QH.
Mortimer, R., PhD, 370 Mill Road, Cambridge, CB1 3NN.
Morton, Miss C. E., MA, MLS, FSA, An Tigh Béag, Glenteenassig, Castlegregory, Co. Kerry, Ireland.
Mosse, Professor W. E. E., MA, PhD, Dawn Cottage, Ashwellthorpe, Norwich, Norfolk.
Mullins, E. L. C., OBE, MA, Institute of Historical Research, University of London, Senate House, London WC1E 7HU.
Murdoch, D. H., MA, School of History, The University, Leeds LS2 9JT.
Murray, A., MA, BA, BPhil, University College, Oxford OX1 4BH.
Murray, Athol L., MA, LLB, PhD, 33 Inverleith Gardens, Edinburgh EH3 5PR.
Myerscough, J., BA, 39 Campden Street, London W8 7ET.
Myres, J. N. L., CBE, MA, LLD, DLitt, Dlit, FBA, FSA, The Manor House, Kennington, Oxford OX1 5PH.

Nef, Professor J. U., PhD, 2726 N Street NW, Washington, D.C. 20007, U.S.A.
Nelson, Janet L., BA, PhD, Dept of History, King's College, London WC2R 2LS.
Neveu, Dr Bruno, 30 rue Jacob, Paris VIe, France.
New, Professor J. F. H., Dept of History, Waterloo University, Waterloo, Ontario, Canada.
Newitt, M. D. D., BA, PhD, Queen's Building, University of Exeter, EX4 4QH.
Newman, A. N., MA, DPhil, 33 Stanley Road, Leicester.
Newman, P. R., BA, DPhil, 1 Ainsty Farm Cottage, Bilton in Ainsty, York YO5 8NN.
Newsome, D. H., MA, LittD, Master's Lodge, Wellington College, Crowthorne, Berks. RG11 7PU.
Nicholas, Professor David, PhD, Dept of History, University of Nebraska, Lincoln, Nebraska 68588, U.S.A.
Nicholas, Professor H. G., MA, FBA, New College, Oxford OX1 3BN.
Nicol, Mrs A., MA, BLitt, Public Record Office, Chancery Lane, London WC2A 1LR.
Nicol, Professor D. M., MA, PhD, King's College, London WC2R 2LS.
Nightingale, Pamela, MA, PhD, 20 Beaumont Buildings, Oxford OX1 2LL.

Noakes, J. D., MA, DPhil, Queen's Bldg., The University, Exeter EX4 4QH.

Nordmann, Professor Claude J., 5 rue du Sergant Hoff, Paris 17, 75017 France.

Norman, E. R., MA, PhD, Peterhouse, Cambridge CB2 1RD.

Obolensky, Professor Sir Dimitri, MA, PhD, DLitt, FBA, FSA, Christ Church, Oxford OX1 1DP.

O'Day, A., MA, PhD, Polytechnic of North London, Prince of Wales Road, London NW5.

O'Day, Mrs M. R., BA, PhD, Open University, Faculty of Arts, Milton Keynes MK7 6AA.

*Offler, Professor H. S., MA, 28 Old Elvet, Durham DH1 3HN.

O'Gorman, F., BA, PhD, The University, Manchester M13 9PL.

O'Higgins, The Rev. J., SJ, MA, DPhil, Campion Hall, Oxford.

Olney, R. J., MA, DPhil, Historical Manuscripts Commission, Quality Court, Chancery Lane, London WC2A 1HP.

Orde, Miss A., MA, PhD, 8 Wearside Drive, Durham DH1 1LE.

Orme, N. I., MA, DPhil, The University, Exeter EX4 4QH.

*Orr, J. E., MA, ThD, DPhil, 11451 Berwick Street, Los Angeles, Calif. 90049, U.S.A.

Ó Tuathaigh, M. A. G., MA, Dept of History, University College, Galway, Ireland.

Otway-Ruthven, Professor A. J., MA, PhD, 7 Trinity College, Dublin, Ireland.

Outhwaite, R. B., MA, PhD, Gonville and Caius College, Cambridge CB2 1TA.

Ovendale, R., MA, DPhil, Dept of International Politics, University College of Wales, Aberystwyth SY23 3DB.

Owen, A. E. B., MA, 35 Whitwell Way, Coton, Cambridge CB3 7PW.

Owen, Mrs D. M., MA, FSA, 35 Whitwell Way, Coton, Cambridge CB3 7PW.

Owen, G. D., MA, PhD, 4 St Aubyn's Mansions, Kings Esplanade, Howe, Sussex.

Owen, J. B., BSc, MA, DPhil, Lincoln College, Oxford OX1 3DR.

Pagden, A. R. D., BA, Girton College, Cambridge CB3 0JG.

Palgrave, D. A., MA, CChem, FRSC, FSG, 210 Bawtry Road, Doncaster, S. Yorkshire DN4 7BZ.

Palliser, Professor D. M., MA, DPhil, FSA, Dept of History, The University, Hull HU6 7RX.

Pallister, Anne, BA, PhD, Dept of History, The University, Reading, Berks. RD6 2AA.

Palmer, J. J. N., BA, BLitt, PhD, 59 Marlborough Avenue, Hull.

Paret, Professor P., Dept of History, Stanford University, Stanford, California, U.S.A.

Parish, Professor P. J., BA, Institute of U.S. Studies, 31 Tavistock Square, London WC1H 9EZ.

Parker, Professor N. G., MA, PhD, LittD, Dept of Modern History, St Salvator's College, The University, St Andrew's, Fife KY16 9AJ.

Parker, R. A. C., MA, DPhil, The Queen's College, Oxford OX1 4AW.

Parkes, M. B., BLitt, MA, FSA, Keble College, Oxford OX1 3PG.

*Parkinson, Professor C. N., MA, PhD, Anneville Manor, Rue Anneville, Vale, Guernsey, C.I.

Parris, H. W., MA, PhD, 15 Murdoch Road, Wokingham, Berks. RG11 2DG.

Patrick, Rev. J. G., MA, PhD, DLitt, 8 North Street, Braunton, N. Devon EX33 1AJ.

Pavlowitch, Stevan K., MA, LesL, Dept of History, The University, Southampton SO9 5NH.

Payne, Professor Peter L., BA, PhD, 68 Hamilton Place, Aberdeen AB2 4BA.

Peake, Rev. F. A., DD, DSLitt, 234 Wilson Street, Sudbury, Ontario P3E 2S2, Canada.

Pearl, Mrs Valerie, MA, DPhil, FSA, New Hall, Cambridge CB3 0DF.

Peck, Professor Linda L., PhD, Dept of History, Purdue University, University Hall, West Lafayette, Indiana 47907, U.S.A.

Peek, Miss H. E., MA, FSA, FSAScot, Taintona, Moretonhampstead, Newton Abbot, Devon TQ13 8LG.

Peel, Lynnette J., BAgrSc, MAgrSc, PhD, 49 Oaklands, Hamilton Road, Reading RG1 5RN.

Peele, Miss Gillian R., BA, BPhil, Lady Margaret Hall, Oxford OX2 6QA.

Pennington, D. H., MA, Balliol College, Oxford OX1 3BJ.

Perkin, Professor H. J., MA, Borwicks, Caton, Lancaster LA2 9NB.

Perry, Norma, BA, PhD, Dept of French and Italian, The University, Exeter EX4 4QH.

Peters, Professor E. M., PhD, Dept of History, University of Pennsylvania, Philadelphia 19171, U.S.A.

Petti, Professor A. G. R., MA, DLit, FSA, Dept of English, University of Calgary, Alberta T2N 1N4, Canada.

Pfaff, Professor Richard W., MA, DPhil, Dept of History, Hamilton Hall 170A, University of North Carolina, Chapel Hill W.C. 27514, U.S.A.

Philips, Sir Henry (E. I.), CMG, MBE, MA, 34 Ross Court, Putney Hill, London SW15.

Phillips, Assoc. Professor John A., PhD, Dept of History, University of California, Riverside, Calif. 92521, U.S.A.

Phillips, J. R. S., BA, PhD, FSA, Dept of Medieval History, University College, Dublin 4, Ireland.

Phythian-Adams, C. V., MA, Dept of English Local History, The University, Leicester LE1 7RH.

Pierce, Professor G. O., MA, Dept of History, University College, P.O. Box 95, Cardiff CF1 1XA.

Pitt, H. G., MA, Worcester College, Oxford OX1 2HB.

Platt, C. P. S., MA, PhD, FSA, 24 Oakmount Avenue, Highfield, Southampton.

Platt, Professor D. C. St M., MA, DPhil, St Antony's College, Oxford OX2 6JF.

Plumb, Sir John, PhD, LittD, FBA, FSA, Christ's College, Cambridge CB2 3BU.

Pocock, Professor J. G. A., PhD, Johns Hopkins University, Baltimore, Md. 21218, U.S.A.

Pole, Professor J. R., MA, PhD, St Catherine's College, Oxford OX1 3UJ.

Pollard, A. J., BA, PhD, 22 The Green, Hurworth-on-Tees, Darlington, Co Durham DL2 2AA.

Pollard, Professor S., BSc(Econ), PhD, Dept of Economic History, The University, Sheffield S10 2TN.

Polonsky, A. B., BA, DPhil, Dept of International History, London School of Economics, Houghton Street, London WC2A 2AE.

PORT, Professor M. H., MA, BLitt, FSA (*Hon. Secretary*), Queen Mary College, Mile End Road, London E1 4NS.

Porter, A. N., MA, PhD, Dept of History, King's College, London WC2R 2LS.

Porter, B. E., BSc(Econ), PhD, Dept of International Politics, University College of Wales, Aberystwyth, Dyfed SY23 3DB.

Porter, H. C., MA, PhD, Faculty of History, West Road, Cambridge CB3 9EF.

Porter, S., BA, MLitt, PhD, Dept of History, King's College, London WC2R 2LS.

Post, J., MA, PhD, Public Record Office, Chancery Lane, London WC2A 1LR.

Potter, J., BA, MA(Econ), London School of Economics, Houghton Street, London WC2A 2AE.

Powell, W. R., BLitt, MA, FSA, 2 Glanmead, Shenfield Road, Brentwood, Essex.

Powicke, Professor M. R., MA. University of Toronto, Toronto M5S 1AI, Canada.

Prall, Professor Stuart E., MA, PhD, Dept of History, Queens College, C.U.N.Y., Flushing, N.Y. 11367, U.S.A.

Prest, W. R., MA, DPhil, Dept of History, University of Adelaide, North Terrace, Adelaide 5001, S. Australia.

Preston, P., MA, DPhil, Dept of History, Queen Mary College, Mile End Road, London E1 4NS.

*Preston, Professor R. A., MA, PhD, Duke University, Durham, N.C., U.S.A.

Prestwich, J. O., MA, 18 Dunstan Road, Old Headington, Oxford OX3 9BY.

Prestwich, Mrs M., MA, St Hilda's College, Oxford OX4 1DY.

Prestwich, M. C., MA, DPhil, Dept of History, 43/46 North Bailey, Durham DH1 3EX.

Price, A. W., 19 Bayley Close, Uppingham, Leicestershire LE15 9TG.

Price, Rev. D. T. W., MA, St David's University College, Lampeter, Dyfed SA48 7ED.

Price, F. D., MA, BLitt, FSA, Keble College, Oxford OX1 3PG.

Price, Professor Jacob M., AM, PhD, University of Michigan, Ann Arbor, Michigan 48104, U.S.A.

Price, R. D., BA, School of Modern Languages & European History, University of East Anglia, Norwich NR4 7TJ.

Prichard, Canon T. J., MA, PhD, Tros-yr-Afon, Llangwnnadl, Pwllheli, Gwynedd LL53 8NS.

Prins, G. I. T., MA, PhD, Emmanuel College, Cambridge CB2 3AP.

Pritchard, Professor D. G., PhD, 11 Coed Mor, Sketty, Swansea, W. Glam. SA2 8BQ.

Pronay, N., BA, School of History, The University, Leeds LS2 9JT.

Prothero, I. J., BA, PhD, The University, Manchester M13 9PL.

Pugh, T. B., MA, BLitt, 28 Bassett Wood Drive, Southampton SO2 3PS.

Pullan, Professor B. S., MA, PhD, Dept of History, The University, Manchester M13 9PL.

Pulman, M. B., MA, PhD, History Dept, University of Denver, Colorado 80210, U.S.A.

Pulzer, P. G. J., MA, PhD, All Souls College, Oxford OX1 4AL.

Quinault, R. E., MA, DPhil, 21 Tytherton Road, London N19.

QUINN, Professor D. B., MA, PhD, DLit, DLitt, DLitt, DLitt, LLD, DHL, Hon FBA, 9 Knowsley Road, Liverpool L19 0PF.
Quintrell, B. W., MA, PhD, School of History, The University, P.O. Box 147, Liverpool L69 3BX.

Raban, Mrs S. G., MA, PhD, Trinity Hall, Cambridge CB2 1TJ.
Rabb, Professor T. K., MA, PhD, Princeton University, Princeton, N.J. 08540, U.S.A.
Radford, C. A. Ralegh, MA, DLitt, FBA, FSA, Culmcott, Uffculme, Cullompton, Devon EX15 3AT.
*Ramm, Miss A., MA, DLitt, Metton Road, Roughton, Norfolk NR11 8QT.
*Ramsay, G. D., MA, DPhil, 15 Charlbury Road, Oxford OX2 6UT.
Ramsden, J. A., MA, DPhil, Dept of History, Queen Mary College, Mile End Road, London E1 4NS.
Ramsey, Professor P. H., MA, DPhil, Taylor Building, King's College, Old Aberdeen AB9 1FX.
Ranft, Professor B. McL., MA, DPhil. 32 Parkgate, London SE3 9X3.
Ransome D. R., MA, PhD, 10 New Street, Woodbridge, Suffolk.
Ratcliffe, D. J. MA, BPhil, Dept of History, The University, 43 North Bailey, Durham DH1 3EX.
Rawcliffe, Carole, BA, PhD, 24 Villiers Road, London NW2.
Rawley, Professor J. A., PhD, University of Nebraska, Lincoln, Nebraska 68508, U.S.A.
Ray, Professor R. D., BA, BD, PhD, University of Toledo, 2801, W. Bancroft Street, Toledo, Ohio 43606, U.S.A.
Read, Professor D., BLitt, MA, PhD, Darwin College, University of Kent at Canterbury, Kent CR2 7NY.
Reader, W. J., BA, PhD, 46 Gough Way, Cambridge CB3 9LN.
Reed, Michael A., MA, LLB, PhD, 1 Paddock Close, Quorn, Leicester LE12 8BJ.
Reeves, Professor A. C., MA, PhD, Dept of History, Ohio University, Athens, Ohio 45701, U.S.A.
Reeves, Miss M. E., MA, PhD, 38 Norham Road, Oxford OX2 6SQ.
Reid Professor L. D., MA, PhD, 200 E. Brandon Road, Columbia, Mo. 65201, U.S.A.
Reid, Professor W. S., MA, PhD, University of Guelph, Guelph, Ontario, Canada.
Renold, Miss P., MA, 24 Kirk Close, Oxford OX2 8JN.
Renshaw, P. R. G., MA, Dept of History, The University, Sheffield S10 2TN.
Reuter, T. A., MA, DPhil, Monumenta Germaniae Historica, Ludwigstrasse 16, 8 München 34, West Germany.
Reynolds, Miss S. M. G., MA, 26 Lennox Gardens, London SW1.
Richards J. M., MA, Dept of History, The University, Bailrigg, Lancaster LA1 4YG.
Richards, Rev. J. M., MA, BLitt, STL, St Mary's, Cadogan Street, London SW3 2QR.
Richardson R. C., BA, PhD, King Alfred's College, Winchester.
Richmond, C. F., DPhil, 59 The Covert, The University, Keele, Staffs. ST5 5BG.
Richter, Professor M., DrPhil habil, Dept of Medieval History, University College, Dublin 4, Ireland.

Riden, Philip J., MA, MLitt, Dept of Extramural Studies, University College, P.O. Box 78, Cardiff CF1 1XL.

Riley, P. W. J., BA, PhD, The University, Manchester M13 9PL.

Riley-Smith, Professor J. S. C., MA, PhD, Royal Holloway and Bedford Colleges, Egham Hill, Surrey TW20 0EX.

Rimmer, Professor W. G., MA, PhD, University of N.S.W., P.O. Box 1, Kensington, N.S.W. 2033, Australia.

Ritcheson, Professor C. R., DPhil, Dept of History, University of Southern California, Los Angeles 90007, U.S.A.

Rizvi, S. A. G., MA, DPhil, 7 Portland Road, Summertown, Oxford.

Roach, Professor J. P. C., MA, PhD, 1 Park Crescent, Sheffield S10 2DY.

Robbins, Professor Caroline, PhD, 815 The Chetwynd, Rosemount, Pa. 19010, U.S.A.

Robbins, Professor K. G., MA, DPhil, Dept of History, The University, Glasgow G12 8QQ.

Roberts, Professor J. M., MA, DPhil, The University, Southampton SO9 5NH.

Roberts, Professor M., MA, DPhil, DLit, FilDr, FBA, 38 Somerset Street, Grahamstown 6140, C.P., South Africa.

Roberts, P. R., MA, PhD, FSA, Keynes College, The University, Canterbury, Kent CT2 7NP.

Roberts, Professor R. C., PhD, 284 Blenheim Road, Columbus, Ohio 43214, U.S.A.

Roberts, Professor R. S., PhD, History Dept, University of Zimbabwe, P.O. Box MP 167, Harare, Zimbabwe.

Robertson, E. M., MA, 4 Chevening Road, Chipstead, nr Sevenoaks, Kent.

Robinson, F. C. R., MA, PhD, 13 Grove Road, Windsor, Berkshire SL4 1JE.

Robinson, K. E., CBE, MA, DLitt, LLD, The Old Rectory, Church Westcote, Kingham, Oxford OX7 6SF.

Robinson, R. A. H., BA, PhD, School of History, The University, Birmingham B15 2TT.

Robinton, Professor Madeline R., MA, PhD, 210 Columbia Heights, Brooklyn 1, New York, U.S.A.

Rodger, N. A. M., MA, DPhil, 40 Grafton Road, Acton, London W3.

*Rodkey, F. S., AM, PhD, 152 Bradley Drive, Santa Cruz, Calif., U.S.A.

Rodney, Professor W., MA, PhD, Royal Roads Military College, FMO, Victoria, B.C., V0S 1B0, Canada.

Roebuck, Peter, BA, PhD, Dept of History, New University of Ulster, Coleraine, N. Ireland BT48 7JL.

Rogers, Professor A., MA, PhD, FSA, New University of Ulster, Coleraine, N. Ireland BT52 1SA.

Rogister, J. M. J., BA, DPhil, 4 The Peth, Durham DH1 4PZ.

Rolo, Professor P. J. V., MA, The University, Keele, Staffordshire ST5 5BG.

Rompkey, R. G., MA, BEd, PhD, Dept of English, Memorial University St John's, Newfoundland A1C 5S7, Canada.

Roots, Professor I. A., MA, FSA, Dept of History, University of Exeter, Exeter EX4 4QH.

Roper, M., MA, Public Record Office, Ruskin Avenue, Kew, Richmond, Surrey TW9 4DU.

Rose, P. L., MA, D.enHist (Sorbonne), Dept of General History, University of Haifa, Haifa, Israel.

Rosenthal, Professor Joel T., PhD, State University, Stony Brook, New York 11794, U.S.A.

Roseveare, H. G., PhD, King's College, Strand, London WC2R 2LS.

Roskell, Professor J. S., MA, DPhil, FBA, The University, Manchester M13 9PL.

Ross, Professor C. D., MA, DPhil, Wills Memorial Building, Queen's Road, Bristol BS8 1RJ.

Rothblatt, Professor Sheldon, PhD, Dept of History, University of California, Berkeley, Calif. 94720, U.S.A.

Rothney, Professor G. O., PhD, St John's College, University of Manitoba, Winnipeg R3T 2MS, Canada.

Rothrock, Professor G. A., MA, PhD, Dept of History, University of Alberta, Edmonton, Alberta T6G 2H4, Canada.

Rousseau, P. H., MA, DPhil, Dept of History, University of Auckland, Private Bag, Auckland, New Zealand.

*Rowe, Miss B. J. H., MA, BLitt, St Anne's Cottage, Winkton, Christchurch, Hants.

Rowe, W. J., DPhil, Rock Mill, Par, Cornwall PL25 2SS.

Rowse, A. L., MA, DLitt, DCL, FBA, Trenarren House, St Austell, Cornwall.

ROY, I., MA, DPhil (*Literary Director*), Dept of History, King's College, Strand, London WC2R 2LS.

Roy, Professor R. H., MA, PhD, 2841 Tudor Avenue, Victoria, B.C., Canada.

Royle, E., MA, PhD, Dept of History, The University, York YO1 5DD.

Rubens, A., FRICS, FSA, 16 Grosvenor Place, London SW1.

Rubini, D. A., DPhil, Temple University, Philadelphia 19122, Penn., U.S.A

Rubinstein, Professor N., PhD, Westfield College, London NW3 7ST.

Ruddock, Miss A. A., PhD, FSA, Wren Cottage, Heatherwood, Midhurst, W. Sussex GU29 9LH.

Rudé, Professor G. F. E., MA, PhD, The Oast House, Hope Farm, Beckley, nr Rye, E. Sussex.

Rule, Professor John C., MA, PhD, Ohio State University, 230 West 17th Avenue, Colombus, Ohio 43210, U.S.A.

*RUNCIMAN, The Hon. Sir Steven, CH, MA, DPhil, LLD, LittD, DLitt, LitD, DD, DHL, FBA, FSA, Elshieshields, Lockerbie, Dumfriesshire.

Runyan, Professor Timothy J., Cleveland State University, Cleveland, Ohio 44115, U.S.A.

Rupp, Professor the Rev. E. G., MA, DD, FBA, 42 Malcolm Place, King Street, Cambridge CB1 1LS.

Russell, Professor C. S. R., MA, Dept of History, University College London, London WC1E 6BT.

Russell, Mrs J. G., MA, DPhil, St Hugh's College, Oxford OX2 6LE.

Russell, Professor P. E., MA, FBA, 23 Belsyre Court, Woodstock Road, Oxford OX2 6HU.

Ryan, A. N., MA, School of History, University of Liverpool, P.O. Box 147, Liverpool L69 3BX.

Ryecraft, P., BA, Dept of History, The University, York YO1 5DD.

Ryder, A. F. C., MA, DPhil, Dept of History, Wills Memorial Building, Queen's Road, Bristol BS8 1RJ.

Sachse, Professor W. L., PhD, 4066 Whitney Avenue, Mt. Carmel, Conn. 06518, U.S.A.

Sainty, J. C., MA, 22 Kelso Place, London W8.

*Salmon, Professor E. T., MA, PhD, 36 Auchmar Road, Hamilton, Ontario LPC 1C5, Canada.

Salmon, Professor J. H. M., MA, MLitt, DLit, Bryn Mawr College, Bryn Mawr, Pa. 19101, U.S.A.

*Saltman, Professor A., MA., PhD, Bar Ilan University, Ramat Gan, Israel.

Samuel, E. R., BA, MPhil, 8 Steynings Way, London N12 7LN.

Sanderson, Professor G. N., MA, PhD, 2 Alder Close, Englefield Green, Surrey TW20 0LU.

Sar Desai, Professor Damodar R., MA, PhD, Dept of History, University of California, Los Angeles, Calif. 90024, U.S.A.

Saunders, A. D., MA, FSA, 12 Ashburnham Grove, London SE10 8UH.

Saville, Professor J., BSc(Econ), Dept of Economic and Social History, The University, Hull HU6 7RX.

Sawyer, Professor P. H., MA, Viktoriagatan 18, 441 33 Alingsas, Sweden.

Sayers, Miss J. E., MA, BLitt, PhD, FSA, 17 Sheffield Terrace, Campden Hill, London W8.

Scammell, G. V., MA, Pembroke College, Cambridge CB2 1RF.

Scammell, Mrs Jean, MA, Clare Hall, Cambridge.

Scarisbrick, Professor J. J., MA, PhD, 35 Kenilworth Road, Leamington Spa, Warwickshire.

Schofield, A. N. E. D., PhD, 15 Westergate, Corfton Road, London W5 2HT.

Schofield, R. S., MA, PhD, 27 Trumpington Street, Cambridge CB2 1QA.

Schreiber, Professor Roy E., PhD, Dept of History, Indiana University, P.O.B. 7111, South Bend, Indiana 46634, U.S.A.

Schweizer, Karl W., MA, PhD, 4 Harrold Drive, Bishop's University, Lennoxville, Quebec, Canada.

Schwoerer, Professor Lois G., PhD, 7213 Rollingwood Drive, Chevy Chase, Maryland 20015, U.S.A.

Scott, H. M., MA, PhD, Dept of Modern History, The University, St Salvator's College, St Andrews, Fife.

Scott, Tom, MA, PhD, School of History, The University, P.O. Box 147, Liverpool L69 3BX.

Scouloudi, Miss I., MSc(Econ), FSA, 67 Victoria Road, London W8 5RH.

Scribner, R. W., MA, PhD, Clare College, Cambridge CN2 1TL.

Seaborne, M. V. J., MA, Chester College, Cheyney Road, Chester CH1 4BJ.

Searle, A., BA, MPhil, Dept of Manuscripts, British Library, London WC1B 3DG.

Searle, Professor Eleanor, AB, PhD, 431 S. Parkwood Avenue, Pasadena, Calif. 91107, U.S.A.

Searle, G. R., MA, PhD, School of English and American Studies, University of East Anglia, Norwich NR4 7TJ.

Seaver, Professor Paul S., MA, PhD, Dept of History, Stanford University, Stanford, Calif. 94305, U.S.A.

Seddon, P. R., BA, PhD, Dept of History, The University, Nottingham NG7 2RD.

Sell, Rev. A. P. F., BA, BD, MA, PhD, Rue de la Golette 11B, 1217 Meyrin, Geneva, Switzerland.

Sellar, W. D. H., BA, LLB, 6 Eildon Street, Edinburgh EH3 5JU.

Semmell, Professor Bernard, PhD, Dept of History, State University of New York at Stony Brook, N.Y. 11790, U.S.A.

Serjeant, W. R., BA, 51 Derwent Road, Ipswich IP3 0QR.

Seton-Watson, C. I. W., MC, MA, Oriel College, Oxford OX1 4EW.

Shackleton, R., MA, DLitt, LittD, DUniv, FBA, FSA, FRSL, All Souls College, Oxford OX1 4AL.

Shannon, Professor R. T., MA, PhD, Dept of History, University College of Swansea, Swansea SA2 8PP.

Sharp, Mrs M., MA, PhD, c/o 96 London Road, Guildford, Surrey GU1 1TH.

Sharpe, J. A., MA, DPhil, Dept of History, The University, York YO1 5DD.

Sharpe, K. M., MA, DPhil, Dept of History, University of Southampton, Southampton SO9 5NH.

Shaw, I. P., MA, 3 Oaks Lane, Shirley, Croydon, Surrey CR0 5HP.

Shead, N. F., MA, BLitt, 8 Whittliemuir Avenue, Muirend, Glasgow G44 3HU.

Sheils, W. J., PhD, Goodricke Lodge, Heslington Lane, York YO1 5DD.

Shennan, Professor J. H., PhD, Dept of History, University of Lancaster, Bailrigg, Lancaster LA1 4YG.

Sheppard, F. H. W., MA, PhD, FSA, 55 New Street, Henley-on-Thames, Oxon RG9 2BP.

Sherborne, J. W., MA, 26 Hanbury Road, Bristol BS8 2EP.

Sherwood, R. E., 22 Schole Road, Willingham, Cambridge CB4 5JD.

Simpson, D. H., MA, Royal Commonwealth Society, 18 Northumberland Avenue, London WC2.

Simpson, G. G., MA, PhD, FSA, Taylor Building, King's College, Old Aberdeen AB9 2UB.

Sinar, Miss J. C., MA, 60 Wellington Street, Matlock, Derbyshire DE4 3GS.

Siney, Professor Marion C., MA, PhD, 2676 Mayfield Road, Cleveland Heights, Ohio 44106, U.S.A.

Singhal, Professor D. P., MA, PhD, University of Queensland, St Lucia, Brisbane, Queensland 4067, Australia.

Skidelsky, Professor R. J. A., BA, PhD, 32 Gt Percy Street, London WC1.

Skinner, Professor Q. R. D., MA, FBA, Christ's College, Cambridge CB2 3BU.

Slack, P. A., MA, DPhil, Exeter College, Oxford OX1 3DP.

Slade, C. F., PhD, FSA, 28 Holmes Road, Reading, Berks.

Slater, A. W., MSc(Econ), 146 Castelnau, London SW13 9ET.

Slatter, Miss M. D., MA, 2 Tuscan Close, Tilehurst, Reading, Berks. RG3.

Slavin, Professor A. J., PhD, College of Arts & Letters, University of Louisville, Louisville, Kentucky 40268, U.S.A.

Smail, R. C., MBE, MA, PhD, FSA, Sidney Sussex College, Cambridge CB2 3HU.

Smith, A. G. R., MA, PhD, 5 Cargill Avenue, Kilmacolm, Renfrewshire.

Smith, A. Hassell, BA, PhD, School of English and American Studies, University of East Anglia, Norwich NR4 7TJ.

Smith, B. S., MA, FSA, Historical Manuscripts Commission, Quality Court, Chancery Lane, London WC2 1HP.

Smith, D. M., MA, PhD, FSA, Borthwick Institute of Historical Research, St Anthony's Hall, York YO1 2PW.

Smith, E. A., MA, Dept of History, Faculty of Letters, The University, Whiteknights, Reading RG6 2AH.

Smith, F. B., MA, PhD, Research School of Social Sciences, Institute of Advanced Studies, Australian National University, G.P.O. Box 4, Canberra, A.C.T. 2601, Australia.

Smith, Professor Goldwin A., MA, PhD, DLitt, Wayne State University, Detroit, Michigan 48292, U.S.A.

Smith, J. Beverley, MA, University College, Aberystwyth SY23 2AX.

Smith, Joseph, BA, PhD, Dept of History, The University, Exeter EX4 4QH.

Smith, Professor L. Baldwin, PhD, Northwestern University, Evanston, Ill. 60201, U.S.A.

Smith, Professor P., MA, DPhil, Dept of History, The University, Southampton SO9 5NH.

Smith, Professor R. E. F., MA, Dept of Russian, The University, P.O. Box 363, Birmingham B15 2TT.

Smith, R. S., MA, BA, 7 Capel Lodge, 244 Kew Road, Kew, Surrey TW9 3JU.

Smith, S., BA, PhD, Les Haies, 40 Oatlands Road, Shinfield, Reading, Berks.

Smith, W. H. C., BA, PhD, Flat A, 110 Blackheath Hill, London SE10 8AG.

Smith, W. J., MA, 5 Gravel Hill, Emmer Green, Reading, Berks. RG4 8QN.

Smyth, A. P., MA, DPhil, FSA, Keynes College, The University, Canterbury CT2 7NP.

*Smyth, Rev. Canon C. H. E., MA, 12 Manor Court, Pinehurst, Cambridge.

Snell, L. S., MA, FSA, FRSA, 27 Weoley Hill, Selly Oak, Birmingham B29 4AA.

Snow, Professor V. F., MA, PhD, Dept of History, Syracuse University, 311 Maxwell Hall, Syracuse, New York 13210, U.S.A.

Snyder, Professor H. L., MA, PhD, 4646 Woodside Drive, Baton Rouge, La. 70808, U.S.A.

Soden, G. I., MA, DD, Buck Brigg, Hanworth, Norwich, Norfolk.

Somers, Rev. H. J., JCB, MA, PhD, St Francis Xavier University, Antigonish, Nova Scotia, Canada.

Somerville, Sir Robert, KCVO, MA, FSA, 3 Hunt's close, Morden Road, London SE3 0AH.

SOUTHERN, Sir Richard (W.), MA, DLitt, LittD, DLitt, FBA, The President's Lodgings, St John's College, Oxford OX1 3JP.

Southgate, D. G., BA, DPhil, The Old Harriers, Bridford, nr Exeter, Devon EX6 7HS.

Spalding, Miss R., MA, 34 Reynards Road, Welwyn, Herts.

Speck, Professor W. A., MA, DPhil, The University, Cottingham Road, Hull HU6 7RX.

Spencer, B. W., BA, FSA, 6 Carpenters Wood Drive, Chorleywood, Herts.

Spiers, E. D., MA, PhD, 487 Street Lane, Leeds, West Yorkshire LS17 6LA.

Spinks, Revd B. D., BA, MTh, BD, Churchill College, Cambridge CB3 0DS.

Spooner, Professor F. C., MA, PhD, The University, 23 Old Elvet, Durham DH1 3HY.

Spring, Professor D., PhD, Dept of History, Johns Hopkins University, Baltimore, Md. 21218, U.S.A.

Spufford, Mrs H. M., MA, PhD, Newnham College, Cambridge CB3 9DF.

Spufford, P., MA, PhD, Queens' College, Cambridge CB3 9ET.

Squibb, G. D., QC, FSA, The Old House, Cerne Abbas, Dorset DT27 7JQ.

Stachura, P. D., MA, PhD, Dept of History, The University, Stirling FK9 4LA.

Stacpoole, Dom Alberic J., OSB, MA, Saint Benet's Hall, Oxford OX1 3LN.

Stafford, Pauline A., BA, DPhil, Athill Lodge, St Helen's Lane, Adel, Leeds LS16 8BS.

Stanley, The Hon. G. F. G., MA, BLitt, DPhil, The Office of Lieutenant-Governor, Fredericton, New Brunswick, Canada.

Stansky, Professor Peter, PhD, Dept of History, Stanford University, Stanford, Calif. 94305, U.S.A.

Starkey, D. R., MA, PhD, 49 Hamilton Park West, London N5 1AE.

Steele, E. D., MA PhD, School of History, The University, Leeds LS2 9JT.

Steinberg, J., MA, PhD, Trinity Hall, Cambridge CB2 1TJ.

Steiner, Mrs Zara S., MA, PhD, New Hall, Cambridge CB3 0DF.

Stephens, J. N., MA, DPhil, Dept of History, University of Edinburgh, George Square, Edinburgh EH8 9JY.

Stephens, W. B., MA, PhD, FSA, 37 Batcliffe Drive, Leeds 6.

Steven, Miss M. J. E., PhD, 3 Bonwick Place, Garran, A.C.T. 2605, Australia.

Stevenson, David, MA, PhD, Dept of International History, London School of Economics, Houghton Street, London WC2A 2AE.

Stevenson, D., BA, PhD, Dept of History, Taylor Buildings, King's College, Old Aberdeen AB1 0EE.

Stevenson, Miss J. H., BA, c/o Institute of Historical Research, Senate House, Malet Street, London, WC1E 7HU.

Stevenson, J., MA, DPhil, Dept of History, The University, Sheffield S10 2TN.

Stewart, A. T. Q., MA PhD, Dept of Modern History, The Queen's University, Belfast BT7 1NN.

Stitt, F. B., BA, BLitt, William Salt Library, Stafford.

Stockwell, A. J., MA, PhD, Dept of History, Royal Holloway College, Englefield Green, Surrey TW20 0EX.

Stone, E., MA, DPhil, FSA, Keble College, Oxford OX1 3PG.

Stone, Professor L., MA, Princeton University, Princeton, N.J. 08540, U.S.A.

*Stones, Professor E. L. G., PhD, FBA, FSA, 34 Alexandra Road, Parkstone, Poole, Dorset BH14 9EN.

Storey, Professor R. L., MA, PhD, 19 Elm Avenue, Beeston, Nottingham NG9 1BU.

Storry, J. G., Woodland View, Huntercombe End, Nettlebed, nr Henley-on-Thames, Oxon. RG9 5RR.

Story, Professor G. M., BA, DPhil, 335 Southside Road, St John's Newfoundland, Canada.

*Stoye, J. W., MA, DPhil, Magdalen College, Oxford OX1 4AU.

Street, J., MA, PhD, Badgers' Wood, Cleveley, Forton, Garstang, Preston PR3 1BY.

Strong, Mrs F., MA, South Cloister, Eton College, Windsor SL4 6DB.

Strong, Sir Roy, BA, PhD, FSA, Victoria & Albert Museum, London SW7.

Stuart, C. H., MA, Christ Church, Oxford OX1 1DP.

Studd, J. R., PhD, Dept of History, The University, Keele, Staffs, ST5 5BG.

Sturdy, D. J., BA, PhD, Dept of History, New University of Ulster, Coleraine, N. Ireland BT52 1SA.

Supple, Professor B. E., BSc (Econ), PhD, MA, St Catharines College, Cambridge CB2 1RL.

Surman, Rev. C. E., MA, 352 Myton Road, Leamington Spa CV31 3NY.

Sutcliffe, Professor A. R., MA, DU, Dept of Economic and Social History, The University, 21 Slayleigh Avenue, Sheffield S10 3RA.

Sutherland, Professor D. W., DPhil, State University of Iowa, Iowa City, Iowa 52240, U.S.A.

Sutherland, Gillian, MA, DPhil, MA, PhD, Newnham College, Cambridge CB3 9DF.

Sutherland, N. M., MA, PhD, 15 Milton Manor Drive, Little Milton, Oxon. OX9 7PT.

Swanson, R. N., MA, PhD, School of History, The University, P.O. Box 363, Birmingham B15 2TT.

Swanton, Professor M. J., BA, PhD, FSA, Queen's Building, The University, Exeter EX4 4QH.

Swart, Professor K. W., PhD, LittD, University College London, Gower Street, London WC1 6BT.

Sweet, D. W., MA, PhD, Dept of History, The University, 43 North Bailey, Durham.

Swinfen, D. B., MA, DPhil, 14 Cedar Road, Broughty Ferry, Dundee.

Sydenham, M. J., PhD, Carleton University, Ottawa 1, Canada K1S 5B6.

Syrett, Professor D., PhD, 46 Hawthorne Terrace, Leonia, N.J., 07605, U.S.A.

Szechi, D., BA, DPhil, 19 Henry Road, Oxford OX2 0DG.

Taft, Barbara, PhD, 3101 35th Street, Washington, D.C. 20016, U.S.A.

Talbot, C. H., PhD, BD, FSA, 47 Hazlewood Road, London SW15.

Tamse, Coenraad Arnold, DLitt, De Krom, 12 Potgieterlaan, 9752 Ex Haren (Groningen), The Netherlands.

Tanner, J. I., CBE, MA, PhD, DLitt, Flat One, 57 Drayton Gardens, London SW10 9RU.

Tarling, Professor P. N., MA, PhD, LittD, University of Auckland, Private Bag, Auckland, New Zealand.

Tarn, Professor J. N., B.Arch, PhD, FRIBA, Dept of Architecture, The University, P.O. Box 147, Liverpool L69 3BX.

Taylor, Arnold J., CBE, MA, DLitt, FBA, FSA, Rose Cottage, Lincoln's Hill, Chiddingfold, Surrey GU8 4UN.

Taylor, Professor Arthur J., MA, The University, Leeds LS2 9JT.

Taylor, Rev. Brian, MA, FSA, The Rectory, The Flower Walk, Guildford GU2 5EP.

Taylor, J., MA, School of History, The University, Leeds LS2 9JT.

Taylor, J. W. R., 36 Alexandra Drive, Surbiton, Surrey KT5 9AF.

Taylor, P. M., BA, PhD, School of History, The University, Leeds LS2 9JT.

Taylor, R. T., MA, PhD, Dept of Political Theory and Government, University College of Swansea, Swansea SA2 8PP.

Taylor, W., MA, PhD, FSAScot, 25 Bingham Terrace, Dundee.

Teichova, Professor Alice, BA, PhD, University of East Anglia, University Plain, Norwich NR4 7TJ.

Temperley, H., BA, MA, PhD, School of English and American Studies, University of East Anglia, Norwich NR4 7TJ.

Temple, Nora C., BA, PhD, University College, P.O. Box 78, Cardiff CF1 1XL.

Templeman, G., CBE, MA, DCL, DL, FSA, Barton Corner, 2a St Augustine's Road, Canterbury, Kent.

Thackray, Professor Arnold W., PhD, E. F. Smith Hall D-6, University of Pennsylvania, Philadelphia 19104, U.S.A.

Thirsk, Mrs I. Joan, PhD, FBA, 1 Hadlow Castle, Hadlow, Tonbridge, Kent TN11 0EG.

Thistlethwaite, Professor F., CBE, DCL, LHD, 15 Park Parade, Cambridge CB5 8AL.

Thomas, Professor A. C., MA, DipArch, FSA, MRIA, Lambessow, St Clement, Truro, Cornwall.

Thomas, D. O., MA, PhD, Orlandon, 31 North Parade, Aberystwyth, Dyfed SY23 2JN.

Thomas of Swynnerton, Lord, MA, 29 Ladbroke Grove, London W11 3BB.

Thomas, J. H., BA, PhD, School of Social and Historical Studies, Portsmouth Polytechnic, Southsea, Portsmouth PO5 3AT.

Thomas, K. V., MA, DLitt, FBA, St John's College, Oxford OX1 3JP.

Thomas, Professor P. D. G., MA, PhD, Dept of History, University College, Aberystwyth SY23 2AU.

Thomas, W. E. S., MA, Christ Church, Oxford OX1 1DP.

Thomis, Professor M. I., MA, PhD, University of Queensland, St Lucia, Brisbane 4067, Australia.

Thompson, A. F., MA, Wadham College, Oxford OX1 3PN.

Thompson, C. L. F., BA, Colne View, 69 Chaney Road, Wivenhoe, Essex.

Thompson, Mrs D. K. G., MA, School of History, The University, P.O. Box 363, Birmingham B15 2TT.

Thompson, D. M., MA, PhD, Fitzwilliam College, Cambridge CB3 oDG.

Thompson, E. P., MA, Wick Episcopi, Upper Wick, Worcester.

Thompson, Professor F. M. L., MA, DPhil, FBA, Institute of Historical Research, Senate House, London WC1E 7HU.

Thompson, R. F., MA, School of English and American Studies, University of East Anglia, Norwich NR4 7TJ.

Thomson, J. A. F., MA, DPhil, The University, Glasgow G12 8QQ.

Thomson, R. M., MA, PhD, Dept of History, University of Tasmania, Box 252C, GPO, Hobart, Tasmania 7001, Australia.

Thorne, C., BA, School of European Studies, University of Sussex, Brighton BN1 9QX.

Thornton, Professor A. P., MA, DPhil, University College, University of Toronto, Toronto M5S 1A1, Canada.

*Thrupp, Professor S. L., MA, PhD, University of Michigan, Ann Arbor, Mich. 48104, U.S.A.

Thurlow, The Very Rev. A. G. G., MA, FSA, 2 East Pallant, Chichester, West Sussex PO19 1TR.

Tomkeieff, Mrs O. G., MA, LLB, 88 Moorside North, Newcastle upon Tyne NE4 9DU.

Tomlinson, H. C., BA, 'Upcott', Wellington College, Crowthorne, Berkshire RG11 7PU.

Tonkin, J. M., BA, BD, PhD, Dept of History, University of Western Australia, Nedlands, Western Australia 6009.

Townshend, D. J. N., MA, DPhil, The Hawthorns, Keele, Staffordshire.

Toynbee, Miss M. R., MA, PhD, FSA, 22 Park Town, Oxford OX2 6SH.

Trebilcock, R. C., MA, Pembroke College, Cambridge CB2 1RF.

Tsitsonis, S. E., PhD, 6 Foskolou Street, Halandri, Athens, Greece.

Turner, Mrs Barbara D. M., BA, 27 St Swithuns Street, Winchester, Hampshire.

Turner, J. A., MA, DPhil, 31 Devereux Road, London SW11 6JR.

Tyacke, N. R. N., MA, DPhil, 1a Spencer Rise, London NW5.

Tyerman, C. J., MA, DPhil, Exeter College, Oxford OX1 3DP.

Tyler, P., BLitt, MA, DPhil, University of Western Australia, Nedlands, Western Australia 6009.

Ugawa, Professor K., BA, MA, PhD, 1008 Ikebukuro, 2 Chome, Toshi-maku, Tokyo 171, Japan.
Underdown, Professor David, MA, BLitt, DLitt, DHL, Dept of History, Brown University, Providence, Rhode Island 02912, U.S.A.
Upton, A. F., MA, 5 West Acres, St Andrews, Fife.

Vaisey, D. G., MA, FSA, 12 Hernes Road, Oxford.
Vale, M. G. A., MA, DPhil, St John's College, Oxford OX1 3JP.
Van Caenegem, Professor R. C., LLD, PhD, Veurestraat 18, 9821 Afsnee, Belgium.
Van Houts, Elisabeth, DLitt, Girton College, Cambridge CB3 0JG.
Van Roon, Professor Ger, Dept of Contemporary History, Vrije Universi-teit, Amsterdeam, Koningslaan 31–33, The Netherlands.
Vann, Professor Richard T., PhD, Dept of History, Wesleyan University, Middletown, Conn. 06457, U.S.A.
*Varley, Mrs J., MA, FSA, 164 Nettleham Road, Lincoln.
Vaughan, Sir (G) Edgar, KBE, MA, 27 Birch Grove, West Acton, London W3 9SP.
Veale, Elspeth M., BA, PhD, 31 St Mary's Road, Wimbledon, London SW19 7BP.
Véliz, Professor C., BSc, PhD, Dept. of Sociology, La Trobe University, Melbourne, Victoria 3083, Australia.
Vessey, D. W. T. C., MA, PhD, Dept of Classics, King's College, Strand, London WC2R 2LS.
Virgoe, R., BA, PhD, University of East Anglia, School of English and American Studies, Norwich NR4 7TJ.

Waddell, Professor D. A. G., MA, DPhil, University of Stirling, Stirling FK9 4LA.
*Wagner, Sir Anthony (R.), KCVO, MA, DLitt, FSA, College of Arms, Queen Victoria Street, London EC4.
Waites, B. F., MA, FRGS, 6 Chater Road, Oakham, Leics. LE15 6RY.
Walcott, R., MA, PhD, 14 Whig Street, Dennis, Mass. 02638, U.S.A.
Walford, A. J., MA, PhD, FLA, 45 Parkside Drive, Watford, Herts.
Walker, Rev. Canon D. G., DPhil, FSA, University College of Swansea, Swansea SA2 8PP.
Wallace, Professor W. V., MA, Institute of Soviet and East European Studies, University of Glasgow, Glasgow G12 8LQ.
Wallace-Hadrill, Professor J. M., CBE, MA, DLitt, FBA, All Souls College, Oxford OX1 4AL.
Wallis, Miss H. M., MA, DPhil, FSA, 96 Lord's View, St John's Wood Road, London NW8 7HG.
Wallis, P. J., MA, 27 Westfield Drive, Newcastle upon Tyne NE3 3XY.
Walne, P., MA, FSA, County Record Office, County Hall, Hertford.
Walsh, T. J., MA, PhD, MB, BCh, LittD(Hon.), FFA, RCSI, 5 Lower George Street, Wexford, Ireland.
Walvin, J., BA, MA, DPhil, Dept of History, The University, York YO1 5DD.
Wangermann, E., MA, DPhil, School of History, The University, Leeds LS2 9JT.
Wanklyn, M. D., BA, MA, PhD, Dept of Arts, The Polytechnic, Wulfruna Street, Wolverhampton, West Midlands.
*Ward, Mrs G. A., PhD, FSA, Unsted, 51 Hartswood Road, Brentwood, Essex.

Ward, Jennifer, C., MA, PhD, 22 The Priory Park, London SE3 9XA.

Ward, Professor J. T., MA, PhD, Dept of History, McCance Bldg., University of Strathclyde, 16 Richmond Street, Glasgow G1 1XQ.

Ward, Professor W. R., DPhil, University of Durham, 43 North Bailey, Durham DH1 3HP.

*Warmington, Professor E. H., MA 48 Flower Lane, London NW7.

Warner, Professor G., MA Dept of History, The University, Leicester LE1 7RH.

Warren, Professor W. L., MA, DPhil, FRSL, Dept of Modern History, The Queen's University, Belfast, N. Ireland BT7 1NN.

Wasserstein, Professor B. M. J., MA, DPhil, The Tauber Institute, Brandeis University, Waltham, Mass. 02254, U.S.A.

*Waterhouse, Professor E. K., CBE, MA, AM, FBA, Overshot, Badger Lane, Hinksey Hill, Oxford.

*Waters, Lt-Commander D. W., RN, FSA, Jolyons, Bury, nr Pulborough, W. Sussex.

Watkin, The Rt. Rev. Abbot Aelred, OSB, MA, FSA, St Benet's, Beccles, Suffolk NR34 9NR.

WATSON, Professor A. G., MA, DLit, BLitt, FSA (*Hon Librarian*), University College London, Gower Street, London WC1 6BT.

Watson, D. R., MA, BPhil, Dept of Modern History, The University, Dundee DD1 4HN.

Watson, J. S., MA, DLitt, DHL, DH, The University College Gate, North Street, St Andrews, Fife KY16 9AJ.

Watt, Professor D. C., MA, London School of Economic, Houghton Street, London WC2A 2AE.

Watt, Professor D. E. R., MA, DPhil, Dept of Mediaeval History, St Salvator's College, St Andrews, Fife KY16 9AJ.

Watt, Professor J. A., BA, PhD, Dept of History, The University, Newcastle upon Tyne NE1 7RU.

Watts, M. R., BA, DPhil, Dept of History, The University, Nottingham NG7 2RD.

Webb, Professor Colin de B., BA, MA, University of Natal, King George V Avenue, Durban 4001, S Africa.

Webb, J. G., MA, 11 Blount Road, Pembroke Park, Old Portsmouth, Hampshire PO1 2TD.

Webb, Professor R. K., PhD, 3307 Highland Place NW., Washington, D.C. 20008, U.S.A.

Webster (A.) Bruce, MA, FSA, 5 The Terrace, St Stephens, Canterbury.

Webster, C., MA, DSc, Corpus Christi College, Oxford OX1 4JF.

Wedgwood, Dame (C.) Veronica, OM, DBE, MA, LittD, DLitt, LLD, Whitegate, Alciston, nr Polegate, Sussex.

Weinbaum, Professor M., PhD, 133-33 Sanford Avenue, Flushing, N.Y. 11355, U.S.A.

Weinstock, Miss M. B., MA, 26 Wey View Crescent, Broadway, Weymouth, Dorset.

Wells, R. A. E., BA, DPhil, Dept of Humanities, Brighton Polytechnic, Falmer, Brighton, Sussex.

Wendt, Professor Bernd-Jurgen, DrPhil, Beim Andreasbrunnen 8, 2 Hamburg 20, West Germany.

Wernham, Professor R. B., MA, Marine Cottage, 63 Hill Head Road, Hill Head, Fareham, Hants.

*Weske, Mrs Dorothy B., AM, PhD, Oakwood, Sandy Spring, Maryland 20860, U.S.A.

West, Professor F. J., PhD, School of Social Sciences, Deakin University, Victoria 3217, Australia.

Weston, Professor Corinne C., PhD, 200 Central Park South, New York, N.Y. 10019, U.S.A.

Whaley, Joachim, MA, PhD, Robinson College, Cambridge CB3 9AN.

Whelan, The Rt Rev. Abbot C. B., OSB, MA, Belmont Abbey, Hereford HR2 9RZ.

White, Professor B. M. I., MA, DLit, FSA, 3 Upper Duke's Drive, Eastbourne, Sussex BN20 7XT.

White, Rev. B. R., MA DPhil, 55 St Giles', Regent's Park College, Oxford.

Whiteman, Miss E. A. O., MA, DPhil, FSA, Lady Margaret Hall, Oxford OX2 6QA.

Whiting, J. R. S., MA, DLitt, 15 Lansdown Parade, Cheltenham, Glos.

Whiting, R. C., MA, DPhil, School of History, The University, Leeds LS2 9JT.

Whittam, J. R., MA, BPhil, PhD, Dept of History, University of Bristol, Senate House, Bristol BS8 1TH.

Wiener, Professor J. H., BA, PhD, City College of New York, Convent Avenue at 138th Street, N.Y. 10031, U.S.A.

Wilkie, Rev. W., MA, PhD, Dept of History, Loras College, Dubuque, Iowa 52001, U.S.A.

Wilks, Professor M. J., MA, PhD, Dept of History, Birkbeck College, Malet Street, London WC1 7HX.

*Willan, Professor T. S., MA, DPhil, 3 Raynham Avenue, Didsbury, Manchester M20 0BW.

Williams, D., MA, PhD, DPhil, University of Calgary, Calgary, Alberta T2N 1N4, Canada.

Williams, Sir Edgar (T.), CB, CBE, DSO, MA, 94 Lonsdale Road, Oxford OX2 7ER.

Williams, Professor Glanmor, MA, DLitt, University College of Swansea, Swansea SA2 8PP.

Williams, Professor Glyndwr, BA, PhD, Queen Mary College, Mile End Road, London E1 4NS.

Williams, Professor G. A., MA, PhD, 66 De Burgh Street, Cardiff CF1 8LD.

Williams, J. A., MA, BSc(Econ), 44 Pearson Park, Hull, HU5 2TG.

Williams, J. D., BA, MA, PhD, 56 Spurgate, Hutton Mount, Brentwood, Essex CM13 2JT.

Williams, P. H., MA, DPhil, New College, Oxford OX1 3BN.

Williams, T. I., MA, DPhil, 20 Blenheim Drive, Oxford OX2 8DG.

WILSON, Professor C. H., CBE, LittD, DLitt, DLitt, DLitt, FBA, Jesus College, Cambridge CB5 8BL.

Wilson, Sir David., MA, LittD, FilDr, DrPhil, FBA, FSA, The Director's Residence, The British Museum, London WC1B 3DG.

Wilson, H. S., BA, BLitt, Dept of History, The University, York YO1 5DD.

Wilson, K. M., MA, DPhil, 8 Woodland Park Road, Headingley, Leeds 6.

Wilson, R. G., BA, PhD, University of East Anglia, School of Social Studies, University Plain, Norwich NR4 7TJ.

Wilson, Professor T., MA, DPhil, Dept of History, University of Adelaide, Adelaide, South Australia.

Winks, Professor R. W. E., MA, PhD, 648 Berkeley College, Yale University, New Haven, Conn. 06520, U.S.A.

Winstanley, M. J., BA, MA, Dept of History, Furness College, The University, Lancaster LA1 4YG.

Winter, J. M., BA, PhD, Pembroke College, Cambridge CB2 1RF.
Wiswall, Frank L., Jr., BA, JuD, PhD, Meadow Farm, Castine, Maine 04421 U.S.A.
Withrington, D. J., MA, MEd, Centre for Scottish Studies, University of Aberdeen, King's College, Old Aberdeen AB9 2UB.
Wolffe, B. P., MA, DPhil, DLitt, Highview, 19 Rosebarn Avenue, Exeter EX4 6DY.
Wong, John Yue-Wo, BA, DPhil, Dept of History, University of Sydney, N.S.W., Australia 20006.
*Wood Rev. A. Skevington, PhD, 17 Dalewood Road Sheffield S8 0EB.
Wood, Diana, BA, PhD, 8 Bartlemas Close, Oxford OX4 2AE.
Wood, I. N., MA, DPhil, School of History, The University, Leeds LS2 9JT.
Wood, Mrs S. M., MA, BLitt, St Hugh's College, Oxford OX2 6LE.
Woodfill, Professor W. L., PhD, 762 Creston Road, Berkeley, Calif. 94708, U.S.A.
Woolf, Professor, S. J., MA, DPhil, University of Essex, Wivenhoe Park, Colchester CO4 3SQ.
Woolrych, Professor A. H., BLitt, MA, Patchetts, Caton, nr Lancaster.
Worden, A. B., MA, DPhil, St Edmund Hall, Oxford OX1 4AR.
Wordie, James R., MA, PhD, 6 The Knapp, Earley, Reading, Berks, RG6 2DD.
Wormald, B. H. G., MA, Peterhouse, Cambridge CB2 1RD.
Wormald, Jennifer M., MA, PhD, Dept of Scottish History, The University, Glasgow G12 8QQ.
Wortley, The Rev. J. T., MA, PhD, History Dept, University of Manitoba, Winnipeg, Manitoba R3T 2N2, Canada.
Wright, A. D., MA, DPhil, School of History, The University, Leeds LS2 9JT.
Wright, C. J., MA, PhD, 8 Grove Road, East Molesey, Surrey KT8 9JS.
Wright, Professor E., MA, Institute of United States Studies, 31 Tavistock Square, London WC1 9EZ.
Wright, Rev. Professor J. Robert, DPhil, General Theological Seminary, 175 Ninth Avenue, New York, N.Y. 10011, U.S.A.
Wright, Professor Maurice, BA, DPhil, Dept of Government, Dover Street, Manchester M13 9PL.
Wroughton, J. P., MA, 6 Ormonde House, Sion Hill, Bath BA1 2UN.

Yates, W. N., MA, Kent Archives Office, County Hall, Maidstone, Kent ME14 1XH.
Youings, Professor Joyce A., BA, PhD, Dept of History, The University, Exeter EX4 4QH.
Young, J. W., BA, PhD, 11 Gordon Avenue, Leicester LE2 1AA.
Young, K. G., BSc(Econ), MSc, PhD, 11 Fawley Road, London NW6.
Young, Mrs Susan H. H., BA, 78 Holland Road, Ampthill, Beds. MK45 2RS.
Youngs, Professor F. A., Jr., Dept of History, Louisiana State University, Baton Rouge, Louisiana 70803, U.S.A.

Zagorin, Professor P., PhD, Dept of History, College of Arts and Sciences, University of Rochester, River Campus Station, Rochester, N.Y. 14627, U.S.A.
Zeldin, T., MA, DPhil, St Antony's College, Oxford OX2 6JF.
Ziegler, P. S., FRSL, 22 Cottesmore Gardens, London W8.

ASSOCIATES OF THE
ROYAL HISTORICAL SOCIETY

Addy, J., MA, PhD, 66 Long Lane, Clayton West, Huddersfield, HD8 9PR.
Aitken, Rev. Leslie R., MBE, 36 Ethelbert Road, Birchington, Kent CT7 9PY.
Ashton, Ellis, MBE, FRSA, 1 King Henry Street, London N16.
Ayrton, Lt-Col. M. McI., HQ Mess, The School of Signals, Blandford Camp, Dorset DT11 8RH.

Baird, Rev. E. S., BD (address unknown).
Begley, M. R., 119 Tennyson Avenue, King's Lynn, Norfolk.
Birchenough, Mrs F. J., 116 Manor Lane, London SE12 8LR.
Bird, E. A., 29 King Edward Avenue, Rainham, Essex RN13 9RH.
Blackwood, B., FRIBA, FRTPI, FSAScot, Ebony House, Whitney Drive, Stevenage SG1 4BL.
Boyes, J. H., 129 Endlebury Road, Chingford, London E4 6PX.
Bratt, C., 65 Moreton Road, Upton, Merseyside L49 4NR.
Bridge, A. E. (address unknown).
Bryant, W. N., MA, PhD, College of S. Mark and S. John, Derriford Road, Plymouth, Devon.
Burton, Commander R. C., RN (ret.), Great Streele Oasthouse, Framfield, Sussex.
Butler, Mrs M. C., MA, 4 Castle Street, Warksworth, Morpeth, Northumberland NE65 0UW.

Cable, J. A., MA, MEd, ALCM, 21 Malvern Avenue, York YO2 5SF.
Cairns, Mrs W. N., MA, Alderton House, New Ross, Co. Wexford, Ireland.
Carter, F. E. L., CBE, MA, FSA, 8 The Leys, London N2 0HE.
Cary, Sir Roger, Bt, BA, 23 Bath Road, London W4.
Chandra, Shri Suresh, MA, MPhil, B½ Havelock Road Colony, Lucknow 226001, India.
Chappell, Rev. M. P., MA, Greymouth Close, Hartburn, Stockton-on-Tees, Cleveland TS18 5LF.
Clifton, Mrs Gloria C., BA, 13 Fontaine Road, London SW16 3PB.
Cobban, A. D., 11 Pennyfields, Warley, Brentwood, Essex CM14 5JP.
Coleby, A. M., BA, Dept of History, The University, Sheffield S10 2TN.
Condon, Miss M. M., BA, 56 Bernard Shaw House, Knatchbull Road, London NW10.
Cooksley, P. G., 14 Wallington Court, Wallington, Surrey SM6 0HG.
Cooper, Miss J. M., MA, PhD, 1 William Street, New Marston, Oxford OX3 0ES.
Cox, A. H., Winsley, 11a Bagley Close, West Drayton, Middlesex.
Cox, Benjamin G., Fairways, 3 St Leonards Avenue, Blandford Forum, Dorset DT11 7NZ.
Creighton-Williamson, Lt-Col. D., 1 Anderson Court, Shepherd's Hill, Haslemere GU27 2NE.

d'Alton, Ian, MA, PhD, 30 Kew Park Avenue, Lucan, Co Dublin, Ireland.

Daniels, C. W., MEd, FRSA, 'Brookfield', St John's Royal Latin School, Buckingham MK18 1AX.

Davies, G. J., BA, PhD, FSA, 16 Melcombe Avenue, Weymouth, Dorset DT4 7TH.

Davies, P. H., BA, 64 Hill Top, Hampstead Garden Suburb, London NW11.

Davis, J. M., BA, 1 Hamilton Road, Harrow, Middlesex.

Downie, W. F., BSC, CEng, FICE, FINucE, MIES, 10 Ryeland Street, Strathaven, Lanarkshire ML10 6DL.

Dowse, Rev. I. R., St Paul's Rectory, 8 Auchnacloich Road, Rothesay, Isle of Bute, Scotland.

Draffen of Newington, George, MBE, KLJ, MA, Meadowside, Balmullo, Leuchars, Fife KY16 0AW.

Dunster, E. R., BA, LCP, 5 Brittania Road, Southsea, Hampshire.

Edgell, The Revd. H. A. R., SB, StJ, The Rectory, Hingham, Norwich NR9 4HP.

Elliott, Rev. W., BA, The Vicarage, Far Forest, nr Kidderminster, Worcs. DY14 9TT.

Enoch, D. G., BEd, MEd, Treetops, 14 St David's Road, Miskin, Pontyclun CF7 8PW.

Firth, P. J. C., 59 Springfield Road, London NW8 0QJ.

Foster, J. M., MA, 3 Marchmont Gardens, Richmond, Surrey TW10 6ET.

Franco de Baux, Don Victor, KCHS, KCN, 10b Rumsey Road, London SW9 0TR.

Frazier, R. Ll., BA, Dept of History, The University, Nottingham NG7 2RD.

Freeman, Miss J., 5 Spencer Close, Stansted, Mountfitchet, Essex.

Granger, E. R., Bluefield, Blofield, Norfolk.

Greatrex, Professor Joan G., MA, The Highlands, Great Donard, Symonds Yat, Herefordshire HR9 6DY.

Green, P. L., MA, 9 Faulkner Street, Gate Pa, Tauranga, New Zealand.

Grosvenor, Ian D., BA, 40 Waterloo Road, Kingsheath, Birmingham.

Gurney, Mrs S. J., 'Albemarle', 13 Osborne Street, Wolverton, Milton Keynes MK12 5HH.

Guy, Rev. J. R., BA, Selden End, Ash, nr Martock, Somerset TA12 6NS.

Hall, P. T., Accrington and Rosendale College, Sandy Lane, Accrington, Lancs. BB25 2AW.

Hanawalt, Mrs B. A., MA, PhD, Indiana University, Ballantine Hall, Bloomington, Indiana 47401, U.S.A.

Hawkes, G. I., BA, MA, PhD, Linden House, St Helens Road, Ormskirk, Lancs.

Hawtin, Miss G., BA, PhD, FSAScot, FRSAI, Honey Cottage, 5 Clifton Road, London SW19 4QX.

Heal, Mrs F., PhD, Jesus College, Oxford OX1 3DW.

Henderson-Howat, Mrs A. M. D., 8 Dove House Close, Wolvercote, Oxford OX2 8BG.

Hillman, L. B., BA, 18 Creswick Walk, Hampstead Garden Suburb, London NW11.

Hoare, E. T., 70 Addison Road, Enfield, Middx.

Hodge, Mrs G., 85 Hadlow Road, Tonbridge, Kent.

Hope, R. B., MA, MEd, PhD, 5 Partis Way, Newbridge Hill, Bath, Avon BA1 3QG.
Hugill, J. A. C., BA, BSc, The River House, Ashton Keynes, nr Swindon, Wilts.

Jackson, A., BA, 14 Latimer Lane, Guisborough, Cleveland.
James, T. M., BA, MA, PhD, 26 St Michael's Close, Crich, Matlock, Derbyshire DE4 5DN.
Jarvis, L. D., Middlesex Cottage, 86 Mill Road, Stock, Ingatestone, Essex.
Jennings, T. S., GTCL, The Willows, 54 Bramcote Road, Loughborough LE11 2AS.
Jermy, K. E., MA, Cert. Archaeol, FRSA, MIM, FISTC, 5 Far Sandfield, Churchdown, Gloucester GL3 3JS.
Jerram-Burrows, Mrs L. E., Parkanaur House, 88 Sutton Road, Rochford, Essex.
Johnston, F. R., MA, 20 Russell Street, Eccles, Manchester.
Johnstone, H. F. V., 32 Jolliffe Road, Poole, Dorset BH15 2HD.
Jones, Rev. D. R., MA, HQ4 Armoured Brigade, British Forces Post Office 17.
Jones, Dr N. L., Dept of History & Geography, Utah State University, UMC 07, Logan, Utah 84322, U.S.A.

Keefe, T. K., BA, PhD, Dept of History, Appalachian State University, Boone, North Caroline 28608, U.S.A.
Keir, Mrs G. I., BA, BLitt, 17 Battlefield Road, St Albans AL1 4DA.
Kennedy, M. J., BA, Dept of Medieval History, The University, Glasgow G12 8QQ.
Knight, G. A., BA, PhD, DAA, MIInfSc, 17 Lady Frances Drive, Market Rasen, Lincs. LN8 3JJ.
Knowlson, Rev. G. C. V., 21 Wilton Crescent, Alderley Edge, Cheshire SK9 7RE.

Lazarus, D., P.O. Box 449, East London 5200, S. Africa.
Leckey, J. J., MSc(Econ), LCP, FRSAI, Vestry Hall, Ballygowan, Co Down, N. Ireland BT23 6HQ.
Lee, Professor M. du P., PhD, Douglass College, Rutgers University, NB, NJ 08903, U.S.A.
Lewin, Mrs J., MA, 3 Sunnydale Gardens, Mill Hill, London NW7.
Lewis, J. B., MA, CertEd, FRSA, 16 Rushfield Road, Westminster Park, Chester CH4 7RE.
Lewis, Professor N. B., MA, PhD, 79 Old Dover Road, Canterbury, Kent CT1 3DB.

McIntyre, Miss S. C., BA, DPhil, West Midlands College of Higher Education, Walsall, West Midlands.
McKenna, Rev. T. J., P.O. Box 509, Quean Beyaw, Australia 2620.
McLeod, D. H., BA, PhD, Dept of Theology, The University, P.O. Box 363, Birmingham B15 2TT.
Meatyard, E., BA, DipEd, Guston, Burial Lane, Church Lane, Llantwit Major, S. Glam.
Metcalf, D. M., MA, DPhil, 40 St Margaret's Road, Oxford OX2 6LD.
Mills, H. J., BSc, MA, Headington, Brockenhurst, Hampshire.
Morgan, D. A. L., MA, Dept of History, University College London, Gower Street, London WC1E 6BT.

Morris, A. R., BSc(Econ), MA, Woolpit End, Duke of Kent School, Ewhurst, Surrey GU6 7NS.
Munson, K. G., 'Briar Wood', 4 Kings Ride, Seaford, Sussex BN25 2LN.

Nagel, L. C. J., BA, 61 West Kensington Court, London W14.
Newman, L. T., LRIC, CEng, MIGasE, AMInst F, 27 Mallow Park, Pinkneys Green, Maidenhead, Berks.
Noonan, J. A., BA, MEd, HDE, St Patrick's Comprehensive School, Shannon, Co Clare, Ireland.

Oggins, R. S., PhD, Dept of History, State University of New York, Binghamton 13901, U.S.A.
Osborne, Irving, M., BEd, Adv.DipEd, FRSA, FCollP, 169 Goodman Park, Slough SL2 5NR.

Pam, D. O., 44 Chase Green Avenue, Enfield, Middlesex EN2 8EB.
Paton, L. R., 49 Lillian Road, Barnes, London SW13.
Paulson, E., BSc(Econ), 11 Darley Avenue, Darley Dale, Matlock, Derbys. DE4 2GB.
Perry, E., FSAScot, 28 Forest Street, Hathershaw, Oldham OL8 3ER.
Perry, K., MA, 14 Highland View Close, Colehill, Wimborne, Dorset.
Pitt, B. W. E., Merryfield House, Ilton, Ilminster TA19 9EX.
Powell, Mrs A. M., 129 Blinco Grove, Cambridge CB1 4TX.
Priestley, E. J., MA, MPhil, 7 Inverleith Place, Edinburgh EH3 5QE.

Raspin, Miss A., London School of Economics, Houghton Street, London WC2A 2AE.
Rees, Rev. D. B., BA, BD, MSc(Econ), PhD, 32 Garth Drive, Liverpool L18 6HW.
Reid, N. H., MA, Wingate, Church Brae, Limekilns, Fife.
Rendall, Miss J., BA, PhD, Dept of History, University of York, York YO1 5DD.
Richards, N. F., PhD, 376 Maple Avenue, St Lambert, Prov. of Quebec, Canada J4P 2S2.
Roberts, S. G., MA, DPhil, 23 Beech Avenue, Radlett, Herts. WD7 7DD.
Rosenfield, M. C., AB, AM, PhD, Box 395, Mattapoisett, Mass. 02739, U.S.A.
Russell, Mrs E., BA, c/o Dept of History, University College London, Gower Street, London WC1E 6BT.

Sabben-Clare, E. E., MA, 4 Denham Close, Abbey Hill Road, Winchester SO23 7BL.
Sainsbury, F., 16 Crownfield Avenue, Newbury Park, Ilford, Essex.
Saksena, D. N., 46 Vigyan Vihar, I.P. Extension Pt II, New Delhi 110 092, India.
Scannura, C. G., 1/11 St Dominic Street, Valletta, Malta.
Scott, The Rev. A. R., MA, BD, PhD, Sunbeam Cottage, 110 Mullalalish Road, Richhill, Co Armagh, N. Ireland.
Sellers, J. M., MA, 9 Vere Road, Pietermaritzburgh 3201, Natal, S. Africa.
Shores, C. F., ARICS, 40 St Mary's Crescent, Hendon, London NW4 4LH.
Sibley, Major R. J., 8 Ways End, Beech Avenue, Camberley, Surrey.
Sorensen, Mrs M. O., MA, 8 Layer Gardens, London W3 9PR.
Sparkes, I. G., FLA, 124 Green Hill, High Wycombe, Bucks.
Stafford, D. S., BA, 10 Highfield Close, Wokingham, Berks. RG11 1DG.

Thewlis, J. C., BA, PhD, Dept of History, The University, Hull HU6 7RX.
Thomas, D. L., BA, Public Record Office, Chancery Lane, London WC2A 1LR.
Thomas, Miss E. J. M., BA, 8 Ravenscroft Road, Northfield End, Henley-on-Thames, Oxon.
Thompson, L. F., Colne View, 69 Chaney Road, Wivenhoe, Essex.
Tracy, J. N., BA, MPhil, PhD, Dept of History, National University of Singapore, Kent Ridge, Singapore 0511.
Tudor, Victoria M., BA, PhD, 33 Convent Close, Hitchin, Herts. SG5 1QN.

Waldman, T. G., MA, 620 Franklin Bldg./I6, University of Pennsylvania, Philadelphia, Pa. 19104, U.S.A.
Walker, J. A., 1 Sylvanus, Roan Wood, Bracknell, Berkshire RG12 4XX.
Wall, Rev. J., BD, MA, PhD, 10 Branksome Road, Norwich NR4 6SN.
Ward, R. C., BA, MPhil, 192 Stortford Hall Park, Bishop's Stortford, Herts. CM23 5AS.
Warrillow, E. J. D., MBE, FSA, Hill-Cote, Lancaster Road, Newcastle, Staffs.
Weise, Selene H. C., PhD, 22 Hurd Street, Mine Hill, New Jersey 07801, U.S.A.
Wickham, David E., MA, 116 Parsonage Manorway, Belvedere, Kent.
Wilkinson, F. J., 40 Great James Street, Holborn, London WC1N 3HB.
Williams, A. R., BA, MA, 5 Swanswell Drive, Granley Fields, Cheltenham, Glos.
Williams, C. L. Sinclair, ISO, The Old Vicarage, The Green, Puddletown, nr Dorchester, Dorset.
Williams, G., FLA, 32 St John's Road, Manselton, Swansea SA5 8PP.
Williams, P. T., FSAScot, FRSA, FFAS, Bryn Bueno, Whitford Street, Holywell, Clwyd.
Wilson, A. R., BA, MA, 12 Tilstone Close, Kidsgrove, Stoke-on-Trent ST7 4HU.
Windeatt, M. C. (address unknown).
Windrow, M. C., West House, Broyle Lane, Ringmer, nr Lewes, Sussex.
Wood, A. W., 11 Blessington Close, London SE13.
Wood, J. O., BA, MEd, 'Avalon', Les Croutes, St Peter Port, Guernsey, Channel Islands.
Woodall, R. D., BA, Bethel, 7 Wynthorpe Road, Horbury, nr Wakefield, Yorks. WF4 5BB.
Worsley, Miss A. V., BA, 3d St George's Cottages, Glasshill Street, London SE1.
Wright, J. B., BA, White Shutters, Braunston, Leicester LE15 8QT.

Young, Assoc. Professor B., MA, PhD, Dept of History, Illinois Wesleyan University, Bloomington, Illinois 71701, U.S.A.

Zerafa, Rev. M. J., St Dominic's Priory, Valletta, Malta.

CORRESPONDING FELLOWS

Ajayi, Professor J. F. Ade, University of Ibadan, Ibadan, Nigeria, West Africa.

Berend, Professor T. Ivan, Hungarian Academy of Sciences, 1361 Budapest V, Roosevelt-tèr 9, Hungary.

Bischoff, Professor B., DLitt, 8033 Planegg C. München, Ruffini-Alee 27, West Germany.

Boorstin, Daniel J., MA, LLD, 3541 Ordway Street, N.W., Washington, DC 20016, U.S.A.

Boyle, The Rev. Leonard E. Boyle, OP, Biblioteca Apostolica Vaticana, Vatican City, Rome, Italy.

Braudel, Professor F., Commission des Archives Diplomatiques, Ministère des Relations Extérieures, 37 Quai d'Orsay, 75007 Paris, France.

Cipolla, Professor Carlo M., University of California, Berkeley Campus, Berkeley, Calif. 94720, U.S.A.

Constable, Giles, PhD, Dumbarton Oaks, 1703 32nd Street, Washington, D.C. 20007, U.S.A.

Crouzet, Professor F. M. J., 6 rue Benjamin Godard, 75016 Paris, France.

Donoso, R., Presidente de la Sociedad Chilena de Historia y Georgrafia, Casilla 1386, Santiago, Chile.

Duby, Professor G., Collège de France, 11 Place Marcelin-Berthelot, 75005 Paris, France.

Garin, Professor Eugenio, via Giulio Cesare Vanini 28, 50129 Florence, Italy.

Gieysztor, Professor Aleksander, Polska Akademia Nauk, Wydzial I Nauk, Rynek Starego Miasta 29/31, 00–272 Warszawa, Poland.

Giusti, Rt Rev. Mgr M., JCD, Archivio Segreto Vaticano, Vatican City, Italy.

Glamann, Professor K., DPhil, DLitt, The Carlsberg Foundation, H.C. Andersens Boulevard 35, 1553 København, V, Denmark.

Gopal, Professor S., MA, DPhil, Centre for Historical Studies, Jawaharlal Nehru University, New Mehrauli Road, New Delhi-110067, India.

Hancock, Professor Sir Keith, KBE, MA, DLitt, FBA, Australian National University, Box 4, P.O., Canberra, ACT, Australia.

Hanke, Professor L. U., PhD, University of Massachusetts, Amherst, Mass. 01002, U.S.A.

Heimpel, Professor Dr H., DrJur, Dr Phil, former Direktor des Max Planck-Instituts für Geschichte, Gottingen, Dahlmannstr. 14, West Germany.

Inalcik, Professor Halil, PhD, The University of Ankara, Turkey.

Kossmann, Professor E. H., DLitt, Rijksuniversiteit te Groningen, Groningen, The Netherlands.

Kuttner, Professor S., MA, JUD, SJD, LLD, Institute of Medieval Canon Law, University of California, Berkeley, Calif. 94720, U.S.A.

Ladurie, Professor E. B. LeRoy, Collège de France, 11 Place Marcelin-Berthelot, 75005 Paris, France.
Leclercq, The Rev. Dom Jean, OSB, Abbaye St-Maurice, L-9737 Clervaux, Luxembourg.

McNeill, Professor William H., 1126 East 59th Street, Chicago, Illinois 60637, U.S.A.
Maruyama, Professor Masao, 2-44-5 Higashimachi, Kichijoji, Musashinoshi, Tokyo 180, Japan.
Michel, Henri, 12 Rue de Moscou, 75008 Paris, France.
Morgan, Professor Edmund S., Department of History, P.O. Box 1504A Yale Station, New Haven, Conn. 06520-7425, U.S.A.

Peña y Cámara, J. M. de la, Avenida Reina, Mercedes 65, piso 7-B, Seville 12, Spain.
Prawer, Professor J., Department of Medieval History, Hebrew University, Il-Jerusalem, Israel.

Rodrigues, Professor José Honório, Rua Paul Redfern 23, ap. C.O. 1, Rio de Janeiro, Gb. ZC-37, Brazil.

Slicher van Bath, Professor B. H., Gen. Fouldesweg 113, Wageningen, The Netherlands.

Thapar, Professor Romila, Dept of Historical Studies, Jawaharlal Nehru University, New Mehrauli Road, New Delhi-110067, India.
Thorne, Professor S. E., MA, LLB, LittD, LLD, FSA, Law School of Harvard University, Cambridge, Mass 92138, U.S.A.

Van Houtte, Professor J. A., PhD, FBA, Termunkveld, Groeneweg, 51, Egenhoven, Heverlee, Belgium.
Verlinden, Professor C., PhD, 3 Avenue du Derby, 1050 Brussels, Belgium.

Wolff, Professor Philippe, Edifici Roureda Tapada, 2ª,7, Santa Coloma (Principality of Andorra), France.
Woodward, Professor C. Vann, PhD, Yale University, 104 Hall of Graduate Studies, New Haven, Conn. 06520, U.S.A.

Zavala, S., LLD, Montes Urales 310, Mexico 10, D.F., Mexico.

TRANSACTIONS AND PUBLICATIONS

OF THE

ROYAL HISTORICAL SOCIETY

The publications of the Society consist of the *Transactions*, supplemented in 1897 by the *Camden Series* (formerly the Camden Society, 1838–97); since 1937 by a series of *Guides and Handbooks* and, from time to time, by miscellaneous publications. The Society also began in 1937 an annual bibliography of *Writings on British History*, for the continuation of which the Institute of Historical Research accepted responsibility in 1965; it publishes, in conjunction with the American Historical Association, a series of *Bibliographies of British History*.

List of series published

The following are issued in collaboration with the distributor/publisher indicated:

Annual Bibliography of British and Irish History
All titles — Harvester Press
Bibliographies of British History
   All except 1485–1603, 1714–1789 — Oxford University Press
   1485–1603, 1714–1789 — Harvester Press
Camden Series
   Old Series and New Series — Johnson Reprint
   Third and Fourth Series* — Boydell and Brewer
Guides and Handbooks
   Main Series* — Boydell and Brewer
   Supplementary Series* — Boydell and Brewer
Miscellaneous titles — Boydell and Brewer
Studies in History
   All titles — Watmoughs Limited
Transactions of the Royal Historical Society
   Up to *Fifth Series*, Vol. 19 — Kraus Reprint
   Fifth Series, Vol. 20 onwards*† — Boydell and Brewer
Writings on British History
   Up to 1946 — Dawson Book Service
   1946 onwards — Institute of Historical Research

Members' entitlements

Fellows and Subscribing Libraries receive free copies of new volumes of series marked*.
Corresponding Fellows, Retired Fellows and Associates receive free copies of new volumes of this series marked†.
Terms for members' purchase of individual titles are listed below.

Methods of Ordering Volumes

Institute of Historical Research—an invoice will be sent with volume.
In all other cases pre-payment is required. If correct price is not known, a cheque made payable to the appropriate supplier, in the form 'Not exceeding £   ' may be sent with the order. Otherwise a pro-forma invoice will be sent.

LIST OF TITLES
ARRANGED BY DISTRIBUTOR

BOYDELL & BREWER

Address for orders: P.O. Box 9, Woodbridge, Suffolk IP12 3DF.

Camden Third Series: All titles now available; a list can be sent on request. Prices range from £10 for original volumes to £30 for the largest reprinted volumes. (£7.50–£22.50 to Members).

Camden Fourth Series: The following titles are available price £10. (£7.50 to Members) unless otherwise indicated:

1. Camden Miscellany, Vol. XXII: 1. Charters of the Earldom of Hereford, 1095–1201. Edited by David Walker. 2. Indentures of Retinue with John of Gaunt, Duke of Lancaster, enrolled in Chancery, 1367–99. Edited by N. B. Lewis. 3. Autobiographical memoir of Joseph Jewell, 1763–1846. Edited by A. W. Slater. 1964. £25.00.

2. Documents illustrating the rule of Walter de Wenlock, Abbot of Westminster, 1283–1307. Edited by Barbara Harvey. 1965.

3. The early correspondence of Richard Wood, 1831–41. Edited by A. B. Cunningham. 1966. £25.00.

4. Letters from the English abbots to the chapter at Cîteaux, 1442–1521. Edited by C. H. Talbot. 1967.

5. Select writings of George Wyatt. Edited by D. M. Loades. 1968.

6. Records of the trial of Walter Langeton, Bishop of Lichfield and Coventry (1307–1312). Edited by Miss A. Bearwood. 1969.

7. Camden Miscellany, Vol. XXIII: 1. The Account Book of John Balsall of Bristol for a trading voyage to Spain, 1480. Edited by T. F. Reddaway and A. A. Ruddock. 2. A Parliamentary diary of Queen Anne's reign. Edited by W. A. Speck. 3. Leicester House politics, 1750–60, from the papers of John second Earl of Egmont. Edited by A. N. Newman. 4. The Parliamentary diary of Nathaniel Ryder, 1764–67. Edited by P. D. G. Thomas. 1969.

8. Documents illustrating the British Conquest of Manila, 1762–63. Edited by Nicholas P. Cushner. 1971.

9. Camden Miscellany, Vol XXIV: 1. Documents relating to the Breton succession dispute of 1341. Edited by M. Jones. 2. Documents relating to the Anglo-French negotiations, 1439. Edited by C. T. Allmand. 3. John Benet's Chronicle for the years 1400 to 1462. Edited by G. L. Harriss. 1972.

10. Herefordshire Militia Assessments of 1663. Edited by M. A. Faraday. 1972.

11. The early correspondence of Jabez Bunting, 1820–29. Edited by W. R. Ward. 1972.

12. Wentworth Papers, 1597–1628. Edited by J. P. Cooper, 1973.

13. Camden Miscellany, Vol. XXV: 1. The Letters of William, Lord Paget. Edited by Barrett L. Beer and Sybil Jack. 2. The Parliamentary Diary of John Clementson, 1770–1802. Edited by P. D. G. Thomas. 3. J. B. Pentland's Report on Bolivia, 1827. Edited by J. V. Fifer, 1974.

14. Camden Miscellany, Vol. XXVI: 1. Duchy of Lancaster Ordinances, 1483. Edited by Sir Robert Somerville. 2. A Breviat of the Effectes

devised for Wales. Edited by P. R. Roberts. 3. Gervase Markham, The Muster-Master. Edited by Charles L. Hamilton. 4. Lawrence Squibb, A Book of all the Several Offices of the Court of the Exchequer (1642). Edited by W. H. Bryson. 5. Letters of Henry St John to Charles, Earl of Orrery, 1709-11. Edited by H. T. Dickinson. 1975.

15. Sidney Ironworks Accounts, 1541-73. Edited by D. W. Crossley. 1975.
16. The Account-Book of Beaulieu Abbey. Edited by S. F. Hockey. 1975.
17. A calendar of Western Circuit Assize Orders, 1629-48. Edited by J. S. Cockburn. 1976.
18. Four English Political Tracts of the later Middle Ages. Edited by J.-Ph. Genet. 1977.
19. Proceedings of the Short Parliament of 1640. Edited by Esther S. Cope in collaboration with Willson H. Coates. 1977.
20. Heresy Trials in the Diocese of Norwich, 1428-31. Edited by N. P. Tanner. 1977.
21. Edmund Ludlow: A Voyce from the Watch Tower (Part Five: 1660-1662). Edited by A. B. Worden. 1978.
22. Camden Miscellany, Vol. XXVII: 1. The Disputed Regency of the Kingdom of Jerusalem, 1264/6 and 1268. Edited by P. W. Edbury. 2. George Rainsford's *Ritratto d'Ingliterra* (1556). Edited by P. S. Donaldson. 3. The Letter-Book of Thomas Bentham, Bishop of Coventry and Lichfield, 1560-1561. Edited by Rosemary O'Day and Joel Berlatsky. 1979.
23. The Letters of the Third Viscount Palmerston to Laurence and Elizabeth Sulivan, 1804-63. Edited by Kenneth Bourne. 1979.
24. Documents illustrating the crisis of 1297-98 in England. Edited by M. Prestwich. 1980.
25. The Diary of Edward Goschen, 1900-1914. Edited by C. H. D. Howard. 1980.
26. English Suits before the Parlement of Paris, 1420-36. Edited by C. T. Allmand and C. A. J. Armstrong. 1982.
27. The Devonshire Diary, 1759-62. Edited by P. D. Brown and K. W. Schweizer. 1982.
28. Barrington Family Letters, 1628-1632. Edited by A. Searle. 1983.
29. Camden Miscellany XXVIII: 1. The Account of the Great Household of Humphrey, first Duke of Buckingham, for the year 1452-3. Edited by Mrs M. Harris. 2. Documents concerning the Anglo-French Treaty of 1550. Edited by D. L. Potter. 3. *Vita Mariae Reginae Anglie*. Edited by D. MacCulloch. 4. Despatch of the Count of Feria to Philip II, 1558. Edited by S. L. Adams and M. J. Rodriguez-Salgado. 1983.
30. Gentlemen of Science: Early correspondence of the British Association for the Advancement of Science. Edited by A. W. Thackray and J. B. Morrell. 1984.

Provisionally accepted by the Society for future publication:

The Acta of Archbishop Hugh of Rouen (1130-64). Edited by T. Waldman.
Cartularies of Reading Abbey. Edited by B. R. Kemp.
Correspondence of William Camden. Edited by Richard DeMolen.
Early Paget Correspondence. Edited by C. J. Harrison and A. C. Jones.
Letters of J. A. Blackwell concerning events in Hungary, 1848-9. Edited by A. Sked.

Supplementary Documents of the English Lands of the Abbey of Bec. Edited by Marjorie Chibnall.
Letters to Sir Reynold Bray. Edited by De Ll Guth and Miss M. Condon.
Clifford Letters, c. 1500–39. Edited by R. W. Hoyle.
The Short Parliament Diary of Sir Thomas Aston. Edited by Judith Maltby.
Journal of Gilbert, second earl of Minto, 1847–1859. Edited by K. Bourne.
The Letters of Henry, Lord Hardinge, Governor General of India, 1844–1848. Edited by Bawa Satinder Singh.
Financial Memoranda of the reign of Edward V. Edited by Rosemary Horrox.
Jean Creton's Prinse et Mort. Edited by J. J. N. Palmer and Mrs L. Stewart.
Indentures of retinue in peace and war, 1272–1485. Edited by N. B. Lewis and M. Powicke.

Guides and handbooks

Main series

1. Guide to English commercial statistics, 1696–1782. By G. N. Clark, with a catalogue of materials by Barbara M. Franks. 1938. (*Out of print*).
2. Handbook of British chronology. Edited by F. M. Powicke and E. B. Fryde, 1st edn. 1939; 2nd edn. 1961; 3rd edn. 1985. £25.00.
3. Medieval libraries of Great Britain, a list of surviving books. Edited by N. R. Ker, 1st edn. 1941; 2nd edn. 1964. £8.00.
4. Handbook of dates for students of English history. By C. R. Cheney. 1982. £5.00.
5. Guide to the national and provincial directories of England and Wales, excluding London, published before 1856. By Jane E. Norton. 1st edn. 1950; 2nd edn. 1984. £12.00.
6. Handbook of Oriental history. Edited by C. H. Philips. 1963. £5.00.
7. Texts and calendars: an analytical guide to serial publications. Edited by E. L. C. Mullins. 1st edn. 1958; 2nd edn. 1978. £8.00.
8. Anglo-Saxon charters. An annotated list and bibliography. Edited by P. H. Sawyer. 1968. £8.00.
9. A Centenary Guide to the Publications of the Royal Historical Society, 1868–1968. Edited by A. T. Milne. 1968. £5.00.
10. A Guide to the Local Administrative Units of England. Vol. I. Edited by F. A. Youngs, Jr. 1980; 2nd edn. 1981. £25.00.
11. A Guide to Bishops' Registers to 1646. Edited by D. M. Smith. 1981. £15.00.
12. Texts and Calendars: II: an analytical guide to serial publications 1957–1982. By E. L. C. Mullins. 1983. £15.00.
13. Handbook of Medieval Exchange. Edited by P. Spufford. 1985. £15.00.

Supplementary series

1. A Guide to the Papers of British Cabinet Ministers, 1900–1951. Edited by Cameron Hazlehurst and Christine Woodland. 1974. £4.50.
2. A Guide to the Reports of the U.S. Strategic Bombing Survey. Edited by Gordon Daniels. 1981. £12.00.

Provisionally accepted by the Society for future publication:

A Handbook of British Currency. Edited by P. Grierson and C. E. Blunt.
A Guide to the Records and Archives of Mass Communications. Edited by Nicholas Pronay.

A Guide to the Maps of the British Isles. Edited by Helen Wallis.
A Guide to the Local Administrative Units of England. Vol. II. Edited by F. A. Youngs, Jr.
Handlist of British Diplomatic Representatives, 1508-1688. Edited by G. Bell.
Scottish Texts and Calendars. Edited by D. and W. B. Stevenson.

Miscellaneous publications

Domesday Studies, 2 vols, Edited by P. E. Dove, 1886. £3.50. (Vol. I out of print.)
The Royal Historical Society, 1868-1968. By R. A. Humphreys. 1969. £1.25.

Transactions, Fifth Series

Vol. 20 onwards. Price £8.50. (£6.38 to Members).

DAWSON BOOK SERVICE

Address for orders: Cannon House, Folkestone, Kent.
Writings on British History to 1946. Prices on request.

HARVESTER PRESS

Address for orders: 17 Ship Street, Brighton, Sussex.
Annual Bibliography of British and Irish History (Editor: D. M. Palliser)

1. Publications of 1975 (1976)
2. Publications of 1976 (1977)
3. Publications of 1977 (1978)
4. Publications of 1978 (1979)
5. Publications of 1979 (1980)
6. Publications of 1980 (1981)
7. Publications of 1981 (1982)
8. Publications of 1982 (1983)
9. Publications of 1983 (1984)

Prices on request.
Bibliography of British History: Tudor Period, 1485-1603. Edited by Conyers Read. 1st edn. 1933; 2nd edn. 1959; 3rd edn. 1978. Price £28.00.
Bibliography of British History: The Eighteenth Century, 1714-1789. Edited by S. M. Pargellis and D. J. Medley. 1st edn. 1951; 2nd edn. 1977. Price £18.95.

INSTITUTE OF HISTORICAL RESEARCH

Address for orders: University of London, Senate House, Malet Street, London WCIE 7HU.
Writings on British History, 1946-1948. Compiled by D. J. Munro. 1973. Price £15.00.
Writings on British History, 1949-1951. Compiled by D. J. Munro. 1975. Price £15.00.
Writings on British History, 1952-1954. Compiled by J. M. Sims. 1975. Price £15.00.
Writings on British History, 1955-1957. Compiled by J. M. Sims and P. M. Jacob. 1977. Price £15.00.

Writings on British History, 1958–1959. Compiled by H. J. Creaton. 1977. Price £15.00.
Writings on British History, 1960–1961. Compiled by C. H. E. Philpin and H. J. Creaton. 1978. Price £15.00.
Writings on British History, 1962–1964. Compiled by H. J. Creaton. 1979. Price £17.00.
Writings on British History, 1965–1966. Compiled by H. J. Creaton. 1981. Price £18.00.
Writings on British History, 1967–1968. Compiled by H. J. Creaton. 1982. Price £20.00.

JOHNSON REPRINT

Address for orders: 24–28 Oval Road, London NW1 7DX.
Camden Old and New Series. Prices on request.

KRAUS REPRINT

Address for orders: Route 100, Millwood, N.Y. 10546, U.S.A.
Transactions: Old, New, Third, Fourth, Fifth Series Vols. 1–19. Prices on request.

OXFORD UNIVERSITY PRESS

Method of ordering: through booksellers.
If members have difficulty in obtaining volumes at the special price, reference should be made to the Society.
Bibliography of English History to 1485. Based on the Sources and Literature of English History from earliest times by Charles Gross. Revised and expanded by Edgar B. Graves. 1975. Price £48 (£36 to Members).
Bibliography of British History: Stuart Period, 1603–1714. 2nd edn. Edited by Mary F. Keeler, 1970. Price £35.00 (£26.25 to Members).
Bibliography of British History: 1789–1851. Edited by Lucy M. Brown and Ian R. Christie. 1970. Price £38.00 (£28.50 to Members).
Bibliography of British History: 1851–1914. Edited by H. J. Hanham. 1976. Price £58.00 (£43.50 to Members).
In preparation
Supplement to Bibliography of British History: 1714–89. Edited by S. M. Pargellis and D. J. Medley. Edited by A. T. Milne and A. N. Newman.

WATMOUGHS LIMITED

Address for orders: 1–7 Albion Place, Britton Street, London EC1M 4RE.
Studies in History is a series of historical monographs, preferably of no more than 90,000 words, intended to help solve the increasing difficulties encountered by historians in getting their books accepted for publication, especially young scholars seeking first publication. Those interested in submitting works for consideration by the Editorial Board should write to the Editorial Assistant, c/o The Royal Historical Society, University College London, Gower Street, WC1E 6BT, from whom further details can be obtained. No typescripts should be sent until asked for.
   1. F. F. Foster: *The Politics of Stability: A Portrait of the Rulers in Elizabethan London.* 1977. £19.60 (£14.00 to Members).

2. Rosamond McKitterick, *The Frankish Church and the Carolingian Reforms 789-895*. 1977. £19.60 (£14.00 to Members).
3. K. D. Brown, *John Burns*. 1977. £19.60 (£14.00 to Members).
4. D. Stevenson, *Revolution and Counter Revolution in Scotland, 1644-1651*. 1977. (Out of print).
5. Marie Axton, *The Queen's Two Bodies: Drama and the Elizabethan Succession*. 1978. £17.50 (£12.50 to Members).
6. Anne Orde: *Great Britain and International Security, 1920-1926*. 1978. £19.60 (£14.00 to Members).
7. J. H. Baker (ed), *Legal Records and the Historian* (Papers read to the 2nd Conference on Legal History, held at Cambridge in 1975). 1978. £19.60 (£14.00 to Members).
8. M. P. Costeloe: *Church and State in Independent Mexico: a study of the Patronage Debate, 1821-1857*. 1978. £19.60 (£14.00 to Members).
9. Wendy Davies: *An Early Welsh Microcosm: Studies in the Llandaff Charters*, 1978. £19.60 (£14.00 to Members).
10. Bernard Wasserstein: *The British in Palestine: The Mandatory Government and the Arab-Jewish Conflict, 1917-1929*. 1978. £21.00 (£15.00 to Members).
11. Michael McCahill: *Order and Equipoise: the Peerage and the House of Lords, 1783-1806*. 1979. £21.00 (£15.00 to Members).
12. Norman Etherington: *Preachers, Peasants and Politics in Southeast Africa 1835-1880. African Christian Communities in Natal, Pondoland and Zululand*. 1979. £19.60 (£14.00 to Members).
13. S. A. G. Rizvi: *Linlithgow and India: A Study of British Policy and the Political Impasse in India, 1936-1943*. 1979. £21.00 (£15.00 to Members).
14. David McLean: *Britain and her Buffer-state: The Collapse of the Persian Empire, 1890-1914*. 1979. £17.95 (£12.80 to Members).
15. Howard Tomlinson: *Guns and Government: The Ordnance Office under the later Stuarts*. 1979. £21.00 (£15.00 to Members).
16. Patricia Crawford: *Denzil Holles, 1598-1680: A study of his Political Career*. 1979. £19.60 (£14.00 to Members).
17. D. L. Rydz: *The Parliamentary Agents: A History*. 1979. £19.60 (£14.00 to Members).
18. Uri Bialer: *The Shadow of the Bomber: The Fear of Air Attacks and British Politics 1932-1939*. 1980. £17.50 (£12.50 to Members).
19. David Parker: *La Rochelle and the French Monarchy: Conflict and Order in Seventeenth-Century France*. 1980. £19.60 (£14.00 to Members).
20. A. P. C. Bruce: *The Purchase System in the British Army, 1660-1871*. 1980. £17.50 (£12.50 to Members).
21. Stephen Gradish: *The Manning of the British Navy During the Seven Years War*. 1980. £19.60 (£14.00 to Members).
22. Alan Harding (ed.): *Lawmaking and Lawmakers in British History* (Papers presented to the Edinburgh Legal History Conference 1977). 1980. £19.60 (£14.00 to Members).
23. Diane Willen: *John Russell First Earl of Bedford*. 1981. £17.50 (£12.50 to Members).
24. Roy Schreiber: *The Political Career of Sir Robert Naunton, 1589-1635*. 1981. £17.50 (£12.50 to Members).
25. W. M. Mathew: *The House of Gibbs and the Peruvian Guano Monopoly*. 1981. £21.00 (£15.00 to Members).
26. D. M. Schurman: *Julian Sl Corbett 1854-1922, Historian of British Maritime Policy from Drake to Jellicoe*. 1981. £19.60 (£14.00 to Members).
27. Scott M. Harrison: *The Pilgrimage of Grace in the Lake Counties 1536-7*. 1981. £17.50 (£12.50 to Members).

28. Angus MacKay: *Money, Prices and Politics in Fifteenth-Century Castile*. 1982. £17.50 (£12.50 to Members).
29. D. Duman: *The Judicial Bench in England 1727–1875: The Reshaping of a Professional Elite*. 1982. £19.60 (£14.00 to Members).
30. J. R. Wordie: *Estate Management in Eighteenth-Century England*. 1982. £21.00 (£15.00 to Members).
31. M. Doughty: *Merchant Shipping and War*. 1982. £19.60 (£14.00 to Members).
32. N. Jones: *Faith by Statute: Parliament and the Settlement of Religion 1559*. 1982. £19.60 (£14.00 to Members).
33. James Barros: *Britain, Greece and the Politics of Sanctions: Ethiopia 1935–1936*. 1982. £19.60 (£14.00 to Members).
34. J. Davis: *Heresy and Reformation in the South-East of England 1520–1529*. 1983. £17.50 (£12.50 to Members).
35. A. J. Pollard: *John Talbot and the War in France 1427–1453*. 1983. £17.50 (£12.50 to Members).
36. E. W. Ives and A. H. Manchester (eds.): *Law, Litigants and the Legal Profession*. 1983. £19.60 (£14.00 to Members).
37. J. Ashworth: *Agrarians and Aristocrats*. 1983. £21.00 (£15.00 to Members).
38. Joyce L. Malcolm: *Caesar's Due: Loyalty & King Charles 1642–1646*. 1983. £21.00 (£15.00 to Members).
39. L. W. Brady: *T. P. O'Connor and the Liverpool Irish*. 1984. £21.00 (£15.00 to Members).
40. J. A. Guy and H. G. Beale: *Law and Social Change in British History*. 1984. £17.50 (£12.50 to Members).
41. R. Holmes: *The Road to Sedan: The French Army 1866–70*. 1984. £21.00 (£15.00 to Members).
42. R. G. Little: *The Parlement of Poitiers: War, Government and Politics in France 1418–1436*. 1984. £17.50 (£12.50 to Members).